Plantation Pedagogy

AMERICAN CROSSROADS

*Edited by Earl Lewis, George Lipsitz, George Sánchez,
Dana Takagi, Laura Briggs, and Nikhil Pal Singh*

Plantation Pedagogy

THE VIOLENCE OF SCHOOLING ACROSS
BLACK AND INDIGENOUS SPACE

Bayley J. Marquez

UNIVERSITY OF CALIFORNIA PRESS

University of California Press
Oakland, California

© 2024 by Bayley Marquez

Library of Congress Cataloging-in-Publication Data

Names: Marquez, Bayley J. 1985– author.
Title: Plantation pedagogy : the violence of schooling across black and indigenous space / Bayley J. Marquez.
Other titles: American crossroads ; 72.
Description: Oakland, California : University of California Press, [2024] | Series: American crossroads; 72 | Includes bibliographical references and index.
Identifiers: LCCN 2023023164 (print) | LCCN 2023023165 (ebook) | ISBN 9780520393707 (cloth) | ISBN 9780520393714 (paperback) | ISBN 9780520393721 (ebook)
Subjects: LCSH: Critical pedagogy—United States. | Slavery—History—Study and teaching—United States. | Indians of North America—Land tenure—History—Study and teaching—United States. | African Americans—Education— United States. | Indigenous peoples—Education—United States.
Classification: LCC LC196.5.U6 M27 2024 (print) | LCC LC196.5.U6 (ebook) | DDC 370.11/50973—dc23/eng/20230719
LC record available at https://lccn.loc.gov/2023023164
LC ebook record available at https://lccn.loc.gov/2023023165

32 31 30 29 28 27 26 25 24 23
10 9 8 7 6 5 4 3 2 1

Plantation Pedagogy

THE VIOLENCE OF SCHOOLING ACROSS
BLACK AND INDIGENOUS SPACE

Bayley J. Marquez

UNIVERSITY OF CALIFORNIA PRESS

University of California Press
Oakland, California

© 2024 by Bayley Marquez

Library of Congress Cataloging-in-Publication Data

Names: Marquez, Bayley J. 1985– author.
Title: Plantation pedagogy : the violence of schooling across black and
    indigenous space / Bayley J. Marquez.
Other titles: American crossroads ; 72.
Description: Oakland, California : University of California Press, [2024] |
    Series: American crossroads; 72 | Includes bibliographical references
    and index.
Identifiers: LCCN 2023023164 (print) | LCCN 2023023165 (ebook) |
    ISBN 9780520393707 (cloth) | ISBN 9780520393714 (paperback) |
    ISBN 9780520393721 (ebook)
Subjects: LCSH: Critical pedagogy—United States. | Slavery—History—
    Study and teaching—United States. | Indians of North America—Land
    tenure—History—Study and teaching—United States. | African
    Americans—Education— United States. | Indigenous peoples—
    Education—United States.
Classification: LCC LC196.5.U6 M27 2024 (print) | LCC LC196.5.U6 (ebook) |
    DDC 370.11/50973—dc23/eng/20230719
LC record available at https://lccn.loc.gov/2023023164
LC ebook record available at https://lccn.loc.gov/2023023165

32 31 30 29 28 27 26 25 24 23
10 9 8 7 6 5 4 3 2 1

CONTENTS

PART ONE
THE FOUNDATIONS OF PLANTATION PEDAGOGY

Introduction: Teaching Slavery and Settlement 3

1 · Plantation Pedagogy, Educative Space, and Currents of Colonialism 28

PART TWO
PLANTATION PEDAGOGY IN THE CURRENTS

2 · Plantation Pedagogy on the Reservation 55

3 · Pacific Currents: Island Plantations and Industrial Schooling 80

4 · Atlantic Currents: Industrial Education and Anti-colonial Struggle in Africa 105

PART THREE
PLANTATION PEDAGOGY AS A TECHNOLOGY OF SETTLEMENT

5 · "Out from Cabin and Tepee": Settlement, Slavery, and the Making of Domestic Space 131

6 · Teachers of Teachers: The Expansion of Plantation Pedagogy through Teacher Training 152

7 · "Better Land, Better Stock, Better People": The School as Experiment Station and Laboratory 176

Conclusion: Learning by (Not) Doing?   197

Acknowledgments   207
Notes   211
Bibliography   271
Index   297

PART ONE

The Foundations of Plantation Pedagogy

Introduction

TEACHING SLAVERY AND SETTLEMENT

When William Hooper Councill spoke at the 1902 commencement of the Carlisle Indian School, he asserted that "no three hundred years of human history have presented such wonderful evolution as the three hundred years of Negro American history." In a history that included both slavery and juridical emancipation, Councill, the Black President of the State Colored Normal School at Huntsville, Alabama, framed slavery as a particularly transformative, even educative, institution, claiming that "four millions of Industrious Christians were evolved in the South from four million savages."[1] The "evolution" continued, he asserted, because "old slave plantations have been turned into industrial schools for the old slaves. Masters' old mansions turned into colleges for slaves, and old slaves are presidents of these colleges."[2] Councill was one such man: a former slave who had become a teacher and then a school administrator of a Black industrial school that would later be chartered as a Black land-grant college, Alabama A&M.[3] Indeed, the transformation of physical plantation space into schools was widespread in the post-emancipation era. Booker T. Washington's Tuskegee Institute was built on purchased plantation land, as were many other Black colleges in the South, such as Florida A&M, Alcorn State, and Prairie View A&M.[4] The conversions that Councill describes from slave to citizen, plantation to school, and former slave to teacher suggest an intimacy between slavery and schooling, with the plantation functioning as a space of both learning and immense violence.[5]

Councill's assertions were meant to serve as examples to his mostly Indigenous audience at Carlisle, an institution that had been created, in the words of its founder Richard Henry Pratt, to "kill the Indian to save the man."[6] In addition to this oft-cited phrase, which has come to signify the violence of boarding school education for Native peoples Pratt was fond of the adage, "the contact of peoples is the best education."[7] Here, the term *contact* indexes colonialism yet attempts to transpose its violence into benevolence by framing colonialism as educative. In other words, Pratt, like Councill, retold white supremacist violence as a story with a redemptive arc in which colonization and slavery become processes of benevolence, striving, and learning.[8] These men were by no means alone; they were carrying forward assertions that apologists for slavery and colonization had long been making. Additionally, though slavery was over as a matter of the law, the plantation was not. At Carlisle, the Colored Normal School, and a host of other institutions, Black and Indigenous students were instructed in what I argue is a form of plantation pedagogy, a form of teaching that draws on human-space relations in an attempt to transform Black and Indigenous peoples as well as land.

THE BEGINNINGS OF PLANTATION PEDAGOGY: THE HAMPTON INSTITUTE

After the Civil War, the landscape of schooling changed significantly in the Southern United States due to the push for schools by formerly enslaved Black communities who sought the education that they had been largely denied in slavery. The Hampton Institute was founded in 1868 as a result of this shift. Although it was established to educate Black students, it was not aimed towards the goals articulated by Black communities, who grounded their desires for education in opposition to slavery and towards freedom.[9] Hampton's educational program was founded on an industrial education model meant to train former slaves in habits of work and industry and accustom them to second-class-citizenship status.[10] This form of education was attractive to the white Southern elite who wanted to maintain a subordinated workforce as well as to Northern philanthropists who operated under assimilatory forms of racist educational thought.[11]

Additionally, the history of the Hampton Institute is one that geographically connects colonial and racialized space across oceans and continents. The founder of Hampton, Samuel Chapman Armstrong, was born in Hawai'i in 1839. He experienced the colonial schooling system of Hawai'i as a member of the elite white missionary class. His father, Richard Armstrong, was a prominent missionary educator and, later, superintendent of the schools for the Hawaiian monarchy, a situation that demonstrates the imperialist influence on the monarchy prior to the illegal overthrow and annexation of Hawai'i.[12] In his youth, Samuel Armstrong toured industrial schools in Hawai'i, which were overseen by his father and were meant to educate the Indigenous population. These schools served as a model for the Hampton Institute insofar as they used a curriculum that required students to work as laborers, particularly in agriculture. They also employed Christian-based moral teachings as key to civilizing Indigenous Hawaiian people. For example, at the Hilo Boarding School, students labored to construct school buildings, cultivate food gardens, and grow sugar cane for sale as a cash crop. The school claimed that student labor was part of their education; it was also integral to keeping the school solvent. Hampton's involvement in Hawaiian education continued for many decades. Armstrong had ongoing relationships with schools like the Hilo Boarding School and the Kamehameha School, and he assisted in founding schools on the islands, like the Kauai Industrial School. Many former Hampton teachers moved to Hawai'i, and some became public intellectuals who wrote editorials in Hawaiian newspapers about Hawaiian education, as did Armstrong and his relatives. Indigenous Hawaiian students would come to attend Hampton and other Indian boarding schools as well.

After his early years observing missionary imperial education in Hawai'i, Armstrong attended college in the United States and served in the Union Army during the Civil War, which eventually led to his employment at the Freedman's Bureau in the area of Hampton, Virginia.[13] He founded the Hampton Institute in this assigned area. Armstrong framed the mission of Hampton around providing industrial training for those who had been formerly enslaved. His stated goal for the Hampton school was to educate "the head, the heart, and the hand," and to provide "cultural uplift" through moral and manual training.[14] He drew this language from the European pedagogue Pestalozzi, who described educating the head, hand, and heart in his framing of industrial education for former serfs in Europe.

Hampton started a smaller program to educate Native peoples in 1877 called the Hampton Indian Program. Once this program was created, the education of Native students was often discussed in comparison to the Institute's larger Black student population. The Hampton Indian program, which lasted for over fifty years and was a key part of the assimilation era of US Indian policy, was typified by the rise of federal Indian boarding schools, which many scholars argue began with the Carlisle Indian School in 1879.[15]

The first Native students at Hampton were "recruited" from the prisoners of war held by Pratt at Fort Marion in St. Augustine, Florida. While they were supposedly given a choice between returning home in the custody of the Bureau of Indian Affairs (BIA) or attending Hampton, the choice was likely not free of coercion as they already had been kept at Fort Marion for over two years.[16]

The Carlisle Indian School was founded in many ways as a direct result of Pratt's involvement in the founding of the Indian Program, and educational programs for the formerly enslaved and Indigenous peoples were also linked in other ways.[17] Estelle Reel, who authored the curriculum for federal Indian boarding schools in 1901, toured Hampton and used its curriculum as inspiration in creating hers. Many Indian boarding schools were interconnected, sharing ideas and transferring students between them. Hampton publications would often write reports on various schools in areas of Indian Country and their progress educating the "savages." Hampton was also integrally connected to US policymaking for Indigenous peoples. Alice Fletcher, a white anthropologist who helped draft and pass the allotment legislation that subdivided reservation lands to be privately owned instead of collectively held by tribes, was involved in recruiting students and creating programs for the school. Associations like the Woman's National Indian Association, the American Missionary Association, the Phelps-Stokes Fund, and the organizers of the Lake Mohonk conferences, where "friends of the Indian" gathered to discuss Indian policy, all had deep connections to Hampton and its Indian program. The board members, funders, invited speakers, consultants, and friends of these organizations overlapped and interacted frequently. As the concentrated involvement of Hampton and its affiliates in various projects aimed at Indigenous peoples reveals, an institution founded to educate former slaves was promoted as ideally situated for the work of "killing the Indian to save the man."[18]

Hampton also inspired the creation of many other educational institutions, including, in 1881, Booker T. Washington's Tuskegee Institute, and the "Hampton model" would become a force across the South, influencing the creation of many more institutions and educational policies.[19] Networks of philanthropists such as the Rockefellers, the Peabody Fund, Anson Phelps Stokes, Julius Rosenwald, and the Slater Fund spread the model by funding various schooling programs and social services throughout the South. This funding contributed to founding new Black schools and training teachers in industrial education; it also pushed out other school models by withholding comparable financial resources. Well-known programs like the Rosenwald Schools and the Jeanes Supervisory Teachers were funded by philanthropists with connections to Hampton, Tuskegee, and the many reformers who supported their projects.

Thus, proponents of the Hampton Industrial School model were integral to the establishment of Black education in the South, including the many Black land-grant schools that have become present-day HBCUs. As the founders of these programs like Armstrong, Pratt, and Washington died or were replaced, new administrators took over and became influential voices in educational policy. These include Hollis Burke Frissell, the former chaplain and second president of Hampton; Robert Moton, Booker T. Washington's successor at Tuskegee and a Hampton graduate; George Washington Carver, the director of Tuskegee's agricultural experiment station; and Jackson Davis, the Virginia Supervisor of Negro schools and a board member of a number of institutions supported by the Rockefeller charities and Phelps-Stokes Fund in the South.

At the turn of the century, the Hampton model expanded beyond Indian Country, Hawai'i, and the Black South, becoming influential in US imperial projects across the Pacific and the Atlantic. For example, the first US director of education for the Philippines (1901–1903), Frederick Atkinson, toured Hampton and many of its associated institutions, citing them as models for a proposed Filipino education system.[20] During his tenure as director of education, Atkinson oversaw the arrival of the first US teachers to the territory, the Thomasites, named after their arrival on the vessel USS Thomas. These teachers were meant to teach English, US civilization, and democracy to Filipinos. Atkinson also oversaw the establishment of the Manila Trade School in 1901.[21] Atkinson was succeeded by David Barrows whose educational programming changed the rhetoric of schooling in the Philippines without significantly changing the industrial focus of the programs themselves.[22] The interaction between Hampton, other US institutions, and institutions in the Philippines was multidirectional, with teachers from US schools teaching in the Philippines and Filipino students attending schools such as Hampton and Carlisle. This created a system of exchange that entrenched plantation pedagogy as a part of the US imperial project in the Pacific.

The Hampton model was also influential in establishing educational institutions in the African state of Liberia, which many scholars have described as a US colony in all but name.[23] The Phelps-Stokes Fund and the American Colonization Society helped fund the Booker Washington Institute of

Liberia in 1929 and looked for staff connected to Hampton and Tuskegee. In fact, US educational reformers sought to incorporate the Hampton model of industrial schooling into education in countries and colonies across Africa through the influence of philanthropic organizations like the Phelps-Stokes Fund and the Rockefeller International Education Board. Thomas Jesse Jones, a former Hampton employee and prolific writer about both Black and Native education in the United States, toured Africa as part of a committee funded by the Phelps-Stokes Fund and authored multiple reports on education in Africa suggesting that colonial governments implement industrial schooling models. He was connected to school reformers across Africa, including men like Charles T. Loram, who argued for the implementation of industrial schooling in segregated South Africa. Across both the Atlantic and the Pacific Oceans, plantation pedagogy was central to imperial education programs. Thus, imperialism was fundamentally connected to earlier histories of slavery and settlement across these geographies.

EDUCATION FOR SLAVERY AND SETTLEMENT

The discourse of industrial education relies on a conception of education as uplifting and even liberatory (albeit to a limited degree). Yet, as numerous scholars have made clear, educational institutions enmeshed within systems of colonial control, segregation, incarceration, and inequality have long functioned to maintain an unjust status quo. At the same time, as other scholars point out, Indigenous and Black communities have co-opted and reframed education for their own purposes.[24] My focus is on how education, the formal institutions that encompass it as well as hegemonic notions of education in "America," is integrally tied to enslavement and settlement and their inherent violence towards land and people, which I call *teaching slavery and settlement*. Consequently, I do not theorize about how to create forms of emancipatory education.[25] Instead, I show that the framing and institutionalization of education for Black and Indigenous peoples has been tied to the assertions that contact with the white race, enslavement, and the settlement of Native lands are, in and of themselves, educational activities. To that end, I begin my analysis when slavery was putatively ended in the United States and a post-emancipation educational system was created. By starting at this moment, I am able to trace how logics of slavery are interwoven with the establishment of post-emancipation schooling.

I draw on archival material from post-emancipation schooling institutions like Hampton, Tuskegee, and Carlisle that demonstrates what educational reformers, teachers, philanthropists, and administrators did in schools during this era, as well as what they said about teaching, schooling, and Black and Native peoples as learners. I use these archives to tell a history not just of what happened in post-emancipation schooling, but also of how education for Black and Native peoples was framed and the material consequences of that framing. Education is a symbolic, ideological, and material process in which symbolic and ideological violence is connected to material violence.[26] Thus, teaching slavery and settlement is a symbolic and ideological project as much as it is a material one.

The way white reformers framed industrial education and the results of that education were often contradictory. These contradictions occur because of a complex set of discourses that support an ideology of education that justifies the violent past and present of colonialization and antiblackness. Throughout this book, I read for concordances and discordances in the assertions of educational reformers about what schooling does. For example, many of these teachers and school leaders stated that education was a means of preparing Black and Indigenous peoples for citizenship, yet they rarely supported enactments of that citizenship such as the right to vote or political participation.[27] Slavery and settlement were so instrumental to this educational discourse that I argue that this form of schooling cannot and will never produce liberation.

There is, of course, an imprecision in using terms like *schooling* or *education* because the ways people learn and the places in which they do so take many forms.[28] I use the term *education* or *educational* to mean a process in which something is *framed* as being learned.[29] This definition may seem overly broad since people learn from all experiences in life. However, I am keenly focused on the framing of what is educational, and by whom, in order to demonstrate what those in power value as learning. Of course, the ideas Black and Indigenous peoples had about what is educational were often, though not always, markedly different from what white reformers valued. There was always contestation over what was and was not deemed educational, especially when forms of schooling were co-opted in order to shift their use for radical ends. The term *teaching*, like the term *education*, can be described in a variety of ways that encompass both formal and informal notions of education. I use the terms *teaching* and *teaches* to indicate what people, spaces, or experiences are described as doing and how those actions are framed as aiding in the process of learning. Thus, what is described by those in power as "teaching" also demonstrates what is structurally valued as part of systems of schooling.

These contested understandings of education and teaching demonstrate why the term *pedagogy*, as "the method or practice of teaching," is also contested. Scholars have engaged in defining which forms of pedagogy entrench inequality and which can facilitate emancipation and liberation.[30] This has led to a great debate amongst scholars as to whether pedagogy can create social change.[31] For example, Khalil Johnson Jr. has noted that the word *pedagogy* is derived from a Greek term for the slave that led children to school and acted as a tutor, which demonstrates that pedagogy is tied to slavery in fundamental ways and thus may not be a liberatory term at all.[32] I use the term *pedagogy* to indicate how teaching is enacted within matrices of power such that the material effects of pedagogy do not always align with what is supposedly taught. When I use the term *power*, I draw from scholars like Antonio Gramsci who have theorized hegemony as power constituted through ideology and scholars like Foucault who have demonstrated that power is also diffuse such that the constitution of the "regime of truth" is always a negotiated process.[33] I draw from this scholarship because, while it may be easy to identify loci of power, it is hard to identify all of power's technologies in their complexity. I trace the material ways that power operates in relation to those who seek to enact power over others through education.[34]

Educational reforms driven by ideologies of dispossession, genocide, and slavery as educational were not unique to the post-emancipation era. For example, European missionaries often framed their encroachment into Native lands and subsequent settlement as necessary for the education of the savage.[35] In fact, schools established by missionaries prior to emancipation share many similarities with the schools examined in this text. Additionally, historians of slavery have noted that slavery was characterized as an educative process in an effort to cast slavery as a benevolent institution. Of particular note is Ulrich Bonnell Phillips's *Life and Labor in the South*, which describes the many spatial iterations of slavery as educative.[36] Donald Warren summarizes as follows: "At its center stood the plantation, a multipurpose institution. It was 'a school' (198), with intentional training and socialization programs for slaves," in which the "'civilizing of the Negroes' was 'a fruit of plantation life itself' (199)."[37] In addition, Phillips situates the plantation as a "homestead," which hints at the fact that the plantation was one of many spatial iterations of European settlement and Indigenous dispossession.

Phillips normalizes the violence of the plantation as everyday life when he describes the plantation's many integrated functions, such as factory, parish, pageant, matrimonial bureau, and boarding house. Therefore, I use the term slavery not just to encompass the specific time period of enslavement but also its afterlife, which continues to reverberate in everyday life after what Hartman calls the "nonevent of emancipation."[38]

Moreover, in addition to the term *colonialism,* I use the term *settlement* rather than *settler colonialism* here and throughout the text. Settlement is a process of dispossession, genocide, and the replacement of peoples and transformation of land that exists across geographic locations and governmental configurations; therefore, settlement does not exist solely in settler colonial states but across colonized spaces globally.[39] Accordingly, I use the term *settlement* to describe a process in addition to a structure that defines nation-state configurations, and I argue that settlement-as-process can exist in tandem and apart from extractive-colonialism-as-process.[40]

While many scholars have noted that either settlement or slavery has been connected to the schooling of Black and Native peoples, fewer have examined how closely intertwined settlement and slavery were. One striking example of this is how Pratt discusses slavery, contact, and education: "The Negro, I argued, is from as a low a state of savagery as the Indian, and in 200 years' association with Anglo-Saxons he has lost his languages and gained theirs; has laid aside the characteristics of his former savage life, and, to a great extent, adopted those of the most advanced and highest civilized nation in the world, and has thus become fitted as fellow citizens among them."[41] Citizenship for Black people becomes possible with the end of slavery, but only because, according to Pratt, slavery, which forced contact with European civilization, prepared them for the role. In relation to Indigenous peoples, Pratt often asserted the importance of "mingling Indians with whites" as part of the educational project of the US state. In this way, settlement (and its inherent violence and genocidal intent to destroy Native populations and communities) was a cornerstone of Pratt's pedagogical outlook, which might explain why he called his memoir "Battlefield and Classroom."[42] Pratt's pedagogy for Indigenous peoples draws from an ideology of slavery as an institution of teaching. "Contact," as used by Pratt, is a term that both encompasses the incredible violence of slavery and colonization and elides the full impact of that violence through the mundaneness of the term.

Based on readings of reformers like Pratt, Councill, and many others who discussed the education of Black and Indigenous peoples, slavery, and settlement, I contend that slavery and settlement as educational processes must be examined in intimate connection.[43] I propose that this history of discussing the "contact of peoples" through slavery and colonialism as educative can best be understood as *plantation pedagogy*, in other words, the teaching of slavery and settlement. Plantation pedagogy was the mechanism through which slavery as an educational project was enacted materially through the spatial formation of the plantation. Additionally, as a spatial unit of settlement, the plantation's existence is impossible without the dispossession of Native peoples. The plantation exists on stolen Indigenous lands for the explicit purpose of transforming the land for capitalist production. Thus, plantation pedagogy privileges space as necessary for teaching slavery and settlement because this form of teaching sought to change not only Black and Native peoples but also their relations to land and the land itself. Through plantation pedagogy, education as the "contact of peoples" was operationalized within a context of primitive accumulation, settlement, and chattel slavery.[44]

CONVERSATIONAL CURRENTS WITHIN, BETWEEN, AND ACROSS BLACK STUDIES AND NATIVE STUDIES

In analyzing the teaching of slavery and settlement, this work is positioned at a meeting point where Black and Native studies engage each other in order to understand our interconnected histories and theorize our political struggles and our futures. At this meeting point, there has been antagonism and disagreement as well as cohesion and comradery.[45] The various tensions that permeate this conversation stem from many factors, including the erasure of Black-Indigenous peoples, histories of Native slaveholding, antiblackness in Indigenous communities, Black educators' roles in teaching and disciplining Native people, Black people settling on Native lands, and Black critiques of Indigenous sovereignty struggles.[46] One example of some of these tensions is Councill's speech at the Carlisle Indian School commencement, which could be read variously as capitulation to white supremacist schooling structures, complicity in the assimilation and genocide of Native peoples, coerced compliance within the larger context of antiblack violence, or a surface-level practice that obscures fugitivity not recorded in the archive. I do not draw out this example to demonize Councill or to argue for his redemption. Instead, I see this speech as an important grounding point for the discussions that must be undertaken between Black and Native studies. These communities have been pitted against each other by white supremacist structures that create zero-sum conditions for life and survival. Black and Native peoples have caused each other harm, acted in solidarity, and at times, ignored each other in favor of our own analyses and political projects. However, the story I tell in this book demonstrates the necessity of talking about these complex moments and particularly the necessity for Black and Indigenous studies to engage with each other and each other's theories. Thus, this book is ultimately intended as a conversation between "us" (i.e., Black and Indigenous peoples) to make sense of the conversations that happened and are still happening about "us" by others, including educational reformers. In desiring to have conversations between, within, and across these positions, spaces, times, and ideas from both Black and Native studies, I am inspired by the many scholars who have engaged and continue to engage in this dialogue, including Leanne Betasamosake Simpson, Kyle Mays, Mark Rifkin, Joyce Pualani Warren, Tiya Miles, Sharron Holland, David Chang, Circe Sturm, Justin Leroy, Chad Infante, and Tiffani Lethabo King.

In order to participate in this conversation between Black and Native studies, I engage with scholars from my own field of Native studies who have theorized about the parameters, tensions, starting points, and places of convergence between our field and Black studies. Scholar of Native literature Mark Rifkin, responding to arguments made in the Afropessimist tradition that there is a fundamental antagonism between Blackness and Indigeneity, argues that Blackness and Indigeneity are not necessarily incommensurable but are not identical and stem from different genealogies that at times have overlapped.[47] Rifkin proposes flesh (ontology) and land (place) as analytics to understand the primary concerns of Black and Native studies and cautions scholars against making claims that conflate antiblackness and settler colonialism as parts of the same power structure. He notes that this "very theoretical unification can short-circuit the process of relation by relying on the analytical structure itself to resolve prominent differences and discrepancies among these movements."[48] Yet, Rifkin also critiques the tendency of theories to "vie for primacy." He quotes Black scholar Justin Leroy, who asks, "What intellectual pathways are foreclosed when slavery and settler colonialism vie for primacy as the violence most foundational to the modern social order?"[49] Rifkin comes to the conclusion that answers cannot be found in conceptualizations of incommensurability or mutual constitution but that "starting from the premise of irreducible difference might generate another set of intellectual and political possibilities, ones based on open-ended processes of relation, negotiation, and translation."[50] Like Rifkin, I am also interested in this process of relation, negotiation, translation, and, ultimately, conversation that happens not from a set of shared understandings or positions that can never be reconciled but from a location between that of impasse and equivalence.

One scholar whose work sits in this in-betweenness and offers space for conversations between Black and Native studies is diasporic Black and Kanaka Maoli scholar Joyce Pualani Warren. Warren reads Indigenous Hawaiian texts, including the tattooing of the Kanaka body, to argue that, within Native Hawaiian epistemologies, Blackness is a constitutive part of Indigeneity. She contends that Kanaka Maoli cosmology positions Blackness not as antithesis to whiteness but as the generative state from which things come into being. Warren reads Indigeneity in connection to Blackness to open up a discussion that circumvents ontological definitions of Blackness that frame it only in opposition to whiteness in order to read Blackness as a generative part of Indigeneity. Warren's work demonstrates how conversations between Black and Native studies can shift orientations in order to engage each other's theories in new ways.[51]

Another key aspect of the conversation between Black and Native studies that must continue is how to engage with each other's political struggles. Rifkin perceptively asks whether the irreducible differences he theorizes present a "difficulty . . . in envisioning roles for non-native people of color within Indigenous projects of resurgence."[52] Indigenous scholar Leanne Betasamosake Simpson addresses this same question in her comparison of marronage as conceptualized in Caribbean studies and Indigenous practices of resurgence, which she theorizes as a form of flight.[53] She understands this flight through the Nishnaabeg concept of constellations, which are "beacons of light that work together to create doorways . . . into other worlds" such that "on a conceptual level, they work together to reveal theory, story, and knowledge representing a mapping of Nishnaabeg thought through the night sky and through time."[54] Through the concept of constellations, Simpson asks penetrating questions that are starting points for further engagement between Black and Native studies, such as, If "constellations exist only in the context of relationships" and are "networks of a larger whole," then "who should we be in constellation with"?[55] In asking this question she indicates that Indigenous peoples should be in constellation with Black communities such that co-resistance can be possible.

I find work like Rifkin, Simpson, and Warren's to be integral and engaged in the process of creating conversations in generative ways between Black and Native studies. While scholars like Rifkin propose concepts such as land and flesh as touchpoints for dialogue between Black and Native studies, I suggest instead turning to the concepts of land and water. While water and land are often viewed as distinct, they touch, overlap, contend for dominance, and constantly affect each other. They are also both concepts that have been theorized in depth by Native and Black studies, yet they are not always discussed together in either field. Additionally, my connection with both water and land comes not only from scholarship but also from my own experience and the stories I grew up hearing. I am Santa Ynez Chumash and grew up in the Santa Ynez Valley, which is a short drive away from the beautiful beaches of Santa Barbara County. From these beaches, you can see out to the Santa Barbara Channel Islands. I grew up with these beaches and views as well as a deep connection to the mountains and valleys covered in brown grasses and studded with oak trees. The creation story I learned about these places connected island, ocean, and land intimately. Our people originated on the islands but moved to the mainland by crossing over a rainbow bridge. Those of us who fell into the ocean became dolphins, and those who made it to the mainland remained connected to our kin on the islands and in the ocean. Because of this background, I have always felt that ocean and land were intimately connected, and both made up a part of who I have always seen myself to be and how I inhabit space.

Land, of course, has always sat at the heart of Native studies. Its dispossession as part of structures of settlement, the extraction of resources as colonists seek to use land for capital accumulation, and the inalienable yet fluid connections Indigenous peoples have to lands and more-than-human kin constitute our understandings of the world. Land is also a shared terrain (or, as Tuck et al. put it, "self-same land") that has been allotted and contested.[56] Tiya Miles and Sharon Holland note that "people of African [origin] ... built metaphysical as well as physical homes on Native lands and within Native cultural landscapes. In the process, they altered their interior worlds as well as those of Native peoples."[57] In his discussion of land struggles between Indigenous peoples, white settlers, and Black communities in Oklahoma, David A. Chang argues that land holds symbolic power and is itself racialized.[58] The racialization of land goes beyond the idea that land is defined in relation to the social construction of race because, as Jean O'Brien and Daniel Heath Justice argue, "what is done to the people is done to land."[59]

In his discussion of allotment, Nick Estes quotes his father, who defined relatives as people who were "related to the same land," which is an apt piece of wisdom in thinking about connections between Black and Native peoples, who have relations to the same lands through histories of violent relocation and dispossession.[60] Thus, using land as an analytic to connect Native studies and Black studies engages in both a spatial and an ontological framing. The space of land holds power that is exercised in a variety of ways, but the land also constitutes forms of Indigenous being such that what is done to land is always intimately tied to the violence done to Native peoples.

Water, fluid and changeable, has a different relationship to human life than that of land. Many scholars of Black studies have engaged in water-based analysis, from Paul Gilroy's classic study of the Black Atlantic to Christina Sharpe's positioning of Blackness as "in the wake" of the slave ship. Noting this lineage of oceanic thinking, Tiffany Lethabo King proposes the concept of the Black Shoals, which is the "liminal space between land and sea" that exists in flux and causes "disruption in movement and flow."[61] She describes shoals as "offshore formations" that serve as a capacious metaphor for understanding Black and Native studies in relation to each other. She argues that, as half land and half oceanic formations, the Black Shoals produce a land/sea hybrid space that frames the ontological condition of Blacks in America both geographically and metaphorically. I seek to connect this idea of shoals and offshore formations to other ways that water has been connected to land within Native studies. For example, Nick Estes and Joseph M. Pierce, in their work tracing allotments of Indigenous lands, note that many original land allotments now sit underwater because of dam projects that have flooded large swaths of Native homelands.[62] These scholars ask how Indigenous resurgence or reclamation of land can happen when the land is itself subsumed. What does (re)connection to land mean when it is underwater? How is this too a liminal space between land and water that centers disruptions of spiritual, legal, and material connections between people and space?

Lenape feminist scholar Joanne Barker makes the argument that water is integral to Indigenous feminisms.[63] She states that water teaches us about movement, transition, and change due to its shifting nature, which has no ending or beginning. For Barker, water is also about interaction. Indigenous scholars demonstrate that water is not a thing apart but always is connected to land and air, as well as living creatures, human and non-human.[64] Most importantly for my own use of fluid analysis, water "shows us the intricacies and intimacies of imperial violence."[65] In order to understand these intimacies, Barker proposes the term "confluence" as an analytic specific to Indigenous feminisms.[66] Confluence as a method provides a lens to view interconnections between theorizing and political movements, such as her examples of intersectionality and assemblage theories as well as the political movements around Standing Rock and water poisoning in Flint, Michigan. Barker's theorization of confluence demonstrates the primacy of a gendered analysis of violence against Black and Native peoples, a contention that King also insists upon as an articulation of how water is a theoretical component of Indigenous theorizing. Christine Taitano DeLisle and Vicente M. Diaz use a feminist lens in relation to land when they call allotment policies "agricultural penetration" and agricultural uplift the "colonial erection."[67] I draw on this feminist theorizing throughout this book, even if it is not explicitly acknowledged in each chapter. In fact, gender and sexuality are implicitly and explicitly important for understanding plantation pedagogy, as will be demonstrated in my discussions of sex-segregated schooling in Hawai'i, the function of domestic space as teaching space, and the roles of female teachers and teacher supervisors in disseminating the Hampton model of schooling.

Following these articulations of land and water, I propose the term *currents of colonialism,* which I define as a form of material and metaphoric movement that maps how systems of colonial power function through transit. Currents "convey an intimacy between people, land, ocean, and time."[68] My understanding of currents is indebted to articulations of movement found in Indigenous studies, such as Jodi A. Byrd's *Transit of Empire* and Mishuana Goeman's theories of (re)mapping, as well as to the work of Jodi A. Byrd, Alyosha Goldstein, Jodi Melamed, and Chandra Reddy who have theorized grounded relationalities that are "situated in relation to land but without precluding movement . . . or other elementary or material currents of water and air."[69] Thus, currents of colonialism is the model I use to theorize colonialism, antiblackness, and settlement and how and why Hampton's pedagogy was influential across a variety of spaces.

Currents were, of course, instrumental to the material process of colonialism and settlement. Ocean currents directly influenced where plantations and settlements were established, and currents materially impacted the shape and form of colonialism and slavery.[70] Current also has the meaning of something that is "of the now" and can be used to denote how something becomes "current" and therefore transferable because of its perceived relevance. In this way, currents are ideological. Currents are also both natural and man-made.

Ocean currents circulate as part of natural processes and are affected by manmade projects that shift their patterns. People even create artificial currents in manmade water structures. Currents affect people and land, but people also try to control and affect them. They have patterns and are hard to change, but they are changeable. Currents can wreck ships and chart new courses. Currents are therefore contradictory, much the way colonial control and power is always challenged and contradicted by that which it can never fully command or harness no matter how hard it tries. The dualities of currents encompass the ways they both direct and are directed for violence and colonial control but also impede and resist this control in various moments. Currents are slippery, allowing for escape routes even when the path seems predetermined. Throughout this text, I use currents to describe how plantation pedagogy was transferred across land and oceans as a "current" form of education and within currents of colonial violence. This transfer thus had directionality and intent but also unintended consequences, incomplete implementation, and moments that could be exploited by people who used these educational institutions for their own purposes. I also propose currents not only as a way to understand the movement of plantation pedagogy but also as another place from which to engage in conversations between Black and Native studies. Currents are a means to understand how power and structures of dispossession move, their incompleteness and contradictions, and how they leave openings for meaningful engagement.

SOLVING EDUCATIONAL PROBLEMS, SOLVING OURSELVES AS PROBLEMS?

I engage Black and Native studies by examining the history of education as a terrain that has historically connected Black and Indigenous peoples and positioned us against each other, eliciting antagonisms between our respective political projects.[71] Indigenous scholar Robert Warrior has asserted that education is a necessary space for engagement when studying Blackness and Indigeneity because of this interconnected history.[72] I sit in this conversation with many other scholars who are opening spaces to engage Black and Native studies in relation to education, such as Khalil Anthony Johnson Jr., Jarvis R. Givens, Sandy Grande, K. Wayne Yang, Eve Tuck, Amanda R. Tachine, Eve L. Ewing, Sara Chase Merrick, and Bryan McKinley Jones Brayboy.

In the post-emancipation era, the language of solving the "Negro problem" and the "Indian problem" were popular and these "problems" were often connected.[73] They were framed as discrete and interactive by educators, reformers, scholars, and philanthropists who believed that when problems were placed together their solutions became interconnected, as in this discussion by H. I. Fontellio-Nanton:

> During the years 1868–1978, Hampton had been demonstrating what could be done in the matter of the "Negro problem." Now, another problem for the school was in the making in Indian territory, here Kiowas, Comanches, Cheyenne and Arapahos had been fighting the white man's encroachment on their lands and their ancient customs. It was from this group of Indians that the sixteen young men became members of the student body of Hampton Institute; thereby creating a problematic situation for the school.[74]

This framing of Black and Native peoples as problems interpellates nonwhite bodies as walking manifestations of structural problems. With these rhetorical moves, reformers diverted attention towards the damage to Black and Indigenous peoples—their bodies and their home spaces—and away from structures of racial and colonial oppression.[75] Locating the problems in the bodies and homes of Black and Native peoples allowed for white reformers to locate the solution to "un-civilizedness" in changing their bodies and the spaces those bodies inhabited.

Framing the problem as a lack of civilization provided a means to continue structures of oppression that only perpetuated views of Black and Native peoples as pathological. Their solutions materially worked to make Black people subservient in the new economic and social organization of the South and to strip Indigenous peoples of their lands and ultimately erase them from the settler spatial imaginary and landscape.[76] Thus, a bait and switch occurs whereby an ontological argument is interchanged with a structural one and an ontological framing is created in the service of material arrangements. This conflation of ontology and materiality is why I am deeply suspicious of the usefulness of changing pedagogy as a form of liberation.[77] I contend that what is learned by the people pedagogy targets is not always the most important aspect of what pedagogy does. What is important is the material relations it seeks to create and how it accomplishes these relations in connection with systems of power.

The intimacy between the discourses about the "Negro problem" and "Indian problem" also points to the intimacy between settlement and slavery.

It is not surprising that the convergence of these "friendships" occurred in the historical moment of both the creation of the post-bellum schooling system for Black former slaves (both by white philanthropists and reformers and Black populations themselves) and the cementing of the reservation system during the height of the Indian Wars in the late 1800s. Attempts by the United States government to pacify and educate Native peoples was a topic of great debate among the same white reformers and philanthropists who looked to create Southern schools. Additionally, this timeframe partially coincided with and led into an era of heightened US imperial ambitions in locations like the Pacific and Latin America, when discourses of civilization were used to justify US interventions abroad. The Black and Red "problems" intersected with the project of US imperialism, which was posited as the solution to the generalized problem of the uncivilized.

Yet the framing of Black, Native, and other subjects of imperialism as problems was also contradictory. If, for example, slavery is framed as educative, then the problem is not really Black people, as the reformers claimed. So then, the problem actually is how to use slavery to educate once slavery has juridically ended. Similarly, in the case of Indigenous peoples, educational institutions framed the resistance to settlement as a problem because settlement itself was considered the educational activity. Understanding how slavery and settlement are tied to the discussion of people as "educational problems" leads me to the conceptual limits of my project for solving educational problems. Finding ways to fix an educational system, which has foundations in teaching slavery and settlement, by defining Native and Black peoples as problems means finding more palatable ways to make *us* less of a problem. While our communities (those of Black and Native peoples) have used education for our own purposes, we are often asked by educational reformers, scholars, and our own institutions how our ideas can be used in mainstream schools. Indigenous- and Black-led projects of learning and study often have nothing to do with the sort of problem-solving that these educational institutions are engaged in. In this way, Black and Native peoples are positioned as needing to give our ideas about learning to the academy in order to solve the problems of an educational system not meant for us. That is not to say that Black and Indigenous peoples do not engage in political struggles around schooling or that we should not have our own educational projects, more so that maybe we should not trust the academy with them. I suggest making a turn toward a refusal to solve educational problems—a refusal to solve ourselves as problems.

A METHODOLOGY OF REFUSAL

To this end, I conducted the archival research for this book from a methodological stance of refusal. Refusal drives how I engage archival sources, how I write about them, and the conclusions I draw from them. A methodology of refusal begins from the idea that a limit is reached at the point of refusal and that this limit reveals core knowledge. Audra Simpson describes this point in her work as the ethnographic limit where the people with whom she spoke collectively refused to speak.[78] Simpson conceptualizes refusal as a generative rather than a limiting method of research that takes into account "the goals and aspirations of those we talk to [to] inform our methods and the shape of our theorizing and analysis."[79] Simpson's theorization of ethnographic refusal also allows for the refusal of academic conventions as central to research because refusal validates the distrust of speaking that Native peoples may have when they know their speech will be heard and transmitted within the context of colonial violence. This also means that refusal can be irreverent at the same time that it is theoretically and analytically complex.[80] Therefore, moments when my writing diverges from academic conventions and takes on conversational or even adversarial tones are part of the generative nature of refusal and a purposeful strategy. The duality of refusal, to say something by refusing to say something or by mixing an academic tone with irreverent critique, is what makes it powerful and what has made it resonate so strongly with Indigenous academics across fields.

Simpson's work has been instrumental for Indigenous peoples engaging in ethnographic work, and I have sought here to apply refusal to the archive. The archive is a difficult place to practice refusal. For one thing, archives are already unevenly representative of the power relations involved in their construction and create enhanced presences and specific silences.[81] These archives are constructed through the silence or the careful control of the voices of Black and Indigenous peoples, constituting a troubling aspect of violence, antiblackness, geocide, and erasure.[82] This leads to the question: what is one refusing in an archive if archives are already terrains for erasure? Some scholars have answered this question by refusing erasure.[83] Scholars like Saidiya Hartman have used creative methods to "elaborate, augment, transpose and break open" what exists in the archives to narrate embodied lives through acts of radical imagination.[84] This approach to the archive seeks to find new ways to speak for those silenced in creative and loving ways, placing the focus on joy, resistance, and rebellion. I find value and beauty in this work, yet

I find myself unsure about this approach to the archive. This is partly because I am wary of the voyeuristic nature of archival research. Tuck and Yang argue that research represents the oppression and pain of the colonized, with the researcher as the "ventriloquist" or "interpreter" of that voice.[85] They draw from Simpson's work on refusal, suggesting that instead of becoming ventriloquists, researchers can refuse to relay stories of pain to the imperial gaze through academic publication.[86] I find this caution especially important when approaching work in the archives because Black and Indigenous peoples often had no chance to refuse what is saved there, thus circumventing the possibility of ethnographic refusal. Consequently, when researching in the archive, refusal necessitates setting your own limits regarding the material you are engaging with. At the outset of my study, I set my limits in a way that resembles K. Wayne Yang's description of the work of artist Ken Gonzalez-Day, who removes the body of the lynched person in lynching postcards, displaying the white mob instead.[87] Yang describes this artistic rendering as a form of refusal that shifts the focus from viewing the violence against the Black body to analyzing the white crowd and their response to antiblack violence. As my conceptual limit I have chosen not to relate the voices of the Black and Indigenous students who attended these schools and instead to focus on the teachers, administrators, reformers, and philanthropists who directed the type of learning the students engaged in.

In refusing to relay the voices of Black and Native students I want to be very clear that I intimately know that Indigenous and Black students and teachers at Hampton and other institutions engaged in fugitivity and found joy and strength within and in spite of these institutions. I know it in my bones as an Indigenous person who has been a student for over half of her life and as a daughter, mother, sister, relative, friend, and teacher of so many Black and Indigenous peoples who have navigated the violence of schooling and resisted it. I have made an intentional choice not to relate the experiences and voices of Indigenous and Black peoples in these schools, but that does not mean they do not exist. I make this refusal as a result of my commitment to think about how Indigenous and Black peoples are portrayed in the academy and as part of my attempt to learn at the limit of my refusals. Simpson notes that there is no way to write in the academy that is "'innocent' of a violence of form, if not content, in narrating a history or present of ourselves."[88] This is, in part, due to the fact that historical narratives of Black and Indigenous peoples' cultural difference are still used to disempower us through a discourse of educational help. Cultural difference narratives confine and order Black and Indigenous peoples within specific representations and create a dichotomy that defines us as a problem. I am wary of this discourse and of how Black and Indigenous voices get used as a part of its propagation.

I know that this move is counter to much of the exceptional scholarship that has occurred in the study of Black and Indigenous education. For example, within the study of Black educational history, a shift took place in the 1990s and early 2000s in which scholars began to depart from studies of how schools were structured to subjugate people of color[89] and turn towards studying the agency of Black communities, who, for example, created buffered educational spaces during segregated periods.[90] This shift was echoed by Indigenous scholars studying the histories of boarding-school and missionary education. Scholars such as Child and Lomawaima began writing from the perspectives of Native students; they documented their experiences within oppressive institutions in order to counter what they saw as the totalizing narratives of previous work on boarding schools.[91] This shift toward studies of resistance placed the gaze upon racialized subjects and their experiences of domination, negotiation, resistance and also of joy, strength, and hopes for the future.

I know that my refusals necessitate a turn away from doing work that centers the resistance, strength, and joy of Black and Indigenous peoples within institutions like Hampton.[92] That refusal can be interpreted as writing them out of existence or creating one-sided narratives that do not show the complexity of Indigenous and Black resilience. My answer to this concern is threefold. First, I believe resistance, resilience, joy, strength, and, above all, agency are always present in institutions such as Hampton, but resistance and challenges to dominant narratives are still often structured by the forms of oppression they react against. Jarvis R. Givens has argued this point persuasively in outlining his concept of fugitive pedagogy.[93] Additionally, scholars of refusal have been careful to note that refusal is not resistance and should not be confused with it.[94] While resistance can be beautiful and generative, there is also a danger in idealizing agency and resistance, particularly in relation to school reform. Framing resistance as the answer to breaking down oppressive structures does not recognize how oppression and resistance co-constitute each other; nor does it acknowledge the flexibility of structures of oppression. In this book, I am interested in learning what I can at the limit point of refusing resistance narratives.

Second, the notion that there is complexity within structures of oppression can be used to obfuscate explicit narrations of how power works.

In presenting my academic work, I have been told many times that I need to pay attention to "complexity," but the complexity that is referred to is often embroiled in what Tuck and Yang call "settler moves to innocence."[95] Data showing that many Native students have fond memories of boarding schools is trotted out by scholars who ask me to discuss "complexity," with the implication that boarding schools must not have been as horrible as they seem if Native peoples could resist and even find joy within them. When people bring up the good relationships Native peoples had with white missionaries in these conversations, they act rhetorically to soften the critique of colonial violence I present in my work. There are ways to do work on Indigenous and Black resilience that does not try to make excuses for the work of settlement, colonialism, and antiblackness, and I applaud the scholars that do this work and cite many of them. However, truthfully, I am still not sure if the academy can be trusted with that kind of work.[96] I worry that, in placing Indigenous and Black voices up for academic display, they can be used in unintended ways by those who wish to obfuscate histories of violence by arguing that it could not have been that bad if Black and Native peoples survived or even (gasp!) felt joy or happiness amidst this violence.[97]

Third, I do not want to participate in manufacturing hope by claiming knowledge about how to decolonize education. I have stated that resistance is not the answer to structures of oppression. I do not believe academics and educators should read solutions into the actions of Indigenous and Black bodies as a means for fixing the educational system or as a strategy for professional advancement by publishing it. Naming Black and Indigenous peoples as solutions rather than problems still places the onus on our bodies to fix educational systems. This is why I refuse to make recommendations for how to improve schooling institutions for Black and Indigenous peoples. The impulse to change education as a solution to social problems is one that is fundamental to the study of educational institutions, but making educational recommendations from historical studies is not a strategy that will make material change.[98]

Because this is a history of education, there is always the pressure to provide information to present day educators based on my findings. My answer to this pressure relies on the poignant analysis of Linda Tuhiwai Smith, who cautions us about the true reach of academic work: "Taking apart a story . . . does not help people to improve their current conditions. It provides words, perhaps, an insight that explains certain experiences—but it does not prevent someone from dying."[99] Deconstructing the history of plantation pedagogy does not mean that I can stop schools from being oppressive, and it does not mean that I now possess the power and ability to change them. Sometimes the answer our work gives is not to make a recommendation at all but to refuse to. A refusal to help reform schools points to a different analysis of why schools may not be the location for change and refuses schools as primary locations of decolonization.

BOOK OUTLINE

This book is presented in three parts, which at times may present chronological disjunctures as it shifts between geographic spaces, sometimes lingering in one space for entire chapters, and other times moving across continents in a span of pages. Thus, currents serve not only as a theoretical model but also as an organizational approach that informs how the chapters of the book unfold. Currents have both predictable and unpredictable elements. Sometimes the paths they take will seem logical and other times jolting. Some currents may run deep and necessitate delving into their depths. These deep dives, such as my theoretical ruminations on currents and plantations, are necessary to understanding the broader conceptual stakes of the project. In other moments, the currents may sweep the reader quickly across vast terrains in a survey of their broad similarities. This is mirrored in the shifts I make between theoretical and historical discussions. Currents often eddy and circle back on themselves, so there may be points where the analysis is iterative, coming back to places and programs discussed in earlier chapters without a conventional chronological trajectory. Drawing on concepts like Rifkin's critique of settler time and assertions of temporal sovereignty, I refuse to tell the story of industrial education in a way that centers chronological change over time.[100] Instead, I skip through space and time in order to focus on continuity and particularly on how the tenets of plantation pedagogy remained remarkably stable across these different moments.

Part one, which includes this introductory chapter and chapter one, presents the foundational concepts of the text in connection to the historical context of the Hampton Institute and its many connected educational programs. Chapter one, "Plantation Pedagogy, Currents of Colonialism, and Educative Space," outlines the concepts of plantation pedagogy and currents of colonialism as well as their connections to each other. Plantation pedagogy operates through proximity to whiteness, labor, and the productive use of space. These pedagogies materially transformed (or attempted to transform) land and relations to space in each of these contexts, demonstrating that land was a main target of plantation pedagogy. Additionally, the plantation not only is a space of slavery but also is intricately bound up with settlement and imperialism. Therefore, plantation pedagogy is not static but moves across currents of colonialism, which is the form of material and metaphoric movement that maps how systems of colonial power function through transit. Chapter one argues for tracing the way that plantation pedagogies are trafficked through currents of colonialism as one action that can be taken in the academy towards understanding how to unravel colonial technologies of schooling.

The second part of the book, "Plantation Pedagogy in the Currents," takes a deeper look at plantation pedagogy across different geographic points. I organize these chapters geographically rather than chronologically in order to frame how plantation pedagogy played out in each spatial sphere, noting its material and discursive shifts and continuities. I take a trip through the currents, stopping at different locations in each chapter. Chapter two presents a close examination of how plantation pedagogy was used for the establishment of education for Indigenous peoples by colonizers across North America. I discuss how industrial-education discourse framed reservations in relation to slavery and utilized proximity to whiteness and labor as part of the educational projects in "Indian Country." Chapter three examines how plantation pedagogy was utilized in Hawai'i both prior to and after the overthrow of the Hawaiian government by the United States and in the Philippines after the Spanish American War. Just as plantation pedagogy did not have to be on a literal plantation to be extended to reservations, the presence of slavery is not necessary for thinking about how plantation pedagogy moved into the Pacific. In the case of the Pacific, however, plantations as physical spaces existed alongside the introduction of plantation pedagogy, allowing for this model of education to interact with plantations in a different form. Plantation pedagogy in the Pacific, therefore, was connected to a justification of slavery without chattel slavery existing in that context. Chapter four examines how plantation pedagogy was transferred to the African continent in a variety of interconnected moments. I examine records from the Booker Washington Institute in Liberia, which was founded as an industrial school in the model of Tuskegee to teach Liberians work and industry, and from Thomas Jesse Jones's tour of Africa, including his subsequent report. Jones was a former Hampton employee and was funded by organizations such as the Rockefeller, Peabody, and Slater funds, which were influential in supporting industrial pedagogy in the Black South. I argue that, when plantation pedagogy was applied in Africa, it was based on the need of colonial governments to squelch decolonial movements through ideologies of uplift and collaboration.

The final section of the book examines the "parts of the machine" of plantation pedagogy as a technology of settler schooling across geographic locations. This section focuses on the material strategies that were used in implementing plantation pedagogy and highlights pedagogical continuity across various locations and temporalities. Chapter five examines the cabin and cottage as a spatial method of instruction, a technological component of plantation pedagogy that functioned across varied locations. Chapter six theorizes why the training of teachers was a key part of the Hampton model by looking at teachers as technological units of spatial expansion for settlement. In particular, I examine the Jeanes Fund teacher supervision model as well as the ideology of teacher training at Hampton and the various other institutes that modeled themselves after Hampton. Chapter seven examines the intimacy between schools and agricultural experiment stations, demonstration farms, and other forms of scientific farming that relied on experimentation as a method of determining farming methods. By reading documents like George Washington Carver's circulars, which were produced as part of the Tuskegee Agricultural Experiment station, I demonstrate that land was a target of plantation pedagogy.

In the conclusion, I signal how plantation pedagogy and its various technologies continue to influence educational discourse through the construct of "learning by doing." I ask how learning by doing is intimately connected to teaching slavery and settlement and in what ways it manifests in the present, using examples such as the conservative backlash against critical race theory. With this conclusion, I demonstrate that plantation pedagogy continues to circulate in currents of colonialism and that knowledge of this circulation might be used to inform critiques of education and work for (non-metaphorical) decolonization.

ONE

Plantation Pedagogy, Educative Space, and Currents of Colonialism

In his 1901 memoir, *Up From Slavery,* Booker T. Washington describes his own early education and admission to the Hampton Institute. Like many other Black people at the time, Washington was seeking an education, which had been legally forbidden to him in slavery, noting in his other writing that he would not have been so invested in learning to read if it had not been denied to him.[1] Yet, instead of being asked to take an academic exam to enter the Hampton Institute, Washington was tasked with sweeping a recitation room. Washington's rhetoric in *Up From Slavery* glorifies this exam, stating that the "sweeping of that room was my college examination, and never did any youth pass an examination for entrance into Harvard or Yale that gave him more genuine satisfaction. I have passed several examinations since then, but I have always felt that this was the best one I ever passed."[2] This exam can be read in a number of ways; we can see it as displaying an overdetermined emphasis on cleanliness in relation to Black bodies or as demonstrating uplift ideology through forms of respectability politics. I have chosen to zero in on the act that was performed, an act of labor done in the service of others. In fact, Washington states that he knew how to clean so well because of his experience working as a servant for a white woman named Mrs. Ruffner. Washington writes, "the lessons that I learned in the home of Mrs. Ruffner were as valuable to me as any education I have ever gotten anywhere since."[3] He received the order to sweep the room and explains, "never did I receive an order with more delight. I knew that I could sweep, for Mrs. Ruffner had thoroughly taught me how to do that when I lived with her."[4] Thus, when Washington arrived at Hampton, his entrance exam framed the kind of acts that would be valued as learning in this space: learning from and laboring for white people in white spaces.

I define the type of learning that was valued, conceived of, and implemented at Hampton as plantation pedagogy. By naming this form of learning *plantation pedagogy*, I draw a line between post-emancipation schooling and earlier legacies of slavery and settlement as violent educational practices. While Hampton drew from many educational institutions and traditions that preceded the post-emancipation timeframe, what made the Hampton model of industrial schooling unique was how it shifted plantation pedagogies so that they could proliferate after the juridical end of slavery. This proliferation was so robust that it expanded not only across the continent but also globally across oceans and temporalties, influencing colonial education in a variety of contexts as US imperial education spread. Thus, the protean and expansive nature of plantation pedagogy is another of its key features. This process of expansion was spatial as much as ideological or political, with land as a subject of education as well as a central feature of how plantation pedagogy was used to educate Black and Native peoples.

HAMPTON AS PLANTATION AND SETTLEMENT

Geographically, Hampton was constructed upon and in concert with the many layers of plantation history and settlement in the tidewater region of Virginia. Hampton's campus is near the original colony of Jamestown, which was both a plantation and settlement. The area currently known as Hampton was originally described by European settlers as Kecoughtan, an Anglicized Indigenous word for the people who lived on that part of the peninsula. These Algonquian-speaking peoples were driven off their land or killed after colonists engaged in a series of attacks in order to secure land and build military forts. When settlers decided that Kecoughtan was too heathen a name, the settlement was renamed Elizabeth City, and later renamed Hampton.[5] The Hampton region also claims one of the first free schools established by settlers, although it was established for the white settler population and not for Black or Indigenous peoples.[6] Therefore, the establishment of slavery and settlement on Indigenous lands always already included the establishment of schools, even at this early stage.[7] In addition to the free school for the white population of Hampton, the plantation itself was of course viewed as educational.[8] For example, Carter G. Woodson, the Black historian of education, poignantly observed that when slaves were brought from Africa they had to "be trained to meet the needs of the environment."[9] Thus, the endpoint of the triangular trade always had an educational component.

Hampton was part of the Chesapeake tobacco cultivation region, with many plantations founded across the peninsula. These plantations largely depleted the soil by 1830, leading to a reduction in large-scale plantation farming on the peninsula. By 1860 approximately 43.2 percent of people in the county surrounding Hampton were enslaved, which was a slightly smaller percentage than other regions of Virginia with larger plantations still operating. However, by 1860 Edwin Ruffin Jr. was credited with introducing the diversification of crops to the region and reinvigorating large-scale farming, making it possible for plantation lands that had been depleted to be profitable in a new way.[10] This allowed for the Hampton Institute, when it was founded, to grow a variety of crops for use by the school as well as for sale.

With the beginning of the Civil War, Hampton, along with the rest of Virginia, sided with the Confederacy. When the North took control of the area, the white population abandoned the town, creating a large population of "contraband of war," the term used for Black people.[11] During the Civil War, the Black population of the Hampton area quadrupled as Black people fled to Union-controlled land.[12] Hampton was established on abandoned land that had formerly been known as the Little Scotland Plantation. The main house on Hampton's campus was built in the original location of the main plantation house.[13] Thus the connection between the spatial layout of the plantation and the construction of the school campus was still pronounced post-emancipation, when the plantation had to take on new forms since it could no longer be tied to juridical enslavement.[14] Hampton, therefore, drew on the spatial and historical legacy of the plantation as an educational space while exceeding the historical definition of a plantation as it reinvented itself in the post-emancipation period.

Many scholars have discussed how the plantation has come to signify something specific in relation to Blackness, antiblackness, and Black modernity. While not fully contesting that this is true, I argue for a more capacious understanding of the plantation that incorporates its profound anti-Indigeneity and deep embeddedness in the project of transforming land and relations to land through settlement, with devastating effects on Native peoples and our nonhuman kin. The history of the plantation is part of global colonial projects of domination that both encompassed and exceeded racialized slavery across these locations. The fundamental action of the plantation was the planting and upheaval of what the land was in order to make it something else, as part of

European settlement and the brutal exploitation of converting non-human life into "resources." This is not to assert colonialism's primacy as an analytic over and above antiblackness or racial capitalism but rather to acknowledge the multiple complex systems of oppression working upon self-same land and shared space.[15] I examine these intricacies in the post-emancipation era to underscore both how the signification of slavery sticks to the plantation and how other relationships, such as settlement and the genocide and dispossession of Native peoples, exist in tandem with, exceed, and are connected to the plantation.

Examining the many-pronged definitions of the term "plantation" demonstrates how the plantation as a concept is far more capacious than a single lineage of slavery.[16] The first definition in the Oxford English Dictionary is of a modern capitalist space: "An estate on which crops such as coffee, sugar, and tobacco are cultivated by resident labor."[17] This definition already occludes two relationships inherent in the plantation: first, that resident labor was historically slave labor (or, at a minimum, coerced contract labor that echoed conditions of enslavement); and second, that the "estate" is preceded by settlement, which only renders the former possible through the dispossession of Indigenous lands. Estates, as spaces conscribed by ownership, only exist as part of colonialism. The second definition of the plantation focuses on "trees under cultivation."[18] This idea of planting trees, though it may seem unconnected, dovetails with the third definition I examine, that of a "colony." A plantation as a "colony or new settlement" derives from the description of the first locations where Europeans settled in the new world.[19] As Houston A. Baker Jr. discusses in *Turning South Again,* the plantation signifies a "transplanting" of people similar to the transplanting of plants, a "laying out of wealth" of the colonizer onto a new spatial plane. This notion of the plantation as a "settlement of persons in some locality, especially the planting of a colony" is the historical formation I bring into focus.[20] The plantation is a space of transplanting both slaves and colonizers into and onto land. Tiffany Lethabo King names this layered space the settlement/plantation, a "hybrid spatial unit," which demonstrates how settlement and slavery are co-eval projects of domination.[21] Similarly, Katherine McKittrick notes that the plantation is central to modernity in that it "fostered complex black and non-black geographies in the Americas and provided the blueprint for future sites of racial entanglement."[22] I suggest that the plantation is a complex form of production and an enduring metaphor that is central to thinking about settlement, slavery, and imperialism together. The history of Hampton perfectly illustrates this layered history of slavery and settlement.

The education students received at Hampton was reminiscent of the labor done on plantations, with Hampton students working long hours in addition to studying. The school was split between the normal school (teacher preparation program) and the night school, which was meant to prepare students to enter the normal program. Normal school students worked two ten-hour days either on the farm or in the various industrial shops, meaning they only went to lessons three days of the week. Night school students worked even longer hours, toiling for six ten-hour days and completing coursework in the evenings after work.[23] The schooling students received was generally elementary level, as the goal was to produce elementary school teachers rather than provide college-level instruction.[24] Outside of coursework and labor, students were subject to strict routines of social discipline based on army drilling.[25]

The students' workdays could involve a number of trades, such as tailoring, knitting, and carpentry. Locations of labor for men included the Huntingdon Industrial works, which was mostly a saw mill and lumber yard; machine shops; the harness shop; the shoe shop; the tin shop; the blacksmith shop; the printing office; and the wheelwright shop. For the girls, the departments consisted of housework; laundry; sewing; cooking; and dairy, which included care of stock animals and butter churning. By and large, the majority of Black male students labored on the school farm with the second largest group working at the Huntingdon Industrial works. Amongst the Black female students, the largest group worked in the housework department, followed by the laundry. Amongst the Native students, farming and carpentry were the most common jobs performed by males and housework or laundry by females.[26] This work often supplied local businesses and provided funds for the school, with students producing goods for local and regional merchants for consumption and sale.[27] Hampton glorified this work in its publications, often focusing on the types of work students accomplished. Discussion of academics was extremely limited. For example, in the book *Everyday Life at the Hampton Normal and Agricultural Institute* there are pictures of students cleaning floors, working in the laundry, ironing, pushing vegetables on a cart, caring for cows, working in greenhouses, gardening, making butter, and polishing silver, amongst other tasks; only two pictures showed students reading or doing any academic work. Both pictures featured Black male students and one picture focuses on religious instruction and reading the Bible.[28]

Despite the number of shops students could work in, James Anderson has argued that Hampton's form of education did not accomplish much in the way of vocational education for its students. In his analysis of the Hampton curriculum, Anderson argues that Hampton's main goal was to work students "long and hard so that they would embody, accept, and preach the ethic of hard toil."[29] This form of education avoided confronting the white planter class, which was reasserting its control of the South.[30] Hampton focused on participation in economic life while at the same time discouraging participation in political life, positioning Black people as agricultural laborers rather than as voters.[31] As Donal Lindsey has stated, Hampton placed an emphasis on the action of emancipation itself rather than on what could actually be changed for Black people post-emancipation.[32] This was a shift from slavery in that people were no longer owned outright but a far cry from full emancipation in any sense of the word. Therefore, this second-class-citizen position was an extension of the plantation and of slavery insofar as Blacks were embraced as agricultural laborers but not as political participants.[33]

Hampton had two farms where students were put to work as agricultural laborers; the original was the Whipple farm and the second the Shellbanks farm, which was located a few miles from the main campus on land that used to be part of the Shellbanks and Canebrake plantations.[34] Shellbanks was a space that served many functions for Hampton. It served as a space of punishment far from the main campus where unruly students could be sent.[35] It was also a space that tied together the past and present of the plantation, harkening back to the tidewater settler planters with its architecture, which was drawn from old plantation buildings, and with the implementation of new scientific farming techniques that were seen as a means to save the Southern agricultural economy.[36] Shellbanks was an integrated farm school, with a newly built farm house where students could learn all aspects of farm life and where they boarded.[37] Students who boarded at the Shellbanks Farm rarely visited the main campus; they worked from 8:00 a.m. to noon daily and had lessons from 1:00 p.m. to 3:30 p.m.[38]

Not all students found the Hampton model as appealing as Booker T. Washington describes in *Up From Slavery*. In 1887, students protested the amount of work they were forced to perform and used the phrase "confined for three years" to define their education, likening it to a convict labor gang. Anderson explains that Hampton "like the reformatories . . . sometimes contracted out student labor to outside entrepreneurs."[39] Thus, Hampton was also a site of Black immobilization. Houston Baker Jr. theorizes the plantation as the organizational structure that is subsequent to the slave ship, a space of caging, making it so that Black bodies cannot move freely.[40]

Connecting the notions of penality, imprisonment, and immobilization allows Baker to draw lines between plantations not only as physical spaces but also as terrains of meaning that have relevance for the study of Black modernity. Baker also notes the importance of transplanting (as discussed above) and how the plantation establishes a "colony in 'conquered' territory." Baker's theorization acknowledges the symbolic dimension of the plantation as well as how it transforms Native lands, Native peoples, and Black people through transplantation. Similarly, Katherine McKittrick describes how the plantation creates a realm of placelessness; it is a realm Black people are never allowed to belong to, one in whch they cannot own the place where they have been transplanted, and a place where violence can indiscriminately be practiced on their bodies. The placelessness and violence that are foundational to the plantation structure future racial geographies such as the prison, or, in this case, the violence of a school like Hampton, which immobilized and imprisoned Black bodies.[41]

Intertwined with the fact that Hampton was like a plantation is the fact that Hampton was also always a settlement, as the history of Kecoughtan before the establishment of the Little Scotland Plantation demonstrates. Thus, it seems almost prophetic that Hampton not only educated Black people but also Indigenous peoples. Booker T. Washington describes his own work with the first Indigenous students at Hampton and the role Black students like himself undertook as models for Indigenous students.[42] Washington's discussion of modeling civilization for Native students likely reflected what he heard from Hampton educators who compared slavery to the reservation. For example, the founder of Hampton, Samuel Chapman Armstrong, wrote that the "western reservation resembles to some extent the southern plantation, and I believe that those of us who have to do with the education and civilization of Indians can learn many things from the dealings of our southern friends with the plantation negro." He continued by asserting that "while we all rejoice in the fact that slavery is a thing of the past, *yet I firmly believe that under the most favorable conditions it was a much more successful school* for training of a barbarous race than is the reservation. *Slavery brought colored men into close contact with his white brother, training him in habits of work.*"[43] Armstrong asserts here that the plantation was a successful school, that labor and "contact" with whiteness are pedagogic, and that the pedagogy of the plantation was missing from the reservation. These assertions formed the basis of the plantation pedagogy practiced at Hampton.

THE TENETS OF PLANTATION PEDAGOGY

The two main tenets of plantation pedagogy are that (1) the plantation is educative through proximity to whiteness, and (2) labor, as a form of teaching, functions through the idealization of the productive use of space. These educative actions were proposed by white reformers as necessary for the civilization of Black people after the Civil War and, as I will show in part two, for the Indigenous peoples of North America and for imperial projects in the Pacific and back across the Atlantic. Throughout this book, I examine the effort the founders, teachers, and promoters of the Hampton Institute put into asserting that these forms of pedagogy would result in learning and so-called civilizational advancement, contingent as that concept was for non-white bodies. I argue that, although the idealized relationships of teaching the other and raising them up are always deferred or partial, this does not mean that plantation pedagogy did not have enduring material effects. Instead of transforming Black and Indigenous peoples, plantation pedagogy has always functioned to create and maintain white access to property and to produce idealized relationships to land and space alongside the maintenance of the organizing structures of antiblackness. Therefore, I reject the claims made by white educators from the later nineteenth and early twentieth centuries that industrial pedagogies assimilated, civilized, and emancipated Black and Indigenous peoples.

This discourse of proximity to whiteness framed slavery as educative through its instruction in labor, which obfuscated the violent realities of slavery and its afterlife. Hampton used slavery as a didactic comparison when discussing the education of Indigenous peoples and other groups subject to US imperialism and colonization. For example, a 1903 reprint in the *Southern Workman* of a speech by professor Kelly Miller, a Black scholar who sought to mediate between the more radical position of Du Bois and the conservative position of white reformers and their protégés like Booker T. Washington, states: "In slavery days the relation between master and slave was very close, and while there came with it much of evil, the Negro race derived from its close contact with a superior race certain very great advantages."[44] Comparisons of this sort were common in Hampton's publications, which used a discourse of Black civilization through proximity to whiteness as an example for Indigenous students to emulate. The concept of "proximity to whiteness" in this chapter denotes physical proximity to white people, spaces, and norms of behavior that is seen as educational in and of itself, regardless of the actions that actually occur through that proximity.⁴⁵ Proximity is rendered pedagogic even without specific pedagogical intent, and in the face of severe cruelty and degradation. While the white educators and reformers discussed in this chapter at times saw their actions as the primary guides, at other times it was simply the space itself, regardless of the white bodies present within these spaces, that was seen as educative.⁴⁶ There was no standard formulation for how proximity to whiteness functioned within industrial education. White educators and reformers who described proximity to whiteness as educative constantly shifted their discourses so that varying amounts and levels of proximity were seen as educative or not, making all supposed gains based on proximity equally effective. White bodies could be present in large numbers or small numbers, and the relationships between them and Black and Indigenous bodies could take a number of forms.⁴⁷ The specifics of the spatial relations shifted as needed to accommodate a variety of scenarios as the pedagogy moved across contexts.

The ideology of proximity to whiteness, for example, is explicitly promoted in an article titled "White Instructors of Negro Pupils," published in a 1903 issue of the *Southern Workman*. The article begins by stating that "education of the highest order usually follows the most accomplished intellectual and spiritual masters."⁴⁸ It continues by describing how enslaved Black people were "brought . . . near to noble men and women," which could be seen as a "happy featyre" of their "hard lot . . . under slavery."⁴⁹ This article describes the large numbers of white teachers who taught in Black schools post-emancipation and particularly argues for the efficacy of Southern white women as teachers of Black students, calling them the "daughters of affluent old time slave-owners."⁵⁰ Further, the article notes that, when it is impractical to have white teachers, Black teachers should have at least been trained by white teachers or have white benefactors to guide them in their teaching and gives the Tuskegee Institute as an example of a Black school that was under white influence.⁵¹ In an article describing Hampton teachers touring the Calhoun School, it is noted that the visit ended with the Black students singing plantation songs. But "drilling by white teachers or by teachers who have been trained by white teachers have taken any of the primitive wildness and peculiar pathos, out of them."⁵² This was described as a benefit and a mark of civilization by the publication. The presence of white teachers was framed as having transformed Black cultural resistance to the plantation into a demonstration of Black learning potential.⁵³

Other traces of proximity as educative appear in transit through educational policy and practice. For example, during school integration in the latter half of the twentieth century, "sitting next to white children" in integrated classrooms was deemed educative, even though Black community leaders offered a social structural critique of the increased resources provided to the white children and a discussion of whether this sitting was symbolic of equality. Despite these critiques, this discourse persists into the present. Test scores or references to cultural markers such as "valuing education" are used to assert that schools with larger white populations are better. Despite the protestations of Black desegregation leaders that sitting next to white children was about proximity to resources and the ability to imagine more equal forms of education, the traces of proximity to whiteness as educative stick to the discourse about school integration, providing a place for slippage in meaning.[54]

Proximity to whiteness as educative also functions through valuing and engaging in labor. Armstrong noted in the above quote that proximity was about "training [Black people] in habits of work," and he lists the various occupations that slavery taught. Even more specifically, Armstrong noted that "the negro was taught to work, to be an agriculturalist, a mechanic, a material producer of something useful."[55] Defining labor as only that which is productive and useful dovetails with settler definitions of Indigenous forms of work as not being useful.[56] Slavery was framed as pedagogic not only because it put slaves in proximity to white masters but also because it settled land and made it useful, which Native land management practices were not thought to do. This ideology was maintained over time at Hampton. The second president of the school, for example, repeats this ideology that proximity leads to productive labor: "... slavery with all its disadvantages taught the negroes the English language, regular habits of industry, and the truths of the Christian religion."[57] I connect the discussion of learning "regular habits of industry" to the transformation of land and relations to it.

Part of what proximity to whiteness does is attempt to erase Indigeneity and detribalize those with whom it comes into contact. This is as true for those who were transported to the Americas on slave ships as for those who lived on the lands that Europeans came to settle. Erasure and detribalization, of course, are always a failed projects, what Joseph Pierce has called the "the impossible mandate of assimilation."[58] Thus, I argue that there is crossover but neither equivalence between antiblackness and anti-Indigeneity nor a singular primacy of one over the other. They intersect in moments like these when Black students are portrayed as needing civilizational uplift through contact with the white race in order to detribalize them fully. The argument that

Indigenous peoples need the same thing was made by proponents of off-reservation boarding schools like Richard Henry Pratt, the funder of Carlisle Indian School. At this intersection, the imagined Venn diagram between antiblackness and anti-Indigeneity almost becomes a circle; yet at other historical moments or when different discourses are highlighted, the diagram shifts so that the sliver of contact might appear miniscule. The shifting crossover is part of the reason why Black and Indigenous communities become pitted against each other; but it also allows for political movements of solidarity. I argue that antiblackness and anti-Indigeneity are a confluence. Neither necessarily powers the other; instead, they coexist in this space of crossover. In this example, "productive labor" indexes both slavery and the transformation of Indigenous lands from land that was seen by settlers as "unproductive" into "useful" space that could make something of value to the capitalist economy (and, in fact, is viewed as something of value to that economy).

However, in Hampton's narrative of slavery as a school, labor does not create property for Black people because they are ontologically defined as property themselves and cannot attain property. In fact, Iyko Day, writing from a Marxist perspective, asserts that there can be no labor in slavery.[59] Labor becomes a pedagogical act that teaches how to relate to space whether or not Black laborers materially gain something through their work.[60] Materially, the pedagogical work of labor transforms land into property or reinforces relations of ownership, rendering the plantation space itself as the pedagogic actor. In the passages quoted above, Armstrong lists occupations such as blacksmith, farmer, mechanic, or carpenter, but he does not include the role of landowner.[61] The Black "students" of the plantation are meant to learn to see land as a relationship of property—for example, to work as homebuilders or as farmers—but their actual ownership of that land is never the point of plantation pedagogy, even if, despite the obstacles they face, they do acquire property. If Black people do acquire land as property, then they "become viewed by white settlers as placeholders on stolen Indigenous lands." In fact, "the truth is white settlers have no problem *giving* Indigenous land to Black people until they want it back."[62] Therefore, plantation pedagogy uses labor not just for capitalist accumulation but also to produce imagined relations to property that both dispossess and seek to eliminate Native peoples, while at the same time deferring the enactment of property relations by Black people in temporal space.

Booker T. Washington made similar remarks regarding labor as pedagogic in his defense of industrial education for Black people in the South:

> While the Negro was not allowed during slavery to learn to read, he was taught to labor. At the close of the war the Negro had a practical monopoly of the common and skilled labor in the Southern states. To a very large extent the economic progress of the South has been and still is dependent upon the degree to which the Negro preserves in freedom that skill in the trades which he learned in slavery. Not only must the Negro laborer preserve and hand down to his children the traditions of what he had already learned, but he must be encouraged constantly to improve and fit himself for the more difficult tasks of a more complicated civilization.[63]

Washington's discussion here borrows from the narrative that slavery was educative and also signals the importance of learning labor in slavery. This valorization of labor contributes to a narrative of civilizational improvement that situates Black people as in need of labor to learn and progress. Washington goes on to discuss how slavery has made Black people rebel against labor as an educative project and that "it has been necessary to teach the masses of the Negro people in the South that freedom means harder, more earnest, and more persistent labor than they ever knew in slavery."[64] By positioning labor as even more necessary in freedom, he uses an educational narrative to serve coercive capitalist accumulation.[65]

The use of labor as an educational tool allows for a form of doublespeak, letting learning stand in for earning the products of that labor. Property is of course always meant to belong to whites, and Black acquisition of property is always a contingent prospect, as is apparent from the deferred promise of forty acres and a mule. The Black students' labor on and outside of Hampton's campus was not meant to actually produce property for Black people. Instead, it functioned as a means to create property for whites, even if it incidentally created property for Black people through their own agentic use of that education. For the Indigenous students at Hampton, the pedagogical process of labor spread to the space of the reservation, merging the educative functions of slavery and settlement. For example, by teaching labor to Indigenous students in the context of the allotment era, Hampton educators used a discourse of learning to work to physically convert reservation trust lands to property so that it could be transferred to white land speculators and settlers. In this way, I conceive of policies like the Dawes Act as pedagogical acts that seek to transform reservation space into plantation space and that view land as a fungible target of education.[66] Thus, the post-Reconstruction plantation is deeply connected to the allotment era of federal Indian policy.

THE PLANTATION AS A SPACE OF EDUCATION

An integral aspect of plantation pedagogy is the transformation of space in addition to the transformation of people. Yet, space as a concept can mean a number of things, including the physical space that is occupied, space as a social relationship, or space as imagination.[67] I rely on definitions of space that understand it as socially produced through interaction embedded in material relations. Thus, land and landscapes, such as plantations, must be understood through social processes. These social processes consist of everyday actions, discourses and representations of space, and spatial imaginaries that work in tandem.[68] Actions and representations of space work directly as part of its social production, while spatial imaginaries help define the desires about what space can be made into. When I discuss space in this chapter, I mean both the physical space as well as the metaphorical and imagined conditions of that space. How space is carved up, its extent, the things to which it is proximate, and the density of populations inhabiting it all become the aspects of that space that imbue it with value. The plantation can be invoked as a physical space or an imagined set of relations.

My discussion of space in this book focuses on colonial and antiblack spatial organization rather than Black and Indigenous conceptualizations of place as locations of "presence, futurity, imagination, power, and knowing."[69] Eve Tuck and Marcia McKenzie discuss how theories of space have moved from those that define space as a "container for matter" or "set of coordinates" through which things move to a more socially produced and dynamic process that is laced with power.[70] Yet, they point out how both these notions disregard Indigenous understandings of place, which emphasize rootedness, specificity, and relationships.[71] I know that Black and Indigenous understandings of place are wholly different than colonial and antiblack ideas of space. The relationships Black and Indigenous peoples develop and maintain with places is not the focus of my analysis of plantation pedagogy—not because I do not believe they exist. I know intimately that these relations do exist and are rich sources of survival, fugitivity, and resistance.[72] I have found in my years of writing that academics are often asked to juxtapose discussions of structures of oppression with an attention to the agency of people within that system as a means to counter totalizing narratives. I am aware that the spatial configurations I discuss could never be total and that Black and Indigenous peoples moved across, through, against, and in relation to these spaces in a variety of ways that challenged, cohered, resisted, and sought to negate these spatial formations.[73] I know that my turn away from describing the relations of place in favor of the relations of space directly contradicts scholars like Tuck and McKenzie who call on us to make the opposite move and center place in our analysis.[74] I focus on the relations of space to trace how they work pedagogically, knowing that Black and Indigenous forms of learning through place are fundamentally different, and I do not wish to confuse the two.[75] Instead, I want this work to unravel the space-making functions of plantation pedagogy, leaving Black and Indigenous forms of place-based learning and relationships outside of the academy and its commodifying impulses. These impulses too often consume Indigenous and Black projects of learning as part of social justice reform efforts that do not materially change conditions for Black and Indigenous youth.

Pedagogy is often associated specifically with teachers, but it can also, of course, be enacted by people in many other professions such as medicine, public health, or policing.[76] In plantation pedagogy it is not always the metaphorical or literal white master who teaches (although it can be and often is), it is also the space of the plantation itself and the various aspects of that space that are educative. In a similar vein, the schoolroom is set up in a specific way—such as how the desks are laid out, which way they are facing, and where blackboards and projector screens are positioned—to teach how the classroom functions. All of these spatial components teach the students where to place their attention and what the dynamics of teaching should look like. Progressive educators often discuss changes in the layout of classrooms as a means to effect different pedagogic methods, such as discussion-based group work rather than lecturing. In my analysis of educational space, I turn to theories of space that denaturalize spatial organization.[77] I take as a starting point that "spaces are organized to sustain unequal social relations," that "these relations shape spaces," and that the discourse of education plays an integral role in the organization and sustainability of these spaces.[78]

The imagining of space is also an aspect of the spatialization of teaching slavery and settlement. Western definitions of space consist of imagined boundaries that encircle imagined concepts of property.[79] These imagined boundaries are enforced, physically limiting and corralling space in order to allow for its ownership—whether by an individual, a corporation, a state, or a nation—in measurable quantities. Imagining space as measurable and bounded produces a form of rational spatial relations that are codified in law and custom.[80] In the production of space as property, Indigenous peoples are displaced and dispossessed of land, and Black and other racialized bodies are made to labor (or do other things) as part of its creation.[81] This process is of course complicated and multipronged because of the different modes of relating, using, connecting, and conceptualizing the created space. I utilize the definition of Mar and Edmonds when thinking about space "not simply as a geographic place to be traveled across, allotted or carved, nor merely defined by the erasure of the colonized by the colonizers," but rather as "a process of production through oppression, resistance, and accommodation, and as both a material place and a phenomenon of the imagination."[82] The idea that space becomes a phenomenon of the imagination and encompasses the transformation of land into property is part and parcel of Western imaginations of civilization and the frontier between civilization and savagery.

Spatial imaginings are harnessed by educational programs, which direct imaginations towards specific spatial formations.[83] The concept of idealized didactic spaces as proposed by Jane Lydon demonstrates how education creates imagined space in the service of settlement within the Australian context. Using the example of Moravian missionaries in Australia, Lydon states that "missionaries were guided by a culturally specific imagined geography that demanded the creation of idealized landscapes intended to teach through example and performance."[84] These imagined geographies, which sought to reorganize aboriginal Australian towns and homes, were meant to create a new gendered and classed (and, I would add to this argument, racial) order.[85] The Hampton industrial education model was also meant to create didactic spaces that sought to reorganize school and home spaces in order to produce specific familial and racialized structures. Idealized didactic spaces are integral to plantation pedagogy, in which forms of teaching are tied to imagining how spaces should be organized and what kinds of ontological and spatial orders they should produce. Space—whether the classroom, the industrial shop, the dorm room, the reservation, or the slave plantation—as a means of instruction is an imagined process meant to have material effects by producing specific relations to land and property and mapping out ontological relations to that property.

THE TIME-SPACE OF PROTEAN PLANTATIONS

As I have argued, the plantation is not geographically situated only in the South but is in fact global; yet it has come to signify something specific about the South and Black modernity, despite historical roots and a capacious reach that exceed that geography. Additionally, the plantation continued to expand

and transform itself further after emancipation with the expansion of US imperialism. With this in mind, I examine some economic and political definitions of the plantation as part of the genealogical and archeological excavation of the plantation's circulating forms. One very well-known example of defining the plantation is Curtin's "plantation complex," which lists six primary features of the plantation: (1) it uses primarily slave labor, (2) it does not have a self-sustaining population, (3) it functions through large scale capitalist production, (4) the owner has authority over the space and the people who work it, (5) it is created to ship goods to distant markets, and (6) political control over the plantation happens from another continent or in another society, what Curtin calls "domination from a distance."[86] Curtin sees the tropical Americas—the Caribbean and parts of South America—as the quintessential example of the plantation complex, which morphed into slightly different instantiations over time, such as the US Southern plantation, which did have a self-sustaining population of slaves. Other scholars in this vein of economic and political analysis have sought to define plantations as engaging in large, centralized agriculture and monocrop production or as a "spatially unified land-factory" in which the growing and processing of a single product occurs in one space.[87]

These definitions are, of course, easily criticized from a variety of angles. They treat slavery as a formation of labor rather than as the complex system of immobilization, fungibility, and imposed placelessness that Black scholars have consistently asserted it was.[88] These definitions also belie the complexity of Indigenous relationships to plantation space, as has been outlined by scholars such as Andres Resendez in *The Other Slavery* and in discussions of Black and Indigenous fugitivity and marronage.[89] They also generalize plantations as pure constructs, emplacing them in a history of colonialism, capitalism, or regional history, irrespective of their status as spatial formations of settlement, genocide, violence, and racial formation across space and time. What is generative in these flawed categorizations of the plantation is the way in which the plantation as a settlement and a location of enslavement is intimately tied to colonialism and empire, whether or not this connection is explicitly made by these scholars. For example, plantations were established in Asia through what Curtin calls "trading post empires," which he describes as distinct from the pure type of plantation complex in "true empires," "settlement empires," or "true colonization" in the Americas.[90] Whether or not these classifications are accurate, they demonstrate how schemes of categorizing plantations are connected with varied forms and registers of colonialism and imperialism.

Across these varied registers the plantation also has a fluctuating temporality. McKittrick discusses what she calls "the uneven time-space workings of plantation logics," which means that there is not a linear relation between the plantation and its protean forms.[91] McKittrick suggests that the plantation is "migratory" with a "built in capacity to maintain itself," yet it is "cloaked as if it is the past as it moves through time."[92] The plantation as such is a spatial formation that temporally does not follow easy rules with clear transformations, endings, or beginnings, especially in relation to violence against Black bodies. A similar concept coined by Anne McClintock is "anachronistic space," a way of discussing Indigenous peoples and spaces as always temporally in the past.[93] I argue that Black students at Hampton also reckoned with anachronistic space since Black education was framed as in stasis or in need of reverting to a previous time: that of slavery. Hampton educators often discussed how their educational system was a mediating stage between slavery and full citizenship, rendering Black education as temporally fixed, while framing it as if in movement. Another key argument Hampton made to describe Black education was that freedom came too soon and that Black progression was not in sync with present-day emancipation. These forms of anachronistically temporalizing Black education connected the education that was offered to the plantation, whether or not schools were geographically in the same space as previous or current plantations (although, to be clear, many in fact were built on former plantation land). Framing Indigenous peoples as in the past made them not of the same temporality as the plantation and in need of learning how to exist in a new temporality, at least until their foretold death.

The temporality of spatial imaginaries of the plantation structure desires of past, present, and future relationships to land. McKittrick notes a number of times that the plantation was built on and transformed "the lands of no one into the lands of someone."[94] She does not explicitly discuss that the lands of no one are Native lands, although she knew and implied that it was not in fact "the lands of no one." I read McKittrick as acknowledging *terra nullius* as a colonialist figuration of space. Part of the transformation of land from belonging to "no one" to belonging to whites was the "planting" of Black people in that land, "not as members of society but as commodities that would bolster crop economies."[95] This connection between the imagined and physical transformation of land and the role of Black enslavement in that process demonstrates the connection between ontological subject-making and the transformation of land. The "planting" of Black people in the land was also a paradoxical process. It created "an economized and enforced placelessness that demanded the enslaved work and thus be chained to the land," which "normalized black dispossession, white supremacy, and other colonial-racial geographies, while naturalizing the racist underpinnings of land exploitation as accumulation and emancipation."[96] In fact, this paradoxical process sets up the discourse that land exploitation and accumulation are what constitute freedom in the United States. These same discourses can be traced through racial uplift ideologies of educators like Booker T. Washington, whose educational model hinged on Black ownership as a means to achieve freedom.[97] Land exploitation and the discourse of emancipation have in fact been linked in a number of ways; for example, emancipation has been used as an argument for the taking of Indigenous lands in policies like the Dawes Severalty Act and the legislative termination of tribal status.[98] The connection between freedom and property is mediated through the space of the plantation, and as Sylvia Wynter writes in *Plot and Plantation,* "the law of the plantation is based on the rights of property."[99] The plantation, through the concept of property, is where the transformation of land, the genocide of Native peoples, and the violence against Black bodies intersect spatially and temporally.

In the words of Katherine McKittrick, the plantation is protean and expands itself temporally and spatially.[100] Because the plantation is protean, its existence across space and time is ubiquitous in what could be termed the Global South as well as within the United States. Lisa Lowe notes this connection in *The Intimacies of Four Continents* and discusses the links between the slave trade and plantation production and Indigenous genocide alongside the eventual transition from slavery to "free" wage labor and contract labor of Asian migrants in the late nineteenth and early twentieth centuries.[101] Through an attention to "linked, but not identical, genealogies, Lowe reads a variety of imperial archives for the connections and intimacies between them.[102] As she notes, "the development of American Industrial capitalism, which depended on slave labor, was deeply connected with the exploitation of agrarian laborers on plantations in Asia and the Pacific Islands, in India and the islands in the Indian Ocean, in Africa, and in Latin America where plantation systems had also been established to profit from imported and Indigenous colonized workers."[103] In addition to exploitative contract labor practices, beginning in the early 1860s, there was also the history of blackbirding in the Pacific, the practice of taking Pacific Islanders by force, coercion, false promises, and so on, to be contract laborers in locations like Australia and Peru.[104] This process was linked to discourses about Pacific Islanders that framed them as connected to Blacks in the United States and to the circulating ideologies of white supremacy that were present throughout the Pacific and Oceania.[105] The circulation of conditions that were similar to slavery and tied to the end of slavery, but were not slavery itself, was connected to the proliferation of plantations as physical spaces across the Pacific, including, for example, the sugar plantations that relied on local Indigenous or imported labor in locations like Hawai'i and the Philippines. The circulation across the Pacific of plantations as modes of production, colonial control, and coerced labor is rarely discussed in relation to similar circulations in the Atlantic during and after slavery, such as the importation of Asian labor into the Caribbean.[106]

In each of these connections, I am left to ruminate on the notion that currents often eddy, moving in circles and doubling back on themselves. For example, the shipping of slaves from Western Africa to spice plantation settlements in Indonesia in the seventeenth century could be seen as yet another iteration of slavery and settlement moving in the currents of colonialism; but this current moves in directions opposite to those that the dominant narrative would predict.[107] None of these formations are exact replicas of each other, yet they are related through their crossing in the currents. Thus, these scholars caution us not to underestimate the pure spatial reach of the plantation, which, despite being constitutive of a complex and shifting modernity, invokes a nostalgic and essentialized image of the old South, fixed in time and anti-modern.[108]

Therefore, if the plantation is a space of intersection crosslinked with the ontological process of slavery, with land seizure and dispossession, with genocide, and with imperial projects of domination, how then can the mechanisms of this space be delineated? That is, what actions can be implemented through the plantation? I argue that plantation pedagogy is expandable and transferable by its very nature, or, as King puts it, the plantation is "a transferable form of disciplinary and spatial power that is used to make colonial and settler colonial space even when the white, settler-master is not present."[109] The act of creating space is always a pedagogic project in addition to a material one.

PLANTATION PEDAGOGY MOVES IN CURRENTS OF COLONIALISM

I conceptualize plantation pedagogy as a technology of settlement. la paperson describes settler colonialism not as something that happened to Native peoples but as something that happened for colonizers and settlers.[110] It therefore functions as a machine that "[runs] on desires for the colonizer's future."[111] Schooling is then part of these "assemblages of machines" whose component parts work in a variety of ways as both individual and interconnected technologies to produce this colonial future. An important aspect of understanding plantation pedagogy as a part of these assemblages of machines is that colonial machines not only seek to biopolitically manage populations, particularly Black and Indigenous peoples, but also aim to support the colonizer's future.[112] This is manifested in the "conversion of land into property, and of people into targets of subjugation."[113] I utilize the concepts of technologies and machines because they are concerned with the "mechanics not just the motives" of colonialism.[114] Colonial motives are often ambivalent in their discourse, but they are consistent in their material effects. Tracing the mechanics of these machines provides information and blueprints for dismantling, sabotage, and scavenging rather than blaming or creating antagonism between Black and Indigenous communities.[115]

These technologies "mutate," "evolve," and "spread" over time.[116] la paperson notes that the Hampton Institute served as a "model for colonial schools throughout the world."[117] He uses the language of trafficking to describe its movement across continents and to connect it to US state colonial violence:

> Colonial schools have been *trafficked* around the world. Colonial schooling in Kenya, Black schooling in the post-Abolition U.S. South, education for pacification of indigenous people in the Pacific, and Indian boarding schools in North America are intertwined through a set of exchanges of peoples, ideas, models, and philosophies never more than a few degrees of separation away from the U.S. Department of War.[118]

la paperson suggests that by tracing models like Hampton's industrial schooling program, historians can create "a map of the trafficking of colonial technologies in radically different lands."[119] This book takes on that project and tracks plantation pedagogy through currents of colonialism across continents and oceans.

The transfer of educational models relies not only on the transit of educational ideas but also on the movements of bodies over both ocean and land. Therefore, the expansion of educational models is both literal—teachers and reformers sailed and traveled across oceans and through various landscapes to teach and propose educational policy—and also figurative in that ideas traveled, moving in patterns that ebbed and flowed. Drawing inspiration from the work of Jodi Byrd and her discussion of the "transit of empire," I trace how the transit of plantation pedagogy illuminates the process of educational diffusion, the intersection of antiblackness and colonialism, and the political and theoretical commitments of Black and Native studies.[120]

I offer the term *currents of colonialism* as a means to examine the transit of plantation pedagogy, its ideology, and its material effects. Currents, like the plantation, is an expansive concept, and its use and meaning has an ambivalence that can contribute to, reify, and challenge colonial dominance. Because of its expansive nature, the term *current* suffers from an overabundance of definitions. The first and most direct is "a body of water or air moving in a definite direction, especially through a surrounding body of water or air in which there is less movement."[121] The scientific descriptions of currents note that they are "continuous, predictable, directional movement of seawater" driven by a variety of processes.[122] Native Pacific scholar J. Kēhaulani Kauanui discusses these definitions in her introduction to the special issue of *American Quarterly* on "Pacific Currents":

> An ocean current is a continuous, directed movement of seawater generated by the forces acting on what physicists call a "mean flow," such as breaking waves, wind, and temperature, with tides caused by the gravitational pull of the moon and the sun. Of course, shoreline conditions and other currents can influence the ocean current's course and power. Ocean currents can flow for great distances, and together they create the great flow of the global conveyor belt, part of the large-scale ocean circulation that plays a dominant part in determining the climate of many of the Earth's regions. Thus "Pacific currents" seems an appropriate metaphor in that the Pacific is too often a forgotten zone, but one of the most capacious.[123]

Like Kauanui, I am interested in the metaphor of ocean currents as a capacious mode of understanding. I see currents as a way to theorize the circulation of colonial thought as well as the movement of people and things through and across currents creating varying colonial structures. Additionally, the idea of a current has many meanings. It can be understood as "an opinion or a feeling that a group of people have"; something that is "used as a medium for exchange"; something that is "generally accepted, used, practiced, or prevalent at the moment"; a "flow marked by force or strength"; "a tendency or course of events that is usually the result of an interplay of forces"; or "a prevailing mood."[124] The notion of something being temporally current, alongside other definitions of currents as forms of movement, forefronts how ideas that move through currents have a strength of purpose, implementation, effect, and affect.

Mel Chen provides a poignant example with their concept of animacy, which is "especially current—and it carries with it a kind of charge."[125] Chen links the concept of a current idea to electric currents, metaphorically describing the former as charged. The metaphorical charge that inhabits something defined as current can also be material. For example, undersea trans-Atlantic cables were constructed to transmit currents of electricity and information but are also subject to the movements and precarity of ocean currents, which affect their construction.[126] In another meaning, transoceanic cables were also part of "current" concerns of a time that privileged technological advancement and communication as a means of consolidating empires.[127] This example is illustrative because it connects the various overlapping meanings of currents and demonstrates the way in which something that is often viewed as a neutral good (i.e., the expansion of technology and communication) actually exists as part of colonial power structures. This way of thinking about something as current demonstrates how ideas become commonplace in circulation.

Each of these literal and figurative meanings constructs an idea of the present, of a general consensus or how the general population feels about something, and of a way to exchange the most recent and most affective ideas and concepts. Most importantly, currents are forms of movement that have directional strength, in combination with and in spite of their meandering paths. Currents can shift or eddy, and their strength may waver, but their directionality can also be predicted, charted, and utilized. This movement can come to define what is considered "of the now" and necessary for progress and advancement. I am interested in currents that transport ideas, in this case educational models and pedagogy, and define them as necessary, important, or common sense. In this way, currents help me understand the spread of both colonial structures of power and, specifically in relation to plantation pedagogy, the spread of educational models. Arguments examining the spread of educational models are often critiqued as being overdetermined by a structural analysis or, conversely, as relying on apolitical diffusion models that do not account for unequal power relations.[128] Understanding educational change as moving in the currents allows for ambivalence and changes in directionality but also for consistency in intent and effect when analyzing how models of education have been transferred through their intimate connection with the implementation of both slavery and settlement.

I define currents of colonialism as the form of material and metaphoric movement that maps how systems of colonial power function through transit. I argue that how currents move can obscure histories and connections but that they can also open up opportunities to understand how systems of power function by tracking their patterns. Lyons and Tengan, in their discussion of Pacific currents, note "the dangers and opportunities for movement that currents present" and that currents "convey an intimacy between people, land, ocean, and time."[129] While their discussion privileges the circulation of Indigenous thought that challenges colonial- and continental-focused ideas, they also note how currents help demonstrate the integral connection of the Pacific to US colonialism. One example of this often-obscured history is the intimacy between the Pacific and the Atlantic as part of the colonization of the Americas. Yokota explains that "Westerners in the early modern period worked tirelessly to establish connections between these two aquatic systems,"[130] including searching for alternate trade routes between the Atlantic and the Pacific such as a Northwest Passage. She contends that the "founding of the United States coincided with the beginning of a new era of European expansion into the Pacific."[131] Her description of this interrelationship shows how the oceanic was connected to the land and the plantation:

> The early American economy rested primarily upon the exploitation of the natural bounty of the land until well into the nineteenth century. Americans exchanged the "raw" materials of their surroundings for the "cooked" products of Europe and China. European American settlers depended upon African slaves and Native Americans to produce and procure crops and natural products that were valued on the global market. Imported slaves provided the labor needed to produce New World crops such as cotton, sugarcane, rice, and tobacco. With the profits from forced labor, slaveholders purchased the imported goods that sustained their lavish lifestyles.[132]

The United States' engagement in the Pacific is often described by historians as part of a linear timeline in which the turn to the Pacific happens after Turner's closing of the frontier, as a way to extend Manifest Destiny even further.[133] Yet, as Yokota demonstrates, the Pacific and Atlantic connections were always integral to the colonial formation of the US.

WATCHING PLANTATION PEDAGOGY
MOVE IN THE CURRENTS

This chapter has moved like the currents I describe, sometimes tarrying in the grammatical or theoretical, other times grounding itself on the shoals of historical context and example, sometimes moving in a line that seems straight, and other times circling back in ways that may appear confusing without a birds-eye view of the circular pattern it creates. When I present my work in formats such as this, I often get asked a version of the following question by a well-meaning scholar who wants to take my meandering path driven by currents and place it into a diagram that can be followed, reproduced, and scaled. This question is, What does this tell us about what we should actually do to make schools better? While the point made in this book is that a refusal to answer questions and to solve "educational problems" is a generative step, I do want to hint towards what I might see as an answer that refuses to reform schools but still offers a method for thinking about what comes next.

To do this, I turn towards theorizations of currents as a methodological choice, much like my methodological commitment to refusal. Lyons and Tengan, in their discussion of Pacific currents, note a piece of Native Hawaiian wisdom that comes from the sea: before swimming you must watch the currents to observe the riptide.[134] I take this moment to think on how this book is about watching the currents of colonialism, seeing how they move and the violence they do, noting the riptides that could drag us under, and how they force us to go in one direction when we might want to swim the other way. This allows us to apply knowledge we already have, such as the admonishments I always got growing up about how to swim out of a riptide by moving at a diagonal rather than directly against the current. I want to know currents in order to know better how to structure my own movements against them, to learn to swim in them in ways that help get me to where I want, toward a non-metaphorical decolonization, towards liberation, towards an abolitionist politic. I know there are other currents too. Ones that move counter to the colonial ones, that fight them, and people that ride them in defiance, swimming through or surfing the waves in different patterns of movement that go with and against the currents.

Watching currents lets us watch for the gaps as strategy and tactic, and we can understand accommodation to Western intrusions through oceanic knowledge: "We know also that going with the 'au' (both 'time' and 'current')—seen in that moment as technological modernity and wrested forms of governance—may be only a short-term strategy until the 'gap' to return to a shore of alternative maternities is found."[135] The knowledge that comes from these gaps gives me strength in writing this, knowing that by mapping currents and what moves on them, maybe we can identify gaps to exploit. Watching currents is definitively not the only thing we can do as Black and Indigenous peoples who want to challenge plantation pedagogy, but it is the only method I feel comfortable sharing in this venue.

PART TWO

Plantation Pedagogy in the Currents

TWO

Plantation Pedagogy on the Reservation

White reformers and educators in the post-emancipation era often compared the reservation to the plantation when they discussed the education of Black and Indigenous peoples. While they framed slavery as a system of education that worked due to its proximity to whiteness and its ability to instill a belief in the value of work, they described the reservation system as secluding Indigenous peoples from whites and, curiously, as a space in which work doesn't appear to happen (at least work as defined by colonial notions of usefulness and productivity). Armstrong claimed that it was good that slavery had formally ended, yet he asserted that slavery was educationally better than the reservation. As a part of this argument, Armstrong calls slavery a "successful school" because it trained Black people to work and become "useful," whereas he implies that the reservation does not elicit the same form of productivity from its occupants.[1] Thus, Armstrong frames the reservation as having no (or at least very little) educational value while the plantation does have educational value, setting the scene for moving plantation pedagogy to the reservation.

In these narratives of slavery as educational, labor is not an act of property creation for Black people because they are ontologically defined as property themselves and cannot attain property. Labor, then, becomes a pedagogical act instead. Labor is discussed by reformers like Armstrong as if it were pedagogical in and of itself, therefore justifying the importance of the act of labor rather than its products. In this way the rhetoric of industrial education performs a sleight of hand whereby gaining property or wealth through labor is substituted with learning through the process of labor. This substitution then contributed to exploitative systems that relied on Black labor without Black communities receiving the supposed benefits of that work. Yet, the labor done by Black students in this model does do something. It transforms land into property or maintains relations of property ownership over other forms of land organization. Plantation pedagogy uses labor not just for capitalist accumulation but also to produce imagined relations to property. At the same time, it defers the enactment of these relations to a future space of racial formations.

Employees of the Bureau of Indian Affairs also employed this comparative rhetoric. Indian Commissioner W. A. Jones wrote a letter to the superintendent of Fort Peck agency in Montana that was reprinted in the Carlisle Indian School publication, *The Red Man,* in 1904, in which he stated:

> If the same policy [i.e., reservations] had been pursued by this government in its treatment of the colored race we would now have conditions in the Southern States similar to that upon Indian Reservations; that race is only two or three generations removed from the barbarous tribes of Africa, but from the fact of their coming in contact with whites, they are practically on an quality with us as far as business and political standing is concerned.[2]

This description echoes in reverse Armstrong's earlier arguments about the plantation and the reservation, noting that, without the existence of the plantation in the South, the conditions of the Black population would be like that of Native peoples. It temporally removed Black people in the South from Indigeneity through the educative force of the plantation's proximity to whiteness, demonstrating the deep anti-Indigeneity and antiblackness of plantation pedagogies' fundamental premises. In the same year, Pratt gave a speech in which he stated, "Bringing Negroes here and scattering them, even under the heel of slavery, has had the effect to give them our language and destroy their own, and to make them a valuable part of our industrial population; and where there have been wider individual opportunities they have risen to enviable place and prosperity."[3] Pratt even goes so far to say that Native peoples "had far more right to rise against us in judgment and greater cause to condemn us than the negro ever had."[4] Firstly, Pratt's remarks make a distinction between the plantation and the reservation, framing the reservation as a space that is fundamentally not educational and possibly even harmful. Secondly, Pratt adds further nuance to the concept of proximity to whiteness as educational with the notion of density. Pratt uses the language of "scattering slaves" across plantation terrains, which he states served an educational purpose, whereas the reservation has the opposite composition, creating a concentration of Native peoples in space that is considered detrimental to their learning.

This chapter examines the comparisons and distinctions made between the reservation and the plantation as educational spaces by industrial educators. I argue that in the same way that the plantation is not just a space of Black immobility but also a space of settlement, the educational production of reservation and plantation space is intertwined. In fact, reservations are locations of, in Katherine McKittrick's words, plantation futures, where the protean plantation expands itself temporally and spatially.[5] In my analysis of plantation pedagogy on reservations, I am interested in how this framing of slavery and the plantation as educative allows for the movement of this form of education into different colonial circumstances wherein its use positions Native peoples in relation to, without being constituted by, Blackness and positions slavery within the process and structure of settlement. This culminates in the teaching of slavery and settlement as coeval processes without equivalent structuring. While the reservation and the plantation are not equivalent, they are connected through the pedagogical projects enacted in both spaces as well as through the material effects of land transformation that occur across these spatial configurations.

A key spatial transformation that occurred as a part of this pedagogical project was the allotment of Native lands, which occurred most famously through the Dawes Act of 1887 but also through myriad other policies proposed by the federal government at the turn of the century. Allotment was a pedagogical process that was integrally connected to the tenets of plantation pedagogy. While allotment has been discussed in combination with Indian boarding schools, as the policies were coterminous and many of the same "friends of the Indian" were involved in both, allotment itself is not often discussed as a pedagogical project. While allotment policies centered landownership, they functioned pedagogically to attempt to transform relationships to land. I frame the loss of land that allotment resulted in not as an unfortunate result of this policy but as an inevitable result of how plantation pedagogies integrally transform Indigenous spaces into settled space. Additionally, when federal policy shifted regarding allotment in the early 1900s, it was reconceptualized by many white educators as a failed project. In this historical moment plantation pedagogy was used as a rhetorical strategy to pivot away from allotment as a political and educational approach. As a part of this shift, educators like Pratt altered their discourse to attack Hampton's schooling model for Black students, while still relying on the underlying logic of plantation pedagogy.

I begin the chapter by describing how Hampton educators and other reformers compared the reservation and the plantation and in what ways this comparison was based on the tenets of plantation pedagogy. I then discuss the places where the rhetorical strategies describing the reservation are contradictory in order to show that the discourse of white reformers who promoted industrial education was often ambivalent, even though many of its effects remained consistent. I then move on to the specific example of allotment policies and their pedagogical dimensions, including how viewpoints on allotment shifted in the early twentieth century. Finally, I move into a series of discussions on how understanding the plantation and the reservation as linked pedagogically may help us examine other plantation futures such as school segregation, prisons, and discourses on crime. I end this chapter by noting moments when these reformers were able to imagine other ways of organizing Black and Indigenous relations to land but foreclosed these imagined possibilities as impossible.

THE PLANTATION AND THE RESERVATION AS OPPOSITIONAL

The reservation, by its very nature, is a space that pauses yet also indexes the violent sweep of settlement. The plantation is a space that is both constitutive of settlement and obscures the structure of settlement at its heart. Thus, comparisons of the reservation and the plantation made by educational reformers can elucidate the overlapping and co-constructed educational projects of slavery and settlement at the same time as they position them in opposition to each other. I explore these discussions of the reservation as a space of containment of Native peoples and a spatial representation of the scale of Indigenous dispossession.[6] It is also a space that is portrayed as restrictive, and often as constantly diminishing. It is described as a space out of time that is destined for disappearance according to settler narratives.[7] Conversely, the plantation is a space that seems ubiquitous. Its temporal and spatial reach is immense and its protean nature signifies how it is fundamental to Black modernity.[8] According to the white educators I read in this text, the reservation is a civilizational black hole where education does not happen and therefore educational policies need to be transferred to that space to allow education to occur.[9] This conception of the reservations led to policies, dating from the post–Civil War era to the mid-twentieth century, that supported Indigenous students being removed from their homes and sent to boarding schools in order to take them away from the bad influences of the reservation.[10] These policies attempted to transfer plantation pedagogy to reservations in such a way that the material effect was to press play on the settlement of Indigenous lands that were not yet integrated into the property relations of the state. They did so by imagining and imposing the property relations of the plantation onto Indigenous lands that had not yet been fully transformed.

The reservation is often discussed in Hampton discourse as a disappearing formation, one that is outside of the march of civilization's time and destined to end. This implies that Indigenous peoples inhabit an alternate temporality—a past that never moves forward—in the discourse of industrial education. Plantation pedagogies' focus on proximity to whiteness is described by white reformers as a means to mitigate the atemporality of reservation space and develop the land to meet the needs of a settler-defined future, a future that Indigenous peoples themselves cannot be part of. Black and Indigenous peoples are then rhetorically conscribed in anachronistic space outside of the settlement's future. The second president of Hampton, Hollis Burke Frissell, demonstrates this mode of thought when he discusses what is lacking in the reservation: "the curse of the reservation has been the separation of the Indian from his White brother. Slavery, as bad as it was, was in many respects a better educational system than the reservation; for it brought the slave in contact with his White master."[11] This is almost identical to the way Armstrong frames the relationship between slavery and the reservation, positioning slavery as an educational project and framing the reservation as in need of the same pedagogical intervention. The reservation, in this formulation, isolates Indigenous peoples from whiteness and civilization. When proximity and labor are absent from space, then it becomes unproductive—the ultimate sin since the process of settlement connected property rights to the use of space. Frissell further laments the inability of the white man to control and enter the reservation in the same way the master controlled and entered the plantation. His argument for proximity relies on a theory of proximal direction. Frances Fisher Kane, a representative of the Indian Rights Association, a society of "friends of the Indian" that attempted to influence US Indian policy under the guise of improvement, also believed the reservation's major problem was its lack of proximity to whiteness, stating that Indian "removal invariably meant a prolongation of savagery. The opportunity and inducements to civilization that existed so long as there was some contact with the whites, ceased to exist when the Indians were thrust out by themselves beyond the frontier."[12] This removal to the frontier necessitates a change in the spatial formation of the reservation to make it educative.

Industrial educators, therefore, arrived at the conclusion that the reservation must be redeemed through plantation pedagogies. For example, if the reservation system was framed as bringing the Indian into proximity with agents of the Bureau of Indian Affairs (BIA) and missionaries, then it could be described as having an educational effect, if only temporarily. Frissell, who described the reservation as a place that was impossible for the white man to enter elsewhere, states the opposite when he describes educational value of the reservations:

> Just as slavery with all its disadvantages taught the negroes the English language, regular habits of industry, and the truths of the Christian religion, so the reservation life, however it may be criticized for its ration system and its separation of the Indian from all other races, has in the hands of faithful agent, and through the influence of devoted missionaries served to bring the Indian to understand something of what white civilization means. But it is essential that the Indian understand that the reservation is only for a time, and that it is to lead to better things.[13]

In this discussion then, the reservation is not completely devoid of proximity to whiteness. In fact, Frissell does note in other writings that some Indigenous peoples had already "benefitted" from proximity to whiteness on reservations. Further on in his discussion he uses the example of the Oneida tribe who had extensive contact with white missionaries and reformers as compared to tribes like the Apaches who did not.[14] Frissell states that "personal contact has been the mainspring of all Indian progress in this country."[15] Therefore, Frissell narrates a history in which the reservation may provide a way for Indigenous peoples to gain exposure to white civilization through a temporary fixity in location—as opposed to roaming as hunter gatherers—providing them access to educative proximity. However, he is clear that this temporary spatial organization of reservations must still be transformed to provide full proximity to whiteness beyond the presence of government agents and missionaries.

The temporary nature of the reservation was a sticking point for industrial educators; for example, Frissell notes, "I believe it is of vital importance that [the Indian] understand that the reservation with its separate life is doomed."[16] The future relations that necessitate the foreseen doom of the reservation is like the promise of citizenship that was extended to Black and

Indigenous peoples, which was continually deferred. Additionally, as Maile Arvin notes in her discussion of Polynesian proximity to whiteness, there is a possessive function to this doom. If Indigenous peoples and reservations are doomed to disappear, they disappear not in opposition to settlement but into settlement through narratives of possession.[17] Arvin's discussion of proximity also demonstrates that the potential proximity to Blackness always creates anxiety in the settler, and the proximity to whiteness promoted by plantation pedagogy in its circulation also transfers a proximity to Blackness that plagued white reformers with questions about whether Blackness would infect Indigenous communities.[18] This rhetorical focus on the reservation and slavery functioned as a means to condense or elongate the spatial location of the reservation in relation to civilization and obscured the brutality of slavery and the violence of Indian removal. Frissell narrates an educational process that is in essence fictional, mapping an educational goal onto the accumulation of land and the genocide, enslavement, and indiscriminate violence that enabled this accumulation.

THE PEDAGOGY OF ALLOTMENT

One of the factors that hindered the educative work of proximity to whiteness, according to white educational reformers, was the density of Indian populations on reservations. Armstrong emphatically stated that "herding" Indians together in too great a density without the interspersed proximity of whites was what made the educational space of the reservation counterproductive to the goals of industrial education. He describes the reservation system as "merely places for herding Indians; temporary, necessary expedients, that, after a given time, may become growing evils. Herding Negroes in like manner would have been a curse to both the white and black races. There has been more sentiment than sense in treating the Indians as a separate people. It was a kindly meant, but, as to its results, a cruel plan."[19] The very word "herding" conjures notions of docility but also covers up a latent fear that a greater density of Black or Indigenous bodies together is dangerous, echoing the fears of slave uprisings or Indian attacks in earlier periods.[20] It may be that reformers at Hampton were influenced by fears of the Ghost Dance movement, which occurred during the second half of the Indian program's tenure at Hampton and was seen as a problem that emerged out of the reservation system. They perhaps believed that the density of Indians could lead to dissidents like those active in the Ghost Dance movement (or "slave" rebellions in the case of Black people) and needed to be quashed.[21]

To counteract the threat of density, I argue that white reformers transported plantation pedagogical practices—labor and the proximity to whiteness—to the reservation in order to transform the reservation space. The same way that the plantation turned land into property and profit, transporting plantation pedagogy onto the reservation was meant to transform the reservation into property. This was particularly meant to be done through agriculture and the allotment of land. Allotment was typified by the Dawes Severalty Act (also known as the General Allotment Act), which passed in 1887 and was implemented haphazardly through numerous federal policies and treaties with Native peoples. Allotment divided Indigenous lands into individual plots to be farmed by single families rather than held in common by tribes as a whole. This was meant to accustom Native peoples to individual land holding and reorganize Indigenous communal lands on reservations into individual farms that were held privately.[22] Allotment policies in their different iterations were often extremely complex. For example, a popular rule was that Indigenous peoples who were allotted land could not sell it for twenty-five years. While this provision was supposedly necessary to avoid the loss of Native lands by immediate sale, it often resulted in long-term leases of Native lands by speculators. There were often stipulations stating that Native peoples did not have true title to the land until they had farmed it for a specific number of years. Additionally, after plots were allotted to individuals, any land that was not allotted was considered leftover and was sold by the government. This meant that, ultimately, allotment resulted in the loss of millions of acres of Native lands when "excess" Indigenous lands were sold to settlers and land speculators or when Indigenous peoples leased their lands or eventually lost or sold it. Allotment policies ended with the 1934 Indian Reorganization Act, when all lands held by Native peoples reverted to lands held in trust by the federal government. However, this resulted in the checkerboarding of many reservations because some plots of land were sold off and others were reverted to trust status. The legacy of allotment has been the dramatic reduction in Indigenous land bases.[23]

Thus, allotment was an integral policy period for Native peoples and the study of it among scholars has been extensive. They have shown that, in addition to the intensive land dispossession, allotment was deeply connected to racialized ideas of Indigeneity and blood quantum, the attempted erasure of Indigenous kinship systems and gender roles, and the entrenchment of the wardship status of Native peoples.²⁴ For example, David Chang, in his study of allotment of the Creek nation's land in Oklahoma, argues that allotment both was deeply imbricated in the construction of white manhood, which was based on the right to take Native lands and transform racialized others, and also initiated a move towards a stricter racial conception of Indigeneity.²⁵ Chang notes that allotment involved far more than "recording a name in a ledger book and assigning a deed to that name" and, in fact, consisted of a "decades long struggle" about whether "it would be accepted and how it would be enacted."²⁶ This struggle over the enactment of allotment policy included overt and covert Indigenous resistance, Indigenous cooperation, as well as Black Creeks and other Black occupants of the area seeing allotment as a tool to create a class of Black landowners.²⁷ Despite the variety of responses to allotment, Rose Stremlau has pointed out that the "participants in this movement to assimilate American Indians displayed a remarkable degree of ideological consensus and tactical cooperation."²⁸ Thus, it was a time when white reformers gathered around a particular consensus on Indian policy despite other differences in opinion.²⁹ I add to this literature by arguing that the policy also contained a specific pedagogic component and that the pedagogy of allotment was the same as plantation pedagogy.

White educators and reformers who promoted industrial education described allotment as a process that was both politically important in terms of converting reservation land into productive space but also, and to them more importantly, educational space. Armstrong describes allotment in a booklet titled *The Indian Question,* written in 1883 and thus prior to the passage of the Dawes Severalty Act in 1887, which obviously supports this kind of legislation and privileged discussions about its provisions. Armstrong states:

> On most of the reservations there is farm land enough along the rivers for Indian agriculture, and abundant pastures; these turned to account by well-directed, consistent effort, would, in a few years, break the miserable herding of Indians, and (always providing for the non-alienation of lands, for at least twenty-five years) whites would settle in their midst, and, in spite of some bad men, the Indian would find contact with a thrifty race the greatest help toward his temporal salvation.³⁰

Note how the same discussion of proximity and labor are used in this description of the reservation as of the plantation. Allotment and the farming of these allotments was intended to break up the density of the reservation, which was seen as threatening. If transformation of Indian lands through allotment did not take place, then the reservation would remain a location of bad influences that would derail the educational goals of schools like Hampton: "There is almost no incentive and no reward for an Indian's labor on a Government reservation. It is heart-sickening to think of students, after years of training in habits of industry and self-help, thrown back into such an atmosphere of miasma."[31] This framing of the "miasma of the reservation" relies on the idea that labor is fruitless unless it happens on private property; labor on reservation land held in trust by the government cannot, therefore, be productive.

The policy of allotment addressed all of these narratives by transforming the space of the reservation itself. The Dawes Act, and other piecemeal allotment policies and amendments to the original act, were intimately intertwined with Hampton's educational goals. One of the main architects of the Dawes Act, Alice Fletcher, was also heavily involved in the creation of the Hampton model cottage program for Indian families and in recruitment for Hampton and later the Carlisle Indian School. Fletcher's argument in favor of allotment was also an educational one, citing the need for individualized farm living to teach and inculcate Indigenous peoples into American life, and she was heavily involved in making sure boarding schools also supported that aim.[32] Allotting Indigenous reservation lands heavily utilized educative reasoning and, ultimately, transported plantation modes of pedagogy to the reservation to aid in the conversion of trust land into private property.

Commissioner of Indian Affairs John Oberly discussed the importance of labor as an educational concept in allotment policy in an article in the *Southern Workman:* "Work among Indians reverts to earlier types and the 'subdivision of labor' attained by modern civilization is not attempted upon Indian reservations ... The Indian must therefore be taught to labor; and, that labor may be made necessary to his well being, he must be taken out of the reservation through the door of the general allotment act."[33] Allotment was meant to change Indigenous peoples' relationships to land from a place held commonly or in trust by the government to one held as property. The owning of property was connected to the notion of labor because, in settler reckoning, private property only accrues value through labor and productivity. Allotment, therefore, became a tool through which plantation pedagogy could be implemented, forcing changed relationships to land and enforcing a concept of labor on that land. The same pedagogical tools used on the plantation (whether literal or in metaphorical terms) are used to transform

Indigenous lands into property that could be inhabited by whites (and sometimes others). In fact, with its educational component, allotment is a prime example of how teaching slavery and settlement dovetail. Similar to how Black labor did not necessarily result in Black landownership, as discussed above, the pedagogical aspects of allotment did not accomplish their stated intentions. For example, there were actually more acres of reservation land in cultivation prior to allotment than after, and allotment drastically decreased the amount of agriculture occurring on reservations.[34] In fact, it can be argued that allotment as pedagogy was never meant to succeed in civilizing Indians or making them farmers and, in fact, the explicit goal of assimilation was undergirded by the goal of spatial control of Indigenous peoples.

The following narrative of the debate regarding Southern Ute allotment and removal is illustrative of the ideologies of education as part of an allotment policy that ultimately reduced Indigenous land holdings. In 1892, the Indian Rights Association wrote a letter to the *Washington Post* detailing their argument against the removal of the Southern Ute tribe to a reservation in Utah because the new reservation had less arable land. The Southern Ute had already been subject to numerous removals and constrictions from their territorial lands across parts of Colorado and Utah when this additional removal was discussed. In this instance, the government was seeking to have them removed from land they had been forcibly relocated to in Southern Colorado, which they were still resisting, to a reservation in Utah that would be combined with other Ute bands.[35] The Bureau of Indian Affairs sought to promote Ute farming and therefore saw no use in moving the Ute people to land that was less suitable for agriculture than the present reservation. Instead, they favored allotting the current reservation so that the Ute people could farm their land as individual property holders. Frances Fisher Kane, the representative of the Indian Rights Association, argued that Indians are savage, ignorant, roving people who don't know their own interests, likening them to "idiots in an asylum."[36] He stated that the Utes would be more in favor of moving to the new reservations so that they could keep leading a "wandering Indian life" than of having their lands allotted, which would be friendly to agriculture:

> This will continue the tribal system rather than make them be civilized. The intercourse with the whites ... is the very thing which the friends of the Indian now regard as a necessity. The day of herding Indians by themselves is past. The reservation system as a means toward civilization has been found to be lamentably wanting. Sooner or later those very Indians must be given land in severalty, if they are to be saved from hopeless pauperism.[37]

Notably "herding Indians" and the trouble of Indigenous density makes a reappearance in this argument, and proximity to whiteness through allotment is proposed as a cure. Fisher Kane goes on to say that the "occupations of the white man will then be open to their children; the latter will not come back from school condemned to the idleness and savagery of reservation life."[38] Through this letter, Fisher Kane and the Indian Rights Association created a clear narrative that allotment solves the educational conundrum of the reservation as a space that can be both educative and degrading. This was meant to be accomplished through allotment, yet the ultimate outcome of allotment was not increased Indigenous farming and civilization but loss of Indigenous lands and impoverishment of Indigenous peoples. Therefore, the real outcome of this pedagogical move is the reordering of legal relationships to land and not the improvement of the lives of the Indigenous peoples on those lands. The ultimate beneficiary is the settler in the same way that the ultimate beneficiary of plantation pedagogy is the master. In this story, the Ute were not ultimately relocated to Utah, and allotments did take place, although the reservation was never completely dissolved and exists to the present day, demonstrating that the hoped-for material outcomes of plantation pedagogy were always partial and never fully accomplished.

ALLOTMENT, OFF-RESERVATION BOARDING SCHOOLS, AND INDIAN EDUCATION POLICY AFTER 1900

This idea of the reservation as a space that would negatively affect Indigenous peoples' education was also clear in the rationale for off-reservation boarding schools. Advocates claimed that by removing Native peoples from reservations, civilizational education would be more effective because labor could be taught in proximity to white civilization. Interestingly, this argument was echoed by Congress as a rationale for not sending Indigenous students to off-reservation boarding schools because, when returned to the reservation, they might "regress," which was interpreted as a waste of the educational effects of removing them from their homes in the first place. In an article in the *Southern Workman,* Elaine Goodale, one of the teachers in the Hampton Indian program, notes the arguments reportedly made in Congress opposing off-reservation boarding schools based in the Eastern part of the US for Native students:

> We made diligent inquiry across the continent on the north, and across the continent on the south, and we could not find that there was one student of all the hundred educated at Carlisle or Hampton, or in any of the schools off the reservation, but had gone back to their savage life in a very short time, except a few that were employed by the Government of the United States.[39]

She quotes a senator who made similar remarks: "I did not find a single instance in all our investigation of any Indian child who had been educated in any of the centers of civilization who had returned to his home who had not also returned to the condition of barbarism in which his tribe was at the time he returned."[40] These descriptions were part of a concerted effort to decrease the congressional appropriations for Indian schools across all areas including reservation day schools and off-reservation boarding schools. Hampton published a response to these accusations detailing the exact circumstances of all 132 students, 47 women and 85 men, stating that "four only have 'lapsed into barbarism.'" Nine other students are reported as "bad" ("lazy, troublesome, evil" but not reverted to tribal ways), forty-two as "doing fairly well," and thirty-two as doing "very well." Those doing very well are listed as working in their trades or on farms or for the women as teachers or homemakers, with eight of these students being married.[41]

In her response on behalf of Hampton, Goodale attempts to assert that the schooling provided by the institution, what I would argue is plantation pedagogy, can penetrate the reservation space and improve it despite lack of proximity to whiteness. This narrative by Goodale posits that an education that shows students how to order and engage in space productively can then be transported and can change other spaces. Essentially, Hampton can design itself as a space to promote labor and property ownership and transport those spatial relations to the reservation through the actions of its students. In fact, the response from Hampton to these congressional allegations was to cite a letter received from Major McLaughlin at the Standing Rock agency detailing the condition of a former Hampton student who had become a teacher: "The substance of the conversation while at Rose Bareface's school was the neatness of the school. Rose's general appearance, deportment, and easy manners."[42] The neatness of her school and her own appearance are central to Hampton's refutation. The space of her school is described as didactic in the same way the space of Hampton is meant to be.

As Congress became more reluctant to fund off-reservation boarding schools, particularly those located in the East like Hampton and Carlisle, in favor of reservations schools, allotment as a policy also fell out of favor among many reformers. It had certainly failed to "civilize" Indigenous peoples (as most reforms with this stated intent have failed, in no small part because of Indigenous resistance), yet the corruption inherent in the process of allotment made many reformers wary and created a turn against the BIA itself. Richard Henry Pratt was initially in favor of allotment and republished propaganda pieces written by Senator Dawes, who sponsored the Dawes Act, in Carlisle newspapers. He also celebrated the "Dawes Bill Day" at Carlisle and printed didactic stories to "teach" their pupils that allotment should be accepted.[43] Yet, Pratt used the decline of the Dawes Bill's popularity to make specific arguments for funding the Carlisle Indian School and locations like it (as opposed to institutions like Hampton) and to directly attack the BIA, which he saw as hostile to his educational projects. Yet the tenets of plantation pedagogy remained very consistent in Pratt's discursive turn, and white reformers consistently tied these educational tenets back to slavery and the Black experience in America.

Proximity to whiteness is clear in Pratt's curriculum, particularly in his rationale for the Carlisle outing program. In the *Annual Report of the Commissioner of Indian Affairs* in 1884, he lays the foundation for his ideas of proximity in the context of off-reservation boarding schools. In a section titled "Planting Out" (in a fascinating connection to the plantation as "planting"), Pratt states that an "Indian boy placed in a family remote from his home (and it is better distant from the school), surrounded on all sides buy [*sic*] hard working, industrious people, feels at once a stronger desire to do something for himself than he can be made to feel under any collective system, or in the best Indian training school that can be established."[44] Pratt advocated for the outing program to serve as an example and educational experience in which contact with white families on small farms would lead to more permanent educational gains. He saw this experience as immersive: "The boy learns to swim by going into the water; the Indian will become civilized by mixing with civilization."[45] His advocating for proximity is also tied to the view of labor as educational, as he notes that if his Native students return to the reservation they will not have to work because they will receive annuities. Therefore, he advocates for the reservations to be abolished so that the "indian, no less than the negro, shall be an unrestricted citizen."[46] This language of allotment, boarding schools, and outing programs as supporting citizenship demonstrates how ideas of freedom that were applied to Black education got mapped onto Indigenous education. In fact, William Bauer has argued that the language of freedom was always heavily implicated in allotment policy.[47] This discourse about freedom in relation to the dispossession of Native lands would repeat itself, acting as a palimpsest, across Indian educational policy discourse, most notably in the 1950s when congress sought to terminate the tribal rights of many tribal groups.[48]

The glorification of labor by Pratt and Carlisle was consistently tied to discourses about slavery as educative even after the decline of allotment policy. In a response to a letter from the California Indian Land Association, Pratt makes his argument against allotment clear:

> The ownership of land is not a civilizer. Indeed, it can be and is made to hinder civilization. Through lands in severalty the government has attempted to make the Indians land tillers, employing farmers to give then some instruction; but that feature of its effort is largely abandoned now, and through the leasing system it is instead making them land-lords with capable Government agents to attend to all the business arrangements of leasing for them.[49]

Pratt argues that landownership alone won't serve an educational purpose and that only "contact with the best of our people ... especially school with our own embryo citizens ..." would be effective.[50] Here, Pratt continues to connect proximity to training in industry and labor as the most pedagogically sound strategy for teaching Indigenous peoples.

Pratt was eventually forced out of his role as the head of the Carlisle Indian school due to his purposeful antagonizing of the BIA. Pratt published a number of scathing critiques of federal Indian policy that BIA director Francis Leupp attributed to Pratt's anger over being overruled when it came to hiring practices at federal Indian boarding schools.[51] In an example of this antagonism, Pratt defended his critiques of the BIA in a series of editorials about his departure from Carlisle, published in a 1904 special issue of the school's paper the *Red Man*. In one of these statements Pratt argues that even though he believed slavery was wrong because it denied liberty, "in our handling of the negro race we still obeyed a great vital principle of all progress in man's affairs, and that was the command to labor. 'In the sweat of his face shall all man eat bread' was not violated in the Negro's case."[52] He contrasts this with the treatment of Native peoples about whom he says, "we have not only ignored the great principle of labor, but have been even more cruel and oppressive than towards the negro."[53] While he concedes that Native peoples were not bought or sold (which is an historical inaccuracy), he also states that denying them the benefits of civilization and placing them on reservations was the true evil. His remedy is directly in line with the tenets of plantation pedagogy:

> Therefore, I proposed and was permitted to bring him away. I placed him in intimate relations with the best of our citizens, and taught him not only theoretical labor in the school, which is the best the school can do, but practical labor by having him go out from the school and actually work for pay among the whites, and this is the essential finishing touch without which, theoretical instructions in the school is comparatively useless.[54]

Carlisle publications often used didactic stories to convey their policy points, such as in an 1896 edition of the *Indian Helper,* which runs a story that begins: "'Why I didn't know Indians worked' said a visitor the other day."[55] The article explains that any race of people can be lazy but places the blame for laziness on space, especially the space of the reservation, which is seen as anti-educational: "The reservation system with its idleness and debauchery is killing the Indian as it would kill any class of people, no matter their color or previous condition. It is not sufficient to get off the reservation with its pitfalls.... We must seize the opportunities that the reservation cannot give. WORK [sic] is the salvation of the Indian."[56] To emphasize this point an interview a reporter conducted with an older Black man, which includes stereotypical Black vernacular language, is relayed. The story concerned the state of Black communities in North Carolina:

> We slavery negros were learned to work; and we knows how, and likes to. We had to work, boss, whether we wanted to or not, and 'twas a good thing for us, for now we knows how to take care of ourse'ves. But the younger niggers are a po' lot; they's lazy and shif'less and theiven'. Oh, yes, they goes to school, some of 'em, and they gits an education, but that's all they gits.[57]

There is no way to know if the person quoted above is real or a fabrication of the writers of this article, as narrative devices such as this were a key strategy used by schools like Carlisle.[58] This type of narrative positions Black people themselves (real or imagined) as promoting plantation pedagogy and making an argument in favor of slavery. The fact that this narrative appeared in the *Indian Helper,* a publication widely read by Indigenous students, also demonstrates the didactic power of example that it sought to create.

In addition to Pratt's editorials attacking the BIA, Carlisle publications printed many other opinions promoting the dissolution of the BIA written by white reformers. Slavery is often used as a comparison in these articles.

One such take appears in an article titled "Our National Dealings with the Indians," reprinted in the *Red Man* by Dr. Lyman Abbott, who was involved in the "friends of the Indian" Lake Mohonk conferences. Abbott argues that the BIA must be abolished and that "this involved placing the Indian on an equality of privilege and opportunity with the Caucasian and the Negro."[59] The idea that dissolving reservations and the BIA is in line with citizenship and equality is one that was common in these discussions and indeed would be used decades later to support the termination of tribal rights in the 1950s, as noted above.[60] Abbott further makes the argument to

> treat them as we have treated the negro. As a race the African is less competent than the Indian; but we do not shut the negroes up in reservations and put them in the charge of politically appointed parents called agents. The lazy grow hungry; the criminal are punished; the industrious get on. And though sporadic cases of injustice are frequent and often tragic they are gradually disappearing relics of a slavery that is past, and the negro is finding his place in American life gradually, both as a race and as an individual.[61]

Another key aspect of Abbott's argument is its genocidal logic. He believes that by getting rid of reservations, Native peoples will disappear, which he sees as inevitable: "let us understand once and for all that an inferior race must either adapt and conform itself to the higher civilization whenever the two come in conflict or else die."[62] Genocidal logic in education for Native peoples has been common from its inception, and attaching this genocidal logic to Black emancipation has also been a tool of the US state to further Indigenous dispossession. I do however want to point out that both the state of slavery as educational, and the argument that, after emancipation, Black people should not be given any special consideration by the government, are integrally connected to genocidal logics applied to Indigenous peoples.

The way that the discourse of plantation pedagogy makes excuses for slavery is made even more explicit in a quote from J. L. M. Curry in an article in the *Red Man* on "The Negro Problem." Curry was a democratic politician from a seceded Southern state, acted as a leader in the Confederate army, and later turned into an educational reformer who worked for both the Peabody and Slater funds promoting industrial education for Black people in the South.[63] In this article, he argues that white settlers used to be pagans but they learned and improved with government direction and work. He calls for white Southerners to educate themselves because if Blacks were to get more education, then it might lead to a Black-controlled government. Curry makes the case that white supremacy rests on better education for poor whites and then makes an argument against the colonization of Black people to Africa:[64] "Slavery brought the negro from Africa from a torrid into a temperate zone. It placed him in family and taught him a new language and a new life. It raised him from a savage African to an American fellow-citizen. By some of the talk we hear, freedom proposes to send him back to savagery or colonize him. Should either transpire it may come to be a pertinent inquiry as to whether freedom or slavery was his best friend ... he is more indebted to slavery than to freedom for what he is."[65] This argument makes clear what Manu Karuka calls an "economy of moral indebtedness."[66] Although Karuka uses this term in relation to Indigenous and Asian American history, it is relevant to this context, where slavery is reframed as educational and then indebtedness is inferred from the granting of that education. I argue elsewhere that the indebtedness becomes a compounding process when Black people are held up as educational models for Indigenous peoples.[67]

In a set of similar discussions about indebtedness to white civilization, Robert Moton, in his address given at the Hampton institute on Indian Emancipation Day, delivered the message to Black students that "morally Congress cannot and does not make you a citizen. It but opens the door through which you may enter into all the blessings that the Anglo-Saxon race, through years of push and energy has made possible."[68] In this speech Moton supports a process of disciplining the Southern Black population into compliance with white notions of citizenship. This sets up the argument that the education of Black people was a moral calling and, in fact, a gift or blessing that Black students should feel grateful for. This discourse serves to both create indebtedness as well as to defer the promises made that Black communities should feel indebted for. In another moment of ambivalence about indebtedness to white civilization, W. N. Armstrong argues that settlers are indebted to Indigenous peoples: "even more than that we were bound to hold him as the 'ward' of the nation; and under that obligation to elevate his condition ... he paid for it in advance, by transferring to us land sufficient in extent to hold empires."[69] Thus, Indigenous disciplining into citizenship was moral insofar as it was tied to compensation for the taking of Indigenous lands, which allowed for future imperial conquest but also entailed a wardship status as "payment" for this so-called debt.

In another issue from 1902, the *Red Man* published a letter from D. A. Sanford, a missionary in Bridgeport Oklahoma, that explicitly links slavery, the detribalization of Black people, and the allotment of Indigenous lands. Sanford argues that slavery did not destroy the negro race but increased it. Yet slavery took away all the negro's many languages, broke up his tribal relations and his old life absolutely and at once; but he had, and I mean to say it with all due respect to contrary opinions, in the main, kindly care, supervision and direction, while the Indians' case has been the exact opposite. Ten millions of negroes brought from the tropics on the other side of the world are English speaking, proclaimed citizens through the slavery method of taking them into our homes as individuals.[70]

His use of the wording "the slavery method of taking them into our homes" downplays slavery's violence intentionally and for the specific purpose of proposing further Indigenous dispossession and genocidal education. This genocidal education is also clear in the educational method of slavery, which was explicitly involved in anti-Indigenous as well as antiblack projects of ontological, epistemological, and material violence. Sanford uses this discussion of slavery to attack the allotment system, particularly the fact that Native peoples were allowed to lease lands, which he argues was detrimental to their development. Pratt responds to Sanford's letter in print and states that "allotting lands in severalty and allowing agents to lease them does away with the sweat. Allotting lands contiguous to each other is still the tribe." He continues, "the best way for a boy to learn to take care of a farm and property is to serve an apprenticeship with a farmer and property holder."[71] This argument rests on the same tenets of plantation pedagogy and demonstrates how even the forcible implementation of private property was not seen as educative unless it followed the tenets of labor and proximity to whiteness. It also demonstrates the flexibility inherent in plantation pedagogy to be integral to both allotment and to the arguments that allotment was a failed project.

THE RESERVATION AND PLANTATION FUTURES

In the comparison discussed so far between the reservation and the plantation it is clear that the educational project is incomplete. The failure of allotment to bring about its stated goal was key to rhetoric that later condemned allotment policy yet still upheld the tenets of plantation pedagogy. In this final section of the chapter, I trace the protean nature of plantation pedagogy, which continued to be tracked in relation to the reservation towards the prison, impoverishment, violence, and death. While I note earlier in this chapter that my goal in making this connection is not to establish equivalency between Black and Native ontologies, experiences, or politics, I do want to think about how the space-time of the plantation is co-constitutive with settlement and how plantation futures bleed into reservation spaces. This section tracks how the comparison between the plantation and the reservation by educational reformers allows the time-space of planation futures and the anachronistic space of the reservation to overlap and infuse each other.

Segregated Schools and Plantation Pedagogy

One location where the futures of plantation pedagogies play out is in the discussion of school segregation and integration. Yet, when a discussion of Indigenous peoples' schooling initiatives is paired with an attention to integration struggles by Black communities, an interesting paradox comes into view. Given the history of boarding schools, from an Indigenous perspective, school integration can be seen as assimilationist, yet in regards to Black education, integration is framed as a remedy for inherently unequal schooling.[72] I call attention to the framing of school integration discourse because the rhetoric of plantation pedagogy is deeply connected to the ideas of integrated schools and assimilation. For example, in his discussion of "The Negro Problem" cited earlier in the chapter, J. L. M. Curry compares missionary education for Native peoples to segregation of Black people in separate schools.[73] Curry's comparison of the education of Native peoples to segregation demonstrates the disingenuous nature of integration discourse when applied to Indigenous peoples.

Similarly, Pratt notes that he viewed Native peoples as "segregated supervised and schooled on reservations remote from contact with [white] people and industries, notwithstanding all the influences of whatever sort that may be doled out to them there." He concludes, "they inevitably continue dependent and undeveloped people."[74] Pratt utilizes an argument based in proximity to whiteness as a means to encourage integrated schooling for Native peoples. In another article published in the *Red Man* in 1903, he takes on the question of whether there should be segregated schools for Cherokees, Blacks, and whites in Oklahoma Indian territory, coming to the conclusion that "separate schools never solved a race problem."[75] The conflation of "race problems" alongside the positing of a solution is important for understanding how plantation pedagogy often attempts to put the political goals of Black and Indigenous communities into conflict.

I draw on this discussion of school integration and segregation by industrial educators to complicate the idea that integration of schools is the only just form of school reform, which has become the common sense of the post–Civil Rights era.[76] In fact, even scholars such as W. E. B. Du Bois questioned the logic of integrated schools and whether Black students might be better served outside of institutions that utilized plantation pedagogies (although of course he did not name them as such).[77] This examination demonstrates that: (1) integration cannot be conflated with all Black political desires, especially when integrationist schooling narratives have been historically directed by white reformers who had an investment in maintaining power relations reminiscent of slavery; (2) when integrationist narratives are applied in the context of the education of Indigenous peoples, the narratives are tied to violent and genocidal schooling systems; (3) integration may not make schools better but may simply shift the forms of proximity to whiteness present in those schools.

The Reservation, Prisons, and Crime

Another aspect of this comparison that can help us think through educational questions in the present is the relationship between schools and prisons. While scholars like McKittrick discuss how the protean plantation segues into the prison and the urban ghetto, not in a linear sense but atemporally, these discourses of public common sense with respect to Blackness do not as often compare the reservation to the prison or to a space of crime. I find that reformers connected to Carlisle and Hampton described the reservation as both a prison and a space overrun by crime in ways that are connected to the protean plantation. Yet, I again caution that the discussion of the reservation as prison-like and crime-ridden is not an exact parallel to the Black experience. However, what I do find is that this construction is integrally linked to education as well as the role of educational space.

The reservation is named as a prison by white reformers and educators because it lacks proximity to whiteness. Pratt states, "We have not bought and sold the Indian, but we have driven him away from his home and held him a prisoner remote from the opportunities and from the knowledge of us and our civilized ways and methods, which would have long ago settled all our differences."[78] In this description two things are occurring. Firstly, the reservation is described as imprisoning Native peoples; Pratt explicitly names its carceral logic. Secondly, through the assertion that proximity "settles difference," Pratt seemingly implies that slavery was the reservation's opposite and (as has already extensively been shown in the discussion above) denies slavery's inherent carcerality. Juxtaposing the reservation as the detrimental carceral space layers further apologies for slavery into plantation pedagogy's sediment. Pratt continues in this line of thought, stating that "the reservation and agency system is a prison system, which feeds our civilization to the Indians in starvation doses and exactly reverses the feeding them to America."[79] Pratt sees the prison as a negative educational space. In fact, the concept that the prison lacks education can be seen in many present-day programs that seek to bring schooling into prisons as a remedy for their carceral logic.[80] It is also a strangely abolitionist stance to take in regards to prisons (albeit metaphorical ones), wherein the prison of the reservation must be abolished. It speaks to the different discourses about the prison and education, the ways they interact, and the necessity for their end. It also demonstrates how discourses of abolition can be bound up in justifications of the plantation in specific moments.[81]

In a 1901 letter to President Theodore Roosevelt, Pratt discusses the reservation as a space of crime. Pratt writes that "in the beginning" the reservation "was alleged to be a protection against vice and wrong doing of the Indians, but without exception it has been the greatest means of introducing vice and crime among them, and the wrong it has done by hindering contact with the higher and nobler things is irreparable."[82] The discourse of protecting Indigenous peoples from crime and bad influence is part of a larger stereotype of Native peoples as simple. Discussions of alcohol in Indigenous communities, for example, are often framed around criminal white influences debasing the noble (but simple) savage. In this particular vignette what I focus on is how space plays a role in the discussion of criminality. In this moment, it is the boundaries of the reservation that prevent anti-criminal influence. In other moments by contrast, proximity and density get discussed as playing a role in criminality. For example, an article titled "The White Man's side, and the Indian's" by the governor of Arkansas, W. M. Fishback, discusses how the proximity of criminals to the reservation and its porous borders are what truly cause criminality: "These criminals who find refuge in this [Indian] Territory are rapidly converting the Indian Country into a school of crime. They are demoralizing the Indians, and are especially stirring young Indians to deeds of theft and blood."[83] The phrase "school of crime" reverses the perceived relationship between crime and education, where crime does not stand in the way of learning but is the pedagogic part of the space. The ambivalence about the role of the reservation in relation to the prison and crime, yet also the intense focus on connecting the two, is tied to the conflicting ways the reservation is seen in relationship to both Blackness and the plantation. Blackness has always been positioned in the United States as inherently criminal; yet by making the plantation the opposite of the reservation a paradox emerges in which the discussion of crime on the reservation would seemingly negate Black criminality. This therefore introduces a level of ambivalence about how to understand the criminality of Native peoples.

ALTERNATE VISIONS OF SPATIAL RELATIONS AND SETTLER ANXIETY

A goal of the educational space-making of plantation pedagogy is to make it harder and harder to imagine spaces and land not as property. The material consequence of industrial education programs was to create private property, as shown by policy initiatives such as allotment. Yet, despite the fact that industrial education props up the discourse of private property ownership and educators espoused this form of education as a path to landownership, it does not actually matter to how plantation pedagogy functions whether Indigenous and Black peoples actually become landowners. As noted above, Pratt makes this reasoning extremely clear stating that "the ownership of land is not a civilizer"[84] because allotment gave Native peoples the right to lease land which was actually counterproductive to teaching Indigenous peoples to labor. Pratt states that proximity to whiteness and labor are truly the crucial educational initiatives for Native peoples, while landownership becomes tangential unless it accomplishes those things. It is learning to labor and doing so in the presence of whiteness that sits at the center of plantation pedagogy regardless of its outcomes. The pedagogical process itself is the goal.

Despite the fact that Native and Black landownership is not necessary for plantation pedagogy to function, what it does do is attempt to render alternate spatial imaginations outside of the gospel of private property impossible. It is important to note that white reformers were able to imagine these alternatives to private property relations and stated so directly; yet they always discounted them through discourses of impossibility. For example, a member of the Lake Mohonk conference, which purported to support Indian rights and did so through an assimilatory framework, reported that she heard someone else discuss allotment of land in severalty, which included the following counternarrative:

> 'I hate a compromise' said a clear-cut little Quaker lady at the conference, in a private conversation; 'It was glorious to work for abolition—it WAS abolition, and nothing less; but now, though I have come to believe that this is the best we can do for the Indians, under the circumstances, I can't throw myself into it with enthusiasm. We promised them the reservations forever; why can't the government keep its word?' The question is, was not the treaty itself compromise; well intentioned, up to the best of our light perhaps but a compromise with barbarism. If the anti-slavery society had set before itself the goal of establishing sixty independent Negro states in South Carolina and Texas, with self government according to the ideas of Ashanti and Uganda, instead of American citizenship and civil rights, would it be a sin and a shame to reconsider?[85]

While obviously this alternative vision is framed as impossible, I still ask what would have happened if white reformers had set up independent Black states instead of incorporated Black people into US citizenship. Would industrial education for Black people still be seen as the means by which to uplift the race? Would slavery still need to be discussed as having educational value? What would the relationship of these Black states be to reservations and Indigenous lands? These ideas had to be categorically dismissed as they would have disrupted the tenets of plantation pedagogy, rebuking the so-called educational nature of slavery and moving towards an alternate framework.

In another example from nine years later, a different imagined alternative is summarily rejected. The *Red Man* printed an article titled "Setting the Negro Apart" based on a lecture at the Monona Lake Assembly, which discussed creating a Black state from the territories of Arizona, New Mexico, and Colorado. This idea was challenged by the author, who states that this would be like creating a Black reservation:

> There would be created an anomalous condition that would vastly complicate, instead of solving, the race problem that has been thrust upon this country. We have only to imagine the future of the negro state overpopulated to realize the inequity of trying to deal with the negro as we have dealt with the Indians.[86]

The rejection of a Black state as an alternate spatial reality invokes the problems with density discussed in relation to the reservation and especially with the direct comparison to Native peoples. It also signals the overpowering antiblack and colonial anxiety over the congregation of too many "others" in one space.[87] One reason that alternatives must be made unimaginable in settlement is to alleviate the anxiety of whites who, though they may deny it, understand that settlement is incomplete. White anxiety always exists in relation to this incompleteness and in relation to the possibilities for other relations to land and political collectivity that Black and Native peoples may imagine for themselves, which could disrupt white power. In fact, Black and Native peoples have always engaged in other forms of non-capitalist and collective governance and placemaking, and these have often been framed as a threat by the state.[88]

These two moments represent how white reformers were perfectly able to think the unthinkable, but that the unthinkable was only conceptualized in order to be rejected. Yet, moments like these also leave space to contemplate how thinking the unthinkable in relation to Black and Indigenous relations to land and property might provide an avenue to critique the narratives of white reformers and the material enactments of plantation pedagogies. Spatial imaginaries sit at the heart of how plantation pedagogy functions, foreclosing alternative spatial arrangements. Yet, both examples are contradictory to the plantation. It is this fact that makes them impossible for white reformers and educators.

THREE

Pacific Currents

ISLAND PLANTATIONS AND INDUSTRIAL SCHOOLING

The story that has often been told about US imperialism is a linear one, in which Manifest Destiny led settlers across a continent and, when the land met the sea, it led the nation to cast out imperialistically across the oceans.¹ Educational publications at the turn of the twentieth century were replete with the imperialistic discourse that argued that the expansion of education to other groups of people justified imperial control and domination. Industrial educational reformers were, of course, participants in this dialogue. For example, the Carlisle Indian School printed the following in the *Red Man* in 1901, referencing the conclusion of the Spanish-American War and American territorial conquest in the Pacific and the Caribbean: "America is no longer bounded by one continuous line along the four oceans as the geographies have so long told us."² White reformers saw the geographic expansion of the United States as necessitating an extension of the role of the United States as a parent-like figure for the less civilized. In an article from the *Southern Workman* in 1901 titled "Aboriginal Industries," the author asked: "Has history no lesson to teach us now that we Americans have extended our role of guardians beyond the Negro and the Indian to include the Philippinos [sic], Cubans, Porto Ricans [sic], Hawaiians, and, in a sense, the Chinese?"³ These excerpts from industrial education publications demonstrate that white reformers did not view the Pacific as isolated from other plantation and colonial geographies.

The linear narrative of US Manifest Destiny as a segue into imperial domination is, of course, a false construction. I posit that these processes can be better understood as shifting and moving circulations of slavery and settlement that took on new formations and meanings in Pacific waters. For example, scholars who have espoused the study of the Black Pacific have pointed to Black life across the Pacific and how these histories are counterpoints to Middle Passage ontologies of Blackness, arguing that Blackness is more unstable in the Pacific context.⁴ I focus specifically on Hawaiʻi and the Philippines in this chapter rather than the interplay between the Pacific and the Atlantic for a few reasons. First, this section engages in discussions of discrete geographies so that part three can consider these geographies in connection. Second, the Pacific merits its own examination because of the unique history of plantation economies without juridical slavery, which existed in contrast to the entrenched nature of chattel slavery across Atlantic oceanic geographies. Consequently, the contours of plantation pedagogy in the Pacific are shaped by a different set of political circumstances.⁵ I trace how the forms and arrangements of plantation pedagogy shifted as the currents of colonialism moved in and out of Pacific Island spaces that both outlawed slavery and were subject to the influence of Western antiblackness and anti-Indigeneity. During this time period, the plantation was also shifting within these Pacific geographies, demonstrating both a connection to the plantations of the US South and a path divergent from them. This meant that the connection between the plantation and schooling also continued to take on new forms as plantation pedagogies that appeared tethered to the context of the post-emancipation South stretched and entwined themselves with island schools.

In the Pacific, plantation economies and plantation pedagogies entwined, separated, and mutually influenced each other. The plantation economy of places like Hawaiʻi and the Philippines is often written about as if it were temporally and contextually distant from slavery. I argue that, just as plantation pedagogy did not have to be on a literal plantation to be extended to reservations, the presence of juridical chattel slavery was not necessary for plantation pedagogy to move through the Pacific. I trace the connections between schools and plantations in the Pacific as part of the currents of colonialism that transported plantations pedagogies onto other soils in an expansion of US imperialism and in relation to multifaceted definitions of the plantation. I argue that the intimacy of the school and the plantation in Hawaiʻi embraced the plantation of the South without reproducing it. Plantations served as units of settlement that worked to gain political control over space in outposts of US empire. By examining plantation pedagogy in Hawaiʻi, including the paradoxical role of plantation pedagogy in the missionary period and after the overthrow, and a counterexample of plantation pedagogy in the Philippines, which disavowed violent genocide and functioned within a form of US imperialism that defined itself against old world forms of domination, I further theorize the links between slavery, settlement, and antiblackness as integral to Pacific imperialism.[6]

THE PACIFIC AND THE ORIGIN AND TRANSFORMATION OF INDUSTRIAL EDUCATION

The Hampton Institute is often credited as the founding location for industrial education for Black and Indigenous peoples, and it is acknowledged that Hampton's roots began in the Pacific. Many scholars have noted that Samuel Chapman Armstrong's upbringing in Hawaiʻi and his father's role as superintendent of public education in the Kingdom of Hawaiʻi deeply influenced how he approached education for Black communities in the South.[7] Armstrong drew on a tradition of the missionary education he saw enacted in Hawaiʻi, which can also be traced across other colonial geographies. For example, in the same way that schools for freed Blacks and early missionary schools for Native peoples existed prior to Hampton and held some of the same beliefs about education, Armstrong's experience with missionary schooling in Hawaiʻi was part of an extended genealogy of white supremacist and colonial educational projects that had long been enacted upon peoples defined as uncivilized. While I argue for the specificity of plantation pedagogies in the post-emancipation time period, I do acknowledge that the roots of Hampton's ideologies and educational practices are diffuse.

However, Hampton was not only influenced by Hawaiian educational institutions, it also had an immense influence on education in Hawaiʻi and eventually in other locations across the Pacific. Informed by white supremacist notions of civilization, Armstrong compared Native Hawaiians to Black and Native peoples in the Americas as a way to legitimate his schooling model. For example, in an oft-quoted statement by Armstrong, he states that "it meant something to the Hampton school, and perhaps to the enslaved of America, that, from 1820–1860, the distinctly missionary period, there was worked out in the Hawaiʻian Islands, the problem of emancipation, enfranchisement and Christian civilization of a dark skinned Polynesian people in many respects like the negro race."[8] This assertion seems to attribute the basis of his schooling model to missionary schooling in Hawaiʻi. Yet a closer reading demonstrates that Armstrong's comparison rests on the concept of emancipation as applied to Indigenous Hawaiian people in the Pacific, a concept that did not have the same meaning in a location without juridical slavery. Based on the history of Hawaiʻi, it could be more accurately stated that missionary educators worked out a scheme to try to create plantation laborers out of the Native populace while also attempting to direct the Hawaiian state towards policies and practices that facilitated colonial extraction. However, the way in which Armstrong links structures of settlement in the context of Hawaiʻi with slavery and emancipation demonstrates how integral missionary schooling in Hawaiʻi was to the construction of post-emancipation plantation pedagogy.

On a material level, the correspondence and exchange between Hampton and Hawaiʻi was extensive, encompassing intimate institutional relationships, student exchanges, curriculum sharing, teacher recommendations, and help in establishing new schools across the islands.[9] The Hawaiian schooling system consisted of a mix between private missionary-run schools and public institutions. During the Hawaiian constitutional monarchy, Hawaiʻi established a centralized schooling system where most schools instructed students in the Hawaiian language, with some specialized schools teaching English. Missionary schools were more likely to teach English, although they often provided instruction in the Hawaiian language as well. The Hawaiian public educational system included elementary school through high school as well as a normal school for teacher training. At the time of the US overthrow there were 140 public schools across the island and fifty-five private institutions.[10] The public school system was heavily influenced by white missionaries, with men such as Richard Armstrong serving as superintendent of public instruction; therefore, while there was a distinction between public and private schools, there was also a commonality of those involved in directing both systems. After the overthrow, the territorial government kept much of the structure of the public school system that had been established under the Hawaiian monarchy.[11]

One of the most important Hawaiian schools in terms of both influencing and being influenced by the Hampton model of industrial education was the Hilo Boarding School. Armstrong cited Hilo as a strong influence on his program at Hampton, and the ideologies of Hampton also strongly influenced the Hilo Boarding School into the early twentieth century.[12] In fact, the connection between these schools continued well after Armstrong's death in 1893, demonstrating that it was an institutional and not just a personal connection that linked these two educational locations. One of

Armstrong's most popular phrases, borrowed from European educational philosopher Pestalozzi, was that Hampton sought to "educate the head, the hand, and the heart," referring to academic, manual, and moral education. The Hilo Boarding School relied on similar rhetoric. For example, Hilo Boarding School pamphlets printed in 1910 state that Hilo valued "the practical side of school life" and educated the "head, heart, and hand." This demonstrates how Hampton's rhetoric influenced Hilo and that, for many decades, it presented itself in relationship to Hampton's widely known motto of industrial schooling.[13] Hilo also had material ties to Hampton; for example, the students took up a collection to help fund scholarships for Hampton students, as described in the same pamphlet.[14] Additionally, the Hilo Boarding School reprinted a 1886 speech by Armstrong in their 1907–1908 catalogue in which Armstrong states that Hilo has "proved the most successful, effective, missionary work at the Hawaiian Islands" and cites Hilo as an inspiration for Hampton.[15] Armstrong's speech continued the comparative discourse between Hawai'i, the US South, and Indian Country, stating: "School training for the Hawaiians, the Africans, or the Indians should, in the great majority of cases be elementary, industrial, earnestly and practically Christian, not attempting the higher scholarship."[16] This description of the type of education supported by industrial education institutions is telling in its focus on industry and work, with labor framed as teaching.

Although Armstrong initially cited Hawai'i as an antecedent to Hampton, with missionary education philosophy in Hawai'i helping to shape Hampton's curriculum, he also wrote a number of editorials and gave speeches that criticized the Hawaiian educational system under the monarchy and made suggestions for its improvement. Armstrong continued to discuss Hawai'i in relation to education for Black students during Reconstruction and the education of Native students in the United States. These comparisons were taken up by other white reformers, educators, and writers who noted the Hampton model's influence on Hawai'i, such as former Hampton employee and later the first "lady principal" at the University of Connecticut, Margaret Kenwill, who published the following in the Hawaiian Gazette in 1891:

> And where can a darker background be found for any similar future experiment than that furnished by the history of the negro in slavery? Where any future more beset with fiery trial and fierce temptation than that of the Indian camp? If, with the cesspool of the slave pen behind and the furnace of the camp before, such results as those obtained by Hampton can be obtained, why despair any people?[17]

The people that need not despair in this quote are Native Hawaiians. Kenwill's discourse proscribes Hawai'i into a temporal space that is after the plantation and slavery of the South and before the reservation, which stretches out before it as a possibility. She situates Hawai'i spatially and temporally as part of a trajectory of industrial education in relation to structures of settlement and antiblackness despite the temporal and spatial reality of Hawai'i as politically and legally distinct from both.

In addition to the connection with Hawai'i, industrial schooling was also important for understanding US imperialism in the Pacific more broadly and Hampton's strong connection to education in the Philippines. Frederick Atkinson, the first director of education in the Philippines after the United States took control, toured Hampton, Tuskegee, and Carlisle in preparation for his posting in the Pacific.[18] Atkinson was instrumental in getting the educational legislation passed that provided funding and an organizational structure for schooling in the Philippines, including provisions for normal, agricultural, and manual training. Atkinson's largest accomplishment consisted of bringing American teachers to the Philippines to teach English while Filipino teachers were being trained. He established the Manila Trade School in 1901 as the first manual training school on the island and established a normal school and vacation normal courses to train Filipino teachers.[19] The elementary schooling curriculum he established (based on a curriculum from his home area in Massachusetts) included drawing and sewing as necessary courses of study. However, while Atkinson was a strong supporter of the industrial schooling model, he was not an effective administrator and fell far short of his ambitions in terms of establishing industrial education across the islands. He was removed from his post in 1902 and, after an interim superintendent who served for less than a year, was succeeded by David Prescott Barrows in 1903.[20] Barrows was less directly connected with the Hampton industrial education program and, in some instances, could even be viewed as in favor of more academic preparation in comparison to industrial education. Still, he toured schools on reservations in the United States that were patterned on industrial education and integrated a great deal of industrial education into the Philippine curriculum. By the end of Barrows's tenure as superintendent of schools, an educational system had been established in the Philippines that included industrial curriculum in elementary schools, high schools with a specialized vocational curriculum such as the Commercial High School, farm schools and farm settlement schools in rural areas, the Manila Trade School, the Philippine Normal

School, and the Central Luzon Agricultural School.[21] Additionally, Barrows's plan for integration and land tenure in the Philippine education system has been compared by scholars to the Dawes Act, which was implicated in the transfer of plantation pedagogy to Indian Country.[22]

On top of the connections these administrators had to industrial education, Hampton and Carlisle Indian school publications held extensive discussions on the imperial project in the Philippines that included topics such as their graduates going to teach in the Philippines, teachers from the Philippines coming to teach in these Eastern schools, and dialogues about whether the Philippines should have independence and what form of education should exist there. In fact, there was a great deal of discussion about the involvement of Black people in both the physical violence of the war and seizure of the government and administration of the Philippines as well as how the Philippines compared to Indian Country.[23] In his remarks at Hampton, Atkinson stated that "if he could only see one school of the type mentioned, it should be Carlisle, as the mingling of seventy different tribes at this institution more nearly approaches the conditions which he expects to meet in the islands."[24] Industrial publications often framed Indigenous peoples of the Americas in relation to Filipinos, based on perceived similar levels of civilization.[25] In one example, Hampton students debated on the topic of whether the Philippines should be granted independence and one of the Native students who was on the winning team in this debate argued for Philippine independence using rhetoric from Hampton that fit with the ideas of individualization, independence, and citizenship.[26] Yet, the publications also compared Filipinos to Black people in the South. This included connecting the independence struggles of Filipinos to the Black freedom struggle or framing the Philippines as a stepping stone for Black people to advance economically within imperial administration.[27]

Indeed, both Hawai'i and the Philippines were talked about extensively by reformers who had a stake in both Native and Black education in the United States. The Lake Mohonk conference, which was held yearly by white philanthropists, educators, and missionaries from 1882–1916, devoted discussions at their meetings to "our island possessions" and their connections to both Indigenous and Black peoples.[28] At the 1903 Lake Mohonk conference, as reported in the *Southern Workman*, there was a discussion comparing the Philippines to the "Negro problem":

> It is enough for our present purpose to say that the social, economic, and educational problems in our islands of the Atlantic and Pacific, offer some

hard nuts to be cracked by the wisdom and justice of the American people, that will require time and patience, as one speaker pointedly remarked, adding that the Philippine problem, to name but one parallel, will require as long or longer.[29]

In this excerpt, slavery and emancipation is made the main comparison for "our lands of the Atlantic and the Pacific," framing US imperialism in relation to the afterlife of slavery. This discussion also allowed for the United States to frame Filipinos as in need of plantation pedagogy in the same way as Blacks in the South and Indigenous peoples on reservations were and to portray the Philippines as yet unready for independence and requiring education for a deferred goal. This was evident at the 1912 Lake Mohonk conference, during which Philippine independence was discussed more vehemently than prior years and participants noted the arguments about the capability of the Filipinos for self-government.[30] These debates consistently pointed to the imperialistic rhetoric of preparing the Philippines for self-government through both teaching and protection, positioning Filipinos as in need of American instruction in order to advance in terms of civilization. With these connections between industrial education in the United States and the Pacific in mind, I examine how plantation pedagogy was implemented in both Hawai'i and the Philippines.

HAWAI'I: CURRENTS OF IMPERIAL INCLUSION

While the plantation economy of Hawai'i was not at its full strength until well after the initial missionary period from 1820 to 1860, the missionary period did lay a foundation for the later supremacy of the sugar plantation economy. The Hawaiian economy in the early 1800s was tied to trade in natural resources, first sandalwood from approximately 1790 to 1830 and then whaling from 1819 to 1860, with peak whaling years in the 1840s.[31] While these forms of trade dominated much of the island economy, missionaries were concurrently involved in attempting to establish plantations and consolidate land holdings. The first recorded growing of sugar on Hawai'i was in 1825 on Oahu, and the establishment of the first white owned sugar plantation in 1836 was followed by many other small sugar plantation experiments. Samuel Armstrong's father, Richard, often cited as the "founder of Hawaiian education," had a sugar plantation in Wailuku in 1840.[32] Noenoe Silva, in her extensive work on the history of Hawaiian education and land theft, asserts that "sometimes the line between mission work and establishing plantations became indistinguishable," calling men like Richard Armstrong "missionary planters."[33] The focus on manual labor in pre-overthrow Hawaiian schools was directly influenced by the need for labor on sugar plantations, and Silva states that manual labor in these schools functioned to "[train] students for a life of labor in the fields," as "missionaries turned these values into immense profits through the plantation economy."[34] Silva also notes the comparisons to slavery inherent in this discourse, as the "Native Hawaiian problem" was compared with the "negro problem."[35] In fact, Nitasha Sharma describes how there were even attempts by these missionary planters to import Black laborers from the US South, although this was eventually abandoned in favor of Asian contract labor.[36] These early planters were not as prolific or as successful as those working in other sugar growing locations such as the Caribbean, yet their presence did influence the policies of the Hawaiian government. The Great Māhele, a process of land redistribution enacted by King Kamehameha III, was a response to the fear of dispossession of Hawaiian lands due to white encroachment, particularly white desire for land to grow sugar. Unfortunately, it paradoxically resulted in further white control of Hawaiian land.[37] After this slow rise and following the 1875 reciprocity agreement, which made sugar imported from Hawai'i to the US duty free, the sugar plantation economy expanded greatly.[38]

The overthrow of the Hawaiian monarchy in 1893 and eventual annexation by the United States was made possible by the consolidation of white missionary and planter power for the purpose of capitalist exploitation that had occurred during the monarchy.[39] In post-annexation Hawai'i the connections between schools and plantations intensified and free labor ideologies permeated Hawaiian industrial schooling. In fact, US-based reformers framed the act of annexation itself as educational and as a way of bringing Native Hawaiians into the fold of the United States. Yet at the same time, these reformers described Hawaiian people as inferior to white Americans. For example, an article titled "Hawaiian Problems" in the February 1902 edition of the *Southern Workman* stated that it was "generally believed in the United States that annexation answered the Hawaiian question," yet "no other territory in the Union presents similar conditions. Thus far annexation has not proved to be the blessing so fondly hoped for. Since the flag was raised there has been turmoil and agitation. To-day the Hawaiian question is more perplexing than ever."[40] In this quote, Hawai'i is framed as a "problematic territory" due to issues of labor and enfranchisement of Native Hawaiian people, both of which were positioned as necessitating education as a solution.

Plantation labor was closely tied to discussions of emancipation and citizenship in Hawai'i. The "Hawaiian Problems" article states that "during the last year the plantations have sought to solve the labor question by importing Negroes from the Southern States and workmen from Porto Rico [sic]. Six languages are now spoken on the streets of Honolulu—a strange medley of peoples out of which to make intelligent American citizens."[41] Hawaiians are also described as "not a commercial people" in relation to other groups, such as Puerto Ricans, Japanese, and Portuguese, who are seen as more fit for labor, particularly labor on the plantations. The parallel between Hawai'i and the South was also taken further, in that the article compared the ability of Native Hawaiians to vote in elections to the enfranchisement of Blacks in the South, rehashing the racist argument that Blacks and Native Hawaiians were both too ignorant to be ready for the vote. In fact, disenfranchising Native Hawaiians was framed as just: "To leave the control of the new territory in the hands of an ignorant minority is to deny the stars and stripes."[42] The remedy given is to provide education towards citizenship which should teach valuing labor so that citizens can be bred and trained. Like in the post-emancipation South, enfranchisement is framed as only possible after education, and education, as an imprecise goalpost, allows for continual deferral.

The Intimacy of the School and Plantation Labor

In addition to the positioning of Native Hawaiian enfranchisement in relation to Black enfranchisement, the plantation figured strongly in white reformers' descriptions of Hawaiian education. The Hawaiian plantation was not a slave plantation, although indentured servitude and other extremely exploitative labor relations did exist. However, the sugar plantation was understood as part of the educational project of civilization, as is seen in this description by Armstrong:

> When I again made the tour of the islands in 1880, the grass cabin was the exception; the partitioned framed house was the rule, but there was the corresponding change in personal habit... There was a marked growth of industrial life from the needs of the good wages offered by the sugar plantations, some Natives making an excellent success as superintendents, making money more easily than they held it.[43]

Armstrong notes a "growth in industrial life" that comes from the plantation space. This industrial life and implementation on the plantation was framed as educative in that it transformed the space of Hawaiian homes and peoples' personal manners. Armstrong discussed wage labor specifically, yet he valued the labor itself rather than wages as the primary driver of Hawaiian civilization. Therefore, this argument, while in favor of wage labor, is not primarily about the system of capitalism, but instead labor in and of itself as moral and educational. Wage labor in this elaboration then leads to a concern with land defined as property, as Armstrong further discusses:

> The development of conservative forces among the Hawaiians is of first importance. It results from a sound practical education and from an interest in property. Creating that interest is to a degree in the power of capitalists. The commercial houses of Honolulu, who are carrying their millions in plantation property, have a deep interest in the condition of the laborer.[44]

This article was written in 1891, two years prior to the overthrow of the monarchy, and these discussions about creating an interest in property are coupled with concerns about Hawai'i as a nation composed of a majority of Indigenous people. Armstrong and other educational reformers were concerned with how to create a feeling of patriotism towards a Hawaiian nation that had white planters in positions of power. To do so, they saw it as necessary to inculcate in Native Hawaiians an imagination of land as property and as something they could and should own.

After annexation, the relation between education and the sugar plantation becomes even more clear in the records of the Hawaiian Land Office and their correspondence with the Department of Education. These records are replete with examples of individual plantations giving up land to expand local schools, particularly to give schools additional space for farms. The establishment of agricultural programs and other industrial programs at these schools was tied to notions of farming and labor as educative; it was also a way for schools to provide their own food for students. The Hawaiian industrial schools, which were not only industrial schools but also reform schools for students who were sentenced on criminal charges, had students labor on plantations directly and grow their own sugar cane on school lands.[45] This is yet another way that the plantation demonstrates its protean form in the Hawaiian context where the plantation, school, and prison become one and the same.[46]

In one account the Boys Industrial School lent students to the local plantation to labor and help bring the crops in. When the superintendent of public instruction questioned this and suggested the program be discontinued, the plantation manager and school teachers wrote stating that the plantation needed the labor for at least one more season. The program was allowed to continue so as to maintain good relations between the Department of Education and the plantation owners (some of whom were one and the same). Records of the Boys Industrial School note the various years when sugar cane was planted, harvested, and sold on school soil, in addition to other food and cash crops, and there is extensive accounting of profits made for the school by its agricultural operations. The school also kept detailed records of runaway students, those who were paroled from the school, and those who were sentenced there. These records demonstrate the work that went into confining boys in the industrial school and lays bare its penal aspect. Many of these students were paroled directly to employment, demonstrating how this prison school for youth was also intimately connected to the island economy, especially local plantations.[47] Thus, plantations used students as low-paid workers when they had need of additional labor, which influenced the shape that schools took, especially schools that were penal in nature, echoing the connections between the plantation as a space of confinement and the prison.

Plantations in Hawaiʻi also had tremendous political influence in the area of education. In a series of letters between the William G. Irwin and Co. plantation to the superintendent of public instruction, W. H. Babbitt, a location described as the Thompson settlement, where former plantation workers lived, is discussed. The plantation manager states that the teachers at the settlement's local school supported anti-plantation sentiment and were therefore creating friction between the school and the plantation. The vice president of the company, W. M. Gifford stated that the plantation "strongly object[s] to government employees, namely, the teachers of the public schools at *Waiʻōhinu,* meddling in plantation affairs and using their influence to stir up dissention in that district."[48] The letters from these plantation officials call for the superintendent to investigate the school, including student attendance and the quality of teaching, as a form of punishment and surveillance because the teachers were meddling with plantation matters. The plantation managers also asserted their right to intervene in local school affairs, stating: "We would also call your attention to the fact that, as a plantation through its heavy investment in the district and through the number of its employees, it should certainly be entitled to representation from the [school] Board," which they saw as unfriendly to plantation influence.[49] While this example is specific to one school and one plantation, the intimacy between plantations and schools in Hawaiʻi was extensive, and it is unlikely that this is the only example of such meddling by plantation owners and managers in school affairs. Many schools implemented agricultural and industrial curriculums, and the grounds of these schools took on aspects of plantations as they cultivated crops for sale. Schools also interacted with the plantations economically, providing current and future laborers for the plantation economy.

Labor, as an educational value, was key to this intimacy between the school and the plantation. This was even evident in Hawaiian private schools, such as the Hilo Boarding School and the Kamehameha School, particularly in discussions about paying tuition. At the Hilo Boarding School, for instance, the school catalogue notes that "in Hawaii . . . experience has shown it to be very inadvisable to encourage scholarship by free gifts at the expense of character which might be formed if the beneficiary were encouraged to earn it by his own efforts."[50] This rhetoric underlies the decision that no free scholarships were offered to students at Hilo and that all boys had to work either in the fields or the industrial shop to earn their tuition. The catalogue also describes how boys worked to support themselves by hiring themselves out as laborers in the local community.[51] In fact in the year 1910–1911, it is noted that the boys hired themselves out 275 days of the year, meaning that seventy-five percent of the calendar year was spent in labor outside of the school.[52] What is important about the amount of labor Hilo students did is not the fact that students worked to support themselves, but that this labor was sanctioned by the school as educational in and of itself. Labor was not just about paying tuition but was seen as part of the education offered by the school.

Similarly, the Kamehameha School emphasized labor as a part of the curriculum, stating that "it is impossible to pick out any part of our work and say 'this is not industrial.' The whole purpose of the school is to fit for life work—life not so much as boys may find it as what they should make it."[53] However, Kamehameha did not describe itself as an industrial school, and in fact, school publications note that it lacked an industrial shop and adequate land and farming facilities, stating instead that the school's "manual training bent" was the most important in terms of its academic value system.[54] For example, it is noted that the school did not have high quality farm land but that this should be viewed as a benefit rather than a detriment to industrial work because "we agree with the late General Armstrong that the best test of educational inspiration is to get students to raise things where it is not easy to raise them."[55] Similar to the Hilo Boarding School, the Kamehameha school also viewed scholarships as inherently making students less educated because they were given as "gifts" rather than worked for. As the annual report of the Kamehameha School noted in 1894, "Kamehameha could get more scholars by the gift method, and would undoubtedly 'turn out' fewer men."[56] These examples demonstrate that labor was considered part of the school's educative function even if the school was not equipped to teach industrial skills. Thus, these cases of Hawaiian schools demonstrate how plantation pedagogy functioned by framing labor as pedagogic and by making labor on the plantation and on the grounds of the school connected enterprises.

Proximity to Whiteness and English Language Education in Hawai'i

Proximity to whiteness, as a tenet of plantation pedagogy, figured prominently in discourses about Hawaiian education and politics. Part of the reason for this was that Hawai'i was seen as a problematic territory in terms of assimilation because of its primarily non-white population.[57] Thus, engineering proximity to whiteness was framed as a necessity in the Hawaiian context both politically and educationally. Additionally, Hawai'i relied on a public school system structure that was founded by the Hawaiian state prior to annexation and primarily educated in the Hawaiian language. Language has always been integrally tied to ideas of race and nation such that targeting the speaking of languages other than English has been a hallmark of US expansion and colonialism more broadly.[58] Juliet R. Kunkel and I have argued elsewhere that the Western idea of a common language naturalizing claims to nationhood and citizenship was reversed in the case of Indigenous peoples, where common language (even when written, such as in the case of the Hawaiian language or the Cherokee syllabary) provided Indigenous peoples no claim to land that was seen as legitimate by the settler state.[59]

An example of how proximity to whiteness as pedagogy interacted with ideologies of language teaching is illuminated in an article discussing the state of English education in Hawaiian schools. In this article, the notion of proximity was deployed to make the argument that the daily interaction with white foreigners was more educative than instruction in the Hawaiian language:

> Hawaiian people of twenty years ago and of to-day show a marked advancement in many of the usages and means of civilized life, and plainly proves

their aptitude to adapt themselves to the requirements of the time, were they favored by greater advantages, and especially that greatest of all for a speedy assimilation—a common intelligible medium between them and the civilization they are striving after. But to say, as some have, said, that this advancement is more owing to their knowing how to read and write in their own language, than to their daily intercourse and commerce with the foreigner, who permeates the country in every direction like a circulating medium . . . is to stultify ones-self or willfully deceive others.[60]

The rhetoric that English now "permeates the country in every direction" demonstrates how English and whiteness was meant to surround Native Hawaiians until the point at which it forcibly permeated them with civilization. This proximity in itself was described as more valuable than education in the Hawaiian tongue because it transmitted civilization rather than knowledge. Knowledge, especially when transmitted in an Indigenous language, was not seen as of the same value as civilization according to plantation pedagogies.

With the influx of plantations run by white sugar planters and the eventual passage of the reciprocity treaty, which ended sugar tariffs on Hawaiian exports to the United States, missionaries believed that relations shifted in the islands such that "the white friends of the Native have become his taskmasters."[61] Whiteness and the sugar plantation as pedagogy permeated the island creating the necessity for labor to act as a teacher and for land to be imagined as property. These connections between proximity to whiteness and labor were integral to how plantation pedagogy was implemented in Hawai'i during the monarchy and after the overthrow.

THE PHILIPPINES: CURRENTS OF IMPERIAL INDEPENDENCE AND DEPENDENCE

The Philippines is a location where plantation pedagogies were transported but where the temporal and geographic context was quite different than the Black South, Indian Country, or Hawai'i. The overthrow of Hawai'i took place prior to the turn of the century, and even prior to that, many white reformers engaged in a rhetoric that sought to deny the ability of Native Hawaiians to appropriately govern themselves (an idea that the Hawaiian rulers had to constantly push back against, sometimes in ways that were damaging to Hawaiian lifeways). By contrast, the Philippines occupied a liminal space between settler colonial inclusion and distant colonial control for decades into the twentieth century. The Philippines was an American possession that experienced immense violence and genocide, which at the same time, was earmarked for eventual independence. This liminal position shaped how plantation pedagogy was implemented in the Philippines. Thus, while there was still a connection between plantations and schools in the Philippines, the link was more aspirational than material, with schools imagined as contributing to plantation modernity rather than being intimately tied together, as they were in Hawai'i. Thus, schools in the Philippines were more institutionally specific and had less crossover between industrial and agricultural institutions at the secondary levels (although they were more integrated at the elementary level).

The pedagogic process of proximity to whiteness in the Filipino context was imagined by white reformers in relation to "readiness" for democracy and therefore independence; independence was theorized as achievable only after close contact with whiteness, which was coded as American democracy. As in other instantiations of plantation pedagogy, labor figured prominently in the schools created in the Philippines. The rhetoric of educational reformers often focused on teaching Filipinos to prepare for "reality," which necessitated labor as a form of learning. The many discussions of Philippine schools by educators and reformers consistently compared Native peoples, Black communities, and Native Hawaiians. This comparative discourse was used to foster confidence in the type of education needed for Filipinos to become civilized, yet Filipino racial status was discussed in more ambivalent ways. This ambivalence in how Filipinos were framed in relation to Black and Indigenous peoples is yet another way that the protean nature of plantation pedagogies emerges.

The connection between schools and plantations in the Philippines occurred on a different timeline than it did in Hawai'i. In the eighteenth century, sugar plantations came to the islands haphazardly and with "the legacy of slavery [which] lingered on in the bifurcated income distribution of sugar societies."[62] As sugar production from other areas, such as the Caribbean and later the US, lessened, this led to further sugar production on Philippine plantations.[63] After the US takeover of the Philippines, sugar production increased further when tariffs were dropped on Philippine imports, and the number of Philippine plantations owned by Americans increased through loopholes in systems of land distribution.[64] In the US imperial era, production of sugar in the Philippines was a constant topic of debate, including in the publications produced by industrial schools. An article in the *Southern Workman* in 1905 titled "Teaching Farming in the Philippines" noted:

> That the sugar industry here is an important one may be easily deduced from the determined opposition of the great sugar interests of the United States to any reduction of the tariff on sugar imported into the United States from these islands. Experts are agreed that this might well become one of the largest sugar markets of the world.[65]

The article goes on to discuss the monetary value of the sugar produced on Philippine plantations and notes that this "revenue could be largely increased," but "the majority of the natives now engaged in this industry are sadly in need of a better knowledge of the principles of cane cultivation."[66] Thus, a large part of the US interest in systems of education for the Philippines was tied to productivity, particularly the cultivation of sugar. American companies were gaining control of Philippine land and developing plantations at increased rates, and the educational system was meant to educate Filipinos to be laborers for those plantations.

Proximity to Whiteness, Citizenship, and American Imperialism

In the Philippines, proximity to whiteness as an educative process hinged on the rhetoric of civilizing and preparing Filipinos for eventual independence under the arm of the US state. This distinguishes it from locations where proximity to whiteness was framed in relation to the assimilation, erasure, or possession of Native peoples like in the US mainland or Hawaiʻi. Yet, despite the fact that the stated intent was for independence rather than takeover, Philippine independence was often framed by educational reformers in relation to education on Indigenous reservations or to educating Black populations to "appropriately" enact voting rights in the Reconstruction South. In the Philippines, the lack of proximity to whiteness was framed through the idea that they did not have a model for moralized labor, which meant that Filipinos lacked the appropriate self-sufficiency for independence. Therefore, proximity to whiteness was meant to teach labor and let labor teach. In this imperial context, where there was often an equivocation between the possibilities of independence or annexation, the discourse of proximity was always coupled with the rhetoric of Western-oriented democracy.

Despite the fact that the political circumstances in which plantation pedagogy was implemented in the Philippines were quite different than in the post-emancipation South, a justification of slavery was still present in many of the discussions of education in the Philippines. For example, a *Southern Workman* article comparing "the Anglo Saxon and the African" stated that Black people would not have advanced as far as they did in slavery if they had been in a place like the Philippines which dealt with a "Latin" influence from Spain instead of an Anglo-Saxon one.[67] In this article, the Philippines is discursively situated as lacking white Anglo-Saxon influence in direct comparison to slavery, which is a paradigmatic example of education through proximity to whiteness. In another article in the *Southern Workman* on education in the Philippines, a discussion of the US "policy toward all child races" mentions that educating Black people in the Reconstruction South was similar to educating Filipinos.[68] These discursive comparisons demonstrate how firmly a justification of slavery as educative continued to be situated at the heart of plantation pedagogy, even when applied outside of a context of juridical slavery.

A similar form of discursive comparison to Indigenous peoples appears in the relationship of allotment to Philippine education. For example, in a 1901 speech delivered to the Indian Nations Education Association and reprinted in the *Southern Workman,* Calvin Woodward, the president of the industrial training school at Washington University in St. Louis, asks:

> What is the aim of Indian education, and how does it differ from the aim, say in the Philippines? In the Philippines it is to build up a people; to make them self-supporting, self-respecting, self-governing; to erect a new and higher civilization on the ruins of an old and lower one. In this case it is easy to see how to go to work with a moral certainty of ultimate success. The Filipinos are to be educated to usefulness and good citizenship just where they are, among their own people, wholly within their present environment. The youth of the islands are not to be trained for American or European employment or for American or European citizenship, but for home employment and for home citizenship.[69]

In contrast with what had happened up until this time in regard to the education of Native peoples, Woodward's conclusion is that land policies that were seen as educational in the context of Indigenous reservations could also be educational in the context of the Philippines:

> The policy of generous allotments of land on which the Indians must support themselves must ultimately become general. This should include a system of Indian education carefully devised to deal with Indian civilization as it now

exists, and gradually to raise it to the plane of respectable American citizenship. In other words, we should deal with the Indians just as we are going to deal with the people of Porto Rico [sic] and the Philippine Islands.⁷⁰

Important to note in this direct comparison is the role of proximity, but in this case proximity to white civilization through imperialism. I argue that this strategy of using education to expose Filipinos to models of self-government, democracy, and citizenship functions as a form of teaching through proximity to whiteness. This is especially stark when allotment policies are framed as preparation for Philippine independence, since allotment was argued as necessary to bring Indigenous peoples in closer proximity to whiteness through the breakup of the reservation. While in one case the Philippines is supposedly being prepared for separation from the US state, it can only do so successfully through closeness to it.

American imperialism was often framed in opposition to European imperialism through the rhetoric of development rather than suppression of colonial others. However, framing American imperialism as developmental also depicted American imperialism as uniquely educational. This functioned to elide the violence of American imperialism by defining it as beneficial. This is evident in the language used by educational reformers that attempted to justify American imperialism because it "developed [them] to their highest capacity" in places like the Philippines in contrast to British "rule" in places like India.⁷¹ This development

> arises from the fact that we are seeking to prepare the people under our guidance and control for popular self-government. We are attempting to do this, first, by primary and secondary education offered freely to all the Filipino people; and, second, by extending to the Filipinos wider and wider practice in self-government, so that by actual experience they may learn the duties of the citizen, his proper sense of responsibility for the government, and the self-restraint absolutely necessary to a wise control of a minority by a majority.⁷²

In this framing, education is part of a process of "guiding" less civilized peoples towards self-government through "experience," a primary part of which was the physical presence of white teachers who could properly convey what civilized experiences should consist of.

An article in the *Southern Workman* titled "The Education of the Stranger" makes a similar comparison between American imperialism and Dutch imperialism in Java, setting out a proximity-based argument in much stronger terms. It notes that the Dutch made the people of Java "understand the desirability of an extremely humble training in the presence of members of the dominant race. The island has been covered by an unparalleled intensive cultivation, and railroads have opened the interior to the markets of the world."[73] In contrast, the US imperial system allows for "contact with the dominant race" to eventually lead to independence, and schools were a cornerstone in this system because they "touch the life of society at all possible points." This imperialist educational perspective and practice proclaimed that "it should deal with all the departments of knowledge needed to further the material as well as the intellectual progress of society."[74] The American imperialist model does not dispute that "contact with a dominant race" is necessary but instead tells a narrative in which it leads to opportunity. Therefore, an important way that the narrative of proximity to whiteness changes in the imperial context is that eventually white people go away. For example, the use of American teachers in the Philippines was described as necessary to train Filipino teachers who would eventually take over the entire schooling system.[75] However, when white teachers left, it was expected that the models they provided would remain.

An article discussing the Lake Mohonk conference of 1904 makes similar claims about how "our connection with these peoples will redound to their great advantage and to our own. We feel that it is our duty to develop in all our dependent peoples what ever is strong and good in them, instead of endeavoring to cast them into the mould of our own racial characteristics, believing that thereby they may contribute to mankind something of permanent value."[76] This is stated in combination with an assertion that industrial education must be pushed as part of this connection so that it can "speedily provide for the unrestricted entry of their products to the markets of the United States."[77] In this moment, it is clear that the connection, which is carried out through imperial proximity to whiteness and training for citizenship, is implemented primarily for economic control and profit.

Teaching Labor and American Economic Imperialism

In the same way that Black and Indigenous peoples were discussed by industrial educators as needing to learn to work, Filipinos were also framed as poor laborers. Filipinos were constructed as being in a "thralldom of inactivity, idleness, and ignorance"; being "behind in the industrial race"; and "not tak[ing] kindly to manual work."[78] This last author concludes that this "prejudice against honest work must be overcome before any great headway can be made in the industrial world."⁷⁹ This discourse of Filipinos not valuing manual work suggests the remedy that education must equip them for work in their natural environment. A member of the Philippine civil service wrote in the March 1912 issue of the *Southern Workman* that "fitting the student for life, for his natural environment life rather than for the legal, religious, or literary profession, seems to characterize Philippine education. More and more emphasis is placed on industrial instruction, domestic science, trades, and agriculture."⁸⁰ The first superintendent of education in the Philippines, Frederick Atkinson, noted in published extracts from his book on the Philippines that the "agricultural nature of the entire country demands its extension; the masses must always remain dependent upon the soil for their maintenance; and the first step that has been taken, it is to be hoped, will be followed soon by other definite ones."⁸¹ These discourses linked the economic development of the Philippines with teaching labor and teaching through labor. Imperialism therefore relied on plantation pedagogy as part of the imperialist goal of the exploitation of resources in other geographies.

These discourses about labor and Philippine education are quite close to discussions of industrial education for Black students in the South. In an article titled "Industrial Education and the Development of the Filipinos," Filipinos are described thus:

> For many years to come, the Filipino must work with his hands. He must be taught that labor is a civilized means of earning his livelihood, and that it is a perfectly dignified proceeding.... Much depends on teaching the masses of people better methods of doing the kind of work which they are engaged in it at present, and training them in other valuable lines of work, of which they are at present ignorant. Let us make of them creatures of larger wants with better facilities to supply those wants. Economic wealth, no one will deny, is conducive to better living. To obtain that wealth, these people must work. Furthermore, it has been found that the most industrious people usually belong to the better and more elevated class of citizens and are the most moral.⁸²

This description is reminiscent of Booker T. Washington's assertion in much of his writing that former slaves needed to learn to re-value labor and learn laboring skills for both practical and moral purposes. In fact, Washington often used the language of "wants," stating that Black people must be taught to want so that they can be taught to labor appropriately in pursuit of those wants.⁸³

In another direct comparison of the labor of Filipinos and Black people, an article titled "Philippinoes [sic] and American Methods of Education" states:

> Mr. Ronald P. Gleason, Director of the Manila Trade School, reports that the Filipinos show the same disinclination for manual labor that the Negroes did when industrial schools were first established in the South. Mr. Gleason thinks that the Filipino boy has as much manual skill as the American boy, that he shows great neatness but is lacking in accuracy and in endurance. It is difficult in the Philippines, as it is also in many parts of the South, to secure regular work. The Filipino, too, like the Negro, has a tendency to stop working as soon as his immediate needs are met.[84]

The Manila Trade School, in fact, often failed to attract students early on because of poor facilities and a lack of tools and machinery to support its curriculum. One of its most successful programs, training in telegraphy to meet the needs of the burgeoning telegraph system, which was in the process of being established across the islands, was transferred one year after this article was written to the Commercial High School so as to make it more accessible to greater numbers of students. Therefore, the Manila Trade School was less able to train laborers during this time, indicating that this likely influenced Gleason's assessment.[85] What this comparison does demonstrate, however, is that while the Filipino people who were targets of American forms of education had never been enslaved as Blacks in the South had been, they were still described similarly as needing to learn to work, whether they actually needed to learn to work or not. Therefore, slavery as an educational project was influential across geographies where slavery was not in practice through the transportation of plantation pedagogies in currents of colonialism. This is why institutions where plantation pedagogy flourished, such as Hampton, Tuskegee, Carlisle, and industrial schools in Hawai'i, were all named as important models for schools in the Philippines even when their models were not fully implemented.[86]

PROXIMITY TO WHITENESS AND THE DEATH OF THE NATIVE

The focus on labor, property, and proximity in discourses of Hawaiian and Filipino education was coupled with the rhetoric that Indigenous peoples were dying, similar to the discourses about Indigenous peoples in the United

States whose life on the reservation was framed as doomed by many of these same reformers. Native peoples on the US mainland and in the Pacific were framed as peoples who would have to be included in a national polity, but that inclusion was in fact an erasure. Armstrong stated this clearly in relation to Native Hawaiian people in the *Hawaiian Gazette:* "As I understand the Hawaiian problem, it is this: To save your institutions if you cannot the people. The *kanaka* is doomed; the land will be occupied for better or worse."[87] Armstrong's use of passive voice frames the doom of Native Hawaiian people as a natural process rather than one that was put into motion by colonialism and violence. It also takes on a note of possession, in which the institutions are saved and absorbed while the people are framed as dying.[88]

In a similar discussion of the "doom" of Native Hawaiian people, W. N. Armstrong states: "the Native race is dying simply out of its contact with the advanced races (for what else is the cause of its decline?)."[89] Once again this decline is discursively framed as natural rather than as part of a structural process of colonial violence:

> Time will work the change fast enough of itself. Eventually foreigners will increase in number, and render the establishment of English schools in every district not only an advantage but a necessity. Time will work other changes too. It will increase the number and influence of the foreign population to such an extent, that every office must of necessity be filled by them, and every Native will from necessity be obliged to learn the foreign tongue and teach his children in it. *Let time, then, work these changes in her own way,* for whenever the English tongue becomes the established idiom, Englishmen will become supreme on Hawaiian soil, and the Native race, like the Native tongue, must yield to the foreigner.[90]

In this example, proximity to whiteness is written about as if it both educated Native Hawaiians and caused their inevitable decline. It is an educational narrative in which Indigenous peoples are made to learn to labor and regard land as property through the mechanisms of the plantation, but the proximity that is necessitated by those plantation pedagogies results in decay and death. It allows for land to be transferred as property to whites and for Indigenous peoples to slowly die off, leaving the white inheritors no way to remedy their "unfortunate" demise. Thus, that which teaches also kills, making even a supposed benevolent enterprise like education a violent endeavor and, at the same time, an endeavor that can disavow its own violent effects because it is framed as a natural good. Through this process, plantation pedagogy worked across locations to turn land into property and to disappear Indigenous peoples.

In the case of the Philippines, the ambivalent discourse about race led to some ethnic groups on the islands being discussed as dying while others were not. Hampton publications were very interested in these different tribal and ethnic groups in the Philippines and wrote about a number of them, showing a similar fascination with Filipino tribal groups as was evident at events like the World Expos. An article titled "Among the Igorots" in the November 1912 edition of the *Southern Workman* asserts that educating them would be unwise because the educational value of proximity to whiteness would also lead to their demise:

> The attempts to educate the Igorot children I regard as picturesque rather than ultimately wise, though I do not speak disparagingly but with full sympathy for the aims and ideals of those who would "raise" the wild people. The Igorots are sufficient unto themselves—there, out in the mountains, amidst beautiful surroundings, ignorant of good or evil. I wish to see them ever happy, care free, and innocent, just as they have ever been—Nature's children.[91]

The notion that these groups would be educated away from primitivity is seen in this context as a sad thing, yet Native peoples were described in parallel terms in the United States and were still subject to the violence of education. In fact, the Igorots were directly compared to Native peoples on the continent in the *Southern Workman's* "notes and exchanges" section in 1904, which stated that the Igorot language was similar to the Creek language and claimed that a Creek interpreter was able to converse with Igorot villagers.[92] This demonstrates one major difference when plantation pedagogy is moved from a location where settlement is more sustained to one where settlement is considered temporary as part of American imperialism.

Similarly, the Negritos of the Philippines are also cited by Hampton publications in relation to their eventual demise. In an article in the *Southern Workman* in 1904 titled "The Negritos of the Philippines," Negritos are both compared to Black people in the South as well as described as "children of nature" who "are probably capable of improvement under proper conditions." The author continues, "but they would soon die out if taken from their mountain homes and placed on the hot plains with the Filipinos."[93] By Filipinos they mean people of Malay origin who the article describes as more industrial and agricultural than these "children of nature." This reveals a second aspect of plantation pedagogy: the genocide and erasure of Native peoples in the pursuit of settlement and establishment of agriculture. In the case of the Philippines, some groups of Filipinos were seen as doomed to disappear while others would continue on as ideal laborers, creating wealth for US plantation owners. Thus, while US imperialism promoted itself as necessary for the education of subject peoples, the tenets of plantation pedagogy proposed that this very education was genocidal to Indigenous peoples across the Pacific. The profound anti-Indigeneity of plantation pedagogy is demonstrated most clearly here in that it can only be fulfilled through genocide.

FOUR

Atlantic Currents

**INDUSTRIAL EDUCATION AND
ANTI-COLONIAL STRUGGLE IN AFRICA**

The Booker Washington Institute of Liberia was founded in 1929 and envisioned as a "Tuskegee in Africa," teaching industrial and agricultural skills to African Natives in Liberia's rural areas.[1] Liberia was a complex location to establish such a school, as its history was deeply connected to colonization societies that sought to end slavery by returning Black people to Africa. Liberia was imagined as a state modeled after US values, but it was populated by former slaves living on the continent from which their ancestors were taken. This complexity is evoked in the following quote from a document titled "Educational Needs and Opportunities in Liberia": "Liberia was established more than a hundred years ago as a country for the freed Negroes of the United States . . . These Negro colonists and their descendants encountered many of the hardships and difficulties of the kind faced by the Jamestown and the Plymouth settlers."[2] The comparison of Liberia to Jamestown and Plymouth evokes a romantic narrative of settlement in a place where the formerly enslaved were to settle. But here, former slaves return to Africa as settlers within the context of the colonization of Africa by white nations looking to extract resources for capitalist consumption by the West.

The Booker Washington Institute of Liberia is one such location where the layered histories of slavery, settlement, and colonization intersect alongside the transfer of plantation pedagogy. Colonization societies began sending Black colonists to Liberia in 1822, and Liberia later declared independence in 1847. The US government did not recognize Liberian independence until 1867 and in fact was heavily involved in Liberian politics and governance after that point as well. Donald Spivey has argued that Liberian independence was exaggerated and the country remained heavily dependent on the United States.[3] Spivey describes the Black colonists of Liberia as "imitating their former slave masters" and pursuing a "'manifest destiny' to bring civilization to native heathens."[4] The idea for the Booker Washington Institute began with Olivia Egleston Phelps Stokes, a member of the Phelps Stokes family that bankrolled the Phelps-Stokes Fund. The planning began in 1919 with an agreement by the trustees of the Phelps-Stokes Fund that a survey of Liberian education was needed, which was carried out by Benjamin Brawley in 1920 with funding from the Phelps-Stokes Fund, the Rockefeller General Education Board, and various US-based colonization societies. This report suggested the need for an institute like Tuskegee in Liberia, but the school was not established until backing from the Firestone rubber plantation was secured after its opening in 1926.[5] The first educational adviser appointed to open the Institute, James L. Sibley, was hired for his experience as a state agent of Negro Rural Schools in Alabama and previous work teaching in the Philippines.[6] This history of Liberia and the Booker Washington Institute illustrates how various interest groups, including philanthropists, abolitionists, and capitalists, were connected in these political and educational efforts. Hampton and Tuskegee were also directly connected to the Booker Washington Institute, helping search for and recommend staff with experience in industrial education.[7]

The movement and circulation of plantation pedagogy to and within Africa was a layered project of both slavery and settlement. This was due to the geographic role played by Africa as the origin location of the slave trade and outpost of European empire and domination. The sediment of slavery's origin story in Africa was overlayed with rhetoric of industrial education that rested on the notion that slavery could be justified for its educational effects. This further suggested that transmitting what slaves learned in the Americas back to Africa could prophetically redeem the African continent from its "darkness." This discourse about slavery, education, civilization, and redemption was popular with many white reformers who sought to justify slavery as necessary despite its brutality—and also amongst some Black reformers who wanted to demonstrate Black civilizational capacity in the face of dehumanization.[8] Yet, industrial educators who discussed Africa also relied on settlement-based educational discourses that harkened back to the rhetoric used to discuss the education of Indigenous peoples in both the US and the Pacific. This layering of the discourses of teaching slavery and settlement meant that much of the discussion about industrial education in the African context was riddled with contradictions, such as whether Africans were Black or Native, what their relationship was to Black Americans, and how the US South could or could not serve as a model for African education.

The idea that US education for Blacks could be useful for Africa is one that has been well discussed in the scholarly literature—such as in Zimmerman's study of the Tuskegee cotton farming experiments in German African colonies and Offut-Chaney's perceptive linking of the establishment of charter schools in New Orleans to Liberian education.[9]

The movement of plantation pedagogy to Africa demonstrates why the separation of colonialism and settler colonialism into distinct types is not useful for understanding settlement in this geography. The debate over whether a state was a settler state or whether it was subject to classic colonialism cannot unearth why settlement as pedagogy and structure was present across a variety of colonial and state formations. Additionally, the implementation of plantation pedagogy in Africa, the space of slavery's origin yet not the space where plantations were first established, added extra layers to the already complicated racial and colonial terrain. I contend that the physical establishments of plantations as part of imperialism and settlement in Africa extended the coterminous project of settlement back to the original location of enslavement's beginning, creating a many-layered enmeshment of slavery and settlement. Arguments made by proponents of industrial education for the implementation of this form of schooling in Africa and for the purposes they stated that it would serve show how education for slavery and education for settlement overlap and merge in new ways in this transferal of industrial schooling models back across the Atlantic.

I begin by examining the terms *cooperation* and *adaptation*. I discuss how each is tied to tenets of plantation pedagogy, in which cooperation serves as coded language for proximity to whiteness, and adaptation indexes labor as educative. From here, I discuss how the tenets of plantation pedagogy in the African context were tied to the focus on economic development in Africa, and the key role that rubber, sugar, and cotton plantations played in that development. Similar to how plantation pedagogy circulated in Pacific currents, I note the intimacy of the plantation and the school, particularly in the case of the Booker Washington Institute of Liberia and the Firestone rubber plantation. I then discuss the ways in which the tenets of planation pedagogy, particularly the deployment of slavery and settlement in the discussion of African education, created ambivalent discourses about slavery and settlement in relation to Africa. Finally, I discuss the political results of this ambivalent educational discourse, which sought to quash decolonial uprisings as well as support US imperialism in Liberia, despite the rhetoric of independence.

AFRICA AND INDUSTRIAL EDUCATION

The transfer of industrial education to the African continent was embedded in Western representations of Africa. A great deal of scholarly work has noted the description of Africa as a "dark continent" and the representations that this has produced of Africa as wild and uncivilized, in which Africans were compared to animals and the continent was depicted as homogenous wilderness.[10] These characterizations are still evident in discussions that treat Africa as a country rather than a continent of over fifty countries, as if all of Africa is the same. This simplification of Africa's diversity has led to broad generalizations of Africa as a space of catastrophe and epidemics as well as white savior complexes about saving Africa.[11] The countrification of Africa in this way is reminiscent of the amalgamation of all Indigenous peoples of North America into the "white man's Indian," which allowed for the proliferation of stereotypes about Indigenous peoples.[12] In fact, the reports on African education funded by the Phelps-Stokes Fund and headed by Thomas Jesse Jones were filled with language that alluded to Indigeneity and settlement. Africa is described by Jones not as the "Dark Continent" but as the "last frontier," where educators face "pioneer conditions" and Africans are not referred to as Black but as Native.[13] Additionally, scholarly discussions of "Africa" (including maybe this one: even though I am aware of the pitfalls, this does not mean I entirely avoid them and I acknowledge my shortcomings) often proliferate these ideas.[14] In my examination of the transfer of plantation pedagogy to Africa, I want to underscore that these rhetorics of generalization and white saviorhood were constitutive of plantation pedagogy.

The report written mainly by Thomas Jesse Jones titled *Education in Africa* is one such example of the countrification of Africa. Along with a committee of American and African educators, Jones, a former Hampton employee who was dubbed the "evil genius of Black education" by W. E. B. Du Bois, headed the creation of a report commissioned by the Phelps-Stokes Fund in 1922.[15] This report was framed as beneficial for educators in Africa who could apply the educational programs created for Black students in the US South by white reformers to the education of Africans in both independent states and European colonies. The connection between education for Blacks in the South and education for Africans was seen as natural by US reformers like Jones who operated based on ideas of racial types deeply tied to antiblackness. The subheading of the report states that it focuses on "West,

South, and Equatorial Africa," but those distinctions are somewhat lost in its attempts to extrapolate about all of Africa from these locations. The first five chapters of the report, representing over one hundred pages of text, are all generalized discussions of the educational conditions in "Africa" as a whole. Individual country or colony-based studies begin in chapter six of the report and include discussions of Sierra Leone, the Gold Coast, Nigeria, South Africa, Angola, the Belgian Congo, and Liberia.[16] A second report on education in East Africa was published three years later in 1925 by the second African education commission, also headed by Jones.[17] Both of these reports focused exclusively on sub-Saharan Africa, ignoring the many geographic and cultural differences across the continent.

These two reports, written by Jones and supported by Northern American philanthropists, were also supported and discussed by European governments, colonial leaders and those in European capitals, missionaries in Africa, and missionary organizations internationally.[18] These reports and projects built on a long history of missionary involvement in Africa and US Black interest in the continent. For example, in 1901 the Tuskegee Institute sent a delegation of teachers and students to teach cotton farming in German protectorates in Africa, and many Hampton and Tuskegee graduates discussed wanting to serve as missionaries and teachers in Africa. Students from various countries in Africa also attended Hampton, Tuskegee, or other US industrial schools and brought these ideas back with them when they returned home. Some scholars have described these efforts as a form of pan-Africanism, although it has also been noted that it was a form of pan-Africanism that was decidedly pro-imperialist.[19] There were, of course, Black political voices that opposed these forms of education in Africa and sought other forms of pan-African organizing, such as the African National Congress in South Africa and the Pan African Congress and its support of decolonization in Africa.[20] Additionally, intellectuals who promoted the importance of African history, like Carter G. Woodson, found that their educational resources circulated widely across the diaspora to educators and activists in Africa.[21] I cannot and do not argue that industrial education was the only influential program of education in Africa, but rather that it was one that white reformers consciously sought to transfer. Morever, it did so using agendas consistent with the tenets of plantation pedagogy and in opposition to African-led political and educational projects that centered decolonization and an end to Black oppression.

COOPERATION AND PROXIMITY TO WHITENESS

Cooperation was a codeword that indexed proximity to whiteness as education and was commonly used by many of the industrial education proponents who were involved in the transfer of plantation pedagogy to Africa. For example, at the Booker Washington Institute in Liberia, the collaboration between the institute and the Firestone rubber plantation often used the language of cooperation to imply the necessity of proximity to whiteness for training Black Natives to be workers. Jackson Davis, a trustee of the institute, employee of the Rockefeller General Education Board, and member of the New York Colonization Society, stated in a memorandum labeled "confidential" and titled "Impression of Liberia—March 31–April 12, 1935" that "Liberia cannot develop without the cooperation of the Western World."[22] This cooperation was necessarily made up of business interests, and Davis stated that "firestone staff are a fine group of American businessmen, competent, broad minded and considerate... Liberia is fortunate in the personnel of its Western business interests."[23] In this example, the exploitative relations between the Firestone Rubber Company and Liberia were reframed as cooperative and tied to educational projects of industrial education.

The focus on cooperation was in part because Africa was described by many educational reformers as a space devoid of white influence. While proximity to whiteness in other geographic areas like the Americas is attributed to slavery and colonization, Africa represents the converse, a space that was not penetrated with white presence but scavenged from the shores, and from which people were taken away and put into a new proximity to white civilization. Thus, white reformers interested in industrial education in Africa had to engage with the question of how to inject proximity to whiteness into the "dark continent." An example of this discourse about proximity to whiteness is an article from the *Southern Workman* written by E. D. Morel, the editor of *The African Mail,* which stated that there was a "colossal section of Africa where Nature seems to have erected a permanent barrier to the up-growth of the white race alongside [Africans]."[24] Robert E. Park, famed sociologist at the University of Chicago and secretary of the Congo Reform Association, would make a similar observation in June of 1912, stating that "Africa must serve a long and hard apprenticeship to Europe, an apprenticeship not unlike that which Negroes in America underwent in slavery." Park pondered, "How far is it possible by means of education to abridge this apprenticeship of the younger to the older races, or at least to make it less cruel and inhuman than it now frequently is."[25] Park uses the language of apprenticeship to denote proximity of Europeans to Africans and even cites slavery in the US as an educative "apprenticeship" similar to earlier language used by proponents of industrial education. He adds to this idea the hope of making the apprenticeship less violent, shifting from the language of earlier educators who lamented slavery's cruelties but found them necessary to a model that repeated the educative aspects of slavery without the same level of cruelty. It was obviously not the case that European colonialism in Africa was nonviolent or nonexploitative. Therefore, what does this discourse do other than try to frame European colonialism in Africa as benign in the same way that slavery was justified as educational in order to obfuscate its violence?

Thomas Jesse Jones, the Phelps-Stokes Fund, and other white missionaries and educational reformers were certainly engaged in justifying European rule in Africa rather than critiquing the violence this rule perpetrated on Africans. In the report on education in Africa, the language of "cooperation" instead of "apprenticeship" is used throughout to signal the necessity of white presence in Africa, with the fifth chapter of the report titled "Cooperation for the Education of Africans." The use of the term cooperation was derived from groups such as the Interracial Cooperation Commission (ICC) in the US South, which consisted of conversations between Northern philanthropists, white Southerners, and conservative Black populations. While the ideal of interracial cooperation may seem progressive for the time of Jim Crow, scholars have noted that the creation of this society served as a means to control race rioting without fundamentally altering Southern race relations.[26] Jones and Tuskegee's principal Robert R. Moton were both involved in initial talks around the ICC, although neither would have been considered leaders of the later work of the group. Moton would speak extensively about "cooperation" and attribute his dedication to it to Hollis Burke Frissell, the second principal of the Hampton Institute.[27] Jones would have therefore been intimately aware that cooperation did not betoken equality or liberation.

In Jones's usage in the report, he stated that "the evidence indicates that the history of the African people resembles that of all other peoples the world, in that their progress has been and will continue to be the result of cooperative relationships with other peoples."[28] Jones would go on to note that it was not just the responsibility of colonial governments and white educators to understand the importance of cooperation; in fact, Jones asserted that "thoughtful Africans are increasingly realizing not only the importance but the necessity of the cooperation of the white group."[29] This white group was, of course, heterogenous. It consisted of colonial administrators, missionaries, and white business interests, among others. Despite this variance in the kinds of whites who came to Africa, the report also noted that if "the negligible number of Europeans are to be successful in transferring the influences of civilization to the African millions they must unite their various contributions and as soon as possible invite Native leadership to share their responsibility."[30] Therefore, Jones and the rest of the commission argued that it was necessary to coordinate efforts between colonial governments, missionaries, philanthropists, and business interests in creating educational programs for Africa. As Moton noted, "these two races are charged under God with the responsibility of showing to the world how individuals, as well as races, may differ most widely in color and inheritance and at the same time make themselves helpful and even indispensable to each other's progress and prosperity."[31] The report concluded that "The misunderstandings between the white and Negro groups the southern states of America are in some respects quite significant for those who must deal with racial problems in Africa and in other parts of the world."[32] This discussion of how Africa required cooperation with Europeans and Americans in order to develop and prosper has aspects of the prophetic in its rhetoric yet at the same time the idea of misapplication. The prophetic aspects echo some of the Black Ethiopianism politics that were based in ideas of Black civilization and Christian prophecy, but the white reformers who coined ideas of cooperation did not support independent Black states.[33]

In the African context, the discussion of proximity to whiteness through "cooperation" was sometimes contradictory. C. T. Loram, a white South African who studied in the United States and had ties to the Hampton Institute, the Phelps-Stokes Fund, and the Rockefeller Foundation, stated in his report on education in South Africa that

> it is possible for a large group, weak in its standard of social life, to drag down a stronger group through its very weakness. The backwardness of the Southern States in the United States of America is partly attributable to the presence of masses of uneducated Negroes, who are dragging down the Whites to a lower level, socially, politically, and economically. Signs of a similar degeneration on the part of the Whites in South Africa are not wanting.[34]

Loram believed that white South Africans had to educate Black South Africans "in self-defense."[35] Loram's discussion inverts the relationship of proximity, theorizing that Black presence degrades rather than that white presence educates. Similar discourse existed around white contact with Native peoples in the Americas, where whites could be seen as educating Native peoples, as in the case of the Carlisle Indian School outing program, or as bad influences that brought drinking, addiction, and crime to reservations, degrading the noble savage. This discourse was also in circulation in relation to Africa. Maurice S. Evans, a representative of the African Society, stated in a 1912 edition of the *Southern Workman* that the "almost unanimous verdict of white colonists is that the effect of contact with our civilization has been to cause deterioration."[36] Thus, I argue that the discourses of degradation and education are mutually reinforcing and that the dialectic is synthesized through educational rhetoric.

In this context, whether or not contact is framed as degrading or educative, plantation pedagogy is proposed as a solution that can fix the problems of contact created by colonialism in whatever form they are framed as taking. The key is that, for Loram, Africans—rather than the South African state—are always positioned as in need of fixing. Loram concludes his discussion of contact and education by stating that "contact with the white has educated the Native," therefore whites "cannot help educating him, if not intentionally than unintentionally"; finally then, since "we have seen that past social contact of the two races has been harmful.... We must attempt to provide a development for each race so that contact, when it takes place at all, should take place at a high level."[37] Loram then proposes industrial education as a solution when segregation is not an option. This argument by Loram was responding to debates around segregation and education of Black South Africans that were circulating in the South African political realm after the 1910 unification of the country between English colonists, descendants of Afrikaner settlers who felt disrespected by English rule, and Black South Africans. The tensions between white populations coupled with antiblack racism resulted in various forms of racial- and class-based labor differentiation that banned Black South Africans from taking certain jobs and living in specified locations reserved for white Afrikaners.[38] Similar to the ICC in the US South, Loram was trying to promote a form of cooperation that did not fully dismantle the program of segregation supported by the white population. Yet, Loram presented proximity and contact as an apolitical process when he stated that "we cannot help educating the Native."

This intimates that colonialism in Africa is inevitable. Loram describes the educative aspects of imitation as a way that "the primitive man adjusts himself to his environment."[39] The language he uses for why the environment changes is revealing: "With the coming of the white man an entirely new environment was created, and the Native's response to this new situation has been a gradual absorption through imitation of as much of the new as he could comprehend."[40] Loram describes the coming of the white man in passive language and neutral terms. Of course, much of the writing by Europeans and Americans at the turn of the century framed colonization in terms of the progress of civilization. For example, H. G. W. Wintersgill wrote, "with the march of civilization the savage tends to more and more abandon his distinguishing characteristics and to adapt himself to the habits of the superior races with whom he is brought into contact."[41] This naturalization of colonization and discussion of contact in non-violent terms is yet another means of justifying colonial and antiblack projects despite their intense violence.

Thus, in this discussion of education in Africa in the early twentieth century, the idea that proximity was educative was embedded into a rhetoric of "cooperation." Cooperation served as a shorthand for promoting white presence in Africa and the educational components of Western colonialism, mirroring the way educators in the US South discussed slavery as educational. These assertions that colonization and white presence in Africa were educative need not actually have been educative. There has always been resistance to European colonialism by colonized peoples, which is likely what created the impetus for a discourse of cooperation as a counterbalance. Yet whether or not cooperation actually happened or taught something to the "Natives" was not the main point of its discursive logic. Cooperation as a form of pedagogy was about extending the reach of colonialism and settlement through the antiblack discourse of African educational backwardness rather than the promotion of actual cooperative projects.

ADAPTATION AND LABOR FOR LIFE

Labor as learning, the second tenet of plantation pedagogy, was also in evidence across many African educational initiatives. For example, the report of Paul Rupel, the principal of the Booker Washington Institute of Liberia, defines the educational model of the school as "learning by doing" and then describes an educational program in which students made bricks to help construct buildings, labored on the school farm, cared for animals, and did other work across the school grounds.[42] R. L. Embree, the educational advisor for

Liberia and president of the College of West Africa, connected this type of labor as education to the development of industry in Africa. He noted that he agreed with the British Empire Advisory Committee on Education report on Africa, which stated, "there is obviously an intimate connection between educational policy and the economic development of a territory. Educational policy must be planned with reference to the line of life pupils may be expected to lead when they leave school." It also argued that "an equally intimate relation exists, or should exist, between the schools and agriculture."[43] Since the employment possibilities in Liberia that were seen as profitable by the Liberian government mainly consisted of farming or work on the Firestone rubber plantation, it was clear that this education consisted of learning to be a laborer and learning through doing labor.

This focus on labor as learning was also discussed using coded language in much of the writing by white reformers. Similar to how *cooperation* stood in for proximity in the language on education in Africa, so too the term *adaptation* stood in for the idea that labor was educative. This switch in terminology also had roots in Black education in the South. Thomas Jesse Jones, prior to touring Africa, wrote a report on Black education in the South for the Phelps-Stokes Fund titled *Educational Adaptations: Report of Ten Years' Work of the Phelps-Stokes Fund, 1910–1920*. In this report Jones describes adaptation as "arising from the needs of the people."[44] Jones specifically references the Hampton Institute in his framing of adaptation, noting that Samuel Armstrong was one of the first educators to prepare his students to meet the circumstances they would face in life. I further interrogate the idea of "education for life" in the conclusion of this work, but in this chapter, I tease out how "educational adaptations" fundamentally indexed the tenet of plantation pedagogy that labor was educational.

Throughout the report on education in Africa, the discussion of adaptation is extensive. The report cites the colonial governor of the Gold Coast, who notes that his government "relate[s] education to the needs of the people" and that this idea was influenced by "American schools for Negros."[45] The introduction to the report states that the "adaptation of education to the needs of the people is urged as the first requisite of school activities."[46] In the section on cooperation in education, the report notes that "it is the right and duty of the government to make certain that African youth are educated so that they may participate effectively in the life of the colony."[47] What is key about educational adaptation in Jones's report is that part of its goal is the differentiation of education, in which some are educated as leaders and scholars, while the masses are educated for agricultural labor or to be workers for Western industry.[48] Jones is clear that the type of educational adaptations that he supports are in line with the Hampton and Tuskegee models of education. Robert Park describes these models as fundamentally based on the principle that "a student should be willing to work for his education." He explains that this experience "dignifies labor because it makes the student feel in the very effort he makes to get his education, the value of common and ordinary labor when preformed with a purpose."[49] This is in response to his assertion that Tuskegee education is designed to meet the conditions that it finds which evidently require the teaching of labor.[50]

In these discussions, the idea of educational adaptation and education for life is also connected to the plantation, to slavery, and to discourses about settlement. Park calls industrial education an "education in social life," which creates an "industrial community" that requires that the school "take the students away from their homes, pluck them out of the ordinary environments, plant them in new soil, and stimulate in them a new and different spirit."[51] Three things are indexed in this concept of teaching. First, that one should be plucked from one place to be planted in another, which echoes the second: the discourse of settlement and colonization, the slave trade, and Indian boarding schools. It also reiterates the planting language of the plantation: planting workers in the industrial community and planting the habits of labor in workers in the same way that crops are planted in the soil.

Given that industrial education was dubbed "education for the new slavery" by Donald Spivey, it is interesting that Jones explicitly mentions slavery in his discussion of educational adaptation. However, Jones attempts to invert the usual argument made by industrial reformers that slavery was educative, stating that not adapting education to the needs of the people is a form of "educational slavery." Jones states that "educational slavery has been painfully apparent both in the retention of certain conventional subjects that have excluded others much more applicable to life, and in the teaching of a subject content that should long ago have given way to results of modern research related to the life of the pupils."[52] While white reformers usually framed slavery as educational in that it taught Black people to work, Jones discursively situates classical education as the equivalent of slavery, shifting the way in which slavery indexes education in his discourse. This may be due to the rhetorical shift he saw as necessary in the African context, where Natives disdained slavery, and Western powers sought to distance themselves from the slave trade. The rhetoric in the South, by contrast, attempted to make slavery seem like a benign social institution in the face of its violent afterlife.[53]

C. T. Loram's writing on educational adaptation in South Africa argues in support of industrial education partly because it makes the Native South African desire material things:

> The more we can increase the Native's legitimate and satisfiable wants, the happier and better we shall make him. To effect this no agency is more powerful than education. The educated Native's wants are considerably more than those of his "raw" brother. To meet these wants he must work. If he works for the white man, we have a better and more permanent servant. If he works for himself, we have a more efficient tradesman or farmer. Not only do the Natives and the individual white man benefit from the increase in the Native's wants, but the State through the Native's improved producing and purchasing power receives a greater share of revenue.[54]

Booker T. Washington made similar arguments in his essay "The Economic Development of the Negro Since Emancipation" where he states, "what is needed is not only to have the individual educated in industry but to have his hand so trained that he will become ambitious; as one man put it not long ago 'He will want more wants.'"[55] Loram frames South African Blacks as not having appropriate wants because of their primitiveness, much in the same way Indigenous peoples were often framed by white educators and politicians in the US.[56] He states that "as producer the Native has in the past done little, because he needed little, but it is clear that as his wants increase, he will be driven to greater productiveness."[57] Loram also connects his discussion to Washington directly by noting that "Booker Washington found the same spirit among the Negroes of the United States, and his classic example of the Negro young man studying French amid squalid surroundings must be familiar to my readers."[58] Loram believed that farming is the "hereditary occupation of the race," with the race being Black people globally.[59] Loram concludes that "for the uplift of the Native race it is necessary that they should make progress along manual and industrial lines"; yet, he continues, "part of our problem is to enable them to do this without entering into 'unfair' competition with the Europeans."[60] The contradiction inherent in this argument is likely because Loram was advocating for industrial education in a manner that did not challenge the segregationist politics of South Africa.

Thus, adaptation, as discussed by Jones, Loram, and others, was a rhetorical stand-in for the language of labor as a form of teaching and learning.

Educational adaption, much like cooperation, does not seek to dismantle segregation or colonial domination and is yet another permutation of plantation pedagogy. Both cooperation and adaptation as educational projects were deeply implicated in the intimacy between the plantation and the school in Africa.

THE PLANTATION AND THE SCHOOL: ECONOMIC DEVELOPMENT AND SETTLEMENT

The physical space of plantations played an important role in the transference of plantation pedagogy across Pacific and Atlantic geographies with much of this connection driven by imperialist resource extraction. The report headed by Jones on education in Africa spends a great deal of time discussing the possibilities of natural resource extraction on the continent. Jones states that a "great misunderstanding" of Africa by those who have not been there relates to the "wealth of resources" it possesses.[61] Jones notes the ability to grow and produce both cotton and sugar, as well as the possibilities of mining, hydro-electricity, and agriculture.[62] While a discussion of the wealth of natural resources and possibilities for development of these resources may seem out of place for a report on education, Jones believes that the form of education necessary for Africa is a kind that will help "the individual to make effective use of his environment."[63] This implies first that Africans are not making effective use of their environment, which was part of the reasoning settlers made in relation to Indigenous peoples in the US, and second that European or US influence is necessary to train African peoples to make correct use of their environment. In this way, Jones bases his educational recommendations for Africa on the success of imperialism, noting that "resources of soil, minerals and water power depend for their development upon the effective education of all the people. Economic prosperity and the educational development of the people are inextricably interwoven. The ultimate test of colonization is not, however, in the exploitation of physical resources. The final test is in the civilization of the Native people."[64] Despite his disclaimer that successful colonization is not the "true test," it is clear that Jones sees the extractive use of African resources as evidence of educational achievement.

Much of this language concerning the wealth of African land and resources is echoed by other publications that espoused industrial education programs. An 1894 edition of the *Southern Workman,* which was published over twenty-five years before the Phelps-Stokes report on Africa, describes a talk given by African missionaries at Hampton extensively discussing the wealth of African land in relation to mining, agriculture, and the river system. Therefore, it is obvious that, even prior to the involvement of Jones and the Phelps-Stokes Fund, industrial education was concerned with development in Africa.[65] These same missionaries also discussed their educational program in Africa, stating: "We'll let him work—sawing wood, weeding your garden, etc... for a few weeks. By and by take a porcupine quill and trace the letters of the alphabet... then he asks for a shirt and builds an upright house." These actions seem to be a non sequitur, yet they are framed as logically connected to each other by these missionaries.[66] Thus, they connect asking for a house to both learning to read and write and to various forms of labor. This reifies the discourse that Africa has rich yet untapped resources and that the establishment of Western ideas of living will bring about colonization's success.

Each of the above examples demonstrates how a focus on the resources of Africa was tied to the ideas of education that these industrial educators and missionaries espoused. In the case of the Booker Washington Institute of Liberia, the progression from the discussion of this intimacy between schooling and economic development to the intimacy of physical plantations and schools is evident. In R. R. Taylor's first report to the US board of directors about the location for the Booker Washington Institute in Liberia, he notes that "as I have observed it, Liberia with a few exceptions such as the Firestone Planation, has very little agriculture, little organized industry, very poor home life measured by anything approaching modern standards."[67] In addition to his discussion of the physical school site, Taylor makes sure to mention exploiting the resources of oil palms and that the cultivation of trees, especially rubber trees, can be profitable for the institute.[68] He imagines the school grounds planted with rubber, coffee, and palm oil trees as well as food crops to export for sale.[69] Taylor's visit was tied quite closely to the Firestone plantation, with the manager at the plantation consulting on plans for the school and providing all Mr. Taylor might need while in Liberia, such as transportation, introductions, and lodging.[70]

Once the Booker Washington Institute of Liberia was opened, the intimacy between the Firestone plantation and the school continued. Various documents from the Rockefeller International Education Board, which helped fund the Booker Washington Institute, the Phelps-Stokes Fund, in addition to the multiple state- and national-level colonization societies mentioned that the plantation had its hands in various aspects of the school's operation. They also discuss what students were trained for when they left the school. Mr. Firestone himself contributed money on multiple occasions to funding buildings on the school grounds as well as the salaries of white American educators employed by the Booker Washington Institute.[71] Firestone employees were consulted on building projects at the school, and they would also arrive at the school without notice and make reports to the board of trustees in America.[72] This surveillance of the school by the plantation echoes discussions by scholars in Black studies of the plantation as a space of both imprisonment and surveillance.[73] Finally, when students graduated the institute, reports from the Rockefeller International Education Board indicate that many went to work for the Firestone plantation directly at far higher rates than they did for other employers.[74] This intimacy between the plantation and the school demonstrates that teaching for slavery and settlement was also tied to extractive colonialism in Africa.

AMERICAN IMPERIALISM AND PRO-COLONIZATION POLICIES THROUGH EDUCATION

The connections between plantations and foreign imperialism were necessary to the landscape of industrial education in Africa, which was deployed strategically to quash political rebellion against foreign colonial powers. For example, in Liberia much of the discussion by the trustees of the Booker Washington Institute centered on making sure Liberia stayed independent of European colonial influence, yet many scholars have argued that Liberia was in essence a US colony in practice if not in name.[75] The Liberian government, which was effectively run by US-born Blacks, was accused of exploitation and oppression of Native Liberians, including by imposing work conditions on Native peoples as part of taxation policies, which were equivalent to slavery.[76] Therefore, despite the fact that Liberia was considered an independent government, the US focus on Liberian independence was in line with their support of colonial governments in other parts of Africa.

Thomas Jesse Jones and the other authors of the Phelps-Stokes report on Africa made no secret of their support for European colonial powers against African self-rule. The report describes both cooperation (proximity) and adaption (labor as education) as important ways to prevent African uprisings against colonial powers.[77] The report notes that the "demand for 'nationalism' and 'self-determination' by Native groups in the continents [is] often feverish [in] character and frequently antagonistic to the possibilities [of] cooperative relations."[78] Cooperative relations was a euphemism in many ways for continued European control, couched in the idea of training Africans for civilization. The report continues by stating: "The only cure for the so-called 'rising tide of color,' and 'the revolt against civilization,' heralded abroad with such anxiety by some alarmists of the present time, is in the development of genuine and sincere cooperation of peoples of all races based upon an education of the Native masses and Native leaders in the common essentials life."[79] Through this education in the "essentials of life," adaptation was described as an educational strategy that would work against decolonization.

In the case of South Africa, the discourse of adaptation and cooperation was often framed in relation to segregation and apartheid as opposed to preventing decolonization. In an article titled "Education among the Bantu of Southwest Africa," Maurice S. Evans, representative of the African Society, argues that with an education that "fit[s] him for his new environment" segregation will pose less of a problem in South Africa and will solve issues of competition feared by white settlers.[80] Therefore, in the case of South Africa, much of the discussion of education was about supporting a settler apartheid government that was both similar to the US in that segregation and settlement co-existed, but also importantly differed. In South Africa, segregation and settlement were aimed at one population rather than two populations—Black and Native—which were framed as distinct from each other. Each of these examples demonstrates that the form of education that white reformers wanted to transfer to Africa was pro-colonial. Decolonial movements were seen as disruptive to a proper education, which relied on cooperation and adaptation.

SEDIMENTS OF SLAVERY AND SETTLEMENT

What is evident from the discourse of cooperation and adaptation in relation to the plantation, slavery, and decolonization is that there is a many-layered set of conditions that connects education in the African context to both slavery and settlement. This layering of the relations to slavery and settlement in Africa is one of the reasons I prefer the term *settlement* as opposed to using *settler colonial* to refer to state formations. Settlement is a material process, and plantation pedagogy happened across various locations in Africa, from independent states to colonies. Distinguishing whether the location is a classic extractive colony or settler colony does not meaningfully map onto the types of educational activities that occurred in these spaces. Additionally, there is not a clear relationship between slavery, settlement, and colonialism across these spaces, with discourses about each constantly cross-referenced and made ambiguous by shifting rhetoric. Thus, in Africa, the interconnection of teaching slavery and settlement is echoed by the layered sediment of slavery and settlement in the landscape of the African continent.

An example of this sediment of slavery and settlement is the relationship between colonial labor extraction and slavery in the Liberian context. Amongst government officials and educational reformers there is discursive ambiguity about whether various forms of coercive labor constituted slavery. Many African Natives saw American migrants as descendants of slaves, and it is described that they looked down on them.[81] Yet, at the same time that many African Natives may have looked down on American Blacks, the American Black–led government of Liberia discussed making slaves of the African Natives as part of national road projects. Native Liberians were conscripted to build roads with no pay in Liberia as a means of paying taxes to the government. W. E. B. Du Bois wrote about this practice and how it led to an investigation by the League of Nations into whether this constituted slavery.[82] Yet, the Rockefeller International Education Board and trustees of the Booker Washington Institute argued that this practice was in no way the same as slavery, stating that "some may say this is forced labor, but I see nothing to get excited about. It is the African pay-as-you-go-plan."[83] In this way, the afterlife of slavery in Liberia is complicated by the settlement of Black former slaves on African soil, pitting Black groups against each other in a discourse about what constitutes enslavement.

In fact, the issue of how to discuss slavery in the African context was ubiquitous in industrial education discourse. According to white reformers, slavery was both uncivilized and no longer part of modern states, yet also a precursor to the possibility of imperialism as a civilizing force. For example, Chauncey M. Depew stated in an 1892 speech at the Hampton Institute that

> we in America had slavery imposed upon us, and it cost millions of lives and thousands of millions of dollars to get rid of it. When America did get rid of it, then it speedily ceased throughout the civilized world; and now there is no civilized nation where slavery exists. The civilized nations of the world send out their navies to prevent the slaver from reaching port. Civilized nations combine to stamp out this evil where it still exists in Asia and Africa.[84]

Here, it is both the presence and absence of slavery that speaks to the educational nature of space. This was common in discourse about the US South as well, in which emancipation was often framed as throwing Black communities into freedom before they were prepared. As William I. Thomas, a professor of sociology at the University of Chicago, argued, places like the US South, Liberia, and Haiti were all locations of crisis that necessitated that Black people "change the pace of the race" since "the negro in slavery never worked at a high rate of energy." Thomas proposed that education in the model of Hampton and Tuskegee would solve this issue by changing the temporality of Black labor.[85] This idea is expressed similarly by a graduation address at Liberia College in 1938, which couched a discussion of slavery in relation to the Roman empire. The speakers stated that Roman and Greek classical education was fundamentally based on the existence of slavery, and therefore, with no slavery, it becomes necessary to prepare people for life differently.[86]

The comparison of Africa to settler states like the United States is also quite stark in the discourse of white reformers. In an address to the League of Nations about the work of the Phelps-Stokes Fund in Africa, Jones notes that one of Liberia's greatest challenges has been controlling the "Natives" in its hinterland.[87] In an address given by President Blyden of the Liberia College during a visit to the Hampton Institute, Blyden compares the state of Liberia to the Jamestown colony in Virginia, with the Black American settlers cast in the mold of John Smith and other British explorers and the Mandingoes of Africa compared to the Choctaw.[88] These comparisons frame Liberia as having a distinct antagonism between settler and Native. However, categorizing Liberia as a settler state is reductive in that it positions Blacks as settlers in relation to Africa, when they themselves are descendants of the enslaved taken from those shores. If Liberia does not exactly fit the classification of settler colonialism, it also overlaps with classic or extractive colonialism. For example, the Firestone plantation's dealings in Liberia are a classic example of the process of extractive colonialism. Therefore, how can one parse the layers of extractive colonialism alongside a set of settlers who came to stay, yet not entirely to replace, but to become a part of and to change? In a way, the settlement of Liberia was founded on Black fugitivity and escape from the US, yet it set up imperialistic relationships and posited Africans as savages to be civilized. This complex layering of slavery and settlement demonstrates why classifying African states in relationship to settlement is a fraught exercise.

South Africa is yet another example of a space that has been differentially categorized as either a settler state or a classic colonialist state, yet is full of layers of contradiction in relation to both slavery and settlement.[89] C. T. Loram, who claimed that US Southern Black education was a good model for South African education, also made arguments that are extremely similar to those made by US settlers about Indigenous peoples, Native Hawaiians, and Filipino Natives. For example, Loram's discussion of the South African Native naturalizes land theft. He stated that the "common opinion that the present Native tribes were the original owners of all the land in South Africa, and that the European peoples have dispossessed them of their ancestral birthrights, is historically untrue."[90] He further compared Indigenous conflict to colonization, stating that "both European and Bantu are in South Africa by right of conquest, and in the matter of race adjustment neither can claim the right of original ownership of the soil."[91] Next, Loram argued that this "conquest" had irrevocably changed relations to land, which could never be reverted to Indigenous land tenure systems, and that this change in land tenure inevitably changed Native peoples, for better or for worse. Loram states: "This idyllic state of affairs was destroyed forever by the new settlers from Europe, who, fired with zeal for more improved methods of farming, demanded that the farms be cultivated more intensively, and that the Crown lands be opened up for European settlement."[92] This change in land ownership and use meant, according to Loram, that "concomitant with the enclosure of the lands and the more intimate relationship between white and black have come marked changes in the social organization of the Bantu people, the passing of the system of communal tenure of land, and the rapid growth of individualism."[93] Therefore, Loram proposes education as a way to direct "the social future of the Black" in this new environment.[94] In this way, Loram uses educational discourse as part of the justification of colonialism and settlement.

This discourse of the change of land tenure, the naturalization of colonization, and how colonization changes the Native leads to the assertion by many white educational reformers that Natives ways are doomed in favor of Western civilization. Loram states that both "the primitive methods of agriculture [and] the primitive method of tribalism must die."[95] He also states that "in the past the Native has made little use of the land. So long as he could obtain sufficient grazing for his cattle, and a small patch of land for cultivation, he was content. As a stock-farmer the Native has not been very successful, and he is probably the worst agriculturist in the world. Although agriculture is the hereditary occupation of the people, it has never been practiced on a large scale."⁹⁶ He argues that "for the new order of things," which is, of course, defined by European control of land, the Native must change his mode of relating to the land and producing crops on the land.⁹⁷

This discussion of Blacks in South Africa is very similar to the discussion of Indigenous peoples of the Americas, Hawai'i, and the Philippines as doomed. What is different in this context is that South African Native peoples are described as "natural agriculturalists" whereas Indigenous peoples often were not, even when they had extensive agricultural knowledge. In the article "Education among the Bantu of the Southwest," Maurice Evans made similar arguments prior to the assertions Loram made in his report on education in South Africa. There, Evans noted that "the ancient way of living as herdsmen is becoming impossible" and that the Native's "social system is disintegrating" due to white influence. He concludes: "to go back to the old life is impossible, the new is full of danger to a race so unprepared for change; the Europeans of South Africa are responsible for this and it is our palpable duty to take steps to minimize or remove the danger and give the native guidance and opportunity for a higher and better life."⁹⁸ This discussion of African life as doomed puts Africa in direct comparison to Indigenous peoples, who were seen as unable to withstand settlement. However, it also frames the South African Native as in need of "guidance and opportunity," which is reminiscent of how slavery and settlement were framed as educational at the same time that they were genocidal.

A final example of the complexity of slavery's sediment in the context of Africa is the discussion of former slave forts in the report on education in African headed by Jones. The report describes these forts as "castles," which have both historic interest and serve as present-day civilizers through their use as spaces for European colonial administration. The report states, "the advantages to Native life provided by the colonial governments have on the whole overshadowed the disadvantages . . . The dungeons of their lower levels point to the cruel slavery of the early centuries. Their upper levels are now transformed into government houses where policies are formulated for the improvement of the people—for building roads, improving sanitation, and providing educational facilities for the Native people."⁹⁹ Describing the forts where Black people were enslaved and kept in dungeons to be transported to the Americas as evidence of European civilization and benevolence is a twisted justification of slavery's overt violence. The sediments of slavery are further muddled by the establishment of plantations across West Africa. The contrast of the new plantation spaces such as the Firestone rubber plantation or cotton plantations in many parts of West Africa with the old slave forts that initially sent enslaved African peoples to the plantation landscape of the Americas demonstrates the atemporality of slavery and the plantation in the African context. Thus, the plantation and plantation pedagogy take on protean forms in Atlantic geographies where the afterlife of slavery is lived differently.[100]

THE CONFLICTS OF PLANTATION PEDAGOGY IN AFRICA

The unique sediments of slavery and settlement in the African context led to conflicts in the discourse and implementation of plantation pedagogy. One such conflict presented itself in the debate at the Booker Washington Institute over the hiring of a Black principal and the firing of a number of Black teachers. When the Booker Washington Institute of Liberia was first founded, it was led by a white educator, James L. Sibley, who died of yellow fever a few months into his work. The subsequent principal and vice principal were both white men with missionary ties. This eventually led to a conflict in which the Black-led Liberian government pressured the Board of Trustees of the Booker Washington Institute to hire a Black principal rather than continuing to hire white educators to lead the school.[101] This conflict was heightened by the fact that a Black man from the US had been acting principle of the Booker Washington Institute for a short time but was demoted and eventually fired by the white trustees. In fact, a number of American Black teachers were fired from the Booker Washington Institute for what the trustees called "lack of cooperative spirit" because they were seen as "not in complete sympathy with the purposes and politics of the institute."[102] It should come as no surprise that American Black teachers in Liberia may have had motives that diverged from those of the white reformers who bankrolled the school. As scholars like Jarvis R. Givens argue, a key thread of Black educational thought is its fugitive nature, hiding its true intent from the white gaze.[103] I do not attempt to theorize what these fired Black teachers in Liberia may have been aiming towards or what their dreams were. I am more interested in the ways that the discourse of Black messianism, which discursively seeks to justify slavery as civilizing American Blacks so that they can return to Africa to save it from heathenism, comes into conflict with the educational tenet of proximity to whiteness.

The board of trustees for the Booker Washington Institute maintained a position opposite to that of the Liberian government. They felt that American Black teachers were too invested in the "Liberian cause" to be effective as principals; they explained that "there is... the conviction in the minds of several who have had experience in Liberia that for the present Liberia needs the influence and services of at least a few white educators and workers."[104] This led to a compromise in which the trustees proposed having a white principal and a white assistant principal, while hiring a Black teacher to also be an administrator at the school under their direction. In the board's inquiries to places like Tuskegee, Hampton, and other industrial schools, they stated that the person to fill this position should be "cooperative" and interested in "interracial relations."[105] The board noted that, in order to be hired, a Black teacher would have to be dedicated to certain goals: "The three purposes which he would serve would be, first, to counteract and to correct the interracial misunderstandings; second, to help the Liberian Government and Liberian leaders to understand the importance of the educational program of the Institute; and, third, to help develop a sound program of education at the Institute."[106] This insistence is likely due to what the board of trustees described as a series of "disturbances" at the Booker Washington Institute where students "complained of excessive work, poor pay, and unsatisfactory food" and where the principal had to appeal to the government for help in "controlling the rebellions [sic] students."[107] The board's position on hiring a white principal demonstrates that the tenet of proximity to whiteness as educative was deeply ingrained at the Booker Washington Institute, yet that cooperation as a project was a contingent one that was likely to be disrupted by the political landscape of Liberia.

This conflict denotes how the layering of the afterlife of slavery, colonial extraction, and settlement in the context of Africa makes classifications of states like Liberia or South Africa as either settler colonial or classic colonial states impossible. It points to the limited utility in trying to separate different forms of settlement, imperialism, and colonialism from each other when they are inherently interlinked. It makes clear that settlement and colonialism cannot be theorized in this context without linking it to the history of slavery and the profound, reverberating effects of antiblackness. Plantation pedagogy's circulation in currents of colonialism was therefore caught in eddies of contradiction, in which some of its main tenets clashed in currents that ran counter to each other, muddying the waters of colonial exchange.

PART THREE

Plantation Pedagogy as a Technology of Settlement

FIVE

"Out from Cabin and Tepee"

SETTLEMENT, SLAVERY, AND
THE MAKING OF DOMESTIC SPACE

A report published by the Hampton Institute in 1900 titled *Out From the Cabin and the Tepee,* written by the second president of Hampton, Hollis Burke Frissell, noted that the Hampton Indian program had the goal of producing "young women... prepared to teach their people the art of homemaking" so that they could bring "back with them to the destitute cabins and tepees the practical knowledge by means of which even the poorest may have clean and attractive homes and surroundings."[1] This discourse of taking Black women "out from the cabin" and Native women "out from the tepee" was tied to larger processes of settlement, antiblackness, and space making. By taking them "out from the Cabin and the Tepee" and putting Black and Indigenous women into domestic programs, Hampton sought to alter the physical spaces of homes through plantation pedagogy. Through programs like the training cottages and the connected home loan program of the Women's National Indian Association (WNIA), the changing of the individual home was connected with the didactic process of allotment, tying together the biopolitical targeting of space with the social construction of womanhood and heteronormativity. This was echoed in programs like the Jeanes supervisory teachers program in the US South, teaching cottages at Hawaiian schools, cottage dorm proposals in Liberia, as well as the transformation of the slave cabin into the teaching cottage as part of progressive education programs during the New Deal era.

The goal of the cottage as a didactic space was, as Frissell states, "Improvement among the Indians in land, homes, and schools."[2] Thus, this chapter traces the connections between land, homes, and schools through the cottage as a space of teaching. Additionally, the pedagogical construction of space was an outcome of plantation pedagogy that was deeply tied to the project of teaching "primitives" to become "men and women," which was an expression of the impositions of Western cis-heteronormative gender roles rather than a true attempt at extending the concept of the human to Black and Indigenous bodies. In this chapter, I address the implementation of domestic education through the cottage as an educational space and conceptualize the cottage as a technology of plantation pedagogy. The pedagogy of the cottage functioned through a scaled use of didactic space, connecting macro spatial pedagogies of land dispossession to micro-level spatial pedagogies of the home and the making of domestic space. Additionally, the small-scale spatial process of "making homes" dovetailed with various larger forms of surveillance, control, and violence that sought to limit non-Western modes of gendered and sexual expression.

Hampton framed the social construction of sex and gender through the discourse of making men and women as a form of creating national domestic space. The formation of national domesticity is, of course, integrally related to imperialism, with the domestic and foreign both relying on the imposition of gendered norms of familial composition and homemaking. This project took shape via the slave cabin, which I argue was a didactic space that both served to justify slavery and to materially represent the supposed degradation of Black people. The teaching cottage at schools like Hampton was a replacement for the slave cabin; it was a pedagogic space that expanded the didactic project of fixing the "negro problem" and furthering settlement. Therefore, the teaching cabin was a piece of machinery in the technology of plantation pedagogy, and one that circulated as plantation pedagogy spread. I connect the allotment act, a macro-level pedagogy that targeted both land and people, to the construction of training cottages on the Hampton grounds and the use of those cottages to train Native women in domestic work, which was a micro-level instantiation of this same pedagogical intent. The micro and macro levels merged when the students who were trained in these cottages received home loans from the Women's National Indian Association (WNIA) to build cottages of their own on allotted reservation land. Ultimately, the teaching cottages intended to produce "homekeeping" as an educational product. Homekeepers, as opposed to homemakers, denoted the supposed degraded domestic status of the Black and Native women that the cottage educated. Homekeepers signaled domestic workers who worked in other people's homes, while homemakers denoted the true domestic ideal of settlement, the white mother.

MAKING MEN AND WOMEN AND CONSTRUCTING CIS-HETERONORMATIVE GENDER IN INDUSTRIAL EDUCATION

Samuel Chapman Armstrong was always very clear that the goal of industrial education was to "make men and women." In *Education for Life,* which details his ideology of industrial education, he states that Hampton "sends men and women rather than scholars into the world."[3] This distinction between "men and women" and scholars is one that is prevalent in industrial education discourse and was echoed in, for example, the famous debates between Booker T. Washington and W. E. B. Du Bois on academic versus industrial curriculum.[4] In the Hampton Institute catalogue from 1876, it is noted that, as an institution devoted to Black education, Hampton "must produce moral as well as mental strength and while making its students first-rate mechanical laborers must also make them first-rate men and women."[5] In this formulation, industrial education produces not only laborers but also a social construct of proper men and women as defined by Hampton's own racial and gendered beliefs.[6] Inherent in this idea of making "men and women" is a gendered and sexualized division of labor in which women's labor is tied to constructions of domesticity. Similarly, an article detailing the Hampton model of education in *The New England Magazine* in 1892, states that "it is the aim of the Hampton Institute to make thrifty, industrious, capable men and women, who will radiate good influences among their people."[7] Thus, the goal was not only to construct ideas of cis-heteronormative gender but also to diffuse and influence other geographies to imitate these forms of "making men and women."

Through the concept of "making men and women," industrial education programs socially constructed the ideal of man- and womanhood in relation to the Black and Indigenous students whom they educated within their walls, fields, and workshops. In studies of gender and sexuality and settler colonialism, scholars have argued that settlers constructed normalized sexual and gendered relations in order to impose a unit of civilization, the family, on Indigenous peoples.[8] The individual family unit was part of imposing private property relations on tribal land and collective living and contributed greatly to policies such as allotment. The imposition of the nuclear family as a unit of civilization drew on stereotypes of Native women as Indian Princesses or as degraded squaws.[9] As Nakano Glenn states in her description of settler colonialism as a race-gender project, settlers blamed Indian women for the "backwardness" of Indian men. In their view, the fact that Indian women did heavy physical labor and were ignorant of modern housekeeping methods accounted for Indian men's laziness and disinterest in material progress. If Indian women could be educated to focus on the household and to desire better furnishings, Indian men would be impelled to work hard to acquire material goods (Stremlau, 2005). Thus, assimilation was intended to instill a sense of gender-appropriate duties and obligations. Ultimately, the aim of Indian schooling was to impose "social death."[10]

Nakano Glenn theorizes how the distinction of gendered labor was necessary for eventual Native disappearance.[11] Similarly, Arvin, Tuck, and Morrill argue that the "paternal organization of citizens into nuclear families, each expressing a 'proper,' modern sexuality, has been a cornerstone in the production of a citizenry that will support and bolster the nation-state."[12] Furthermore, they write, "it is important to note that in many cases, the enforcement of 'proper' gender roles is entangled in settler nations' attempts to limit and manage Indigenous peoples' claims to land."[13] Therefore, constructing cis-heteropatriarchal gender roles both bolsters settlement and aids in the dehumanization of those who are seen as deviant from those roles. For example, I have argued in other work that the portrayals of Black and Native women are intimately interconnected because their gendered representations are tied to land dispossession and genocide.[14] I am deeply indebted in this analysis to Black studies scholars who have also addressed the role of cis-heteropatriarchy in relation to Black women. This has often been discussed in relation to the pathologization of Black women and households headed by Black women, as well as to the demonization of Black reproduction.[15] Iconography such as the mammy served to index Black womanhood as in service to white womanhood and, as Hortense Spillers notes in her iconic essay, "Mama's Baby Papa's Maybe: An American Grammar Book," slavery ruptured bonds of kinship, breaking families and gendered relations, resulting in an ungendering of Black flesh.[16] This results in what she and Christina Sharpe both theorize as an untethered signifier when Blackness abuts words like woman or girl.[17] These theorizations are important for understanding how Black women were framed as in need of learning settler cis-heteropatriarchal gender roles, as slavery was seen as rupturing Black ties to gender.

The construction of cis-heteropatriarchal gender roles as part of industrial education also effected the material construction of schools, particularly whether men and women were educated together, also known as "coeducation." Former Hampton teacher of ten years, Margaret Kenwill, who moved to Hawai'i to work on industrial education projects, wrote in the *Hawaiian Gazette* about how coeducation for white students as well as Black and Native students in the United States was a structure that should be transferred to Hawai'i. The rationale behind coeducation in this article hinges on sexual relations being policed between men and women and on a production of womanhood that obeyed white protestant ethics:

> It is an axiom that no nation of race ever rises above the level of its women. We get what we demand. If we command respect, we receive it. The Hawaiian girl needs to learn self-respect and to demand respectful and courteous treatment at the hands of her brothers. The thing that must strike every observer is that she does not expect it or ask it or receive it. She has yet to learn what belongs to her. She can nowhere do this better than in school, where boys and girls mingle in class room, or dining room, or social hall, under proper and competent surveillance. In a country where the proprieties of family and social life are lacking, where familiarity is the rule, the need of co-education is self-restraint and self-respect is more imperative than elsewhere. Mutual respect is a certain outcome when men and women stand equal in the classroom.... Nowhere the 'flower of the kingdom" is selected and sent to different schools, kept separate and apart for the number of years, and at just the time when the society of each is most attractive to the other; it is a little wonder that when set free they should throw restraint to the winds. Daily companionship in classroom and dining hall in the presence of their teachers would by very familiarity lessen the danger in their homes, where such restraint should be withdrawn.[18]

The comparison here between Hawai'i, which had single-sex education, and the United States, where there were many coeducational institutions, demonstrates how ideas about gender and sexuality were embedded in the space of schooling institutions. The narratives of Native Hawaiian women lacking self-respect and seen as degraded by Native Hawaiian (and, of course, white settler) men is structured through antiblack and settler notions of gender and domesticity. In this instance, the insistence on women's presence through coeducation is related to the way Indigenous women's presence made race particularly salient at Hampton and the co-occurring degradation of Black women and places that degradation narrative in the context of coeducation of the sexes as a race-gender project.[19]

This is demonstrated further in a section of the Hampton University catalogue from 1876:

> The question of co-education of the sexes is, to my mind, settled by most favorable experience with the present plan. Our school is a little world; the life is genuine; the circle of influence is complete. The system varies industry and cheapens the cost of living. If the condition of woman is the true gauge of civilization, how should we be working, except indirectly, for a real elevation of society by training young men alone? The freed woman is where slavery left her. Her average state is one of pitiable destitution of whatever should adorn and elevate her sex. In every respect the opportunities of the sexes should be equal, and two years of experience have shown that young men and young women of color maybe educated together to the greatest mutual advantage, and without detriment to a high moral Standard.[20]

This explanation of coeducation for Black students is wary of behavior that is not of a "high moral standard," a euphemistic way of describing how Black women were represented as degraded or without morals and tied to the view of Black procreation as threat. Roberts notes that Black procreation has always been seen as a problem and that Black women in particular have been seen as bearers of an incurable immorality through their procreation.[21] Armstrong and others at Hampton attempted to construct coeducation as a means to assuage the fears associated with the procreation of Black women in their state of perceived ungendered depravity. By stating that Hampton was creating men and women, Hampton attempted to mitigate the fears of white southerners who did not want Black people to be educated at all. However, in doing this, it also reinforced the idea of Black women as already degraded and in need of elevation as well as the idea that coeducation specifically benefits, uplifts, and constructs women as vulnerable beings.

This same rationale for coeducation is discussed in relation to the Native women and men who came to Hampton after 1878. Winona lodge was a women's dormitory built specifically for Native women and this description of the social activities of the lodge reinforces these discourses on the benefits of coeducation:

> By the little socials at "Winona" at which the young men are entertained by the young women, the two sexes are put in their proper relation, social graces are acquired, and a strong impression is made upon the character of the participants who find, like other young people, that this innovation upon the Indian social system is a very pleasant one. The Indian students have their own table in the school dining-hall, the girls sitting opposite the boys. The boys have their own dormitory, known as the Wigwam, and their own company in the Institute battalion; but in the normal school, negroes and Indians work together.[22]

The cis-heteropatriarchal notion of the sexes being in proper relation is a hallmark of teaching slavery and settlement. The type of man and woman that institutions like Hampton attempted to make reinforced western notions of sex and gender in opposition to other modes of being. Hampton constructed gender roles as a key part of its pedagogy because gender and sexuality was a crucial way that its civilizational program was articulated and women students were the means to create civilization change. This change hinged on the relationship between gendering, domesticity, and the operation of power.

DOMESTICITY AS DEFINING BOTH CIVILIZATION AND SAVAGERY IN INDUSTRIAL EDUCATION

Domesticity is integrally related to nation building and imperialism.[23] Amy Kaplan discusses the integral role domesticity plays in the colonial project of civilizing racialized people, arguing that it "monitors the borders between the civilized and the savage but also regulates traces of the savage within itself."[24] This spatial organization, which defined the home as a separate domestic sphere reserved for women, also defined the national domestic against the foreign racialized being. As Kaplan explains, "the shared racial underpinnings of domestic and imperialist discourse through which the separateness of gendered spheres reinforces the effort to separate the races by turning Blacks into foreigners."[25] Stoler and Sánchez-Eppler both extend this analysis by showing how notions of domesticity shape the trope of the infantilized Native, who is seen as a child despite their adulthood.[26] Piatote explains that "from the perspective of Native American polities during the assimilation era, the categories of foreign and domestic were not so much proximal as coterminous."[27] Piatote cautions us to pay heed to multiple registers of domestic discourse. This is exemplified in a discussion of the "Lexington cottage" at Hampton, which was used to house Native women students prior to the construction of the women's dorm on campus. The text uses a language of colonization that is more often reserved for international contexts: "twelve of the Indian girls ... were colonized in the Lexington Cottage."[28] The spatial register of the home is tied to the register of the nation by connecting the domestication of space to the broader project of imperialism. Thus, the pedagogy of the home space as enacted at Hampton was directly connected to other spatial scales of domination.

The focus on domesticity in industrial education and its role in constructing sex and gender relations is clear in the way Hampton described its Indian program. In an article from the *Southern Workman* in 1889, Armstrong argued that "the family is the unit of civilization, and the conditions of pure family living are the first things to be created in educating men and women. Hence the co-education of the sexes is indispensable."[29] If the family is the unit of civilization, then the domestic sphere and education within the domestic sphere are paramount to Hampton's educational project. Consequently, a necessary part of justifying the domestic sciences as part of industrial education programs was portraying Black and Indigenous women as degraded and not "true women."[30] In a similar vein, in his report *Indian Education in the East,* which details Hampton's efforts to raise funds to enroll more Native women as students, Armstrong stated that the "deep degradation of Indian women calls for an earnest effort on their behalf."[31] Hampton construes itself as remedying this degradation through industrial curriculum. An article highlighting Hampton in the *New England Magazine* notes that the "sewing room is a place where work is made a delight." It continues, "The teachers cultivated, sympathetic, earnest women, ladies in the truest sense of the word, make this 'home,' indeed. How much it means for the Indian race, that the dignity of a true womanhood is being cultivated to take the place of its brutally degraded squaws, must be apparent to anyone."[32] By making "womanhood" the terrain of struggle for civilization, industrial educators created dual narratives of Black and Native women that served to justify their educational program.

Native and Black women were described as both the saviors of their races and the most degraded subjects of their races. The training Hampton offered provided them a means of improving their racialized and gendered lot through homemaking, housekeeping, or teaching, particularly teaching in the industrial education model. The idea that Native women were both degraded within their communities, the ultimate example of Indian savagery on display, and also the instrument through which Native peoples could be saved from degradation is evident in discussions about race and gender at Hampton. Armstrong's pedagogy focused on Black and Native women because he believed that they represented the location where spatial relations might be altered for further settlement. Armstrong theorized that a program of industrial education could work in Indian camps without teaching as a mode of altering space: "The success of the education of our Indians turn on the conditions which await them on their return to their homes ... The girls have no foothold on which to attempt to breast it. The boys have their trades, and can separate themselves from their old homes and their camp life. There is absolutely no position of dignity to which Indian girls can look forward to."[33] This contrast between boys and girls serves to further entrench the notion that to be a Native woman is to live a degraded existence, one that even training in civilization cannot alter. Industrial education's answer to this narrative of degradation is teaching, as demonstrated by the argument made in Armstrong's 1882 annual report of the school:

> Should the United States Government ever find it possible to keep their treaty with the Sioux tribe, which provides for a school and suitable teacher for every thirty children in the tribe, the way might open for a solution of the knotty problem. Schools in the Indian camps, under judicious and vigorous supervision (such as in a few cases already established by the missionaries), not unlike the log-cabin school-houses to which our graduates go in the South, would give honorable work, full of inspiration, to our best Indian girls; while the children idling about the camp in the hope of existing on our government rations, would be taught the first principles of industry and virtue.[34]

The school on the reservation would serve, then, two purposes. It would continue the transformation of Indigenous women to be agents of civilizational change themselves and make the reservation space a satellite of Hampton. This discussion of the school as a means for expansion echoes the transportation of plantation pedagogies to reservation space.

THE SLAVE CABIN AND THE COTTAGE

Hampton's project of making men and women rested on a simultaneous degradation of Black and Native women and an attention to them as bodies through which civilization is enacted. As a part of this project, the discourse of taking the slave women out of the cabin is based on ideas of both the slave woman as degraded and also her home space as deficient. By taking the body out of one space and putting it into a new space, industrial education makes space a pedagogic tool. This new space is often labeled as the cottage rather than the cabin, although the two terms are often used synonymously, and it can be difficult to distinguish between them. In the context of industrial education and the post-emancipation time frame, the distinction between the cabin and the cottage is best demonstrated by the report of the Third Annual Hampton Negro Conference in 1899. The report described the cabin as a crude one-room house, as opposed to a cottage that had multiple rooms and sturdier construction.³⁵ This distinction would have been well known; Barbara Mooney has described it as the "iconography of the ideal home," which Black families were made to desire. This desiring of the "comfortable tasty framed cottage" was part of assimilation through architectural practice.³⁶

The slave cabin, in fact, has a long history in relation to ideas of education and civilization. W. E. B. Du Bois described slave cabins as "rude inadequate shelters" that did not have the "niceties of the civilized home."³⁷ According to Du Bois, this cabin was not adequate to learn white civilization, and it also divorced slaves from their African customs: "the continuity of negro family tradition has been broken and the traditions of the white environment never learned."³⁸ He goes on to say the plantation created bad and filthy habits in slaves; there was no need to have "thrift" because food and necessities were always provided. This narrative, by a scholar who would later go on to theorize race and antiblackness in less damage-centered ways, demonstrates how the cabin was seen as indexing the degradation of slavery on Black flesh even by some Black scholars. In fact, many scholars have noted that slave cabins were described by slave holders as a paternalistic gift, through which the white master saw himself as the head of both the Black and white family; slave holders therefore used the home as a means of teaching their charges. In this way the cabin was a space of teaching as well as a space of warped caring that sought to muddle the violence of enslavement with educational language.³⁹

Therefore, the idea of taking the Black woman out of the cabin, as stated by Frissell at the start of this chapter, is somewhat of a contradiction. The slave cabin, which was originally a pedagogic space in the context of teaching slavery, was reframed as a space of degradation where, after emancipation, learning cannot happen; the ideal of the "tasty framed cottage," then, becomes the slave cabin's replacement. Yet, in many ways, the cabin and the cottage are one in the same, both serving the pedagogic purpose of expanding settlement. In fact, the slave cabin is fundamentally similar to the pioneer cabin, which served as an instantiation of Western encroachment. Thus, I argue that it is not the removal of Black women from the cabin that is the most important outcome of the cottage as a pedagogic technology. In fact, the cabin/cottage is more of a trap, creating a double bind where to be in it or outside of it can both be construed as part of Black degradation. Only by making the cabin/cottage part of settlement that transforms the landscape towards white domination is the cottage a space of production.

MAKING NATIVE HOMEMAKERS THROUGH THE SPACE OF THE COTTAGE

Hampton's domestic curriculum was designed spatially to produce women who could maintain a home with the stated purpose of creating and transforming land through homemaking. A key example of this process is the family cottages built on Hampton's grounds. The Hampton cottage system for Native families was created in concert with Alice Fletcher, a white anthropologist who was also instrumental in the drafting and passing of the Dawes Act, as discussed in previous chapters. She recruited married couples to come and live as a family unit in small cottages constructed on the Hampton grounds. The program began in 1882 and ended in 1891, bringing twenty-three Indigenous families to Hampton. The families were meant to learn homemaking skills to transfer back to the reservation and to serve as examples of proper homemaking to the Native students at Hampton. This program worked in concert with a homebuilding loan program developed by the Women's National Indian Association (WNIA) in 1885 which furnished loans to Native families to build Western-style homes on allotted lands.[40]

One document discusses Native families at Hampton, the beginning of the program, and the families who were brought to live in these model cottages in detail. It describes the genesis of the cottage program in this way: "urged by Miss Alice Fletcher who ... realizing their need, and that of all tribes, for a higher ideal of home life ... begged that Hampton receive a few married couples and train them in model housekeeping on such a scale as would be feasible on the reservations in the West."[41] The purpose of the cottage program was twofold. It provided training and was itself a mechanism of training through modeling domestic organization. This blurred the line between homemaker and teacher, and I would argue, was instrumental to Hampton's construction of women as homemakers/homekeepers. Fletcher "herself chose [the] first families Noah La Flesche and wife, Philip Stabler, wife and baby." It is noted that the "husbands were taught the carpenter's trade, assisting to plan and put up the two three-roomed cottages built back of Winona for their use." They learned how to be carpenters and the women to keep house, and materially, this education was followed with funds to build homes on their own allotments.[42] The La Flesche family had a long history with boarding schools and assimilatory politics, with various members having attended Hampton and other white-run schools.[43] In tracing the trajectory of the Stablers at Hampton, the connection between domestic training and allotment of lands is made visible. The Stablers directly benefitted from the WNIA's home loan program after finishing their stint at Hampton. In fact, Noah La Flesche and Phillip Stabler were the only candidates considered for the first loan in the program, and Samuel Armstrong was part of the committee that approved the awarding of the loan to Stabler.[44]

As Mathes notes, "in addition to cultivating manliness among Native American men," the purpose of the WNIA home loan program was to "stimulate Native women to participate in the economic and social relations that it symbolized."[45] The ideology of the program drew from an understanding that space was didactic: "middle-class white women drew upon already potent beliefs in the power of a well-ordered home to influence individuals' moral character and upon women's crucial role in transforming architectural space into 'home' through their industry, refinement, and taste."[46] These homes worked didactically on Indigenous women but also served to showcase the civilizational process: "reformers supported the erection of model homes on reservations in an effort to create architectural spaces in which 'women's work' was visible as the work of civilization and thus of nation-building; such spaces were also designed to incorporate Native American women into the nation by defining their domestic work as the power behind evolutionary progress."[47] These understandings of the home as influencing both women's characters and showcasing the civilizational project of education are illustrative of the didactic power of space in Hampton's curriculum.

After the La Flesches and the Stablers, six more Native families were brought to Hampton before the program abruptly ended.[48] Bringing entire families to Hampton was ultimately a short-lived project due to a variety of issues, including cost, childcare while the parents attended classes, and the spread of similar model homes across reservations, western boarding schools, and reservation day schools.[49] However, the explanation given in the "Indian Families" document focuses more on the deficiency of Indigenous families as well as the importance of the program, again mentioning the WNIA home loans:

> After some years it was deemed best to give up bringing on families. Apart from the problems introduced into school life and the fact that some who were brought were not far enough advanced to be examples, there was no longer the same need of object lessons in the East since educated Indians, some of them former Hampton students, were marrying and setting up

homes of their own in the West. Hampton's experiment had also helped to inspire Mrs. Sara T. Kinney of Connecticut to organize a Home Building and Loan Committee in the National Indian Association which lent money without interest to aid young Indians in the erection of model homes.[50]

The intimate tie between the model family cottages and the physical building of homes on the reservation through the home loan program is exemplary of the connection between the micro and macro spatial constructions of settlement. The cottages at Hampton were meant to take Native women and their families out of the "tepee" and then to make sure they could not return to the "tepee" by providing a means for construction of Western-style homes on allotted lands. Allotment, the model cottages, and WNIA home loans were part of an intertwined effort to transform Indigenous homes and lands through a domestic spatial pedagogy.

Once it was decided that bringing families was no longer a supported programmatic goal, the cottages transitioned to serving as educational models for female Indigenous students. This became a popular pedagogical method that spread throughout the Indian boarding school system.[51] The focus of these model homes was to provide a space that Hampton reformers saw as closely mirroring the conditions girls would be in when returning to homes on allotted lands. By transforming the "tepee" into the Western home, the home becomes a small scale version of the transformation of Indigenous space into settlement, which was part of the larger program of allotment of Native lands. Of the four model-family cottages constructed "one . . . is now used to teach the Winona girls practical housekeeping under the conditions which are likely to surround them when they return to the west."[52]

The notion of fitting women to the conditions that would surround them was a common theme in discussions of the Hampton domestic program for both Black and Indigenous women. In fact, a large portion of the rhetoric of industrial education in general was to fit students to the life they were most likely to lead. As many scholars of Black education have persuasively argued, industrial education was tied to preparing Black people for assuming subservient roles as laborers in the South's new economic organization.[53] Black students were described as in need of this type of education to be improved upon, but with the qualification that they would not be improved so much that they would not be fitted for the life they were intended to lead in the South. The distinction between the cottages and the domestic program Black women attended was made clear in how the work was described:

> The girls prepare and serve a certain number of meals each week with simple appliances such as they are likely to have at home; for in the regular cooking classes of the Institute the work is done with "modern improvements" such as would hardly be obtainable on Indian Reservations. In every department at Hampton it is the aim, while showing the students the best methods of living not to unfit them for the life they will probably lead, but to fit them to make the best of it and to improve it.[54]

Thus, Black and Indigenous women were framed as needing to be taught domestic arts to be uplifted, but not so much that they would desire something beyond what their "less modern" homes could provide.

In line with fitting Native women for the conditions of the reservation, the cottages served a specific didactic purpose different from other domestic facilities at Hampton. In the same file as the document on Indian families is a description of the housekeeping cottages; it discusses how they differed from the other domestic didactic spaces at Hampton: "the school had its regular cooking classes, under a skillful teacher, but its big cook stove was for coal and its cupboard was stored with the appliances and convenience of a New England kitchen. For such girls as must return to a one or two-roomed cabin . . . a course in housekeeping of a very primitive nature seemed a most desirable supplement to the lessons of the cooking school."[55] The cottages served a specific purpose outside of the domestic programs, which was necessitated by the perceived primitivity of the conditions of reservation homes. Defining Native homes as primitive was key to how Hampton constructed Native women as homemakers; they were homemakers but only of the lowest variety. In fact, to educate Native women to expect more than that would not fit them to their conditions. Therefore, Native women were educated as homemakers who were already deficient in comparison to the cult of domesticity that upheld the national imagination. Native women might be homemakers in a primitive home on the reservation, but that role was transitional in the transformation of the reservation into settled space.

Ultimately the goal of educating Native women as homemakers who could manage primitive homes on allotted lands was tied to their own disappearance. This is illustrated best in the suggestions that this education fit Native women for marriage to white men. In an article in the *Southern Workman*, it is stated that "the majority of the marriages are between whites and Indians" and that "as a rule the educated girls marry white men."[56] Similarly, Samuel Armstrong is quoted as discussing what happens to Native women students when they return to the reservation: "On the Indian girl rests most heavily the weight of past and of present surroundings ... one of the five, an earnest Christian, wrote; 'Hard to be good woman out here;' she finally married a white man of good repute. She has recently brought her family near to her home."[57] Marrying a white man was the ultimate example of the proper Indigenous homemaker because it allowed for the transfer of Indigenous lands to white men as well as eventually for the erasure of Indigenous women altogether through their absorption into whiteness. The marriage was seen as a form of possession, leading to settler inheritance of Indigeneity and Indigenous lands.[58]

THE COTTAGE AS AN EDUCATIONAL TECHNOLOGY IN PACIFIC AND ATLANTIC CIRCULATION

The iconography of the cottage was not only integral to both slavery and settlement but it also circulated widely in currents of colonialism through US imperial projects. The cottage appears as a pedagogic space at schools founded by missionary educators in Hawai'i and in plans for schools funded by US philanthropists in Liberia. In fact, the idea of the home as an educative space appears in discussions of education programs across reports on the Philippines, Africa, and Hawai'i. As plantation pedagogy circulated, parts of its machinery, like teaching cottages, were transported and sometimes transformed as they were implemented in new contexts.

Thomas Jesse Jones's *Education in Africa* report states that the "home is recognized as one of the most fundamental institutions of human society." Since "the primitive family lacks many of the most vital requisites of healthful home life, including often even the decencies that are required for the training of the children," Jones explains, "the schools must therefore plan to make use of every school activity for the training of the youth in the essentials of home life."[59] Jones was specific that this training was more important for women than for men, arguing that "village life cannot effectively or permanently be improved without distinct elevation of African womanhood."[60] Jones also discussed how the school and the home/cottage should be merged in educational programs in Africa. For example, the report notes, "the schoolroom type will give way to the school-home type. To the classroom there will be added rooms where home activities will be taught. The teacher's home may become a part of the school plant.... Thus will the school home merge into the village homes and become a leaven for the transformation of the community."[61] In outlining this connection between home and school, Jones drew on his knowledge of programs in the US South that had been supported by the Rockefeller Foundation and Phelps-Stokes Fund, such as Jeanes Fund teachers and Rosenwald schools, which used traveling supervisory teachers as both a way to improve schools and teaching and improve local homes.

At the Booker Washington Institute of Liberia, where Jones served on the board of trustees and where the Phelps-Stokes Fund had a great deal of influence, the principal discussed how cottages might figure in the work of the school. The school was planning to build a dormitory for students and was constantly seeking funding to complete the project (including from the Firestone rubber plantation). The principal, Paul Rupel, suggested that a more fitting model might be having a series of cottages for the students rather than a large dormitory. He made similar arguments as Hampton did to justify the training cottages for Native families–that cottages would teach important lessons about home life. While the students of the Booker Washington Institute of Liberia were either all male or mostly male in the early years of its instruction, the principal noted that having cottages could later be used for married students or students with families. Rupel cited a missionary school in Nigeria that used this model and, in fact, made students construct their own houses as part of the educational process. He then discussed how the Booker Washington Institute could be "similar to the brick buildings which Firestones are building in the labor camps."[62] This plan was denied by the board, who noted that they thought it would be too expensive—but the trustees did agree that it was a solid educational idea. Therefore, even though the plan was not implemented, it was not for want of desire, but for want of material resources. The dorm at the Booker Washington Institute was eventually built with significant funds contributed by the Firestone Plantation.

The cottage as a space of teaching made a similar material and discursive circulation in Hawaiian Education. Derek Taira writes about the Kamehameha School for Girls which used the same language as Samuel Armstrong about "making women."[63] Taira states that Kamehameha "invade[d] and undermine[d] students' indigenous identities in order to convert them into 'useful servants of civilization.'"[64] He describes how the Kamehameha School for Girls constructed a "senior cottage" as a means to teach a small number of girls in a "real home atmosphere."[65] The Kamehameha School for Girls was designed to educate the children of Hawaiian royalty during the monarchy, but this method of teaching was also implemented in the Boys and Girls industrial schools, which were juvenile reformatory schools that committed their students for various crimes. The Girls Industrial School "was built on the cottage plan, with the idea in mind of giving these girls training in home-making, something very essential to the class of children coming under our care."[66] This system was recommended the next year for the Boys Industrial School because "the system obviates the old time dormitory and individualizes each boy. It is infinitely easier and better to have twenty boys housed in a home-like cottage. Training becomes a part of their existence. The cottage supervisors act as their adopted parents. Here are taught them the ethics of life and before them constantly are wholesome home environs."[67] This organization was also mimicked by the housing types used on Hawaiian sugar plantations, which, during the same time frame (1920s), began constructing primarily single-family cottages for their laborers rather than multifamily or barrack-like units.[68]

In the case of the Philippines, the construction of cottages was not proposed as a means of teaching in the same ways as the Hawaiian and African examples, since many of the Filipino communities consisted of Western-style homes due to Spanish colonization.[69] Yet, the description of the home as an educative space was consistent, demonstrating how the physical structure of the cottage was not needed in order for the cottage to be deployed as a discursive technology of teaching. Funie Hsu argues that education in the Philippines was a location of "playing imperial house," where "the schoolhouse became a political theatre for staging a public performance of home, in which colonial domesticity would be imposed."[70] Anne Paulet also notes how the teaching of domestic relations in the Philippines was tied to the use of domestic training in Indian boarding schools, particularly through the focus on ideas of sanitation and hygiene that were stressed in Filipino schools.[71] In the context of the Philippines, then, the teaching of domesticity and the connection between the home and the school served as a part of the specific flavor of US imperialism. The changing of Filipino homes was more about imperial shifts in rule than it was about teaching how to live in a home for the settlement of an "empty" country.

In each of these cases, the cottage and the home as a technology of plantation pedagogy circulated, sometimes shifting in its use and implementation. It also adapted to the differing goals of imperial powers across these spaces, which ranged from absorption to preventing decolonial uprising to preparing a country for "home rule"—all while capitalizing on the imperial extraction of resources.

HOMEKEEPING: SPACE IS WHAT MAKES THE WOMAN

Emily Huntington, one of the Hampton Indian program teachers, in a "Statement on Domestic Science" at Hampton, calls Black and Native women "the home keepers if not the home makers of the land."[72] This quote highlights an important aspect of Hampton's domestic program. While it trained Black and Native women in domestic arts, they were not in fact the ideal homemakers of the cult of domesticity; they were the offshoots of that narrative. White women occupied the place of the homemakers of the lands; they could make homes and settle, while Black and Native women were trained to keep house as a part of the spatial expansion of settlement and slavery. Since homemaking was an integral part of Hampton's domestic curriculum and the way in which it created "women," this section turns to how the cottage as an educational technology taught homemaking. But instead of homemakers, it really sought to produce homekeepers.

In addition to the model cottages described above, the women's dormitories were another educative space that worked to make women into those that could keep a home for others. The Indian women's dorm, named the Winona lodge, completed in 1881 and funded in part by Olivia and Caroline Phelps Stokes, was discussed in detail in Hampton publications.[73] The *Southern Workman* notes in 1882 that "there has been a marked improvement during the year in the self-respect and ambition shown by the girls, and a corresponding increase of courtesy on the part of the boys; though much is left to be desired in both directions. The new building for the girls, though still uncompleted, has been a strong stimulus to them."[74] Later that year, the *Workman* notes the completion of the building and its effect on the first class of Indigenous women:

> Years of instruction could not do for the Indian girls what a building of their own has accomplished immediately. They feel its influence in the dim morning twilight, as they get up for their early breakfast, and close the doors quietly, and soften their voices and go lightly down stairs that they may not wake others. It puts their rooms in order for the day, and sweeps out the corners of the corridors, and clears the windows.[75]

The talk of the impact of the building and the educational value of it as a space where students labored was widespread. The *Southern Workman,* which wrote articles chronicling the creation of the Winona lodge, from raising money to the beginning of building to its completion and use, noted how "the building of Winona [did] more for them than any teaching had."[76] It was because space was seen as pedagogic that the building had such an effect on Native women. The inside of the dormitory served as a proxy for the home and mimicked the didactic properties of space writ large. In the previous chapter, reservations and plantations were imagined as didactic spaces that existed across large swaths of the landscape; on the grounds of Hampton, the dorm served a didactic purpose equivalent to the classrooms.

One way that the didactic space of Winona Lodge functioned was by producing women to be household workers. Hampton teacher Cora Folsom, in her text *Guiding the Indian,* discusses the mechanisms through which the dorm produced Native women as workers:

> She is neat and orderly, but has never known by experience what it is to have a room of her own—*a miniature home* for which she is individually responsible. We give her such a room, and she is required to make it comfortable, pleasant and pretty. Her bed-linen and towels are her own, marked with her name. Her clothing is also hers, and after the first is purchased, planned and made by herself. On her wash-day she takes her little bag of clothes and bedding to a room fitted up with individual tubs, and there does her washing and later her ironing, all without the aid of machinery. At a certain time her mending must be done, and her clothes pass inspection. Most Indian girls sew well and many can make their own clothes when they come to us, but as a rule, they lack both taste and judgment in dressing themselves. They have seldom had the experience that would teach them to get the best material for the money and to make it up in a suitable and becoming way. At Hampton every girl is given a daily task for which she is paid, and with this money much of her clothing is purchased by herself from the stores in town. In this way a girl is forced to learn something in regard to the use of money and the relative value of different materials.[77]

The quote begins by discussing the dorm room as a miniature home, one where the Native woman has individual responsibility. There is a segmenting of responsibility in line with individualist Western paradigms, which is spatially created by separate rooms. Providing for a family is by nature a collective enterprise, but the dorm takes women from families, partitions them, and makes tasks individualized through a particularized orientation to space. Folsom then details the various tasks the women perform, including changing bed linen, laundering linen and towels, and mending clothes. While these tasks might be broken up and done collectively, having them be solely responsible fits them for the role of taking on these tasks for an entire home as a servant. Each task discussed could be a list of tasks for a housekeeper, fitting Native women to serve others by serving themselves within the miniature home of the dorm.

More explicitly, the dorm as training ground was also structured so that Native women worked for and served their teachers. In a report titled *Concerning Indians* published by the Hampton Institute, Winona Lodge is described thus: "All of the Indian girls, from eight to twenty-four years old, make their own clothes, wash and iron them, care for their rooms, and a great many of them take care of teachers' rooms. Besides this they have extra work such as sweeping, dusting and scrubbing the corridors, stairs, hall, sewing room, chapel, and cleaning other parts of the building."[78] The Native women in the Winona dorm cared for their own rooms, their teachers' rooms, and the common areas of the dormitory. The didactic space of the dorm, constituted by individualistic partitioning in which students became servants to their teachers, sought to create girls who could either be homemakers in a cottage on an allotment or homekeepers who could do the tasks needed as servants in a white home. Girls who could keep house for others, serving their teachers and their school, were able to serve the settler in various capacities. In fact, Hampton also pioneered outing programs, which were popular across many federal Indian boarding schools. These programs sent Indigenous women to be domestic servants in white homes, which they framed as continuing the educative process.[79] Black women were also subject to training that "fitted" them to be domestics as they had similar experiences in their own dormitories.

When Black and Native women were taken "out from the Cabin and the tepee," as Hollis Burke Frissell suggested they should be, where did they go, and what was the final destination meant to be? For Black women, being taken "out from the cabin" often meant being educated to be domestic laborers. Black and Native women may be taken out from the cabin and the tepee, but the end destination was not always a cottage of their own; often it was the space of another's home. This meant that the end point was not owning a "tasty framed cottage;" instead, the cottage served as a transit space that was moved through for training or work but never inhabited. Native women also moved through the cabin and cottage as a transit space. But in their transit, they were meant to be possessed by whiteness to such a degree that this possession required their death, or at least a death of sorts. These processes siphoned off the number of Black and Native women who would have had a stake or claim to settlement through home ownership. The teaching of slavery and settlement does not grant power through property acquisition to those it assimilates. The cottage absorbs Native and Black women into it as it takes them out, but renders them placeless, bodyless, and adrift even as they merge with its walls and floors. The cottage represents the placeholder space, that which can be given by the settler—that is, until they want it back.[80] Which they always do. For nothing is ever given by power which is not demanded back.

SIX

Teachers of Teachers

THE EXPANSION OF PLANTATION PEDAGOGY THROUGH TEACHER TRAINING

Hampton, officially named the Hampton Normal and Agricultural Institute, combined a focus on agricultural education with the training of teachers. A normal school, in fact, is the type of institution that eventually morphed into present-day teacher training programs at universities, and thus the training of teachers was integral to Hampton's educational program since its founding. The teacher training model that Hampton engaged in and promoted was firmly entrenched in plantation pedagogy. For example, an article in a 1903 edition of the *Southern Workman* discussed the importance of "white instructors [of] negro pupils."[1] This could appear contradictory as Hampton was engaged in the project of training Black teachers to teach in Black schools across the South and encouraged its Indigenous students to pursue teaching as a vocation. However, the article resolves this tension by stating that Black communities needed their own teachers and leaders but that it "devolved upon white people to be leaders of leaders and teachers of those teachers."[2]

Thus, Hampton's teacher education program engaged in one of the key tenets of plantation pedagogy, proximity to whiteness, by positing the necessity of whiteness in the training of teachers. That whiteness could then be diffused through Black teachers who were appropriately trained. This process was described in the "Twenty-Fourth Annual Report of the Principal" of Hampton as creating "living epistles" who could spread Hampton's gospel of labor and work.[3] Teacher training was meant to expand the reach of Hampton's influence and pedagogic goals and resolve the tension between the segregationist impulses of the post-emancipation South and the tenet of plantation pedagogy that proximity to whiteness was educative. Teacher training as a technology of plantation pedagogy allowed for proximity to whiteness as educative to be diffused via the production of teachers who were not white but who could spread whiteness as ideology. It also allowed the mechanics of plantation pedagogy to be scaled beyond the labor power constraints of the white teacher population. By making plantation pedagogy scalable, it allowed for the exponential expansion of plantation pedagogy into colonial and imperial space.

James Anderson has written about how white educators at places like Hampton as well as the white philanthropists and reformers that supported them sought to control the ideological narrative of education by training teachers in what they saw as the best mode of education.[4] Anderson's analysis rightly engages with the question, Who decides who becomes a teacher? and demonstrates that this question is part of a power struggle over the use and purpose of education. As Eve Tuck and Julie Gorlewski note, the question of who decides who can become a teacher can be broken down into two questions: Who decides? and, Who becomes a teacher?[5] This break down is important because it addresses both who creates the structures through which teacher training is enacted and how different people are filtered through that system. Tuck and Gorlewski view this dual process as part of the expansion of the settler nation state, where the public trust of producing teachers has relied on the genocide and removal of Native peoples and the subjugation of Black people.[6]

While one aspect of industrial teacher training programs was to control the ideologies of teachers by restricting who could become a teacher and what these teacher-candidates were taught about pedagogy and curriculum, teacher training's most enduring effects were not always in the actual production of trained teachers. In fact, these institutions did not always train a significant number of teachers or train them well. Instead, these programs consistently worked to expand the material practices of slavery and settlement regardless of whether teaching happened as it was intended.[7] Ideologies of learning are always contested. The fugitive practices of Black teachers always existed inside and against teacher training programs like those at Hampton, as did the secret practices and resistances of a variety of groups subject to industrial schooling.[8] The ideological battle over controlling what teachers believe and what they teach is one that will always be incomplete. I turn away from discussing teacher's resistance, not to invalidate it, but to allow it the space to be secret outside of academic display. Instead, I examine the material aspects of teacher-training programs that often evaded resistance and cemented slavery and settlement, such as the creation and expansion of schools and the improvement and expansion of homes and homesteads across an array of contested geographies. Programs like the Jeanes supervisory teachers, which had ties to Hampton and its funders, explicitly engaged in school and home expansion and improvement projects that were tied to settler notions of productivity and capitalist production. Technologies of teacher training persist and enact material changes whether or not they transmit the ideologies they aim to. The teacher is both a product of industrial education—albeit sometimes a faulty product in the eyes of the institution—and one of its technologies of material expansion. Hampton and other schools produced teachers to transmit ideas, but the teachers also functioned as part of an integrated system that expanded settlement and plantation futures.

NORMAL SCHOOLS AND THE HAMPTON NORMAL PROGRAM

Normal schools were developed to train teachers in the first part of the nineteenth century as a means to provide large numbers of teachers for the burgeoning common school system. These institutions were run by both state and private colleges and increased greatly in number by the end of the nineteenth century.[9] Hampton was founded after emancipation in the midst of this extreme growth of the normal school model, when teachers were needed not only for common schools but Black teachers were needed for segregated schools in the South. Segregation in public institutions in the South required a parallel private system for the production of Black teachers, and the proliferation of private normal schools like Hampton sought to control the type of teachers that were trained to teach Black students.[10]

Hampton's normal program for Black—and a small number of Native—students was structured as a three-year program of study, in which Black students were required to take a year between their second and third year of schooling to do a teaching placement in a local school. Native students were not required to take this year as there were not many locations in the East where they could teach other Native students.[11] This three-year program was not the only one offered to students at Hampton. There was a night school in which students worked during the day and took classes at night in preparation for the normal school. There was also the separate Indian program, which taught Native students English and prepared them for the normal program, providing similar knowledge as the night school; far fewer Native students, however, entered the normal program compared to Black students. All of these programs were in addition to the industrial and manual labor components of the school, which were integrated across the Hampton curriculum. Hampton explained that "a large proportion [of Black graduates] teach in the free colored schools of the South, though the salaries paid are rarely sufficient to do more than help out their income, which must be earned by farming or other labor."[12] Therefore, teaching and labor were intertwined within the lives of Black teachers and in Hampton's material and ideological practice.

The normal school curriculum consisted of classes in science, geography, history, Old Testament history, reading, language and grammar, writing, arithmetic, music, drawing and the theory and art of teaching.[13] In their discussions of the theory and art of teaching, Hampton publications explain that some of the main educational philosophies taught to students in their final year of the program were based on the writings of Pestalozzi and Froebel, two European educational theorists who would have been well known at the time of Hampton's founding. In examining Pestalozzi's theories on teaching and education, it is obvious that he was greatly influential for Armstrong in creating his schooling model. A Swiss educator who focused on educating the poor, Pestalozzi was credited as creating an approach of "learning by head, hand and heart," which Armstrong appropriated as part of Hampton's model. Pestalozzi believed that education must train individuals based on their own interests and abilities and that society would progress by training the individual. Having lived through the abolition of serfdom, Pestalozzi believed in training students for "practical capacity" and in manner suited for the life they were likely to lead. He was heavily influenced by enlightenment thought that glorified the individual, the role of the individual in society, and exclusionary European humanist perspectives.[14] In his discussion of the history of industrial education, Beyer identified Pestalozzi as one of the major influences on industrial education in the United States broadly.[15]

Froebel, a student of Pestalozzi, was a German educator and the creator of the concept of the kindergarten. Froebel's theory focused on respecting children as individuals, play-based learning, and self-directed play. While this might seem somewhat at odds with an institution like Hampton that trained many adult learners and was extremely regimented, some aspects of Froebel's theorizing can be seen in Hampton's ideology. Froebel centered education on the interaction with the objects that surrounded the child in their environment. This focus dovetailed with manual and industrial labor as forms of learning for adults as well as with Enlightenment ideas defining property as the mixture of a people's work with the environment to produce something of value. Froebel is also credited with supporting the role of women as teachers, a position Hampton would also take in relation to Black and Indigenous women.[16]

Hampton can also be placed in the context of what Meyerhoff describes as the "education-based mode of study." As opposed to modes such as Indigenous community-based study or Black fugitive study, the education-based mode has always functioned through a vertical imaginary by portraying education as a romantic plot in which the student has to overcome obstacles. The romantic plot portrays teachers and students as heroic figures, and therefore the institution of schooling itself becomes heroic since it trains students to achieve their own glory by overcoming hardship. This was also a vertical mode of schooling that employed techniques of governance in which students were expected to be obedient to the teacher, who is constructed as the holder and transmitter of knowledge. This mode of study creates "binary figures of value and waste" and "an affective economy of credit and debt" in which some students are written off as failures, and others are celebrated as successes, with their success always connected to an indebtedness to the heroic institution of schooling.[17] Meyerhoff perceptively argues that certain modes of study are related to modes of world making, and that the education-based mode of study is related to the capitalist/colonialist mode of world making.[18] This mode of education is also integrally tied to European philosophies of humanism, which scholars in Black studies have heavily critiqued as fundamentally based on antiblackness.[19] By examining the Hampton normal program and its offshoots, I interrogate teacher training not as a neutral good and part of the romance plot of education to be celebrated but as part of the technologies of plantation pedagogy.

HAMPTON TEACHERS AS EXPANSIONARY UNITS OF SLAVERY AND SETTLEMENT

Hampton's rhetoric often addressed how many teachers the institution produced as well as the spatial reach of its influence. In 1876, Hampton produced a map of Virginia and some sections of surrounding states showing all of the schools where Hampton-trained teachers from the past five years were teaching (see figure 1).[20] During the commencement of 1882, Dr. Samuel Eliot, a professor and later head of a girl's normal school in Massachusetts, addressed the school:

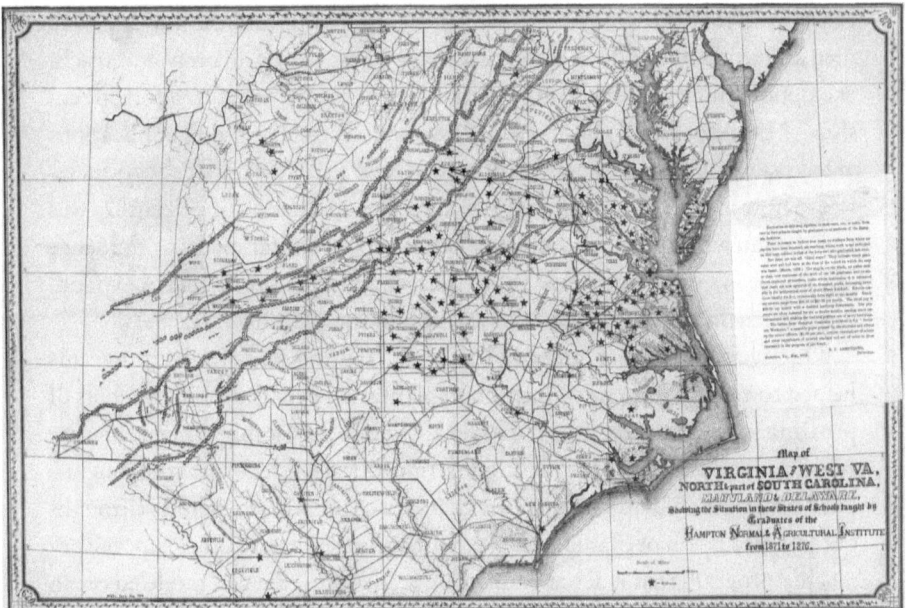

FIGURE 1. Map of the distribution of Hampton teachers. *Credit: Library of Congress, Geography and Map Division.*

Why to look back on such a work for one year is to look on something like a miracle,—that a school founded in Virginia in the dark period following the war should train a sufficient number of teachers to take forty thousand children into their arms! These seven hundred or more graduates, most of them today teachers, are the witnesses of the fruitfulness of the school.[21]

Hampton publications are full of statements like these, which propose the specific numbers of students it has reached through its training of teachers as well as spatial imaginings of its influence in maps like figure 1. The *Southern Workman* notes "over 700 colored and 300 indian trained workers have been sent out among their people. The great majority of both are doing well; many as teachers, farmers, mechanics, laborers; good examples. The majority are teachers and farmers and own good houses."[22] Yet again, the pairing of teaching and labor, particularly farming, demonstrates how teachers were not meant to just transmit ideologies but were also producers on settled land mimicking the production of the plantation.

Teaching was framed by the school as a means of spreading civilization in addition to spreading the Hampton program of industrial education. In a speech printed in the *Southern Workman,* Chauncey M. Depew notes, "How is it proved that the white race is worthy of citizenship and the power of free men and women? It is done through schools where there are competent teachers; opportunities to learn and to demonstrate that they are fitted for citizenship."[23] I cannot and do not take this assertion from Hampton's publications at face value. Whether or not teachers produced citizens was not always material to how Hampton's influence grew since the production of citizenship was and is contested. Instead, I view the rhetoric about the far-reaching influence of Hampton's teachers as a means to understand Hampton's role in expanding settlement as a material outcome through the training of teachers.

One way in which Hampton's teacher training and similar programs helped to expand settlement is through plantation pedagogy and its tenets of proximity to whiteness and labor as pedagogic. While it might not seem that training Black teachers to teach industrial education to Black students utilized proximity to whiteness as part of its structure, there are hints throughout the discussion of Hampton's teacher training and the Jeanes supervisory teacher program that it actually did. The Jeanes program was modeled on an early program piloted by Hampton that sought to place Hampton-trained teachers in rural areas to further train local teachers who had more limited experience in educational institutions. Jackson Davis, the supervisor of Negro schools in Virginia, was a strong supporter of this model and was able to leverage funds from the Anna T. Jeanes Foundation to support the first supervisory teacher program at the state level in 1908. The first Jeanes teacher was a Black teacher named Virginia Rudolph appointed to Henrico County, Virginia. Ms. Rudolph traveled around the county and provided support for local teachers as well as example lessons in various forms of industrial and domestic work. As the program expanded throughout Virginia and eventually into other Southern states, at least half of the supervisory teachers that were employed were educated at either Hampton or Tuskegee. As a teacher supervisory and training program, the Jeanes teachers' funding, oversight, and goals overlapped with other organizations trying to influence Black education in the South. For example, the Jeanes program provided funding to teachers to attend Hampton and Tuskegee summer teacher institutes and hired Hampton and Tuskegee graduates as supervisors. The board of the Jeanes teacher program overlapped with those that ran the Slater fund, the Phelps-Stokes Fund, and the Rockefeller General Education Board, all of which sought to influence Black Southern education.[24]

The Jeanes supervisory teachers and Hampton-style normal school programs operated under the assumption that educational proximity to whiteness could be spread by diffusion from white teacher to Black teacher or supervisor to Black teachers and students. While this was often framed as the transmission of Hampton ideology, there was also a persistent assertion that nearness to whiteness physically or in terms of thought was necessary for learning. This nearness, of course, existed in the context of the afterlife of slavery and continued colonization. For example, in an article in the *Southern Workman,* Jackson Davis discussed how the Jeanes teacher program "meant the bringing together of the best white people and the best colored people in working out a common problem."[25] Discussions of the Jeanes teacher program also relied on the language of cooperation, which was shorthand for engaging with the educational potential of proximity to whiteness. In another publication on the work of the Jeanes teachers, Davis noted that, when they worked together with the community, it created "a better understanding of the society of which they are a part" and "a cooperative attitude in all matters in which community action is essential."[26] It is a small wonder that this discourse was used in the context of the Jeanes teachers as Davis was on the board of trustees of the Booker Washington Institute of Liberia, where cooperation was also touted as a necessary component of the school's success. Similarly, in an article presented at the Southern Sociological Conference in 1913, it was stated that the work of the Jeanes teachers created "a cooperative movement for improvement."[27] Cooperation, as a shorthand for proximity to whiteness, was deeply entrenched in the Jeanes supervisory teacher program. Thus, these programs sought to resolve the paradox between proximity to whiteness as an educational strategy and segregated schooling through the discourse of cooperation.

Labor as a form of teaching was also integral to the way teacher training was framed at Hampton and other teacher training programs in industrial schools. For example, the training given by industrial teachers was described in this manner: "The immediate outcome of such training is that every Negro child learns how to do some particular piece of work and to do it well. The effect is not simply economic, it is highly intellectual and moral. . . . He comes to feel that work is not only dignified but pleasurable."[28] Reframing labor not only as a process of learning but also as producing pleasure sought to encourage students to substitute work for other pleasures that were denied students. The action of production, which in settlement is what makes property and material wealth, was framed not as subjugation but as learning and leisure. The merging of labor, learning, and pleasure related a moralized and pleasurable notion of work that promoted the narrative of slavery as a benevolent institution since "work," broadly defined, is deemed benevolent. It is this substitution of labor for both learning and leisure that makes the justification of slavery as educative particularly cunning. Whether or not this connection between work and pleasure was believed by Black students, and there is evidence that it often was not, the link between work and learning was still enacted on the land; therefore, the enactment of this instruction changed the land, even if it did not change the minds and hearts of the students.

The Jeanes Fund supervisory teacher program, as an offshoot of the Hampton teacher training model, was particularly acknowledged for the various material effects it was able to produce. These effects can be divided into three main categories: (1) school expansion and improvement, (2) home expansion and improvement, and (3) the production of goods. This resulted in a solidification of settlement practices in Black-majority communities and Black contributions to colonial capitalist production, as well as the further expansion of this model of supervisory teaching into imperial projects across oceans and continents. The material projects that Jeanes teachers engaged in functioned to alleviate white anxiety about Black rebellion through the surveillance of Black students and teachers, which is a key component of plantation futures.

School Expansion

A key action that Jeanes teachers took in rural areas was the expansion and improvement of school buildings and grounds, which they reported to the State Supervisors of Negro Schools. Jackson Davis describes two schools that the first teacher, Virginia Rudolph, helped with improvements: the Barton Heights School and the Sydney School. Davis noted that at Barton Heights, they "fenced in the yard, granolithic walk, set out hedges, trees, and rosebushes, [and] whitewashed the trees and fence."[29] The Sydney School, which was near the former Curls Neck Plantation, had plantation workers come to the school to do similar work, including fencing the yard, adding gravel to the walkway, building a porch and benches, putting in hedges, building a belfry, and installing a bell.[30] While these improvements were described in minute detail in reports on the work of the Jeanes teachers, the work was not the only aspect of these projects that was reported. For each of these school improvement projects, Davis also reported how much money the school collected from the local Black community and how much was expended for the work. For example, the Barton Heights School collected over $50.00 and only spent

$10.95, and the Sydney School only spent $1.50 of the $5.30 collected because of the donation of labor by plantation workers.[31] However, this was not the only source of funding. The Jeanes Fund, under the determination of the Rockefeller General Education Board and in consultation with both Hampton and Tuskegee, also directed private funds to school improvements.[32] Despite this contribution, the "school improvement" that was part of the goals of the Jeanes teacher program often came at the expense and free labor of the Black community as opposed to the state or the school system.[33]

Jeanes teachers often sought to set up community associations for "self-help" in rural Black communities.[34] This focus on self-help was framed as both a cost-saving measure and a good investment, since communities that contributed to their own improvement were framed as a more secure investment. The Jeanes teachers were instructed to

> introduce into the schools such simple forms of industrial work as may be needful and helpful, and will tend to show the connection between the school and the daily life of the community. You should by word and example endeavor to promote orderliness, promptness, and cleanliness, being particularly careful, for the sake of the influence on the children, that the schoolrooms and school surroundings, no matter how poor, be kept neat and tidy, and in as good condition as possible.[35]

This connection between school and community demonstrates the intimacy between schooling and the changing of land and space. School buildings had to both model and mimic the spaces around them, in order that their role as reinforcers of norms of settlement remained influential. The programs sought to make Black community members believe in this work, but they were determined to carry it out whether or not this occurred. The improvement of the school itself was part of the skeleton of settlement and the plantation that was embedded in the landscape of the South.

The Penn School of St. Helena Island was often cited in Hampton publications as an institution that improved local farming practice. St. Helena Island was primarily inhabited by a Black Gullah community that industrial educators viewed as particularly rural and backwards in regards to education, farming, and civilization.[36] The Penn school included a farm and described its purpose as teaching "the youth of the Sea Islands to live happy, useful lives on the farm."[37] Therefore, the expansion of the school also expanded agriculture, which was seen as a superior use of land compared to Indigenous uses. The Penn School was, therefore, engaged in expanding settlement through the "productive" use of space. The school sought to inculcate students into this project of settlement by "growing [a] sense of responsibility among the pupils for the care and protection of the school buildings and property."[38] This ideology, however, did not need to succeed fully for the school to transform land through agriculture or for it to mark the landscape in myriad ways. Schools have always been foundational to the world making of settlement. For example, the expansion of common schooling dovetailed with the enactment of Indian removal, which demonstrates how schools expand through Indigenous erasure.[39] The industrial school in particular was a natural outgrowth of the plantation, with its fields for farming, industrial shops, and large dorms and houses that were often built on plantation grounds. Thus, the school served as the bones of the expansionary practices of settlement.

Home Expansion and Improvement

The Jeanes Fund teachers did not confine themselves to helping improve school buildings; they also fostered campaigns to improve local homes around the schools because they held that "the influence of . . . teaching is almost immediately apparent in the homes."[40] White reformers felt that an improved school would draw Black families to buy or live in homes and farms in the vicinity of the school: "It was not surprising that thrifty Negro farmers began to buy small tracts of land near this school and to build simple but comfortable cottages."[41] Through programs like homemakers' clubs, home garden projects, and offering cooking, sewing, or other domestic lessons inside of local homes, Jeanes teachers inserted themselves into community homes in an effort to change them and make them more attractive and efficient. This effort demonstrates the ways that industrial education linked schooling to the domestic sphere. In materials on the Jeanes teacher program, this ideology was directly stated: "They make education real and genuine by connecting the schools with the home and community needs of the people and they organize and guide the people in many practical undertakings that develop self-help and a sense of responsibility."[42] Similarly, Thomas Jesse Jones, in reporting on some of the accomplishments of the first Jeanes teacher, Virginia Rudolph, noted the beautification of local homes in the area she worked.[43] The expansion of home ownership/home occupation and the beautification of homes was directly connected to Black respectability politics, capitalist concepts of property ownership, and understandings of cis-heteronormative domestic relations, as demonstrated by the cottage as a technology of plantation pedagogy. This process of schools affecting homes closely resembles some of the ways that the allotment program was discussed for Native peoples—as creating a pride in home ownership and a well-kept house.

Another way in which Jeanes teachers influenced their communities was in their cooperation with the farm demonstration movement.[44] The farm demonstration movement was instituted as a result of Tuskegee's Agricultural Experiment Station in the early twentieth century. Also known as the "Tuskegee moveable school," this project, which sent farmers out into communities to demonstrate how to make their farms produce more, was supported by both the federal government and white philanthropists.[45] The cooperation between the farm demonstration staff and Jeanes teachers involved homemaking and gardening clubs among young Black women and teaching lessons in gardening, canning, sewing, and cooking during the summer months. It was stated by a paper at the Southern Sociological Conference that "in many ways the summer work of these teachers has proved of even greater value than their work with the schools, for they are touching directly the homes of the people and bringing about improvements there that are having a far-reaching effect."[46] The same paper described the improvements in local gardens across multiple Southern communities. Certain aspects of the home—if it had been whitewashed, had a fence, or if the yard was weeded—were attributed to the influence of the Jeanes teacher program.[47] This intense focus on home gardens, which was connected to the focus on agriculture and farming generally, demonstrated how changes in the home mirrored the changes made to the landscape as part of settlement. Home improvement was directly tied to the work of school improvement and teaching, dovetailing with the home's role as a technology of plantation pedagogy.

Production for the "Wealth of State"

The practices of school and home improvement discussed in the previous sections have been interpreted by scholars as forms of Black striving in and against white supremacy as well as a means of asserting Black humanity against allegations of Black civilizational savagery.[48] Without discrediting the intentions of Black community members, I read the work of these programs in relation to the larger pattern of the accumulation of land and wealth by various agencies of the US state and white capitalists as part of the project of settlement. This is not meant to demonize Black farmers who were seeking survival in the afterlife of slavery. Living in the afterlife of slavery and ongoing settlement means that, as part of our existence inside structures of power, everyone is complicit in these projects.[49] I want to draw attention to the way that power sought to co-opt Black striving for its own ends and how these operations of power work to entrench settlement and plantation futures. Thus, I focus on how teacher training programs were engaged in a form of wealth production that ultimately did not benefit Black farmers and community members.

The Jeanes supervisory teacher program was often justified by its proponents as a good investment. One example reports that having a Jeanes teacher in a community created material improvements that doubled the value of the teacher's salary.[50] On St. Helena Island, it was noted that having a Jeanes teacher helped increase crop yields of local farmers; in addition, the teacher contributed to a "gradually awakened sense of need for better things in a primitive community where the conservatism of the Islander and the comparatively unexacting conditions of soil and climate make it easy for a people to be content with too little. There is no progress where there are no wants."[51] This is, once again, very similar to the rhetoric of Black educators like Booker T. Washington who discussed increasing wants in order to increase community economic power. Yet, the wants that were meant to increase were in alignment with capitalist understandings of property ownership. Property ownership as a concept has been integral to the settlement of the United States and dispossession of Native peoples, in addition to making all other types of relationships to land seem impossible. The work of Black farmers was framed by white educators as creating "wealth for the state" rather than for themselves (although sometimes they did create personal wealth against all odds). In an article in a 1912 edition of the *Southern Workman,* Jackson Davis stated, "Because our educational machinery has failed in the past to fit the negro for rural life, wherein lies his greatest opportunity for happiness and gain to himself and the state, is no reason why we should condemn negro education; but it is an excellent reason why we should change the character of that education in order that he may know how to produce more, live better, and add to the common wealth of the state."[52] The idea of producing more is part of European ideologies of value that exalt the mixture of human enterprise and land to create wealth, commodifying land and what it can produce. When land is targeted for its output and productivity, the land is changed in service of settlement whether or not the people on it want to be in service to it.

Anxiety about Black Rebellion and Surveillance

Industrial teacher training programs in the South also sought to manage white anxiety about Blackness. Black communities were conscripted into acts of settlement but were also disciplined according to white fears that dated back to fears of slave rebellion as well as ideologies that framed Blackness as pathological. In fact, schooling programs that sought to cement Black people into the process of settlement through labor also sought to alleviate anxieties about settlement itself (which is always an unstable production in that those it has displaced refuse to die or be quiet). This demonstrates how white anxieties about Blackness and the incomplete nature of settlement are interwoven. Education became one way to alleviate these anxieties in the post emancipation era, and teacher training in particular was integral to that project.

A common discourse spread by white educational reformers in the post-emancipation era was that education would reduce the perceived high level of Black criminality. W. D. Weatherford, the student secretary of the international committee of the YMCA, argued in the *Southern Workman* that "we must set ourselves definitely to a policy of aggressive training because the ignorant Negro is a menace to the health of the entire community in which he lives"; he explained, "the ignorant negro is far more frequently a criminal than is the better trained Negro."[53] Similarly, the associate principal of the Penn school argued that "shiftlessness, crime, and pauperism come from lack of definite training."[54] She also cited a speech by Booker T. Washington in which he stated that no graduates of either Hampton or Tuskegee have been imprisoned or charged with crimes—a fact that is highly disputable considering the criminalizing of Blackness itself in the Jim Crow South. Washington made this statement to soothe white fears and trepidation that educating Black people would cause uprisings in the South:

> The records of the South show that 90 per cent of the colored people in prisons are without knowledge of trades, and 61 per cent are illiterate. This statement alone disproves the assertion that the negro grows in crime as education increases. If the negro at the North is more criminal than his brother at the South, it is because of the employment which the South gives him and the North denies him. It is not the educated negro who has been guilty of or even charged with crime in the South; it is, as a rule, the one who has a mere smattering of education or is in total ignorance.[55]

The discursive linking of education, criminality, and labor is one that still exists in the present day, with educational or work-based programs proposed as a means of alleviating or preventing crime.[56] These ideas about education as an antidote to criminality were integral to plantation pedagogy and its justification of slavery as educational. Yet, education would and will never be enough to fully alleviate the white anxiety about Blackness—which, as the converse of whiteness, is always viewed as a threat.

This same rhetoric was echoed by the proponents of the Jeanes supervisory teacher program who asserted that in various Southern communities, Jeanes teachers "condemned the common dances and festivals which nearly always resulted in drinking and a cutting or shooting affray, and urged amusements of a different kind."[57] Jeanes teachers were described as working against this "criminal element" in Black communities. These teachers, then, were not just pedagogues but also figures of surveillance and correction. This surveillance included Jeanes teachers making "suggestions" about how teachers should be using their time, in terms of both the formal curriculum and the care of homes and school grounds.[58] The Jeanes teachers were not meant to be supervisors in the strictest sense, but they functioned as such in that they reported to the state supervisors of Negro education, such as Jackson Davis, who were well connected to Hampton, Tuskegee, and white philanthropic foundations.

These aspects of the Jeanes supervisory teacher program (school expansion, home expansion, settlement, mitigating the anxiety over Black criminality, and producing "wealth for the state") were not something that only occurred in the South but across geographies. Robert Park, in fact, presciently called graduates of Tuskegee "colonies of graduates," who could transfer outward the effects of industrial education to the masses.[59] This was prescient because Tuskegee and other industrial education programs indeed attempted to transfer their educational ideas extensively into colonial space. Therefore, teacher training, which was an integral part of Hampton, Tuskegee, and other industrial schools in the United States, became a key part of the colonial expansion of industrial schooling, particularly in Africa, but also in other geographies of US imperialism.

COLONIES OF TEACHERS: INDUSTRIAL TEACHER TRAINING FROM THE ATLANTIC TO THE PACIFIC

While in the US South the production of Black teachers was a prolific enterprise, similar programs in other geographies remained uneven in terms of actually producing teachers. While this unevenness in the number of teachers produced was part of the way teacher education worked in general (for example, normal schools never produced a sufficient number of teachers for common schools, and teacher education programs still do not produce enough teachers today), the number of teachers these programs produced was not the only effect of teacher education. Thus, I examine how teacher education fit into the varying goals of settlement, imperialism, and domination across the currents of colonialism.

One of the places in which the Jeanes supervisory teacher program was transferred extensively was through the work of US philanthropists in Africa. The report on Education in Africa headed by Thomas Jesse Jones included multiple references to the Jeanes supervisory teacher program and recommended the implementation of similar teaching supervisory programs in colonies across Africa as a strategy to control what he saw as uneven teaching across missionary-sponsored schools.[60] Similarly, Charles T. Loram was a proponent of the Jeanes model for South Africa.[61] One of the reasons that these models of teacher training were seen as integral in the context of Africa was that reformers framed Africa as in need of agricultural education in the same way as the US South. For example, Jones quoted Armstrong in the *Report on Education in Africa:* "The temporal salvation of Negroes for some time to come is to be won out of the ground. Teaching and farming go well together in the present condition of things. The teacher-farmer is the man for the times. He is essentially an educator throughout the year."[62] Note how the connection between labor and learning/teaching and farming is also connected to the concept of winning or, put another way, conquering.

Later in the same report, there is a discussion of how schools and teachers should influence the homes of African students. The report's language closely resembles discussions of the impact of Jeanes teachers on their communities in the South:

> Wherever possible, arrangement should be made for practice in the homes of the community. Special attention should be given to the kinds of food and the methods of cooking in the pupils' homes. Canning and preserving vegetables and fruits and the effective care of the kitchen garden are essential parts of the instruction.[63]

In these ways, there were close parallels between the programs proposed for countries and colonies in Africa and those in place in Southern states. In describing what he saw as necessary for schooling institutions in African colonies, Jones stated that African schools should first give an agricultural education; second, they should be equipped with special departments to train teachers in agriculture; and finally, should create outreach programs to teach farmers how to "cultivate more effectively their plots of ground or to work on the large plantations."[64] Institutions like the Overtoun Institute near Lake Nyasa, located on the present day border between Malawi, Tanzania, and Mozambique, and the Lovedale school in South Africa were modeled on Southern normal schools, including their use of summer teacher institutes and outreach programs in communities to improve local homes.[65] Therefore, the type of educational institutions proposed for many areas of Africa mirrored those that existed in the US South for Black communities. Of course, white philanthropists like Jones were not as successful at implementing these programs across the Atlantic, largely due to the number of parties involved in African education, which included European governments, various missionary groups, independent African governments, and numerous other philanthropic organizations. Therefore, while the training of teachers in Africa was heavily discussed by educational reformers, it was not implemented nearly to the same extent as it was in the US South.

In Indian Country and Hawai'i, the notion of training teachers was discussed as well but not to as great an extent as in the African context. This could be because there was a lesser need for teachers in these locations because of the high number of white missionary teachers who went to reservations and to Hawai'i. The Carlisle Indian school stated that "the aim of the Carlisle School is to train Indians as teachers, homemakers, mechanics, and industrial leaders who find abundant opportunity for service as teachers and employees of the Indian service leaders among their people, or as industrial competitors in the white communities in various parts of the country."[66] Carlisle's publications often listed the occupations of previous graduates, and the December 1909 edition of the *Indian Craftsman* listed all known graduates of the school and their current jobs; approximately thirty of these students were working as teachers.[67] Yet, teacher training in Native boarding schools has not been discussed at length in scholarly literature. It may be that the numbers were too low to be viewed as part of the primary function of these institutions, especially in comparison to the number of Black teachers trained during the same time. But it is important to note that the ideology of training teachers was an integral aspect of many of these schools even if they did not train at large scale. By stating that a main goal of Carlisle was to train teachers even when it did not produce many teachers in comparison to other industrial schools, Carlisle demonstrates the ambivalent nature of teacher training outcomes. While the training of teachers in Native boarding schools may have produced a negligible number of Native teachers, it did produce other material outcomes in the name of educating teachers, such as the support of allotment policies and the disruption of Indigenous family and community ties. The outcomes of teacher training should be measured not just in the production of teachers and the way teachers teach, but in the material outcomes of their pedagogy.

In Hawai'i, the outcome of teacher training was similar. Because many of Hawai'i's teachers, most of whom were white missionaries, were imported from the mainland, only one normal school with the explicit purpose of training teachers existed on the islands during the early part of the twentieth century. In fact, reports on the number of teachers of different races in Hawai'i in from 1931 to 1932 demonstrate that Native Hawaiians only made up twenty-two percent of teachers on the islands, with whites making up over forty percent (almost double the number of Native Hawaiian teachers); the rest was made up of other racial groups brought to the islands for labor, such as Chinese, Japanese, Portuguese, and Koreans.[68] Interestingly, the idea of supervisory teachers was part of Hawaiian schooling beginning in the 1850s, prior to the founding of Hampton, demonstrating the influence Hawaiian schools had on later teacher training programs in the South. While he was the superintendent of schools in Hawai'i, Richard Armstrong utilized school inspectors to report on schools across the islands, leading to a wealth of documents about the types of surveillance these schools were subject to.[69] Therefore in Hawai'i, there was less of a focus on training teachers, possibly because it served as an outpost for missionary teachers seeking service outside of the continental United States.

Similar to Hawai'i, initially there was a large influx of white American teachers to the Philippines. The first white teachers (and eventually a small number of Black teachers, including, for a short period of time, Carter G. Woodson) arrived in 1901 on the US army ship *Thomas* and were referred to as the Thomasites; this term would later be used to refer to all white teachers in the Philippines during the early years of US control.[70] Fred Atkinson, discussed the necessity of establishing normal schools and teacher training institutes. He noted that in 1905 there were 750 American teachers to 2,500 Filipino teachers, and stated:

> One of the handicaps which the work has thus far felt most seriously is the common lack of efficient native teachers, something that is hardly

surprising in view of the facilities for normal training which previously existed. The supervisory character of the work of the American teacher often takes him away from the particular town school, which is left in charge of some native assistant, and the imperative need of better trained Filipino instructors then becomes apparent. This normal work is without doubt second in importance only to the general primary instruction itself, and indeed is a part of the latter, supplying the means for its furtherance. In conjunction with the central normal school in Manila, have been organized five tributary institutions, in certain important provincial centers. It has an attendance of some three hundred and twenty-five from the various provinces; has a corps of special American teachers; and a dormitory system for the young women. The grade of work done is excellent, and a trained body of young men and women is being graduated that will without question raise the quality of the native teaching force to the degree that is desired.[71]

Atkinson's focus on training Filipino teachers under the imported white teachers demonstrates the nature of US imperialism in the Philippines, an imperialism that was not meant to rely on constant proximity to whiteness in order to educate. Instead, white teachers were meant to work in the Philippines so that their influence and proximity would educate Filipino teachers and by proxy Filipino students, mimicking the diffusional tactics of Black teacher training in the US South. Atkinson's successor, David P. Barrows, also discussed the need to train teachers, noting in 1910 that "the creation and training of this great corps of young native men and women, qualifying them as instructors in a foreign language, preparing them by normal courses, institutes, vacation schools and assemblies and by daily training classes to teach, not only the common primary branches, but industrial work, hygiene, simple domestic science, local government and village improvement, gardening and agriculture is the most notable achievement of the Bureau of Education."[72]

Across these spaces, the language of wants and of schooling and education creating wealth was very similar to that discussed in relation to teacher education in the US South. For example, in a discussion of education for Filipinos, M. Friedman stated, "Let us make of them creatures of larger wants with better facilities to supply those wants. Economic wealth, no one will deny, is conducive to better living. To obtain that wealth, these people must work. Furthermore, it has been found that the most industrious people usually belong to the better and more elevated class of citizens and are the most moral."[73] Friedman introduced this idea of creating wants in an extensive discussion of the natural wealth of the Philippines, where he argues that "it rests with the Filipino, by skill and brawn, to convert these raw materials into wealth."[74] This is similar to how areas of Africa were discussed by Jones in the report on Education in Africa and to the discussion of making more "wealth for the state" through education and teacher training in the South. Material production was a key aspect of plantation pedagogy, and the agents of material expansion and production were teachers.

In this way, teacher training, productivity, wealth, work, and wants were interwoven across colonial space. An excellent final example of this appears in the same article on the Philippines by Friedman, which cites the many other locations globally where industrial education models were transferred:

> Booker T. Washington's school at Tuskegee, and the Hampton Normal and Agricultural School in Virginia show what thorough training in agriculture and the mechanical trades is doing for the colored race in the United States, while the large government industrial schools at Carlisle, Pa.; Phoenix, Arizona; Lawrence, Kansas; and Chilocco, Oklahoma; together with some three hundred other industrial schools, are doing their share in making of the American Indian a self-supporting, useful citizen. Industrial work in the trades has been introduced in Honolulu and is proving a great success. Soon after the American occupation industrial work was introduced in the schools of Porto Rico [sic] and is growing rapidly. These few examples show that the world is awake to and cognizant of the great importance of this mode of training as an equipment of its young for the struggles of life.[75]

With this discussion of industrial education in the Philippines, Friedman narrates the story of this form of schooling as a movement from its origins to its own type of manifest destiny. The "colonies" of teachers it created were part of the expansion of settlement across the US continent, Hawai'i, and part of imperial ventures in the Atlantic and the Pacific that sought to increase US wealth and influence.

TEACHING TO TEACH AND THE FEMINIZATION OF TEACHING

Hampton took pride in its program of "teaching to teach," which can be compared to Meyerhoff's concept of an "educator of educators."[76] While Meyerhoff frames the "educator of educators" in relation to theorists like Paulo Freire whose work was meant to teach educators how to critically interrogate power relations, the concept can also be applied to the establishment of normal schools, which were explicitly meant to create educators of educators and to teach to teach. For example, on the twenty-fourth anniversary of the Hampton institute program, a speech was given by Evalina A. Davis titled "How the Way Opened." A reporter provided a summary, explaining that Davis began with "pictures of the old plantation and the new little farms now occupying it, and how the speaker's own way opened by the influence of a Hampton graduate teacher." She described the teacher as having "the determination of an exslave father that his children should have the blessing he had missed."[77] Davis spoke about the influence of a Hampton-trained teacher who taught her and her eventual attendance at Hampton to learn to teach. She described it as a spiral moving outward where the expansion of the outer circle was driven by the foundational teaching of old plantation life. In the same year in the annual report by the principle of Hampton, it was noted that

> the school should and could be, even more than it is, a far reaching light and influence in this part of the country. Its graduate teachers, whose school houses dot thickly this and neighboring states, should be supplemented by a traveling ministry of practical education.... An institution like this doubles its power for good when it can reach the field workers with wise and helpful influence.[78]

This same report described Hampton's graduates as "living epistles, bringing back the knowledge of civilized and Christian life to transform their early haunts," and notes that of the 193 Hampton graduates they had tracked, twenty-two were teachers.[79] Yet an often underexamined aspect of this teacher training was the way that women like Davis figured into this professional training: Hampton's program of "teaching to teach" was part of the feminization of the teaching profession that occurred at the turn of the century.[80] Labaree has argued that, since normal schools were academically more akin to high schools than colleges, they served more women. Therefore, the increasing feminization of teaching was paired with a view of teacher education as lower status. The large scale of normal school expansion, especially to women, further underpined its professional status.[81] As a normal school, Hampton was part of this shift towards the feminization of teaching and the lowering status of teachers as professionals. Of course, Hampton trained many men as teachers as well, but in this section, I focus on the specific language Hampton used to frame teaching as an occupation for Black and Native women.

When discussing the necessity of teaching both Native and Black women as a means of social uplift, Samuel Armstrong noted that

> teaching is the career for Indian girls, as it has been the one way for colored girls of the South to be more than drudges: it is their only field for a womanly ambition. The increase of the educational fund for Indians creates some hope for their girls, on whom rests the hope of the race.[82]

The assertion that Hampton trains women for more than duties as homemakers links teaching as a professional occupation to improving Indigenous and Black communities. Thus, teaching simultaneously provides a vocation for Indigenous and Black women and a home for the legions of Black and Indigenous children that are seen as bereft of an education that transmits the virtues of industry. Civilizational change through education is framed as magnified by training teachers, which expands the reach of industrial education beyond the grounds of Hampton and fuels its discourse of educational change.

The feminization of teaching is evident in Hollis Burke Frissell's writing when, as noted in the previous chapter, he stated that training Native women was meant to "teach their people the art of homemaking."[83] In this framing, homemaking is instructive, and the outcome is a clean home, which has moral value within a white protestant work ethic. A clean home can be on an allotment or on a tenant farm. The argument for homemaking as teaching is tied to transforming racial relations. In his text *The Indian Question,* Armstrong states, "Let us first supply our own teachers for the Indians, and then fit *them* to become their own teachers: to make these is to make the people . . ."[84] This same model was common for Black schools in the South; as Armstrong notes, "The system of Negro free schools in the South is vitalized by a number of strong, central institutions that train the picked youth of the race as teachers." Additionally, the Indian program trained Black women as teachers of domestic arts by having them teach Indian students.[85] Eastern boarding schools were seen as part of a larger system that encompassed reservation day schools in relation to off-reservation boarding schools in the same way that one-room schoolhouses in the South were related to normal schools: "This is, I think, the true relations of Eastern charity to the Indian; excellent boarding and industrial schools at each important Agency, to train the best boys and girls to teach the rest, both in school and by their good example."[86] Teaching, then, is seen as part of a didactic program that exponentially expands settlement.

To end this section, I note another report about where graduating students from Hampton ended up, in this case Native women students. The report discusses a number of Native women graduates of Hampton and notes that one married a white man and became a homemaker, one became a servant, and another was set to become a teacher: "Of the two others, younger, [sic] one is waiting an opportunity to return to Hampton for two years more training, with view of becoming a teacher."[87] A teacher is seen as an acceptable solution and on par with becoming a housewife or a domestic worker and another way of using a Hampton education. Becoming a teacher may be seen as a better outcome than becoming a housewife or a housekeeper in that it is a more professionalized career (albeit a low status one); teaching was also framed as means for Indigenous and Black women to take control over their own education and make changes for their communities. However, even if Hampton only trained a few teachers, and only some of those teachers reproduced their industrial and domestic curriculum, the expansion could still be exponential. There is a dual emphasis on lifting Black and Native women up from drudgery but at the same time producing teachers to transform Indigenous peoples through the teaching of homemaking, which worked to further processes of Indigenous dispossession, such as allotment. Thus, producing teachers could be as useful to the goals of transforming Native communities as producing house wives and housekeepers was. The training of teachers was coupled with the expansion of domestic training, which was coupled with the transformation of spatial relations of settlement, such as the carving up of reservations and the imposition of single-family land ownership. Preparing women for teaching was intimately intertwined with discussions of domesticity and homemaking in that it was meant to be the extended arm of domestic education, expanding the domestic reach of Hampton.

These various examples of teacher training across the currents of colonialism demonstrate that attempting to change the ideology of teacher training does not and cannot undo the materiality of schools that dot the US landscape or the ways land was targeted for change through these programs as a means of wealth production. Teachers as expansionary units of settlement have helped cement settlement into the landscape over time. Teacher training for Black and Native peoples has been, of course, co-opted for other purposes as a means to transform systems of power throughout history. Yet, I argue that, because normal schools have historically created both ideas about what teaching is and physical structures of teaching that are imprinted on the landscape and that act as radiating influencers of settlement, teachers have been misidentified as necessary agents of change. That is not to say that teachers don't do awesome things (I know; I was one, and I know many other amazing teachers). However, focusing on teacher education may not be the best location for school change in the same way that schools may not be a necessary site of decolonization. Teachers can and do still engage in political struggles, but I am wary of asserting that these struggles can enact the misnamed and paradoxical project of "decolonizing schools."

SEVEN

"Better Land, Better Stock, Better People"

THE SCHOOL AS EXPERIMENT STATION AND LABORATORY

Sociologist Robert Park, in describing the Tuskegee Institute, noted that it "has become a great experimental station in racial education.... The questions which were raised for discussion will affect native races in all parts of the world."[1] The term "experimental station" refers to the fact that many universities and industrial schools housed federally and state funded agricultural experiment stations on their campuses. At Tuskegee and other Black agricultural colleges, the work of these experiment stations was often positioned as integral to the solving of "the race problem" through the implementation of scientific farming. For example, in 1912, Jackson Davis defined the "Negro Problem" as Black farmers owning a lot of land but making poor use of it.[2] By defining the problem as one of making use of land, agricultural experiment stations were proposed as a method to find solutions.

Thanks to the influence of the Hampton model of education, which centered farm labor, Tuskegee was always deeply engaged in agriculture as part of its curriculum. But Tuskegee also systematically influenced farming in the geographic areas around the school by establishing Black farmers conferences in 1892, two years after the Morrill Act extension of 1890, which expanded land-grant colleges to segregated Black institutions. These conferences inspired similar events across the South and more institutions modeled after Tuskegee's program were established both privately and with Morrill Act funding. In 1896, Tuskegee hired George Washington Carver to head the agriculture department; as part of his work, he lobbied for an experiment station to be established at Tuskegee as they were being built at other Black land-grant institutions. The work of the experiment station was directly tied to programs like the farmers conferences, which sought to disseminate scientific farming information to Black farmers. They did so by publishing bulletins about the work of the station, which were written in practical and simple language so as to appeal to farmers; establishing farmer's institutes; and offering the Tuskegee short course on agriculture, in which local farmers were brought to the experiment station to learn.[3] The farm education piloted at Tuskegee eventually morphed into the demonstration farm and moveable school concepts, deeply influencing the eventual Smith-Lever legislation that authorized the development of cooperative extension programs at land-grant colleges. The Tuskegee moveable school initially consisted of a wagon, and later a truck and other vehicles, that would drive to different areas of the community surrounding Tuskegee demonstrating farming ideas.[4] The moveable school has widely been discussed in scholarly literature as a form of expanding access to agricultural education. However, it can also be understood as indexing Western expansion through the symbolism of the wagon as a primary transportational mode of settlement. The moveable school shifted people across space to implement new relationships to land through farm instruction and thus echoed some aspects of settlement, even in its distinct project. Therefore, even if the moveable school was not engaged in homesteading it signified settlement in the context of Black tenant farm geographies.

Demonstration farms were operated by demonstration agents who put scientific farming into practice and sought to show how it worked and inspire other farmers to do the same. This practice was spread by Seaman Knapp, who got the program funded through the US Department of Agriculture and established demonstration farm agencies, first in areas around Tuskegee and Hampton, which were instrumental in the founding of the program, and later in many other locations. John B. Pierce, one of the first state-based farm demonstration agents, was a Hampton graduate.[5] In describing these demonstration farms, Knapp wrote in the *Southern Workman* that, although these farms were not experimental in the way they approached farming, he saw them as experimental because they were improving Black farming, especially as opposed to immigrant farming, which he saw as a threatened replacement for Black labor.[6] Beyond farming, these demonstration farms were conceived of as experiments in Black social and economic improvement. They were described as a way that the work of experiment stations could be "delivered to the present day farmer" to produce "better land, better stock, better people."[7] Knapp's description displays how demonstration farming, as one aspect of plantation pedagogy, targeted both people and land as subjects of change and, in fact, also targeted animals/non-human kin. Each of these were seen as teachable components of the demonstration farm model such that all aspects of settlement (land, people, and animals) were part of the educational product.

I argue that agricultural experiment stations, the Tuskegee moveable school, and demonstration farms were a part of the technology of plantation pedagogy, which not only targeted Black and Native peoples as subjects who needed to change how they farmed land but also targeted land in order to transform the land itself and people's and non-human's relationships to it. Thus, these programs were directly engaged in creating a pedagogic relationship between the institution and the land on which it was built as well as between the students and teachers and the land on which they learned. Thus, land, much like the bodies of Black and Native peoples, was seen as an appropriate subject of experimentation, and often one that institutions had limited accountability to. Agricultural experimentation attempted to teach the land to be different and do things differently—in terms of the composition of the soil, the types of plants that it nourished and even the amount of water that it absorbed. Through this process of transforming land, scientific farming practices reinforced a world view based on cultivation and development of land as necessary for civilization; they also reinforced property-based and hierarchical relationships to land based on what could be produced from it and used for profit. This pedagogic practice aimed at land is also part of what traveled as plantation pedagogy and circulated in currents of colonialism. While these programs did not always have the effects on Black and Native peoples that they proposed (because resistance always accompanies ideological educational projects such as these), the effects on the land were often far more consistent and far reaching. This, then, is another moment when the protean plantation, the plantation as changeable through time and space, continues to expand and perpetrate antiblack violence—here, in the form of the experiment station and the laboratory. This violence is far-reaching in that it permeates people, their connection to land, the land itself, and non-human kin and is also still fundamentally connected to the plantation as schooling.

SCHOOLS, AGRICULTURAL EXPERIMENT STATIONS, AND SCIENTIFIC FARMING

The genealogy of agricultural experiment stations is one that has roots both in the violent settlement of the Americas and the establishment of plantation slavery and in European Enlightenment thought, which established experimentation as the means of producing valid knowledge. The need for the scientific study of farming was a product of colonial-imposed monocrop farming, which depleted soil mineral concentrations. Monocrop farming—particularly of tobacco, sugar, and cotton cultivation in the Americas—was deeply implicated in the spread of colonialism and plantation slavery. One of the first aims of scientific farming was to use chemical analysis of soil to study which nutrients plants needed to thrive and to develop fertilizers to revitalize depleted soil. Thus, scientific farming's development was also tied to the reinvigoration of plantation economies, which were threatened by soil depletion due to the poor implementation of monocrop farming. The outcomes of monocrop farming make evident the violence of colonial farming practices. Forcing the land to produce in specific ways can be done, but the long-term outcomes are that the land eventually can no longer continue to thrive under such violence.

The use of the scientific method to investigate agricultural factors such as soil composition was based in Enlightenment ideas of reason, the scientific method, and the dichotomy between man and nature. This was noted by historians of agricultural experiment stations, such as in a document produced by the United States Department of Agriculture in 1962 titled "State Agricultural Experiment Stations: A History of Research Policy and Procedure;" the history begins with the Enlightenment and the establishment of the scientific method. The document notes that scientific methods were eventually applied to agriculture, and this became popular with groups such as the Royal Society and the American Philosophic society. Early settler leaders like Washington and Jefferson were strong proponents of agricultural science and during the colonial period of US settlement many agricultural societies were founded to experiment with the best forms of farming in various parts of the United States. By 1860, over nine hundred agricultural societies existed for this purpose in the US.[8] This timeframe is tied to the depletion of the soil from plantation economies, a problem colonists were actively involved in combatting during the lead up to the Civil War, through both agricultural experimentation and the expansion of plantation slavery.

Despite the presentation of agricultural science as based in truth, scholars in science studies as well as in feminist and cultural studies have challenged the concept that science is neutral, natural, or the only way to learn about the world.[9] Bruno Latour and Steve Woolgar, in their ethnographic examination of laboratory life, note how scientific experiments, far from being perfect examples of the scientific method, are actually heavily socially constructed.[10] Latour and Woolgar posit that scientific facts and findings are produced through a contested process rather than a pre-existing truth, and that they become reified and entrenched over time based on the credibility and legitimacy given to scientific experimentation. Thus, the public is made to accept facts that are constructed in the laboratory and are represented as natural truth, despite possible contradictory information.[11] Additionally, the rise of science and Enlightenment thought coincided with European colonial expansion. Scholars in Indigenous studies, Black studies, and ethnic studies have levied many critiques against the presumed impartiality of scientific inquiry as well as the way research as a process has positioned BIPOC people as biased, incompetent, or unfit to do research, particularly research on their own communities.[12] Denise Ferreira Da Silva critiques science as a tool of colonialism and its role in constructing race and racism.[13] Similarly, Sylvia Wynter posits that science is heavily implicated in the overdetermination of the white cisgender heterosexual man as the model of the human. She proposes alternative forms of knowing, what she calls Scientia, as a means to counter hegemonic Western science.[14] In fact, Western notions of science are implicated in creating the false dichotomy between humans and the natural world.[15] Viewing humans and the natural world as separate is also part of the mechanism through which people can be framed as targets of pedagogy while land is described as simply being "cultivated" or "developed" rather than taught as part of a colonial process.

Since the scientific process is so embedded in the rise of agricultural experiment stations and their integration into schooling institutions, it should not be surprising that schools like Hampton and Tuskegee were referred to rhetorically using the language of experimentation. For example, Reverend Daniel Merriman of Massachusetts gave an address at Hampton in which he called the school an experiment that "has been reflected upon educational institutions of the north, bringing them into closer and more helpful contact with the realities of their problem."[16] The idea that industrial schools like Hampton were experiments was seen as a reflection of the "experimental" spirit of the United States. For example, Chauncey Depew stated in an 1892 edition of the *Southern Workman* that solving the race problem after the Civil War happened because the United States is a "nation of experimenters."[17] In these ways, schools are framed as both experiments and products of experimentation, firmly placing them within the cycle of the scientific method. The plantation, which I have argued is a space of schooling, has also been described as an experiment. Britt Rusert defines what she calls the "experimental plantation" as "an enclosed site from which empirical knowledge is produced, extracted, and transplanted from tropicalized lands and bodies."[18] Rusert's understanding of the term experimental includes scientific definitions but also includes medical and agricultural experimentation as privileged sites for understanding the "experimental regimes" of the plantation.[19] Rusert focuses on the pairing of experimentation with sugar cane production and medical experiments on slaves as ways that land and bodies were both used to produce knowledge through surveillance and enclosure. Thus, plantation pedagogy has a distinctly experimental component to its technology, and the intersection between industrial schooling, experiment stations, and scientific farming is a crucial lens for examining how it functions.

Additionally, while many histories of experiment stations focus on their connections to universities, few note the intense intimacy between agricultural experimentation and pedagogic thought. One of the first-documented agricultural experiment stations was Hofwyl, established in Bern, Switzerland, by Philipp Emanuel von Fellenberg in 1799. The educational theorist Pestalozzi, whose work heavily influenced Hampton's educational program, wrote about Hofwyl, and his pedagogy was used to establish a school in connection with agricultural experimentation. Von Fellenberg called Hofwyl an "educational colony" because of its extensive outreach activities and the proliferation of its ideas. Thus, Hofwyl became a model for many agricultural schools that engaged in agricultural experiments across the European continent. Other early agricultural experiment stations in Europe include the Durham Laboratory in Scotland and various German agricultural experiment stations, including the Moeckern experimental station, both of which were established in the 1840s and 1850s and were extremely influential in the establishment of the first formalized agricultural experiment stations in the United States.[20]

Experiment stations and demonstration farming also played a role globally outside of Europe. Both European and American imperial exploits created experiment stations in places in Africa and the Pacific during the twentieth century to take material advantage of the resources in those locations. Some examples in Africa included "the Gezira Scheme (Sudan), the Office du Niger (French Soudan), the Tanganyika Groundnut Scheme, [and] the *Compagnie*

Générale des Oléagineux Tropicaux (CGOT, Senegal)."[21] This also was followed with a proliferation of experiment stations once colonial control ended, where newly formed nations sought to expand Westernized notions of development.[22] While some historians of imperialism have distinguished between plantation and yeoman farm–based agricultural colonies, the use of experiment stations moved between both of these types and demonstrates the connection between the plantation as a space and form of pedagogy and the idea of the small farmer as an expansionary unit of the plantation.[23]

In the case of the United States, the historiography of agricultural experiment stations often begins with the establishment of the Department of Agriculture by Abraham Lincoln in 1860 at the beginning of the Civil War. Land-grant colleges were established by the Morrill Act two years later in order to connect federal programs for agriculture and institutions of higher learning. The Morrill Act was later extended to fund segregated Black institutions in 1890. Prior to the 1890 extension, private institutions like Hampton served the de facto role of "land grant" colleges for Black communities in that they often garnered federal support for programs sponsored by the Department of Agriculture, such as demonstration farms. The Morrill Act was discussed as part of a series of "farmer's legislation" signed by Lincoln that included the Homestead Act and the Transcontinental Railroad Act. Scholars have critiqued each of these acts as instrumental to the process of settlement, dispossession, and genocide enacted against Indigenous peoples over the subsequent decades.[24] In fact, the Morrill Act was marketed to Eastern farmers both as a way to restore the fertility of the soil that had been pilfered by colonial commercial farming and as a way to help Eastern farms compete with newly settled land in the West, as Indigenous peoples were further dispossessed and murdered as part of the expansion of the US settlement.[25] Included among these land-grant institutions were experimental stations, which were established piecemeal depending on institutional interest and funding, with the first station established in 1875 at the University of Connecticut.[26] Following this period of legislation during the Civil War and extending into the Reconstruction and Jim Crow eras were a variety of additional legislative acts that bolstered financial support for and organization of agricultural experiment stations. The 1887 Hatch Act and its 1890 Morrill Act extension funded agricultural research programs at land-grant colleges and segregated Black institutions in the South, and these were further extended by the Smith-Lever Act in 1914, which funded substations and extensions of the experiment station work.[27]

TEACHING PEOPLE AND TEACHING LAND AT TUSKEGEE

Tuskegee was one location where schooling for Black communities, agricultural experiment station work, and demonstration farming occurred in the same institutional and geographic setting. Tuskegee was also an institution that had one of the clearest connections to Hampton. Booker T. Washington often spoke of Samuel Armstrong as the most influential mentor of his life and consulted him regularly in regard to founding Tuskegee. Tuskegee became a premier institution for spreading the Hampton model of industrial schooling. While Tuskegee did not educate Indigenous peoples directly, it laid a foundation for how agricultural experimentation and scientific farming could work in concert with schooling in ways that would influence a variety of institutions across the Pacific and Atlantic. One of the key players to establish how Tuskegee would engage in a project of scientific farming for racialized communities was George Washington Carver, who ran the Tuskegee agricultural experiment station. Between 1898 and 1942, Carver published over forty bulletins for circulation amongst Black farmers in Alabama as part of his work for the Tuskegee agricultural experiment station. The purpose of these bulletins was to disseminate information on scientific farming produced by the experiment station to the average Black farmer in language they could understand and providing techniques that they could apply with limited resources.[28]

Carver is best known for his advocacy of the peanut and in particular his connection to peanut butter, to which his agricultural work was related. The peanut appears in a number of his circulars, including a bulletin published by the experiment station in 1917 titled "How to Grow the Peanut."[29] Peanuts in themselves are a fascinating study in the connection between colonialism and slavery. Peanuts were initially grown in South America and the Caribbean and were transplanted worldwide as part of colonial food transfer and commodification to become integral food staples in other parts of the world, such as the African continent and parts of Asia. Yet they maintained an association as a food fit for savages (i.e., Indigenous peoples) and were thus associated with the "uncivilized," such that they were used as a staple food for slaves as a well as for livestock. Peanuts eventually outgrew this association, but this "New World" food that was deemed appropriate to feed slaves and that slaves survived on through their own agency was a historical marker of the intimacy of colonialism, settlement, and slavery.[30]

However, one of the recurring themes that emerges across many of Carver's circulars is not related to food crops but is concerned with how to improve soil composition. In the third published bulletin in 1899, Carver outlines the various experiments with fertilizers conducted by the Tuskegee Experiment Station. Many other circulars reiterate the findings of this bulletin, such as the editions that cover growing cow peas, cotton cultivation, and "how to build up worn out soils."[31] Much of the scholarly work on Carver's circulars has demonstrated how they disseminated knowledge in understandable language in order to change Black farming practices; however, I argue that Carver's work acted not only to teach people but also to teach land to work differently. In "Fertilizer Experiments on Cotton," published in 1899, Carver outlines how to prepare soil to cultivate cotton, which includes deep plowing with the goal of "pulverizing" soil to make it "even and mellow."[32] This act of "taming" the soil is described as if the soil itself has a life, and one that tends toward the wild and unregulated (much as how the Indigenous peoples who belonged to the land were framed).[33] In the circular, Carver suggests that Black farmers add various types of fertilizers and lime to the soil. The lime, while not a fertilizer, would act to loosen both hard clay soil and compact sandy soil so that fertilizers could be better rendered throughout the layers of the soil. Carver noted that lime was best used on soil in "poor mechanical condition, such as the worn-out soil many tenant farmers farmed that had historically been depleted by monocrop farming."[34]

In bulletin six, "How to Build up Worn out Soil," published in 1905, Carver adds further detail regarding how land needs to be instructed and made to change. He states that the farmer should "fill in ditches with pine tops, hay, bark, old cotton stalks, leaves, etc., in fact, rubbish of any kind that would decay and ultimately make soil."[35] The next step he suggests includes stump removal and plowing to increase the "water holding potential of the soil." He states that this reduces the need for terraces, which he calls "ragged and weedy" and can increase the overall amount of cultivatable land.[36] He states that these processes are necessary to improve both the aesthetics and efficiency of the land and discusses how his method for building up the soil can improve the land's "latent fertility" such that "maximum fertility" can be achieved.[37] Carver's discussion of soil improvement in bulletin six is bolstered by a historical approach that makes an argument for scientific farming as related to civilizational change. He notes that ancient Egyptians understood the value of crop rotation to maintain soil fertility, but "as the population of the world increased and civilization advanced, it became imperative that all farming operation should become more intensive and less extensive."[38] This connection to ancient Egypt indexes histories of African civilization as advanced that in many ways are in line with projects of African-centered history, yet it also makes an argument for the inevitability of capitalist farming practices in the face of demographic change brought on by colonialism and the industrial revolution. In tying scientific farming to the concept of "advancing civilization," Carver is situating these practices in and against Indigenous agricultural practices and land relationships.

Part of the argument Carver makes when he suggests these alterations to land (teaching land to work and learn a different composition) is that cotton can continue to be grown anywhere and in any type of soil in Alabama and may be profitable for the Black tenant farmer.[39] Thus, Carver's educational program as scientific farming is related to recovering the profitability of cotton farming and recovering remnants of the plantation economy in the post-emancipation Alabama landscape. He also suggests that these methods of scientific farming are of use to schools, with multiple circulars that directly address how his scientific farming discoveries can be implemented in rural schools and school gardens.[40] Therefore, the school and the plantation continue to be entangled insofar as they are both invested in what the land produces and how it produces it and not just in who is made to produce things for whom. In this way, plantation pedagogy continues to manipulate the land for settlement and plantation spatial expansion, which is contiguous with projects of teaching Black and Native peoples.

EDUCATION AND EXPERIMENT STATIONS ACROSS THE CURRENTS

While many histories of agricultural experiment stations and demonstration farms are either US- or Western-centric, these institutions also peppered the colonial landscape across both the Pacific and the Atlantic. In the same ways that agricultural experiment stations were deeply tied to educational institutions in the United States, they were intimately connected in the colonial context. Experiment stations and demonstration farms were described by white reformers not only as important for the development and settlement of colonial space but also as pedagogic projects to teach the populations of these spaces how to appropriately interact with land in a productive and efficient manner. Much in the way other technologies of plantation pedagogy circulated in eddying movements that were non-linear, the proliferation of agricultural experiment stations also gradually transplanted ideas and institutions that shifted across contexts.

In 1901, the first agricultural experiment station in the state of Hawaiʻi was established at the University of Hawaiʻi, Manoa, which was the land-grant university of the newly annexed state. In fact, the experiment station preceded the establishment of the university by six years.[41] However, just as experiment stations were established by the US government on the mainland, this institution had precursors in non-governmental agricultural societies. For example, the sugar planters societies in Hawaiʻi developed experiment station programs to test the best ways to cultivate sugar on the islands during the missionary period. In this way, agricultural experimentation was part and parcel of the imperial exploitation by white sugar planters, who sought to reap profit from Hawaiian soil during the Hawaiian monarchy. After the establishment of the first US government funded experiment station in Hawaiʻi, other extension stations were established across the islands. For example, an experiment station, which currently exists in Hilo, on the island of Hawaiʻi, is located in the same area as a station that was first established in concert with the Hilo Boarding school, one of the progenitors of Hampton.[42] The Hilo Boarding School catalogue highlighted their experimental farming program, which worked in cooperation with the US Department of Agriculture through the establishment of a cooperative agricultural experiment station. This mirrored how Tuskegee also cultivated a relationship with the Department of Agriculture in order to establish an experiment station on their grounds. Experiment stations also proliferated in locations that were influenced by US imperialism after formal imperialism ended. For example, the Philippine government established agricultural experiment stations as a means of demonstrating their development and capacity for independence in the early 1900s.[43]

In colonial Africa, experiment stations also were a key part of strategies of colonial control by European and American governments. German colonies in Africa established many agricultural experiment stations in the Gold Coast region and described the purposes of these stations as multifaceted. They functioned to surveil and control the Native population, while also educating them to become a pliant workforce for development: "These will be essentially military stations on agricultural foundation;" and "German officers are to train Negro soldiers for defensive purposes. For the working of plantations, the labor of free natives, and, to a smaller extent, foreign work people."⁴⁴ In his report on Education in Africa, Thomas Jesse Jones cited experiment stations in locations such as the Congo, Nigeria, and the Gold Coast and specifically noted how these stations were connected to schools. For example, the Assuantsi experiment station on the Gold Coast established a cooperative relationship with a local missionary-run industrial school. Assuantsi was one of five experiment stations across the colonies of the Gold Coast established by European colonizers.⁴⁵ Jones lauded this connection between agricultural experimentation and schools as a model that other European colonizers in Africa should encourage. Furthermore, the educational programs in Liberia, which were funded by US philanthropists and businesses, were also deeply invested in agricultural experiment stations in connection with educational institutions. When the Booker Washington Institute of Liberia was looking to hire educators, it privileged those who had experience working at agricultural experiment stations because they wanted the school to have an experimental component to its agricultural program.⁴⁶ This program never fully developed, largely due to budgetary constraints, despite the fact that the institute hired staff who had experience at experiment stations and supported agricultural experimentation programs.

Besides the extensive discussion of experiment stations that existed across Africa, Thomas Jesse Jones also theorized about the importance of both experiment stations and demonstration farms in his vision for Africa's future. In the chapter on "educational adaptations" in the report he headed on African education, he noted that demonstration farms would be important "experiments" for understanding the African condition.⁴⁷ He stated that missionary schools across colonial Africa were "experiment stations in which the educational adaptations are initiated and tested."⁴⁸ Jones concluded that European governments should recognize the value of schools as "experiment stations where new methods of education should be tried."⁴⁹ These discussions by Jones demonstrate that the agricultural experiment station, the demonstration farm, and the school were all enmeshed in the social construction of science and Western ideas of experimentation. The connection between schools and experimentation also served as a precursor to programs that sought to improve schooling through experimentation and demonstration-based programs, which treated colonized bodies as subjects to be experimented on. Thus, the establishment of schools, demonstration farms, and agricultural stations in Africa have had a long legacy in the "development" that the West has continued to impose on African states in the neo-colonial era.⁵⁰ In fact, whether or not these demonstration farms actually influenced local farmers in Africa, they have continued to be used discursively as a form of development imposed from outside of the continent.

In addition to this international movement of agricultural experiment stations as a technology of plantation pedagogy, these programs were also integral to how the US sought to enforce developmental programs in Indian Country. Experiment stations were common at Western land-grant institutions, which sought to transform what was framed as "non-productive" Indigenous lands into settlements that produced crops efficiently. Two examples of how experiment stations were expanded to reservation space were the Pima Egyptian cotton cooperative station in Arizona and the various experimental and demonstration programs on the Navajo Nation discussed by Thomas Jesse Jones in his report *The Navajo Problem*.[51]

Jennifer Bess discusses the history of the Pima Egyptian cotton cooperative station, which was founded in 1907 as both a demonstration farm and cooperative project between the US Department of Agriculture and the Bureau of Indian Affairs (BIA).[52] The project was implemented on the Pima Indian School farm and sought to grow Egyptian cotton in the Southwest using the Pima and other Indigenous peoples in the area as cheap wage labor for local cotton farmers. Pima cotton, now considered the only American varietal similar to Egyptian cotton, was a strand established from Egyptian cotton. It was grown for a time on the South Carolina Sea Islands and then eventually was grown as part of the Pima cooperative project, where it got its name.[53] Cotton, of course, has always been a commodity that was deeply embedded in the histories of slavery, settlement, and imperialism across multiple continents. The cotton economy was instrumental in the expansion and entrenchment of slavery in the South and the eventual outbreak of the Civil War. Cotton was also a crop that required a great deal of land and resources to farm and necessitated more and more land to make a profit, which accelerated Indigenous dispossession. In addition, cotton is a commodity that defies the lines of the Columbian exchange, having been grown and used across continents in the "new" and "old" worlds.[54] During the early 1900s when the Pima cotton strain was being developed, the boll weevil infestation in the Southern cotton region led to the expansion of cotton growing in other regions of the US, and this marked a turn to the possibility of Indigenous labor across the Southwest, which was positioned by white growers in opposition to Southern Black labor.

The head of the BIA, Francis E. Leupp, described the Pima cooperative farm as having the educational purpose of preparing Pima people to take allotments and transition from commonly held reservation land to individual land owning. However, this was in many ways secondary to the goal of providing labor for large scale white farmers in the region, which demonstrates once again that the stated goal of a pedagogy (for example, teaching Natives to farm their own allotted land) was often not the most important outcome of pedagogic projects.[55] Bess also quotes Leupp, who compared Pima farmers to Black farmers on plantations: "Even the little papoose can be taught to weed the rows just as the pickanniny in the south can be used as a cottonpicker."[56] While Leupp discusses the transformation of young Black and Native bodies into laborers, he also describes teaching land to produce a new form of cotton that is not native to the space. Thus, the agricultural experiment station participates in both the training of people and the training of land in order to produce something of value for white colonizers in the context of settlement and to introduce plantation agriculture to new geographies and climates.

Experiment stations on reservations encompassed more than agriculture; they also addressed the management of livestock. In a report titled *The Navajo Problem,* which was written by Thomas Jesse Jones, the same former Hampton employee who wrote the reports on education in Africa, Navajo farming and herding practices are discussed at length. Khalil Anthony Johnson Jr. has noted that Jones was integral to Indigenous education, participating, for example, in the pivotal document, the Meriam Report, which discussed conditions in Native Boarding Schools.[57] I draw parallels between Jones's support of agricultural experiment stations and demonstration farms in Africa, as described above, and his support of similar programs on the Navajo Nation as a means of solving the "Navajo problem." The "Navajo problem," as described by Jones and other US government agents, was one of overgrazing, where Navajo livestock, particularly sheep, were blamed for soil erosion on the reservation. Daniel Perlstein has persuasively argued that this focus on soil erosion was not brought on by environmental concerns but by the threat it caused to the Hoover Dam and other capitalist electricity projects in the region.[58] Ultimately, the government focus on erosion led to the culling of the Navajo-Churro herds, during which thousands of Navajo livestock were killed, with disastrous effects on Navajo well-being.[59] Navajo-Churro sheep were viewed as inferior stock in terms of creating wool for trade or meat for sale, which overlooked the spiritual and cultural relationship that Navajo people had with this breed as well as the use of this specific wool in Navajo weaving practice.[60] As part of this non-human genocide of Navajo life, the concept of laboratories, experimentation, and demonstration were key to how the US government conceptualized the post-genocidal aftermath.[61] Jones described the many livestock demonstration areas across the reservation established by the US government where Navajos were shown how to "properly" graze sheep for profit. This was coupled with government sheep-breeding laboratories, which sought to fundamentally change Navajo herding practices, including the type of sheep kept by Navajo herders. Additionally, there were agricultural extensions and farm supervisors employed across the reservations who worked in concert with livestock demonstration areas, whose goals were to change the "primitive practices" of Navajo farmers and herders.[62]

The example of Navajo herding and the genocide of Navajo livestock demonstrates how technologies of plantation pedagogy are continually implicated in targeting various forms of Indigenous life for death, including nonhuman life. This could also be said about the way that these institutions targeted land as a subject of experimentation. As part of settlement and plantation agriculture, land was subjected to a similar form of genocide, stripped of its shape and made to produce crops that depleted it, fundamentally altering its existence. Experiment stations, as noted above, were established because of this genocidal project against the land that sought to use and possess it in and beyond death and regeneration.[63]

PLANTATION LABORATORY TO LABORATORY SCHOOL

In the case of agricultural experiment stations, the experimentation happens on land and to land. Thus, the land is both the location and subject of experimentation. While I have discussed land as a subject of experimentation in detail, I will end this chapter with a discussion of land as a location of experimentation—that is, land as laboratory. I draw from Britt Rusert's discussion of the "laboratory life of the plantation" to assert that, because plantation pedagogies worked in concert with agricultural experiment stations and other forms of teaching that relied on concepts of scientific experimentation, the plantation laboratory is a fundamentally educational project. I therefore argue that the laboratory, the farm, and the school are connected entities that cannot be untangled. The plantation also cannot be disentangled from the settlement as they are one and the same space, where enclosure acts on lands and bodies and is part of the creation of private property. In fact, Rusert notes that the general idea of enclosure, both the broad concept of enclosing public space for production and the idea of creating a closed system, was integral to the creation of the plantation laboratory as a perceived closed space of experimentation.[64]

The plantation laboratory does not end with abolition but extends beyond emancipation much the way plantation pedagogy shifted but did not disappear after emancipation.[65] Black (and other racialized) bodies were seen as appropriate subjects of experimentation to be used in a variety of ways. Rusert discusses how Tuskegee made Black bodies the subjects of research by experimenting medically on them, a practice that has undoubtedly continued in the afterlife of slavery. She connects the Tuskegee Institute's agricultural education and manual labor programs to the later Tuskegee syphilis study, which, she notes, functioned through the containment and enclosure of Black bodies in a way that produced a contained population for experimentation. Thus, Tuskegee is a plantation laboratory insofar as it is a space "where the containment of black students within the enclosures of an abandoned plantation-turned-college campus, paired with public health-style maintenance of personal hygiene, extended plantation systems of slave health 'care' into the twentieth century."[66] Other connections between Rusert's description of the plantation laboratory and my understanding of plantation pedagogy and settlement include how sanitation is used for the purposes of a "recuperation of dirt." She writes that there was "a purifying intimacy imagined between the bodies and the soil of the Black Belt caus[ing] Washington to forward a model of human 'planting.'"[67] The plantation is a literal space of planting but also a planting of a settlement/colony, and a planting of bodies into that space as a means of settlement and as a containment of Blackness. Rusert connects this intense focus on hygiene at Tuskegee to Washington's experiences with the Hampton Indian Program and its obsession with "colonial purity."[68] By framing the plantation as a non-threatening space, akin to the way the plantation is presented as a school, the plantation as laboratory normalizes the plantation as an "organic component of the Southern landscape."[69]

Therefore, at the same time that Black bodies were experimented on, land was also seen as something to be changed and experimented on through the location of the agricultural experiment station. This experimentation was not only about the construction of facts about how to farm effectively but was also pedagogic in that it attempted to teach the land. Through experiments with fertilizers, soil, and new plant species, plantations—and later experiment stations and demonstration farms—attempted to teach the land to act differently. Thus, in addition to the bodies of Black and Indigenous peoples, land was a target of pedagogy and experimentation. In this way, agricultural study, experimentation, demonstration, and teaching is implicated in settlement and colonialism beyond the ideological transference of ideas because it directly transformed land. This transformation was framed through capitalist notions of value and work in order to increase production in combination with Western ontologies of what constituted how humans were supposed to interact with the world. I need to stop briefly here and clarify that when I speak about the teaching of land for the purpose of production, I do not wish to confuse this with Indigenous epistemologies of land or land-based pedagogies. Just because Indigenous peoples may create programs where they learn through interaction with land does not mean that land is targeted pedagogically in the same way.[70] In fact, Indigenous epistemologies have not framed land as a potential subject of experimentation in the same ways as Western epistemologies.[71] I leave discussion of these projects of learning and study outside of this text because I know they are fundamentally different and because I want to allow for these projects to have space outside of the commodifying impulses of the academic context.

For an example of how the plantation laboratory is applied to Indigenous peoples and to the land, I turn to an example from the writing of Thomas Jesse Jones, whose reach as an educational reformer spanned the US South, Indian Country, and Africa. Jones described agriculture as integral to public welfare and stated that the Bureau of Experiment Stations was integral to "the study of agricultural education and industrial training in the common schools."[72] Jones discussed this project not just in practical terms of the curriculum but also in terms of the relationship between this form of schooling and settlement: "The study of land or nature as a factor in production brings up the question of the influence of the environment upon the economic life of the individual ... the discussion is extended to the influence of these elements upon character. Equally interesting and, in a sense, more profitable is the discussion of the ability of man to conquer his environment."[73] In this discussion, teaching land to produce more is viewed through the lens of the conquest of the environment, and in fact, he implies that conquest is the natural form of human interaction with the world. Jones then goes on to describe two "Indian boys" who undergo an experiment, investing different amounts of money into their land; he explains how the one who invests more can become more profitable through farming.[74] Jones connects Black and Indigenous peoples' learning to farm to the concept of freedom as tied to assimilation:

> The Study of the distribution of colored and Indian populations showing that a large majority of these races are living in country districts and are immediately dependent upon farming makes the great importance of a knowledge of agriculture quite apparent to the thoughtful pupil. The importance is emphasized by the fact that rural life offers the freedom of activity necessary to the development of a people in the process of assimilating the customs of another people.[75]

Here, freedom becomes tied to the transformation and development of land; it is framed as the ability to engage in capitalist production and in Western ideas of interacting with the world. It is not the ability to choose how to live in relationship with the land. Additionally, this rhetoric linked the training of land and the training of people, but not in a causal manner in which one produces the other. The training of people to do things and believe things is in dialectical relationship to the training of land.

As Jones discussed in his report on education in Africa, schools, like farms, were seen as sites of experimentation. Additionally, this experimentation was coupled with the proliferation of schools as sites of expanded settlement. A clear example of this connection is the Penn School on St. Helena Island, a school that Jones discussed as an excellent example of industrial education in much of his writing. The Penn School is described in the *Southern Workman* as both a "social settlement" and an "experiment station." After they had been tried at the Penn School, its teachers and graduates expanded its practices into the community.[76] If the school was a manifestation of society and settlement, then to view it as an experiment was to understand the production of settlement as a process of experimentation in which a more perfect form of settlement and control was always sought because of its very elusiveness. In this final section, I show how the idea of the Penn School as a "social settlement" and "experiment station" coalesces into discourses of progressive education in which the school is set up to be both an "embryonic society" and a laboratory for working out effective pedagogy.[77]

Progressive education, exemplified by the work of scholars such as John Dewey and inclusive of scholars such as Pestalozzi and Froebel, is often described as a form of education opposed to traditional or classical education.[78] Progressive education in many ways sits at the root of many critical and radical critiques of schools such as critical pedagogy.[79] Thus the tenets of progressive education have become enmeshed in both mainstream schooling practices and radical schooling practices such that these ideas about learning are not often contested and have become normalized.[80] I read progressive educational theories, particularly the work of John Dewey, as an extension of the technologies of plantation pedagogy.[81] Dewey's educational theorization focused on how education had to change to "meet the needs of society" much in the same way that Armstrong and Washington framed industrial education as "education for life."[82] In fact, Dewey specifically discusses industrial education as part of his educational theory: "We cannot overlook the factors of discipline and of character building involved in this kind of life: training in habits of order and of industry, and in the idea of responsibility, or obligation to do something, to produce something in the world."[83] This discussion of production by Dewey is firmly entrenched in Western concepts of production in which "the world without relationship to human activity is less than the world."[84] Yet Dewey describes the production as less important than the learning that happens as part of that production; he writes, "the aim is not the economic value of the products, but the development of the social power of insight."[85] This is much the same as how plantation pedagogy framed labor as pedagogic regardless of whether it produced profit, which justified work programs in educational institutions that were not profitable for the school.

In discussing his idea of the school as a laboratory, Dewey almost echoes the words of Thomas Jesse Jones, noting that "the school would be an experiment station in education."[86] These experiments would point to how students could work to overcome obstacles to production, and Dewey even cited the colonization of the Americas as an example of this process.[87] In fact, much of Dewey's understanding of development is based upon scales of civilization, in which the child is at the same stage of development as the savage, and thus the child should be taught about modes of "primitive" life in their first introduction to learning by doing.[88] This comparison of the stages of child development to European ideas about savagery and civilization produces a linear narrative in which Indigenous death and disappearance or Black death and pathologization are inevitable steps in a trajectory of progress that commodifies the violence committed against Black and Indigenous bodies as part of the making of society. Additionally, Dewey was clear that science and experimentation were key aspects of creating a proper education for society. This was mirrored in how industrial education proponents like Jones discussed science education in relation to settlement. Jones describes elementary science as "designed for rural people who are exceedingly primitive and who place superstitious interpretations upon natural phenomena;" he therefore believed it would help these populations to move towards vocational work in relation to the natural environment.[89] Dewey's laboratory school included a garden, shop, and relations to business, like a mini pioneer homestead or a mini plantation; thus, Dewey's laboratory school is much like the plantation/settlement.

The proliferation of schools, demonstration farms, and experiment stations targeted land and changed land in material ways that furthered plantation futures and entrenched settlement in the landscape. Yet, another result of the intimacy between the school and the experiment station is in how the school itself is viewed as a space of experimentation. One way in which this continued into mainstream education was through Dewey's laboratory schools. But, in general, schools as laboratories or experiments exemplify spaces that are framed as integral to solving societal problems. Thus, the discourses of school improvement that are so ubiquitous in the present are also implicated in this history of plantations, laboratories, and experimentation. Agricultural experimentation, as one technology of plantation pedagogy, was a driver of the formation of the school as experimental space. Thus, the protean nature of plantation pedagogy continues to expand itself into temporal and spatial formations that would otherwise appear unconnected to plantation politics.

Conclusion

LEARNING BY (NOT) DOING?

> Ignorant and inexperienced, it is not strange that in the first years of our new life we began at the top instead of at the bottom; that a seat in Congress or the state legislature was more sought than real estate or industrial skill; that the political convention or stump speaking had more attractions than starting a dairy farm or a truck garden. A ship lost at sea for many days suddenly sighted a friendly vessel. From the mast of the unfortunate vessel was seen a signal, "Water, water. We die of thirst." The answer from the friendly vessel at once came back, "Cast down your bucket where you are."
>
> **BOOKER T. WASHINGTON**
> *The Atlanta Compromise Speech, September 18, 1895*

> Whereas true civic education is not political action itself but rather preparation for life.
>
> *A Resolution of the State Board of Education of Georgia, June 3, 2021*

In June of 2021, the Georgia State Board of Education approved a resolution that was part of the growing conservative backlash against teaching about race and racism in K-12 public schools. This resolution was reported on by news outlets in relation to the use of the term *critical race theory* by conservatives as a dog whistle to signal curriculums that address histories of racism. While the resolution contained language that indexed critical race theory—for example, "the United States of America is not a racist country, and ... the state of Georgia is not a racist state"—there was a less discussed part of the resolution that I focus on here, which is presented in the above epigraph.[1] I was drawn to this particular part of the resolution because first, it was taken as a given, starting with the term *whereas,* rather than in the list of resolutions. Secondly, because the notion that civic education is "preparation for life" so precisely echoed much of the language used by industrial educators such as Armstrong, Washington, and Pratt. In fact, a parallel can be drawn between this moment from the 2021 resolution in Georgia and another moment when political life and education were on rhetorical display in the same state: Booker T. Washington's Atlanta Compromise speech, which famously urged Blacks in the South, "Cast down your bucket where you are." This speech has widely been interpreted as calling for a turn away from political action towards economic accumulation and a politics of self-help through labor.[2] Thus, Washington's project was education in preparation for life both in that it drew on the tenets of industrial education and in that it was practically oriented towards a model of economic accumulation rather than political action. The extensive debate about whether Booker T. Washington's project of economic self-help has a redemptive arc by defining it as fugitive or whether it was a successful approach for navigating the violence of the Reconstruction South is not a debate that I choose to engage in here.[3] Instead, I point to how the ideology of education as "preparation for life" abdicates projects of abolition and decolonization and is fundamentally tied to the teaching of slavery and settlement.

The following selection from Booker T. Washington's lesser read work titled *My Larger Education: Being Chapters from My Experience* and published in 1911 is illustrative of how teaching in preparation for life is linked with teaching slavery. As a part of education in "preparation for life," a key component is that one must "learn by doing" so that learning can be applied to the real experiences one will face rather than abstract concepts. Washington describes his background in learning by doing thus:

> I have gotten a large part of my education from actual contact with things, rather than through the medium of books. I like to touch things and handle them; I like to watch plants grow and observe the behaviour of animals. For the same reason, I like to deal with things, as far as possible, at first hand, in the way that the carpenter deals with wood, the blacksmith with iron, and the farmer with the earth. I believe that there is something gained by getting acquainted, in the way which I have described, with the physical world about you that is almost indispensable.[4]

This discussion of learning from the physical world is one of the ways in which Booker T. Washington's educational discourse comes across as the most relatable and in which his pedagogy seems the most benign. The notion of learning from the physical world with a hands-on approach would seem to be universally applicable and benign. It is certainly much more palatable than the message of "cast down your bucket where you are." Yet, preceding this discussion of learning from the physical world, Washington spends a number of paragraphs describing how being born a slave benefitted him educationally and socially. He bases his construction of learning from the natural world on the intimacy he acquired with nature during enslavement. He describes how his privations in slavery led to his first "intimate acquaintance with animals" because he had to learn to find food and often would take Indian corn fed to the animals and eat it for breakfast.[5] Despite admitting that he had to eat food that was deemed animal feed, Washington emphatically states, "if I had not been a slave and lived on a slave plantation, I never would have had the opportunity to learn nature."[6] Thus, Washington's conceptualization of learning by doing is grounded in his experiences in slavery. It is this connection that makes me wary of educational models based on "learning by doing" or "preparation for life;" the history of Westernized education for Black and Indigenous peoples has been driven by ideologies that assert that dispossession, genocide, and slavery have at least some educational value in spite of their violence.

Progressive education models, best exemplified by the theorizations of John Dewey, also focused on learning by doing and education that was tied into the real life of the community. While these models are often presented as distinct from past forms of teaching, they discursively signal much of the rhetoric of industrial education.[7] Daniel Perlstein and Sam Stack describe an instantiation of progressive education in the West Virginia mining community of Arthurdale, where a school was built as a part of New Deal era model communities.[8] On the school grounds was a cabin that had been built by the county's first white settler, John Fairfax, and Perlstein and Stack describe how the use of the cabin by the school "embodied Dewey's ideas and school and community bonds."[9] In this cabin, the teachers used "pioneer activity" to teach both industrial and academic topics, demonstrating that the school was grounded in the mythologies of settlement as making a benevolent community.[10] Yet, what was not explicitly noted by the community school in its curriculum was that this cabin was not actually a white pioneer cabin but a cabin that Fairfax built for his slaves to live in. This slave cabin symbolically stood in for a settler cabin and was part of teaching students towards their own bonds with the settler community and the US state on a site of slavery's afterlife.[11] I note this example of the slave cabin and its utilization for "pioneer" teaching activity as a part of progressive educational programs to demonstrate how learning by doing in the context of progressive education was implicated in the longer project of plantation pedagogy. Therefore, the conclusion to this book interrogates the concept of learning by doing and learning in preparation for life as part of the historical formation of plantation pedagogies and of the ever-shifting scope of plantation futures that transcend temporal and spatial geographies.

I begin by engaging in what might be called a meditation on the concept of *doing*, where I sit with the word in order to understand its many-faceted meanings and their relationship to the project of teaching slavery and settlement. The concept of *doing* might seem an odd one to tarry with after having tarried with such weighty concepts as the *plantation* and such expansive concepts as *currents*. Yet, this is exactly why I want to spend time with the notion. *Doing* is a word we take for granted. A normalized idea of what it means to exist in the world, or otherwise stated, "the activities in which a particular person engages."[12] Yet I do not take this one meaning of doing as the only meaning or even the most important one. Doing can also be defined as "effort" or "activity," with synonyms being "work" and "labor." Doing as consisting of activity, work, and labor is linked to Western concepts of the value of production and work as human activities, which run in contrast to Indigenous modes of relation. Further still, the concept of doing has many other informal meanings. It can mean "a beating or a scolding," indexing that doing is a violent process.[13] The verb "to do" has meanings such as "to perform," "to work," "to solve," "to make," or "to work for a living" but also can indicate "to beat up or kill," "to swindle," "to have sex with," or "to finish or be over."[14] The violent and libidinal connotations of doing stick to the word even as its everyday meanings appear obvious. Each of these formal and informal definitions are the "doings" of settlement and slavery.

In relation to education, learning by doing is often discussed as learning through action or project-based learning.[15] However, the idea of learning by doing in the classroom also has a temporality. Time is constructed in classrooms such that it is tied to efficiency and production.[16] If a student learns by doing, then if they are not actively doing something, they must not be learning. This leads to classroom structures like the "do now," an activity students are expected to engage in as soon as they enter the classroom in order to immerse them in the productive flow of the work of learning. The constant attention to making sure students are "on task" is a form of monitoring the level at which they are engaged in "doing."[17] Lesson plans written by teachers require objectives that must be met through action (SMART goals that are Specific, Measurable, Achievable, Relevant and, most importantly, Time-based).[18] In all of these ways, doing is enacted in the daily lives of students and teachers in classrooms.[19]

Doing also takes on different meanings politically and culturally. Julius B. Flemming Jr., for example, has argued that asking Black people to be patient and not do things has historically been deployed as a weapon against Black communities who make demands from the state. Asking Black people to "slow down" or wait for change has been a consistent tactic to defer the inclusion of Black people in the political fabric of the United States. Conversely, Black patience itself has been used as a form of action; for example, sit-ins were forms of patience deployed for political action that Black people repurposed against repressive state authority.[20] On a similar note, as my friend Juliet R. Kunkel has pointed out, a labor strike, a form of radical engagement against capitalism, is a form of "not doing" that accomplishes a political and material goal. Conversely, Kevin Quashie posits a theory of Black quietness, in which he questions the necessity of publicness in the performance of justice-based political work and moves towards theorizing the expressive interiority of Black quietness.[21] Black quietness, according to Quashie offers an alternate way to conceptualize Black resistance outside of the dominant cultural aesthetic of a more outward focused form of resistance. In this way, doing as a mode of political resistance becomes a dominant cultural construct that can obscure the intimate power of not doing, or at least not doing in the public eye.[22]

Ultimately, doing is a material process. Doing is a process of violence. Doing is a death drive.[23] Both settlement and slavery are violent enterprises replete with various means of exploiting both people and land, which are reframed as progress. This includes the physical and metaphorical rape of people and land, as indexed by the idea of America as "virgin land."[24] In addition to the violent and libidinal implications of doing, doing also indexes finality. The possessive settlement of land and people is framed as part of the origin story of the US state, where settlement is narrated as both inevitable and complete and slavery as a sad, but closed, chapter in a far-off past. This narrative seeks to close off recognition of settlement as an ongoing condition of existence and of how slavery reverberates through daily life.

Thus, I interrogate doing to move toward a thought experiment about a possible politics of not doing. How can not doing be conceptualized as an active pursuit in contrast to and in opposition to colonial doing? Is there an opposition of doing, and what would it consist of? What could the effects of not doing be? To engage these questions, I look to scholarship and conversations that have begun to engage these questions. For example, Funie Hsu's work on the commodification of mindfulness engages Buddhist cultural and religious understandings as a practice of "not doing," which Daniel Perlstein has reminded me might be the very thing that is needed in a world where the doing of things has slowly destroyed the planet through global warming and ecological disaster.[25] While I do not present "not doing" as an answer to how to make schools better, I do present it as a location for thought, especially in relation to the violence of doing and the way learning by doing has long been implicated in slavery and settlement.

Thus, what I might be suggesting (*might* is the key word here) is a learning by refusal. A refusal to learn by doing; a turning towards a practice of not doing provides a conceptual limit from which to learn. Learning by refusal is texturally different than learning by resistance. I will not repeat my arguments against commodifying the resistance of Black and Indigenous peoples as an answer to solving the problems of schooling, but I will repeat that resistance as a theory of change is a tenuous one that is always tied to the structures of power it is reacting against. Not doing also does not mean not living, not surviving, not striving, not relating. Not doing is just as active as doing. For example, Saidiya Hartman states throughout her text *Wayward Lives, Beautiful Experiments* that the Black girls she writes about demonstrated a waywardness that was a refusal to settle.[26] A refusal to settle, a not doing of settlement, does not negate the other ways they lived out their social lives, as Hartman's poignant work demonstrates.[27] Learning through the limit of refusal, learning by not doing, might (or might not) allow for an engagement with other ways that Indigenous and Black lives are lived at the limits of existence, including the climate catastrophe, capitalist dystopia, genocide, and apocalypse. A refusal of learning by doing can point to the futility of schools as sites of social change much the way a refusal to solve educational problems does.[28]

This text has made the argument that settlement and slavery can both be viewed as educational processes. As a location of both slavery and also of settlement, the plantation becomes a site where the educational projects of settlement and slavery come together. I therefore have drifted through an examination of the plantation's pedagogy. Plantation pedagogy (1) privileges space as necessary to teaching slavery and settlement and (2) examines how this form of teaching not only sought to change Black and Native peoples but also (3) delineates how this form of teaching also sought to change land and relations to it. By defining proximity to whiteness and manual labor as forms of pedagogy, education as the "contact of peoples" was operationalized within the context of plantation labor for profit and land accumulation. The chapters in this book have demonstrated these aspects of teaching slavery and settlement across the geographies of the post-emancipation South, Indian Country and the imaginaries of US Western expansion, the islands of the Pacific, and back across the Atlantic to locations in Africa such as Liberia, South Africa, and the colonies of the Congo and the Gold Coast. This movement of plantation pedagogy across currents of colonialism has contributed to the dispossession of Native peoples, to anti-decolonial politics in Africa, and to US imperialism. Plantation pedagogies have produced a varied set of technologies that have circulated across these geographies and merged and shifted as they moved in these currents, expanding their use across spatial and temporal locations. These technologies included the use of the cottage as a spatial form of teaching, teacher training as a mode of settler expansion, and the linked intimacies of the school and modes of scientific farming.

This set of arguments has moved in uneven and circular patterns towards a critique of learning by doing, which is threaded throughout the creation and circulation of plantation pedagogy and its various technologies. My critique of learning by doing has three main components.

First, the learning outcomes of pedagogy are always contingent and subject to resistance, co-optation, and other forms of rebellion, and this includes plantation pedagogy. Students resist enacting what they are supposed to learn and find other ways to engage in learning and study. Ideological ideas can be transmitted through pedagogy but also can be rejected or repurposed. Scholars of education have documented this over and over, from the way Black folks used segregated schools for their own ends to Indigenous children's resistance to boarding schools.[29] However, just because the learning-based outcomes of pedagogy are contingent does not mean that pedagogy does not have material outcomes that can be reproduced regardless of whether pedagogy does what it says it does. In many ways, the effects of plantation pedagogy on land far outlast the effects it has had on people.

Second, learning by doing and "educating for life" should be viewed as suspect when done in institutions of education funded or regulated by the state. The first reason to be suspect of learning by doing is because of the way it reinforces the status quo, which in the United States, is wrapped up in colonialism and antiblackness. Learning in preparation for life reifies current social structures and disavows other futurities that center Black and

Indigenous well-being. Additionally, educating by doing often centers "solving problems," whether it be learning to build something for a new purpose or solving the race problem in the South, as Booker T. Washington described his work at Tuskegee. In this way, learning by doing is deeply linked to ideologies of educational research that propose that with the right pedagogy, the right way of "doing" something, the problems of the educational system can be fixed and can fix society.

Third, plantation pedagogies have plantation futures. I view plantation futures not only as the prison industrial complex or the ghetto, as described by Katherine McKittrick, but in schools where students are told to wear uniforms to look professional, are told financial literacy can solve poverty, or are inculcated into the romantic narrative of education and the ideals of property ownership and work.[30] These plantation futures include John Dewey's laboratory school and ideologies of progressive education, which have deeply influenced present-day schools as well as aspects of critical pedagogy. While there is a broad consensus that progressive education is part of the project of critical education, innovative scholars have made the argument that this form of pedagogy can have effects opposite to their intention in terms of inspiring students to fight for social change. Progressive education based on constructivist educational ideologies can also have material effects on workers, such as teachers who become displaced by educational researchers considered experts in their fields.[31] These plantation futures also extend to educational intervention programs—for example, when STEM education is framed in relation to the historical narrative of the Tuskegee moveable school or when the conservative backlash against critical race theory utilizes the language of education as preparation for life as part of its justification.[32]

As I have noted throughout this book, because I am a scholar of education, when I present my critiques of educational systems, I am always asked, "So, then what do we do?" Therefore, I will end with a question: If education is not in preparation for life, what is education for? Or maybe, more precisely, is there an education outside of the concept of preparation for life? What life is imagined when education prepares students for it? Further still, what if what is needed is not to reorder education but to reorder life? Many radical scholars of education have suggested ways other forms of education may look, such as Eli Meyerhoff's theorization of modes of study, Jarvis R. Givens's fugitive pedagogy, Leanne Betasamosake Simpson's landed pedagogy, or Moton and Harney's concept of Black study. I do not know that there is one answer or that the answer is best shared in academic forums, yet I know that work that questions foundational assumptions about education is imperative to working towards Indigenous and Black futures.

While I stand firm in my refusal to give answers and, in fact, see that refusal as a generative and ethical choice, one thing I am sure of is that pedagogy is not an answer in and of itself. Changing forms of pedagogy does not change the material ways that slavery and settlement are woven into educational systems even if it might do other things, like challenge antiblack and colonial epistemologies. Despite the ways pedagogy can be used to interrogate forms of knowledge, pedagogy on its own cannot dismantle plantation futures nor decolonize as both are material as much as epistemological projects. Thus, if the framing of slavery as education requires abolition and the framing of settlement as education requires a non-metaphorical decolonization, then refusal to solve educational problems requires a politic of abolition/decolonization that refuses schooling as a project that can accomplish these goals. As the project of abolitionist university studies notes, abolition indexes both the end of slavery but also the destruction of schools that have been built upon slavery.

This is not to say that schooling is not a site of political engagement or one that should be abandoned for projects of thought that do not engage in the material world.[33] Instead, it is a plea to be honest with ourselves about what interventions in schools can and cannot do. As my friend Theresa Burruel Stone has noted, our project as educators is what we do while schools exist in the form they do now, knowing that this form is part and parcel of the violence of settlement and slavery and must be ended. As Juliet R. Kunkel has shown me, maybe our role in institutions of learning is not about changing them or decolonizing them but about scavenging in their wreckage.[34] As la paperson's work explores, we are cyborgs already caught up in the machinery of settler colonial schools, but we are disloyal to them and looking for opportunities for sabotage. Ultimately, in thinking about education and its place in abolition/decolonization, I am left with a final observation rather than an answer: education is directly related to the creation of space and the transformation of land and people. Therefore, a politicized response to plantation pedagogy cannot only counter the transformation of people and the way they think about and engage in the world but must engage with the materiality of space and land in projects that seek to center Black and Indigenous futures.

I end with gratitude to the many scholars who have come before me who have been engaging in the dialogue between Black and Indigenous studies and a call for continued engagement, particularly around the field of education. I do not offer the work of this book to create rifts and pit Black and Indigenous communities against each other but to demonstrate the necessity of recognizing our interrelations. Kelly Limes Taylor states: "Shared conversations about decolonization and abolition likely require that Black and Native peoples first establish which stories about ourselves, each other, and the world around us are true for us, and true for the world we want to see."[35] I have told a story about educational history. I feel a truth in it. I hope this can be a baseline for further conversations.

ACKNOWLEDGMENTS

I wrote this book as a California Indian out of place on Piscataway land and former plantation land and am therefore deeply grateful for the many scholars, friends, and colleagues as well as my loving family that have supported me in my writing from this sense of displacement.

To the many people who read and commented on the book manuscript in whole or in part, thank you for the deep attention and care you gave to my work: Joy Esboldt, Leah Faw, Jarvis R. Givens, C. Darius Gordon, Daniel Marcus Green, Eva Hageman, Talia Leibovitz, Dinorah Sanchez Loza, David Antonio Maldonado, Mahasan Offut-Chaney, Daniel Perlstein, Frankie Ramos, Rachel Roberson, M. R. Sauter, Alyse Schneider, Theresa Burruel Stone, and Rachel Williams. Thank you to the many folks who spent time reading my earlier dissertation work, including Susanna Castro, Omar Davila Jr., Vianney Gavilanes, Nathan Gong, Derrika Hunt, Gabriela Borge Janetti, Patricia Baquedano López, Franklin Mejia, Sara Chase Merrick, and Maryam Moeini Meybodi. Thank you to Michele Frazier and Laura J. Rosenthal from the UMD Faculty Affairs office for your work facilitating faculty writing groups and to Jessica Enoch from the UMD ADVANCE program for putting together the summer writing group facilitated by the lovely Beth Goodbe. Particular thanks to my writing partners, Theresa Burruel Stone for your many months of meeting over Zoom to share writing and give generous comments, and Chad Infante for spending endless Fridays eating almond based pastries at Vigilante Coffee while writing together and reading each other's work. Thank you to all of the employees of the College Park We Work office, where a great deal of this book was physically written, especially to Angela and Bethany. Deep love and thanks to Juliet R. Kunkel for the immense time she spent reading every single chapter I wrote, her incisive commentary, grammatical editing prowess, and friendship. I feel deeply privileged to have colleagues like Sara E. K. Fong and Khalil Anthony Johnson Jr. who also study the intersection between Black and Indigenous education who are truly outstanding scholars and interlocuters and who I also consider friends.

A great deal of thanks to the editorial team who helped will this book into existence. Thank you to Megan Pugh for your thoughtful read-throughs of my work, critical and caring commentary, and organizational prowess. Thank you to Niels Hooper for believing in this project and shepherding it through the publication process, and to Naja Pulliam Collins for your work in helping get the book prepared for production. In the production process I am grateful to Stephanie Summerhays, Nora Becker, Artemis Brod, and Hazim Abdullah-Smith. Thank you to Alejandra Dubokvscy, Mark Rifkin, and all of the anonymous reviewers who read my manuscript during the peer review process for your time and dedication and the incredibly helpful and constructive feedback you provided.

The mentorship I received has helped make me the scholar I am today and deeply contributed to this piece of scholarship. Thank you to Sandy Grande for supporting me during my Ford Post-doctoral fellowship and for organizing the book workshop at the University of Connecticut. Thank you to Nate Acebo, Jarvis R. Givens, Mishuana Goeman, Audra Simpson, and Khalil Anthony Johnson Jr. for your wonderful feedback during the UCONN book discussion event. Thank you to my mentors through the National Academy of Education/Spencer Foundation, Bryan Mckinley Jones Brayboy and Tyrone Howard. Thank you also to the many Ford Fellows who offered profound advice and support, including Koritha Mitchell and Rayshawn Ray. Thank you to my graduate school dissertation committee who initially helped me grapple with the ideas I engage in this book, Patricia Baquedano López, Daniel Perlstein, and Beth Piatote, and to the many other faculty mentors who helped shape my thinking, especially Lisa García Bedolla, Thomas Biolsi, Michael J. Dumas, Keith Feldman, Shari Huhndorf, Zeus Leonardo, David Montejano, Evelyn Nakano Glenn, Na'ilah Suad Nasir, Michael Omi and Janelle Scott.

I could not have completed this book without the help of archivists and archive employees. Thank you to Donzella Maupin and Andreese Scott at the Hampton University Archives. Thank you to Laura Zepka at the Williams College Special Collections. Thank you to Elizabeth Pooloa for helping facilitate my visit to the Hawaiian Mission Children's Society Archive even when you did not have a full-time librarian. Thank you to the staff at the Hawaii State Archives for all of your help in pulling documents and files. A deep and profound thank you to Bethany J. Antos at the Rockefeller Archive Center for facilitating my access to documents digitally during the Covid-19 pandemic.

I am deeply grateful for the many supportive students and colleagues around me. Thank you to the members of the American Studies Department at UMD for your support, care, and being amazing colleagues: Asim Ali, La Marr Jurelle Bruce, Robert Chester, Jason Farman, Perla Guerrero, Eva Hageman, Christina Hanhardt, Nancy Mirabal, Jamila Moore Pewu, Mary Corbin Sies, Psyche Williams-Forson, and Janelle Wong. Great thanks to the many other scholars and friends at UMD who have been supportive of work here including Neel Ahuja, Neda Atansoski,

Ralph Bauer, Patricia Cossard, Anahi Espindola, Andrew Fellows, Shay Hazkani, Diana Marsh, Karin Rosemblatt, Angela Stoltz, and Ruth Zambrana. I am also incredibly grateful for the amazing students I have had the privilege of engaging with and who have taught me so much, including the members of my settler colonial theory seminars: Victoria Alexander, Mateo Arango, Elisabeth Asher, Hannah Cameron, Chrystal Charity, Lydia Curliss, Caroline He, Prisma Herrera, Tori Justin, Manuel Mendez, Sam Menefee-Libey, Tapaswinee Mitra, Evelyn Nkooyooyo, Jazmin Pichardo, Eden Rivera, Gabriela Salas, Daniel Stott, Justine Suegay, and Nina Versenyi. Also, the students I have been lucky enough to mentor whose keen thinking has taught me so much, especially Lydia Curliss, Prisma Herrera, Danielle La Place, Kylee Manganiello, and Gabriela Salas. Thanks to my TA Ian Miller for doing all the grading so I could ready the book manuscript for production.

I am also grateful for the support I have received from external and internal fellowships. Thank you to the Ford Foundation, the National Academy of Education/Spencer Foundation, the College of Arts and Humanities at UMD College Park, the Independent Scholarship, Research, and Creativity Award at UMD College Park, the Student Mentoring and Research Teams Program at UC Berkeley and my wonderful research assistant Skye Fierro, the UC Berkeley Center for Race and Gender, and the Joseph A. Myers Center for Research on Native American Issues.

My family and loved ones have held me up and kept me going through the process of writing and working on this text. My partner and love Javier and my daughters Miranda and Persephone have borne the brunt of my writing schedule and been my sources of joy and rest in the midst of stress and deadlines. My mother, Cynthia Lopez, is the rock which tethers me and gives me strength. My brother Tyler Lopez makes me laugh and keeps me from taking myself too seriously. Juan Stephens will never let me live down a typo or back out of an argument whether it be about the nature of truth or politics. My sister, Jennifer McCool and my amazing nieces and nephew Emma McCool, Jessica McCool, and Keegan McCool always provide love and support even when from afar and are all brilliant in their own right. Aunt Jo, I wear the necklace you gave me and think of home when I am far away knowing your love is always with me. To all of my many grandparents, aunties, uncles, cousins, nieces, nephews, and other family members whose love I feel daily even when we are separated, your love sat with me as I wrote. To my family who have passed, especially those that passed as I worked on this project, I miss and love you and felt you with me too.

NOTES

INTRODUCTION: TEACHING SLAVERY AND SETTLEMENT

1. *The Red Man and Helper* 17, no. 31, (1902): 1. I use and capitalize the term *Black* as a political stance following Dumas, who understands it "as a self-determined name of a racialized social group that shares a specific set of histories, cultural processes, and imagined and performed kinships. Black is a synonym (however imperfect) of African American and replaces previous terms like Negro and Colored..." The terms *African American* and *Negro* are used in specific quotes or in relation to sources that use those terms. The term *former slave* is a discursive construct that is used in some moments, yet I know that slavery has an afterlife that remains present. Therefore, there is no "former" with respect to slavery in that slavery's violence still reverberates in our present. I use this as a term that references a legal codification rather than an ontological one. In contrast, I do not capitalize *white*. Some scholars have made the argument that white should be capitalized because, in capitalizing Black, we are drawing attention to the structural determinants of Blackness as a group and to a label that has the structural position of white as its converse. My non-capitalization is not a theoretical move akin to this argument, but a political stance. I capitalize Black because, in the simplest sense, it is what Black publications and many, but not all, Black scholars themselves do. White supremacist organizations make a point of capitalizing white; therefore I don't. I choose to leave the capitalization (or non-capitalization) of white, Black, and other terms used in quoted text as they are written since my choices are political rather than grammatical and therefore do not require the correction of others. Michael J. Dumas, "Against the Dark: Antiblackness in Education Policy and Discourse," *Theory Into Practice* 55, no. 1 (2016): 12; La Marr Jurelle Bruce, *How to Go Mad Without Losing Your Mind: Madness and Black Radical Creativity* (Durham, NC: Duke University Press, 2020); Eve L. Ewing, "I'm a Black Scholar Who Studies Race. Here's Why I Capitalize 'White,'" *Zora,* July 2, 2020, https://zora.medium.com/im-a-black-scholar-who-studies-race-here-s-why-i-capitalize-white-f94883aa2dd3; Kwame Anthony Appiah, "The Case for Capitalizing the *B* in Black: Black and White are Both Historically

Created Racial Identities—and Whatever Rule Applies to One Should Apply to the Other," *The Atlantic,* June 18, 2020, https://www.theatlantic.com/ideas/archive/2020/06/time-to-capitalize-blackand-white/613159/.

2. *The Red Man and Helper* 17, no. 31, (1902): 1.

3. Earl E. Thorpe, "William Hooper Councill," *Negro History Bulletin* 19, no. 4 (1956).

4. Josephine McCann Posey, *Succeeding Against Great Odds: Alcorn State University in Its Second Century* (Jackson: University Press of Mississippi, 2017); Gerald Moorehead et al., "Prairie View A&M University (Alta Vista Agricultural and Mechanical College of Texas for Colored Youth)," *Society of Architectural Historians Archipedia,* https://sah-archipedia.org/buildings/TX-01-PF1; Derrick E. White, *Blood, Sweat, and Tears: Jake Gaither, Florida A&M, and the History of Black College Football* (Chapel Hill: University of North Carolina Press, 2019).

5. I take critiques by scholars such as Jarvis R. Givens to heart that, in the context of antiblack oppression, we can understand Black complicity with white industrial education as a means to gain monetary or political influence for fugitive purpose. Yet, whether or not Councill or other Black industrial educators were enacting a fugitive educational project for Black communities, it is necessary to analyze how their actions worked within schooling systems designed by white reformers that were meant to assimilate Indigenous peoples. Jarvis R. Givens, *Fugitive Pedagogy: Carter G. Woodson and the Art of Black Teaching* (Cambridge, MA: Harvard University Press, 2021).

6. David Wallace Adams, *Education for Extinction: American Indians and the Boarding School Experience, 1875–1928* (Lawrence: University Press of Kansas, 1995).

7. Richard Henry Pratt, "The Advantage of Mingling Indians with Whites," cited in Paul Francis Prucha, *Americanizing the American Indians: Writings by the "Friends of the Indian," 1880–1900* (Cambridge, MA: Harvard University Press, 1973), 260–271. When I speak of those Indigenous to North America, Indigenous Hawaiians (Kanaka Maoli), and other Indigenous peoples globally, I will utilize the term *Indigenous peoples.* I use tribally specific phrasing whenever possible, and I use the term *Native* rather than *Native American* or *American Indian* to refer to groups collectively. I do so not out of definitional accuracy but as a political stance. The word *native* carries a variety of connotations. It has been used by settlers who oppose immigration, and it gets taken up by settlers to mean belonging to America. *Native* is also used to distinguish plants native to a region from species that have been transplanted, some of which can be invasive. I claim the word *Native* decoupled from *American* because the two are overlapping in space yet opposed in meaning. More simply, I use the term because it is often what I refer to myself as in my own head and when in the company of other Native peoples. I make no claim about the opinions of other Native peoples regarding this term, nor do I advocate its usage. I also make no claim to it being right. I use the white settler construction *Indian* when it relates

to the historical contexts in which that word was used. All the collective terms I have mentioned are in themselves imprecise and problematic since they amalgamate Indigenous peoples into a fictive pan-Indianness or globalized pan-Indigeneity. I use *Indian* in this context because schools such as Hampton were instrumental in the construction of "Indianness" as both label and identity. Additionally, boarding schools and other colonial institutions, which brought together many tribal peoples, were instrumental in creating pan-Indian organizing and constructing pan-Indian identities that are constantly in tension with the hegemonic concept of the "white man's Indian." Many of these terms often also take on legal definitions within both the US nation state and international bodies such as the United Nations. Each term is a social construct that has real effects and affects within a multitude of contexts. When quoting texts from other authors, I leave the terms and their capitalization or non-capitalization as they are written. Robert J. Berkhofer Jr., *The White Man's Indian: Images of the American Indian from Columbus to Present* (New York: Vintage Books, 1979); Paige Raibmon, *Authentic Indians: Episodes of Encounter from the Late Nineteenth-Century Northwest Coast* (Durham, NC: Duke University Press, 2005); Adams, *Education for Extinction;* K. Tsianina Lomawaima and Theresa L. McCarty, *To Remain an Indian: Lessons in Democracy from a Century of Native American Education* (New York: Columbia University Press, 2006); Robert A. Williams Jr., *The American Indian in Western Legal Thought: The Discourses of Conquest* (Oxford: Oxford University Press, 1992); United Nations General Assembly, Resolution 61/295, United Nations Declaration on the Rights of Indigenous People A/61/L.67.1 (September 13, 2007).

8. Eli Meyerhoff, *Beyond Education: Radical Studying for Another World* (Minneapolis: University of Minnesota Press, 2019).

9. Hampton is the most paradigmatic example of what scholars in abolitionist university studies have labeled the "post-slavery university." The concept of the post-slavery university has reframed the historiography of universities by understanding them in relation to capital accumulation and views the emancipation era as a key time when the university was reconfigured as forms of accumulation shifted. I also argue that it is necessary to examine the post-slavery university because a distinct form of teaching slavery without having juridical slavery was fashioned in these institutions. Abigail Boggs et al., "Abolitionist University Studies: An Invitation," *Abolition,* August 28, 2019. https://abolitionjournal.org/abolitionist-university-studies-an-invitation/.

10. Donald Spivey, *Schooling for the New Slavery: Black Industrial Education, 1868–1915* (Westport, CT: Greenwood Press, 1978).

11. William H. Watkins, *The White Architects of Black Education: Ideology and Power in America, 1865–1954* (New York: Teachers College Press, 2001); Spivey, *Schooling for the New Slavery;* James D. Anderson, *The Education of Blacks in the South, 1860–1935* (Chapel Hill: University of North Carolina Press, 1988).

12. Maenette Kapeʻahiokalani Padeken Ah Nee-Benham and Ronald H. Heck, *Culture and Educational Policy in Hawaiʻi: The Silencing of Native Voices* (Mahwah,

NJ: Lawrence Erlbaum, 1998); J. Kēhaulani Kauanui, *Paradoxes of Hawaiian Sovereignty: Land, Sex, and the Colonial Politics of State Nationalism* (Durham, NC: Duke University Press, 2018).

13. Armstrong replaced the original Hampton-area Freedman's Bureau employee, who was considered to be too much of an abolitionist. It was assumed that Armstrong, by contrast, would support the return of land to the Southern planters who had abandoned the region. Anderson, *The Education of Blacks in the South*.

14. Donal F. Lindsey, *Indians at Hampton Institute, 1877–1923* (Urbana: University of Illinois Press, 1994), 2.

15. Brenda J. Child, "The Boarding School as Metaphor," *Journal of American Indian Education* 57, no. 1 (2018).

16. Of the over seventy prisoners who were imprisoned at Fort Marion, seventeen chose to attend Hampton at Pratt's invitation. This may have been preferable to being released to BIA custody, which was what the other prisoners who might have been unclear about the parameters of release, faced. The majority of prisoners did end up returning to their homes. Diane Glancy and Rachel Gould, *Fort Marion Prisoners and the Trauma of Native Education* (Lincoln: University of Nebraska Press, 2014); Sarah Kathryn Pitcher Hayes, "The Experiment at Fort Marion: Richard Henry Pratt's Recreation of Penitential Regimes at the Old Fort and Its Influence on American Indian Education," *Journal of Florida Studies* 1, no. 7 (2018).

17. In his later writing, Pratt argued that Native students would be better trained in institutions separately from Black students so they could use whites as their civilizational model. This argument was directly related to his former work at Hampton. Richard Henry Pratt, *Battlefield and Classroom: Four Decades with the American Indian, 1867–1904* (New Haven, CT: Yale University Press, 1964), 213.

18. Adams, *Education for Extinction;* Prucha, *Americanizing the American Indian;* Roger W. Buffalohead and Paulette Fairbanks Molin, "'A Nucleus of Civilization': American Indian Families at Hampton Institute in the Late Nineteenth Century," *Journal of American Indian Education* 35, no. 3 (1996).

19. Lindsey, *Indians at Hampton Institute;* Anderson, *The Education of Blacks in the South;* Spivey, *Schooling for the New Slavery;* Watkins, *The White Architects of Black Education*.

20. Fred Washington Atkinson, *Education in the Philippine Islands* (Washington, DC: United States Bureau of Education, 1902); Anne Paulet, "To Change the World: The Use of American Indian Education in the Philippines," *History of Education Quarterly* 47, no. 2 (2007).

21. Peter James Tarr, *The Education of the Thomasites: American School Teachers in Philippine Colonial Society, 1901–1913* (Ithaca, NY: Cornell University, 2006); Dinah Roma-Sianturi, "'Pedagogic Invasion': The Thomasites in Occupied Philippines," *Kritika Kultura* 12 (2009).

22. Barrows has been interpreted by historians as diverging from Atkinson's ideologies of schooling, yet materially his programs incorporated a great deal of the industrial education that Atkinson supported. Chester L. Hunt, "Education and

Economic Development in the Early American Period in the Philippines," *Philippine Studies* 36, no. 3 (1988); Kenton J. Clymer, "Humanitarian Imperialism: David Prescott Barrows and the White Man's Burden in the Philippines," *Pacific Historical Review* 45, no. 4 (1976); Paulet, "To Change the World."

23. Christine Whyte, "Between Empire and Colony: American Imperialism and Pan-African Colonialism in Liberia, 1810–2003," *National Identities* 18, no. 1 (2016); Barbara Lüthi, Francesca Falk, and Patricia Purtschert, "Colonialism without Colonies: Examining Blank Spaces in Colonial Studies," *National Identities* 18, no. 1 (2016); Magdalene S. David, "The Love of Liberty Brought Us Here (an Analysis of the Development of the Settler State in 19th Century Liberia)," *Review of African Political Economy* 11, no. 31 (1984).

24. Pierre Bourdieu and Jean-Claude Passeron, *Reproduction in Education, Society and Culture,* trans. Richard Nice (London: Sage, 1990); Samuel Bowles and Herbert Gintis, *Schooling in Capitalist America: Educational Reform and the Contradictions of Economic Life* (Chicago: Haymarket Books, 1976); Michelle Alexander, *The New Jim Crow: Mass Incarceration in the Age of Colorblindness* (New York: The New York Press, 2010); Jean Anyon, *Ghetto Schooling: A Political Economy of Urban Educational Reform* (New York: Teachers College Press, 1997); Sandy Grande, *Red Pedagogy: Native American Social and Political Thought* (Lanham, MD: Rowman and Littlefield Publishers Inc., 2004); John Willinsky, *Learning to Divide the World: Education at Empire's End* (Minneapolis: University of Minnesota Press, 1998); K. Tsianina Lomawaima, "The Unnatural History of American Indian Education" in *Next Steps: Research and Practice to Advance Indian Education,* eds. Karen Gayton Swisher and John W. Tippeconnic III (Charleston, WV: Eric Clearinghouse on Rural Education and Small Schools, 1999); Bryan McKinley Jones Brayboy, "Toward a Tribal Critical Race Theory in Education," *The Urban Review* 37, no. 5 (2005); Givens, *Fugitive Pedagogy;* Heather Andrea Williams, *Self-Taught: African American Education in Slavery and Freedom* (Chapel Hill: University of North Carolina Press, 2009); Joyce E. Williams and Ron Ladd, "On the Relevance of Education for Black Liberation," *The Journal of Negro Education* 47, no. 3 (1978); Christopher M. Span and James D. Anderson, "The Quest for 'Book Learning': African American Education in Slavery and Freedom," in *A Companion to African American History,* ed. Alton Hornsby Jr. (Malden, MA: Blackwell, 2005); Noelani Goodyear-Ka'opua, *The Seeds We Planted: Portraits of a Native Hawaiian Charter School* (Minneapolis: University of Minnesota Press, 2013); Matthew Wildcat et al., "Learning from the Land: Indigenous Land Based Pedagogy and Decolonization," *Decolonization: Indigeneity, Education & Society* 3, no. 3 (2014); Jeff Corntassel and Tiffanie Hardbarger, "Educate to Perpetuate: Land-Based Pedagogies and Community Resurgence," *International Review of Education* 65, no. 1 (2019).

25. For two well-known examples, see Paolo Freire, *Pedagogy of the Oppressed,* trans. Maya Bergman Ramos (New York: Continuum, 1996) and Marie Battiste, *Decolonizing Education: Nourishing the Learning Spirit* (Vancouver: University of British Columbia Press, 2017).

26. I draw the term *symbolic violence* from Bourdieu and Passeron, *Reproduction in Education*.

27. Anderson, *The Education of Blacks in the South*.

28. Haim Eshach, "Bridging In-School and Out-of-School Learning: Formal, Non-Formal, and Informal Education," *Journal of Science Education and Technology* 16, no. 2 (2007); Meyerhoff, *Beyond Education*.

29. I italicize *framed* here to indicate that learning is not always an outcome of education and in fact some students actively resist learning things that are meant to be taught.

30. Freire, *Pedagogy of the Oppressed;* Henry Giroux, *On Critical Pedagogy* (New York: Bloomsbury, 2011).

31. Michael W. Apple, *Can Education Change Society?* (New York: Routledge, 2012); David F. Labaree, "The Winning Ways of a Losing Strategy: Educationalizing Social Problems in the United States," *Educational Theory* 58, no. 4 (2008).

32. Bayley J. Marquez, Jarvis R. Givens, and Khalil Anthony Johnson Jr., "Black and Indigenous Pedagogy and Politics" (presentation, University of Connecticut, Storrs, CT, April 14, 2022).

33. Antonio Gramsci, *Prison Notebooks*, ed. and trans. Joseph Buttigieg, vol. 2 (New York: Columbia University Press, 2011); Michel Foucault, *Power/Knowledge: Selected Interviews and Other Writings, 1972–1977*, ed. Colin Gordon, trans. Colin Gordon et al. (New York: Pantheon Books, 1980).

34. In order to understand power in relation to Western thought, I draw from Hobbes, for whom power was a "present means, to obtain some future apparent good," and from Nietzsche's concept of the "will to power," which denotes the domination of both other people and one's environment. Thomas Hobbes, *Leviathan: Or the Matter, Forme, and Power of a Commonwealth, Ecclesiastical and Civil,* ed. A. R. Waller (Cambridge: University Press, 1904); Friedrich Nietzsche, *The Will to Power,* ed. Walter Kaufmann, trans. Walter Kaufmann and R. J. Hollingdale (New York: Vintage Books, 1967).

35. Lomawaima, "The Unnatural History of American Indian Education"; Francis Paul Prucha, *American Indian Policy in Crisis: Christian Reformers and the Indian, 1865–1900* (Norman: University of Oklahoma Press, 1976).

36. Ulrich Bonnell Phillips had connections to the Rockefeller-funded General Education Board, which funded both domestic and international educational programs that drew from the Hampton model of industrial schooling. Ulrich Bonnell Phillips, *Life and Labor in the Old South* (Columbia: University of South Carolina Press, 2007).

37. Donald Warren, "Slavery as an American Educational Institution: Historiographical Inquiries," *Journal of Thought* 40, no. 4 (2005): 46, citing Phillips, *Life and Labor in the Old South,* 196–201.

38. Saidiya V. Hartman, *Scenes of Subjection: Terror, Slavery, and Self-Making in Nineteenth-Century America* (Oxford: Oxford University Press, 1997).

39. Patrick Wolfe, "Settler Colonialism and the Elimination of the Native," *Journal of Genocide Research* 8, no. 4 (2006); Patrick Wolfe, *Settler Colonialism and*

the *Transformation of Anthropology: The Politics and Poetics of an Ethnographic Event* (London, New York: Cassell, 1999); Lorenzo Veracini, *Settler Colonialism: A Theoretical Outline* (Houndmills, UK: Palgrave Macmillan, 2010); Lorenzo Veracini, "Introducing: Settler Colonial Studies," *Settler Colonial Studies* 1, no. 1 (2011); Lorenzo Veracini, "'Settler Colonialism': Career of a Concept," *The Journal of Imperial and Commonwealth History* 41, no. 2 (2013).

40. Wolfe, "Settler Colonialism and the Elimination of the Native"; Veracini, "Settler Colonialism."

41. From *Annual Report of the Commissioner of Indian Affairs to the Secretary of the Interior,* dated 1890 (Washington, DC: Government Printing Office, 1824–present (1877–1913)), cited in Lindsey, *Indians at Hampton Institute, 1877–1923,* 23.

42. Pratt, *Battlefield and Classroom.*

43. Lomawaima and McCarty, *To Remain an Indian;* Grande, *Red Pedagogy;* Lomawaima, "The Unnatural History of American Indian Education"; Brayboy, "Toward a Tribal Critical Race Theory in Education."

44. Iyko Day, "Being or Nothingness: Indigeneity, Antiblackness, and Settler Colonial Critique," *Critical Ethnic Studies* 1, no. 2 (2015); Siddhant Issar, "Theorising 'Racial/Colonial Primitive Accumulation': Settler Colonialism, Slavery and Racial Capitalism," *Race & Class* 63, no. 1 (2021); Manu Karuka, *Empire's Tracks: Indigenous Nations, Chinese Workers, and the Transcontinental Railroad* (Berkeley: University of California Press, 2019).

45. In addition to the scholarship I cite in this section, some examples might include: Vine Deloria Jr., "The Red and The Black," in *Custer Died for your Sins: An Indian Manifesto* (Norman: University of Oklahoma Press, 1969); Theodore Walker Jr., "The Black and the Red: Responding to Sioux and Other Native American Instructions on Red-Black Solidarity," *Journal of Religious Thought* 55, no. 2/1 (1999); Frank B. Wilderson III, *Red, White and Black: Cinema and the Structure of US Antagonisms* (Durham, NC: Duke University Press, 2010); Jared Sexton, "The Vel of Slavery: Tracking the Figure of the Unsovereign," *Critical Sociology* 42, no. 4–5 (2016); Zainab Amadahy and Bonita Lawrence, "Indigenous Peoples and Black People in Canada: Settlers or Allies?" in *Breaching the Colonial Contract: Anti-Colonialism in the US and Canada,* ed. Arlo Kempf (Dordrecht, NL: Springer, 2009).

46. Kyle T. Mays, *An Afro-Indigenous History of the United States* (New York: Beacon Press, 2021); Claudio Saunt, *Black, White, and Indian: Race and the Unmaking of an American Family* (Oxford: Oxford University Press, 2005); Khalil Anthony Johnson Jr., "'Recruited to Teach the Indians': An African American Genealogy of Navajo Nation Boarding Schools," *Journal of American Indian Education* 57, no. 1 (2018); K. Keith Richard, "Unwelcome Settlers: Black and Mulatto Oregon Pioneers," *Oregon Historical Quarterly* 84, no. 1 (1983); David A. Chang, *The Color of the Land: Race, Nation, and the Politics of Landownership in Oklahoma, 1832–1929* (Chapel Hill: University of North Carolina Press, 2010); George Junne et al., "Dearfield, Colorado: Black farming Success in the Jim Crow Era," in *Enduring Legacies: Ethnic Histories and Cultures of Colorado,* ed. Arturo J. Aldama, Elisa Facio, and Daryl Maeda (Denver: University Press of Colorado, 2011); Anthony W. Wood,

Black Montana: Settler Colonialism and the Erosion of the Racial Frontier, 1877–1930 (Omaha: University of Nebraska Press, 2021); Sexton, "The Vel of Slavery"; Wilderson III, "Red, White and Black."

47. Mark Rifkin, *Fictions of Land and Flesh: Blackness, Indigeneity, Speculation* (Durham, NC: Duke University Press, 2019).

48. Rifkin, *Fictions of Land and Flesh*, 16.

49. Rifkin, *Fictions of Land and Flesh*, 28–29.

50. Rifkin, *Fictions of Land and Flesh*, 30.

51. Joyce Pualani Warren, "Reading Bodies, Writing Blackness: Anti-/Blackness and Nineteenth-Century Kanaka Maoli Literary Nationalism," *American Indian Culture and Research Journal* 43, no. 2 (2019); Joyce Pualani Warren et al., "Genealogizing Pō: The Relational Possibilities of Blackness in the Pacific," *Ethnic Studies Review* 44, no. 3 (2021).

52. Rifkin, *Fictions of Land and Flesh*, 27.

53. *As We Have Always Done: Indigenous Freedom Through Radical Resistance* (Minneapolis: University of Minnesota Press, 2017). Rifkin would disagree with Simpson's conceptualization of Indigenous resurgence as flight since, in his discussion of marronage, he argues that the maroon matrix risks reinforcing narratives of Indigenous replacement. Rifkin, *Fictions of Land and Flesh*.

54. Simpson, *As We Have Always Done*, 17, 212.

55. Simpson, *As We Have Always Done*, 215–218, 228–229.

56. Eve Tuck, Allison Guess, and Hannah Sultan, "Not Nowhere: Collaborating on Selfsame Land," *Decolonization: Indigeneity, Education & Society* 26 (June 2014).

57. "Introduction: Crossing Waters, Crossing Worlds," in *Crossing Waters, Crossing Worlds: The African Diaspora in Indian Country*, ed. Tiya Miles and Sharon Patricia Holland (Durham, NC: Duke University Press, 2006), 2–3.

58. Chang, *The Color of Land*.

59. Daniel Heath Justice and Jean M. O'Brien, eds., *Allotment Stories: Indigenous Land Relations Under Settler Siege* (Minneapolis: University of Minnesota Press, 2022), xi.

60. Nick Estes, "The World of Paper, Restoring Relations, and the Lower Brule Sioux Tribe," in *Allotment Stories: Indigenous Land Relations Under Settler Siege*, eds. Daniel Heath Justice and Jean M. O'Brien (Minneapolis: University of Minnesota Press, 2022), 48.

61. Tiffany Lethabo King, *The Black Shoals: Offshore Formations of Black and Native Studies* (Durham, NC: Duke University Press, 2019), 4.

62. Estes, "The World of Paper"; Joseph M. Pierce, "Allotment Speculation: The Emergence of Land Memory," in Allotment *Stories: Indigenous Land Relations Under Settler Siege,* ed. Daniel Heath Justice and Jean M. O'Brien (Minneapolis: University of Minnesota Press, 2022).

63. Joanne Barker, "Confluence: Water as an Analytic of Indigenous Feminisms," *American Indian Culture and Research Journal* 43, no. 3 (2019).

64. Zoe Todd, "Fish, Kin and Hope: Tending to Water Violations in Amiskwaciwâskahikan and Treaty Six Territory," *Afterall: A Journal of Art, Context and Enquiry* 43, no. 1 (2017); Kim TallBear, "An Indigenous Reflection on Working Beyond the Human/Not Human," *GLQ: A Journal of Lesbian and Gay Studies* 21, no. 2–3 (2015).

65. Joanne Barker, "Confluence: Water as an Analytic of Indigenous Feminisms," 6.

66. Barker, "Confluence," 13.

67. Christine Taitano DeLisle and Vicente M. Diaz, "Itinerant Indigeneities: Navigating Guahan's Treacherous Roads through CHamoru Feminist Pathways," in *Allotment Stories: Indigenous Land Relations Under Settler Siege,* ed. Daniel Heath Justice and Jean M. O'Brien (Minneapolis: University of Minnesota Press, 2022), 150–152.

68. Paul Lyons and Ty P. Kāwika Tengan, "Introduction: Pacific Currents," *American Quarterly* 67, no. 3 (2015): 546.

69. Justice and O'Brien, *Allotment Stories,* 68, citing Jodi A. Byrd et al., "Predatory Value: Economies of Dispossession and Disturbed Relationalities," *Social Text* 36, no. 2 (2018).

70. Curtin notes how the location of plantations in the Caribbean was influenced by currents. Philip D. Curtin, *The Rise and Fall of the Plantation Complex: Essays in Atlantic History* (Cambridge: Cambridge University Press, 1998).

71. Deloria, "The Red and The Black"; Kim Cary Warren, *The Quest for Citizenship: African American and Native American Education in Kansas, 1880–1935* (Chapel Hill: University of North Carolina Press, 2010); Fikile Nxumalo, "Decolonial Water Pedagogies: Invitations to Black, Indigenous, and Black-Indigenous WorldMaking," *Occasional Paper Series* 2021, no. 45 (2021): 6; Meseret Hailu and Amanda Tachine, "Black and Indigenous Theoretical Considerations for Higher Education Sustainability," *Journal of Comparative & International Higher Education* 13, (Summer 2021); George Sefa Dei, "Indigenous Anti-Colonial Knowledge as 'Heritage Knowledge' for Promoting Black/African Education in Diasporic Contexts," *Decolonization: Indigeneity, Education & Society* 1, no. 1 (2012); Django Paris, "Culturally Sustaining Pedagogies in the Project of Black and Indigenous Solidarities on Turtle Island," in *Education in Movement Spaces: Standing Rock to the Chicago Freedom Square Movement,* ed. Alayna Eagle Shield et al. (New York: Routledge, 2020).

72. Robert Warrior, "Lone Wolf and DuBois for a New Century: Intersections of Native American and African American Literatures," in *Crossing Waters, Crossing Worlds: The African Diaspora in Indian Country,* ed. Tiya Miles and Sharon Patricia Holland (Durham, NC: Duke University Press, 2006), 185.

73. See, for example, Samuel Chapman Armstrong, *Education for Life* (Hampton, VA: Press of the Hampton Normal and Agricultural Institute, 1913), 45.

74. H. I. Fontellio-Nanton, *Indian Education at Hampton Institute: 1878–1923,* Indian Education Collection, Hampton University Archives, 4.

75. Sophie Rudolph makes a similar argument in *Unsettling the Gap: Race, Politics and Indigenous Education* (New York: Peter Lang, 2019).

76. Anderson, *The Education of Blacks in the South;* Patrick Wolfe, "Land, Labor, and Difference: Elementary Structures of Race," *The American Historical Review* 106, no. 3 (2001); Wolfe, "Settler Colonialism and the Elimination of the Native."

77. Ontology, which is used as a synonym of metaphysics and is defined as the study of "being," is of particular importance to those scholars in Black studies who have argued that the construction of the category *human* and of the concept of being itself excludes Blackness. Thus, ontology is centered in Black studies because asserting Black being or pointing out the construction of Black non-being have been central to Black political projects such as Black Lives Matter but also to the history of the Black diaspora. To name only a few scholars engaged in this work: Hortense J. Spillers, "Mama's Baby, Papa's Maybe: An American Grammar Book," *Diacritics* 17, no. 2 (1987); Calvin L. Warren, *Ontological Terror: Blackness, Nihilism, and Emancipation* (Durham, NC: Duke University Press, 2018); Zakiyyah Iman Jackson, *Becoming Human: Matter and Meaning in an Antiblack World* (New York: New York University Press, 2020); Sylvia Wynter, "Unsettling the Coloniality of Being/Power/Truth/Freedom: Towards the Human, After Man, its Overrepresentation—An Argument," *CR: The New Centennial Review* 3, no. 3 (2003); *Britannica,* s.v. "Ontology," accessed June 28, 2022, https://www.britannica.com/topic/ontology-metaphysics.

78. Audra Simpson, "On Ethnographic Refusal: Indigeneity, 'Voice' and Colonial Citizenship," *Junctures: The Journal for Thematic Dialogue* 9 (2007): 74–77.

79. Simpson, "On Ethnographic Refusal," 68.

80. Simpson gives a good example of this duality when she critiques the double consciousness articulations of post-colonial studies: "I am me, I am what you think I am and I am who this person to the right of me thinks I am and you are all full of shit and then maybe I will tell you to your face." Simpson, "On Ethnographic Refusal," 74.

81. Michel-Rolph Trouillot, *Silencing the Past: Power and the Production of History* (Boston: Beacon Press, 1995).

82. Linda Tuhiwai Smith, *Decolonizing Methodologies: Research and Indigenous Peoples* (London: Zed Books, 1999); Kathleen Washburn, "New Indians and Indigenous Archives," *PMLA* 127, no. 2 (2012); Katherine McKittrick, "Mathematics of Black Life," *The Black Scholar* 44, no. 2 (2014); Jamila J. Ghaddar, "The Spectre in the Archive: Truth, Reconciliation, and Indigenous Archival Memory," *Archivaria* 82, no. 1 (2016); Ashley Glassburn Falzetti, "Archival Absence: The Burden of History," *Settler Colonial Studies* 5, no. 2 (2015).

83. Nicole M. Brown et al., "Mechanized Margin to Digitized Center: Black Feminism's Contributions to Combatting Erasure within the Digital Humanities," *International Journal of Humanities and Arts Computing* 10, no. 1 (2016); William J. Bauer Jr., *California Through Native Eyes: Reclaiming History* (Seattle: University of Washington Press, 2016); Roberta Price Gardner et al. "(Re) Membering in the

Pedagogical Work of Black and Brown Teachers: Reclaiming Stories as Culturally Sustaining Practice," *Urban Education* 55, no. 6 (2020).

84. Saidiya Hartman, "A Note on Method," in *Wayward Lives, Beautiful Experiments: Intimate Histories of Riotous Black Girls, Troublesome Women, and Queer Radicals* (New York: W. W. Norton & Company, 2019).

85. Eve Tuck and K. Wayne Yang, "R-Words: Refusing Research," in *Humanizing Research: Decolonizing Qualitative Inquiry for Youth and Communities,* ed. Django Paris and Maisha T. Winn (Thousand Oaks, CA: Sage, 2013), 223. Gayatri Chakravorty Spivak, "Can the Subaltern Speak?" in *Marxism and Interpretation of Culture,* ed. Cary Nelson and Lawrence Grossberg (Basingstoke, UK: Macmillan Education, 1988).

86. Tuck and Yang, "R-Words: Refusing Research," 223.

87. Tuck and Yang, "R-Words: Refusing Research," 237.

88. Simpson, "On Ethnographic Refusal," 69.

89. Anderson, *The Education of Blacks in the South;* Carter G. Woodson, *The Mis-education of the Negro* (Trenton, NJ: Africa World Press, 1933).

90. Vanessa Siddle Walker, *Their Highest Potential: An African American School Community in the Segregated South* (Chapel Hill: University of North Carolina Press, 1996); Vanessa Siddle Walker, "Organized Resistance and Black Educators' Quest for School Equality, 1878–1938," *Teachers College Record* 107, no. 3 (2005); Williams, *Self-Taught.*

91. Brenda J. Child, *Boarding School Seasons: American Indian Families, 1900–1940* (Lincoln: University of Nebraska Press, 2000); K. Tsianina Lomawaima, *They Called it Prairie Light: The Story of the Chilocco Indian School* (Lincoln: University of Nebraska Press, 1994).

92. I am indebted to La Marr Jurelle Bruce's theorization of the Afromantic for this discussion.

93. Givens, *Fugitive Pedagogy.*

94. Carole McGranahan, "Theorizing Refusal: An Introduction," *Cultural Anthropology* 31, no. 3 (2016).

95. Eve Tuck and K. Wayne Yang, "Decolonization Is Not a Metaphor," *Decolonization: Indigeneity, Education & Society* 1, no. 1 (2012).

96. Examples of such work include Givens, *Fugitive Pedagogy;* Bruce, *How to Go Mad Without Losing Your Mind;* Sara Chase, "Na: tinixwe Education as a Site for (Re)newed Words and Worlds," (PhD diss., University of California, Berkeley, 2020).

97. I draw my thoughts here from conversations with La Marr Jurelle Bruce about his upcoming work on the Afromantic and from personal conversations with Patrick Johnson on Black joy.

98. I am inspired in this line of thinking by the practice of Michael J. Dumas who often answered questions at public talks with this assertion.

99. Smith, *Decolonizing Methodologies,* 3.

100. Mark Rifkin, *Beyond Settler Time: Temporal Sovereignty and Indigenous Self-Determination* (Durham, NC: Duke University Press, 2017).

1. PLANTATION PEDAGOGY, EDUCATIVE SPACE, AND CURRENTS OF COLONIALISM

1. Booker T. Washington, *My Larger Education: Being Chapters From my Experience* (Garden City, NY: Doubleday, Page, 1911).
2. Booker T. Washington, *Up From Slavery: An Autobiography* (New York: A. L. Burt, 1901), 53.
3. Washington, *Up From Slavery*, 44.
4. Washington, *Up From Slavery*, 52.
5. Lyon G. Tyler, *History of Hampton and Elizabeth City County, Virginia* (Hampton, VA: The Board of Supervisors of Elizabeth City County, 1922). http://lawlibrary.wm.edu/wythepedia/images/4/48/TylerHistoryOfHampton1922.pdf
6. Tyler, *History of Hampton*, 22. This text notes that "Benjamin Syms, of Virginia, left the first legacy by a resident of the American Plantation for the promotion of education. By his will, made February 12, 1634–'35, he gave two hundred acres on the Puquosin, a small river which enters the Chesapeake Bay, a mile or less below the mouth of York River, with the milk and increase of eight cows, for the education and instruction of the children of the adjoining parishes of Elizabeth City and Kiquotan, 'from Mary's Mount downward to the Poquosin river.'" The money arising from the first increase of the cattle was to be used to build a school house, and the profits from the subsequent sales of cattle to support the teacher." This would become the Syms-Eaton School, touted as America's first free school.
7. In addition to viewing the plantation as educational, settlers viewed the establishment of churches as educational for Indigenous peoples, as was the first church established at Kecoughtan by English settlers. Tyler, *History of Hampton*.
8. Craig Steven Wilder, *Ebony and Ivy: Race, Slavery, and the Troubled History of America's Universities* (New York: Bloomsbury, 2014); Leslie Maria Harris, James T. Campbell, and Alfred L. Brophy, eds., *Slavery and the University: Histories and Legacies* (Athens: University of Georgia Press, 2019); Sharon Stein, "Universities, Slavery, and the Unthought of Anti-Blackness," *Cultural Dynamics* 28, no. 2 (2016); Alfred L. Brophy, "Forum on Slavery and Universities: Introduction," *Slavery & Abolition* 39, no. 2 (2018). Other projects that take up this work include the Universities Studying Slavery Consortium and the Lemon Project at the College of William and Mary, first introduced to me by Vineeta Singh; Billy Hawkins, *The New Plantation: Black Athletes, College Sports, and Predominantly White NCAA Institutions* (New York: Palgrave Macmillan, 2013); Bianca C. Williams, Dian D. Squire, and Frank A. Tuitt, eds., *Plantation Politics and Campus Rebellions: Power, Diversity, and the Emancipatory Struggle in Higher Education* (New York: SUNY Press, 2021); T. Elon Dancy, Kirsten T. Edwards, and James Earl Davis, "Historically White Universities and Plantation Politics: Anti-Blackness and Higher Education in the Black Lives Matter Era," *Urban Education* 53, no. 2 (2018); Lisa Hinrichsen, "'A Curious Study': 'The Autobiography of an Ex-Coloured Man', Pedagogy, and the Post-Plantation Imagination," *African American Review* 48, no. 1/2 (2015); Laurette Bristol, "Practicing in Betwixt Oppression and Subversion: Plantation Pedagogy as

a Legacy of Plantation Economy in Trinidad and Tobago," *Power and Education* 2, no. 2 (2010): 167.

9. Carter G. Woodson, *The Education of the Negro Prior to 1861: A History of the Education of the Colored People of the United States from the Beginning of Slavery to the Civil War* (Washington, DC: Association for the Study of Negro Life History, 1919), 1.

10. Tyler, *History of Hampton*.

11. Tyler, *History of Hampton*, 52. The term "contraband of war" originated during negotiations made in the Hampton area.

12. Donal F. Lindsey, *Indians at Hampton Institute, 1877–1923* (Urbana: University of Illinois Press, 1994), 7.

13. The little Scotland Plantation was owned by William E. Woods and was bought by George Whipple of the American Missionary Association for the Hampton Campus. The main house on campus was built where the original plantation house once stood. Edward H. Bonekemper III, "Negro Ownership of Real Property in Hampton and Elizabeth City County, Virginia, 1860–1870," *The Journal of Negro History* 55, no. 3 (1970).

14. For another discussion of this post-emancipation moment, see Abigail Boggs et al., "Abolitionist University Studies: An Invitation," *Abolition*, August 28, 2019. https://abolitionjournal.org/abolitionist-university-studies-an-invitation/.

15. Eve Tuck, Allison Guess, and Hannah Sultan, "Not Nowhere: Collaborating on Selfsame Land," *Decolonization: Indigeneity, Education & Society* 26, (June 2014).

16. This grammatical approach to examining the plantation is inspired by the work of Christina Sharpe's "anagrammatical" and Spiller's "American Grammar" as well as my own engagement with theories of racial grammar. Christina Sharpe, *In the Wake: On Blackness and Being* (Durham, NC: Duke University Press, 2016); Hortense J. Spillers, "Mama's Baby, Papa's Maybe: An American Grammar Book," *Diacritics* 17, no. 2 (1987); Bayley J. Marquez, "'No Women Involved': Settler Colonial Racial Grammars in Black and Indigenous Education," *Feminist Formations* 33, no. 3 (2021).

17. *Oxford English and Spanish Dictionary*, s.v. "Plantation," https://www.lexico.com/en/definition/plantation.

18. *Merriam Webster*, s.v. "Plantation," https://www.merriam-webster.com/dictionary/plantation.

19. *Dictionary.com*, s.v. "Plantation," https://www.dictionary.com/browse/plantation; *Merriam Webster*, s.v. "Plantation," https://www.merriam-webster.com/dictionary/plantation.

20. Other definitions and descriptions Baker offers include "colonization"; "to send prisoners, etc. to the plantation i.e. to penal service, or indentured labour in the colonies"; a "method of treating criminals of all kinds much in favour during the 17th century"; "plantation-Negro"; "plantation-slave." Houston A. Baker Jr., *Turning South Again: Re-thinking Modernism/Re-reading Booker T* (Durham, NC: Duke University Press, 2001), 84.

21. Tiffany J. King [Tiffany Lethabo King], "In the Clearing: Black Female Bodies, Space, and Settler Colonial Landscapes," (PhD diss., University of Maryland, 2013), 33.

22. Katherine McKittrick, "On Plantations, Prisons, and a Black Sense of Place," *Social & Cultural Geography* 12, no. 8 (2011): 949.

23. James D. Anderson, *The Education of Blacks in the South, 1860–1935* (Chapel Hill: University of North Carolina Press, 1988), 54–55; Lindsey, *Indians at Hampton Institute*.

24. Even the schoolwork focused on labor. For example, Anderson describes how the curriculum outlined the difference between free and enslaved labor and the importance of the laboring class. Anderson, *The Education of Blacks in the South*, 50.

25. Anderson, *The Education of Blacks in the South*, 49.

26. "Fourteenth Annual Report of the Principal, for the School and Fiscal Year Ending July 1st, 1883," *Southern Workman* 12, no. 6 (1883), Hampton University Archives, 71–73.

27. "Fourteenth Annual Report of the Principal," 73; Anderson, *The Education of Blacks in the South*, 49.

28. Hampton Institute and Richmond L. Miner, *Everyday Life at Hampton Institute* (Hampton, VA: Hampton Institute, 1907), https://catalog.hathitrust.org/api/volumes/oclc/6876351.html.

29. Anderson, *The Education of Blacks in the South*, 34–36.

30. Anderson, *The Education of Blacks in the South*, 33.

31. Anderson, *The Education of Blacks in the South*, 37–38.

32. Lindsey, *Indians at Hampton Institute*, 7.

33. Anderson, *The Education of Blacks in the South*, 44.

34. Helen Ludlow, "The Shellbanks Farm School," *Southern Workman* 34, no. 10 (1905): 533.

35. Lindsey, *Indians at Hampton Institute*, 124; Ludlow, "The Shellbanks Farm School"; "Hampton Incidents," *Southern Workman* 34, no. 9 (1905): 509.

36. Ludlow, "The Shellbanks Farm School," 534–535.

37. Ludlow, "The Shellbanks Farm School," 538.

38. Ludlow, "The Shellbanks Farm School," 538, 540.

39. Anderson, *The Education of Blacks in the South*, 61.

40. Baker Jr., *Turning South Again*, 84.

41. McKittrick, "On Plantations, Prisons, and a Black Sense of Place," 950.

42. Washington, *Up From Slavery*, 96–99; I discuss this model in my article: Bayley J. Marquez, "The Black Model Minority: Slavery, Settlement, and the Genealogy of the Model Minority," *Du Bois Review: Social Science Research on Race* 19, no. 1 (2022).

43. Samuel Chapman Armstrong, "Indian Education in the East," *Southern Workman* 9, no. 11 (1880): 114, Hampton University Archives. My emphasis.

44. Kelly Miller, "The Anglo Saxon and the African," *Southern Workman* 17, no. 1 (1903): 9.

45. Proximity as a learning concept has been proposed by other scholars in the twentieth century, most notably by Vygotsky in his formulation of zones of proximal development. Vygotsky's concepts, which were conceived in the 1920s and 1930s and popularized in the 1980s, are instructive in understanding how white reformers

may have seen proximity as an educative process, even if they are anachronistic. Vygotsky theorized that learning and development happen in relation to the social context, and his concept of zones of proximal development delineated important learning moments when what an individual can accomplish themselves and what they can accomplish with help overlap. He theorizes this moment as a part of the developmental process that connects the individual with society. Leonardo and Manning examine this theorization in relation to race, asking "how these theories play out when we understand the signs and tools of society as racial, which are driven (not determined) by the exclusionary power of whiteness." They propose that the connection between learning and society happens in the context of white supremacy where "the ideology of whiteness mediates individual and collective development." It necessitates the help that is given be white because of the context of white supremacy. The idea that proximity to whiteness was an educative process founded in slavery, settlement, and industrial education would link these ideas of learning through proximity across nonlinear time such that the traces of learning by being near whiteness linger in Vygotsky's educational theory of proximity. Zeus Leonardo and Logan Manning, "White Historical Activity Theory: Toward a Critical Understanding of White Zones of Proximal Development," *Race, Ethnicity, and Education* 20, no. 1 (2017): 3; Luis Moll, "Vygotsky's Zone of Proximal Development: Rethinking Its Instructional Implications," *Infancia y Aprendizaje* 13, no. 51–52 (1990).

46. This comes closest to Dumas's framing of school integration programs as working through proximity to whiteness since integration is about "sitting next to white children." Dumas, "Sitting next to White Children: School Desegregation in the Black Educational Imagination," (PhD diss., City University of New York, 2007).

47. In "The Vel of Slavery," Sexton critiques the false idea that proximity to whiteness is emancipatory or good for Native peoples because it is part and parcel of Native genocide. He calls Blackness the antipode of whiteness (590). Yet proximity to whiteness as educative was imposed on both groups. In this sense, proximity to whiteness upheld slavery as an institution that taught a population that was whiteness's antipode. The project of educating Blacks to be "men" when it is an impossibility, according to scholars of Afropessimism, is part of upholding antiblack logics because, ultimately, it reinscribes the status of slavery as rightful. Jared Sexton, "The Vel of Slavery: Tracking the Figure of the Unsovereign," *Critical Sociology* 42, no. 4–5 (2016): 590.

48. G.S. Dickerman, "White Instructors and Negro Pupils," *Southern Workman* 32, no. 12 (1903): 610.

49. Dickerman, "White Instructors and Negro Pupils," 611.

50. Dickerman, "White Instructors and Negro Pupils," 612.

51. Dickerman, "White Instructors and Negro Pupils," 614.

52. "A Trip through the South II. A Last Conference," *Southern Workman* 22, no. 5 (1884): 82.

53. One could also read Black agency into this description by a white author by noting the fugitive potential of singing Black plantation songs in white run schools.

I know this potential exists and want to signal it without this being the focus of my analysis.

54. Dumas, "Sitting Next to White Children."

55. Armstrong, "Indian Education in the East," 114.

56. For example, see Joanne Barker, "For Whom Sovereignty Matters," in *Sovereignty Matters: Locations of Contestation and Possibility in Indigenous Struggles for Self-Determination,* ed. Joanne Barker (Lincoln: University of Nebraska Press, 2005).

57. Hollis Burke Frissell, "The Attitude of the Indian To White Civilization," n.d. Box 1, Hollis Burke Frissell Papers, Hampton University Archives, 3.

58. "Allotment Speculation," 67.

59. Iyko Day discusses how there is no labor in a slavery system (according to Marxist theory). With this in mind, labor being taught isn't meant to be labor in the Marxist sense. Iyko Day, "Afro-Feminism Before Afropessimism: Meditations on Gender and Ontology," in *Antiblackness,* ed. Moon-Kie Jung and João H. Costa Vargas (Durham, NC: Duke University Press, 2021), 71.

60. Examples of this include tenant farming and sharecropping systems as well as poverty level wages in the present.

61. While many Black educators, such as Booker T. Washington, did include ownership of land as a goal, it is notable that this goal is not always present in the discourse of white educators. This demonstrates the fault lines in the alliance between white and Black educators, despite their rhetorical agreement on pedagogy.

62. Tuck, Guess, and Sultan, "Not Nowhere," 8.

63. Booker T. Washington, "Relation of Industrial Education to National Progress," *The Annals of the American Academy of Political and Social Science* 33, no. 1 (1909): 6.

64. Washington, "Relation of Industrial Education to the Progress of the Negro," 6.

65. This is connected to Du Bois's critique in *Black Reconstruction* that Reconstruction failed because of the need for Black labor in capitalist production. William Edward Burghardt Du Bois, *Black Reconstruction: An Essay Toward a History of the Part Which Black Folk Played in the Attempt to Reconstruct Democracy in America, 1860–1880* (Philadelphia: A. Saifer, 1935).

66. Hampton used labor as a teaching mechanism to continue an ontological positioning of its Black students as fungible, pedagogically reproducing the ontological relations of the plantation. Fungibility, or the use of the Black body for any purpose, including, but not exclusive to, labor, has been argued in Black studies to be the overarching analytic for understanding antiblack ontology. King argues that it is necessary to place fungibility at the center of this analysis to critique theorizations from settler colonial studies that analyze Black relations to Native peoples through discussions of labor only. Fungibility covers labor as one such use of the Black body but expands its use outside of capitalist relations. I hold fungibility close when I discuss the labor of Black students, knowing it is but one ontological placement that industrial education sought to make in relation to Black flesh. Yet I ana-

lyze the discussion of labor because its place in industrial education is paramount for understanding the functioning of plantation pedagogy, including understanding land, and not just bodies, as fungible. Tiffany Lethabo King, "Labor's Aphasia: Toward Antiblackness as Constitutive to Settler Colonialism," *Decolonization: Indigeneity, Education & Society*, 2014, https://decolonization.wordpress.com/2014/06/10/labors-aphasia-toward-antiblackness-as-constitutive-to-settler-colonialism/.

67. la paperson, *A Third University Is Possible* (Minneapolis: University of Minnesota Press, 2017).

68. Edward W. Soja, *Postmodern Geographies: The Reassertion of Space in Critical Social Theory* (London: Verso, 1989).

69. Eve Tuck and Marcia McKenzie, *Place in Research: Theory, Methodology, and Methods* (New York: Routledge, 2015), xiv; Henri Lefebvre, *The Production of Space* (Oxford: Blackwell, 1991).

70. Eve Tuck and Marcia McKenzie, *Place in Research*, 6, citing Karen Barad, *Meeting the Universe Halfway: Quantum Physics and the Entanglement of Matter and Meaning* (Durham, NC: Duke University Press, 2007).

71. Tuck and McKenzie, *Place in Research*, 6, 21.

72. Examples of these placemaking projects include the Black Land Project, Native Like Water, Mapping Indigenous L.A. and many other scholarly works. Black Land Project, "Black/Land Gathers and Analyzes Stories About the Relationship Between Black People, Land and Place," accessed July 20, 2020, http://www.blacklandproject.org/; Native Like Water, "Native Like Water: Conservation, Health, Outdoor Science & Culture 'An Experience of a Lifetime!'" accessed July 20, 2020, https://www.nativelikewater.org/; "Mapping Indigenous LA," accessed July 20, 2020, https://mila.ss.ucla.edu/; bell hooks, *Belonging: A Culture of Place* (New York: Routledge, 2009); Mishuana Goeman, *Mark My Words: Native Women Mapping Our Nations* (Minneapolis: University of Minnesota Press, 2013).

73. Goeman, *Mark My Words;* Audra Simpson, *Mohawk Interruptus: Political Life Across the Borders of Settler States* (Durham, NC: Duke University Press, 2014).

74. Tuck and McKenzie, *Place in Research*.

75. Excellent examples of scholarship on place-based learning include Leanne Betasamosake Simpson, "Land as Pedagogy: Nishnaabeg Intelligence and Rebellious Transformation," *Decolonization: Indigeneity, Education & Society* 3, no. 3 (2014); Wildcat et al., "Learning from the Land: Indigenous Land Based Pedagogy and Decolonization," *Decolonization: Indigeneity, Education & Society* 3, no. 3 (2014); Omari L. Dyson, *The Black Panther Party and Transformative Pedagogy: Place-Based Education in Philadelphia* (Lanham, MD: Lexington Books, 2013); Fikile Nxumalo and Stacia Cedillo, "Decolonizing Place in Early Childhood Studies: Thinking with Indigenous Onto-Epistemologies and Black Feminist Geographies," *Global Studies of Childhood* 7, no. 2 (2017).

76. I would like to thank the brilliant graduate student Danielle LaPlace for discussing the pedagogic components of medicine and public health with me and in her work. Additionally, see Damien Mason, "Command Presence: Video

Observations of Police Civilian Encounters and the Practice of Coercive Force by Law Enforcement," PhD diss., (University of California, Berkeley, 2020).

77. Tracey Banivanua Mar and Penelope Edmonds, "Introduction: Making Space in Settler Colonies," in *Making Settler Colonial Space: Perspectives on Race, Place and Identity,* ed. Tracey Banivanua Mar and Penelope Edmonds (New York: Palgrave Macmillan, 2010), 5.

78. Sherene Razack, "When Place Becomes Race," in *Race, Space, and the Law: Unmapping a White Settler Society,* ed. Sherene Razack (Toronto: Between the Lines, 2002), 1.

79. Simpson, *Mohawk Interrupus.*

80. What Moreton-Robinson might call "white possessive logics." Aileen Moreton-Robinson, *The White Possessive: Property, Power, and Indigenous Sovereignty* (Minneapolis: University of Minnesota Press, 2015).

81. Razack, "When Place Becomes Race," 22.

82. Mar and Edmonds, "Introduction: Making Space in Settler Colonies," 15.

83. My use of spatial imaginings is deeply influenced by Michael J. Dumas's concept of the Black educational imagination. Dumas, "Sitting Next to White Children."

84. Jane Lydon, "'Fantastic Dreaming': Ebenezer Mission as Moravian Utopia and Wotjobaluk Resistance," in *Making Settler Colonial Space: Perspectives on Race, Place and Identity,* ed. Tracey Banivanua Mar and Penelope Edmonds (New York: Palgrave Macmillan, 2010), 220.

85. Lydon "'Fantastic Dreaming.'"

86. Philip D. Curtin, *The Rise and Fall of the Plantation Complex: Essays in Atlantic History* (Cambridge: Cambridge University Press, 1998), 11.

87. Ulbe Bosma, Juan Giusti-Cordero, and Roger Knight, eds. *Sugarlandia Revisited: Sugar and Colonialism in Asia and the Americas, 1800–1940* (New York: Berghahn Books, 2007), 10–11.

88. Baker Jr., *Turning South Again;* Katherine McKittrick, *Demonic Grounds: Black Women and the Cartographies of Struggle* (Minneapolis: University of Minnesota Press, 2006); Katherine McKittrick, "On Plantations, Prisons, and a Black Sense of Place"; Tiffany Lethabo King, "The Labor of (Re) Reading Plantation Landscapes Fungible(ly)," *Antipode* 48, no. 4 (2016).

89. Andres Resendez, *The Other Slavery: The Uncovered Story of Indian Enslavement in America* (Boston: Houghton Mifflin Harcourt, 2016); Neil Roberts, *Freedom as Marronage* (Chicago: University of Chicago Press, 2015); Adam Bledsoe, "Marronage as a Past and Present Geography in the Americas," *Southeastern Geographer* 57, no. 1 (2017).

90. Curtin, *The Rise and Fall of the Plantation Complex,* 14.

91. McKittrick, "On Plantations, Prisons, and a Black Sense of Place," 952, 955.

92. Katherine McKittrick, "Plantation Futures," *Small Axe: A Caribbean Journal of Criticism* 17, no. 3 (42) (2013): 3, 5, and 9.

93. Anne McClintock, *Imperial Leather: Race, Gender, and Sexuality in the Colonial Contest* (New York: Routledge, 1995).

94. McKittrick, "Plantation Futures," 8.

95. McKittrick, "Plantation Futures," 8.

96. McKittrick, "On Plantations, Prisons, and a Black Sense of Place," 949.

97. Booker T. Washington, *Up From Slavery;* Booker T. Washington and William Edward Burghardt Du Bois, *The Negro in the South, his Economic Progress in Relation to his Moral and Religious Development.* The William Levi Bull Lectures for the Year 1907, (Philadelphia: GW Jacobs, 1907).

98. Wilcomb E. Washburn, *The Assault on Indian Tribalism: The General Allotment Law (Dawes Act) of 1887* (Philadelphia: Lippincott, 1975); Donald L. Fixico, *Termination and Relocation: Federal Indian Policy, 1945–1960* (Albuquerque: University of New Mexico Press, 1986).

99. Sylvia Wynter, "Novel and History, Plot and Plantation," *Savacou* 5, no. 1 (1971): 8.

100. McKittrick, "Plantation Futures."

101. Lisa Lowe, *The Intimacies of Four Continents* (Durham, NC: Duke University Press, 2015), 71.

102. Lowe, *The Intimacies of Four Continents,* 11.

103. Lowe, *The Intimacies of Four Continents,* 170.

104. Gerald Horne, *The White Pacific: US Imperialism and Black Slavery in the South Seas After the Civil War* (Honolulu: University of Hawaii Press, 2007).

105. Horne, *The White Pacific.*

106. Lowe, *The Intimacy of Four Continents.*

107. Frenise A. Logan, "The British East India Company and African Slavery in Benkulen, Sumatra, 1687–1792," *The Journal of Negro History* 41, no. 4 (1956).

108. Amy Clukey and Jeremy Wells, "Introduction: Plantation Modernity," *Global South* 10, no. 2 (2016); Hinrichsen, "A Curious Study."

109. King, "In the Clearing," 44.

110. la paperson, *A Third University Is Possible,* 4.

111. la paperson, *A Third University Is Possible,* xiii. Yet, la paperson also notes that colonial machines do not only run on desires for the colonizer's future, but paradoxically also produce Indigenous futures simultaneously. I have argued in the introduction that I know that Indigenous and Black futures are always intertwined with, pushed back against, and affected by colonizer futurity, but my focus in this book is on the mechanisms driving systems of power.

112. la paperson, *A Third University Is Possible,* 2.

113. la paperson, *A Third University Is Possible,* 2.

114. la paperson, *A Third University Is Possible,* 5.

115. I do not hide that I have malicious intent in seeking to understand these machines. I do so in order to harm them, even as I am implicated in them, much the way la paperson describes himself as a piece of "colonialist scrap" that is "disloyal to colonialism," otherwise known as a "cyborg" that enacts "agency in assemblage." la paperson, *A Third University Is Possible,* xvi, xxiii. In discussing ways of engaging these machines I also draw from the work of Moten and Harney in their theorization of the undercommons, Jarvis R. Givens's work on fugitive pedagogy, and Juliet R. Kunkel's discussion of scavenging. Fred Moten and Stefano Harney, "The University

and the Undercommons: Seven Theses," *Social Text* 22, no. 2 (2004); Jarvis R. Givens, *Fugitive Pedagogy: Carter G. Woodson and the Art of Black Teaching* (Cambridge, MA: Harvard University Press, 2021); Juliet R. Kunkel, "The Eugenic University," (PhD diss., University of California Berkeley, 2021).

116. la paperson, *A Third University Is Possible,* 2, 4.
117. la paperson, *A Third University Is Possible,* xvii.
118. la paperson, *A Third University Is Possible,* xvi. My emphasis.
119. la paperson, *A Third University Is Possible.*
120. Jodi A. Byrd, *The Transit of Empire: Indigenous Critiques of Colonialism* (Minneapolis: University of Minnesota Press, 2011).
121. *Oxford English Dictionary,* s.v. "Current," https://www.lexico.com/en/definition/current.
122. "Ocean Currents," Resource Library Collection, National Geographic, accessed November 3, 2020, https://www.nationalgeographic.org/topics/resource-library-ocean-currents/?q = &page = 1&per_page = 25.
123. J. Kēhaulani Kauanui, "Imperial Ocean: The Pacific as a Critical Site for American Studies." *American Quarterly* 67, no. 3 (2015): 633.
124. The first definition is from *Cambridge Dictionary,* s.v. "Current," https://dictionary.cambridge.org/us/dictionary/english/current; all subsequent definitions are from *Merriam Webster,* s.v. "Current," https://www.merriam-webster.com/dictionary/current.
125. Mel Y. Chen, *Animacies: Biopolitics, Racial Mattering, and Queer Affect* (Durham, NC: Duke University Press, 2012), 10.
126. Peter J. Hugill, "Communication and Empire," *The Geographical Review* 98, no. 3 (2008); Daniel R. Headrick, *The Tentacles of Progress: Technology Transfer in the Age of Imperialism, 1850–1940* (Oxford: Oxford University Press, 1988).
127. Headrick, *The Tentacles of Progress;* Michael Adas, "A Field Matures: Technology, Science, and Western Colonialism," *Technology and Culture* 38, no. 2 (1997). For a modern example, see Michael Kwet, "Digital Colonialism: US Empire and the New Imperialism in the Global South," *Race & Class* 60, no. 4 (2019).
128. Thomas Clayton, "Beyond Mystification: Reconnecting World-System Theory for Comparative Education," *Comparative Education Review* 42, no. 4 (1998); Mark B. Ginsburg et al., "National and World-System Explanations of Educational Reform," *Comparative Education Review* 34, no. 4 (1990); Francisco O. Ramirez and John W. Meyer, "Comparative Education: The Social Construction of the Modern World System," *Annual Review of Sociology* 6, no. 1 (1980); John W. Meyer, Francisco O. Ramirez, and Yasemin Nuhoğlu Soysal, "World Expansion of Mass Education, 1870–1980," *Sociology of Education* 65, no. 2 (1992); Francisco O. Ramirez, "The World Society Perspective: Concepts, Assumptions, and Strategies," *Comparative Education* 48, no. 4 (2012).
129. Paul Lyons and Ty P. Kāwika Tengan, "Introduction: Pacific Currents," *American Quarterly* 67, no. 3 (2015): 546.
130. Kariann Akemi Yokota, "Transatlantic and Transpacific Connections in Early American History," *Pacific Historical Review* 83, no. 2 (2012): 205.

131. Yokota, "Transatlantic and Transpacific Connections in Early American History," 205.

132. Yokota, "Transatlantic and Transpacific Connections in Early American History," 208.

133. Lawrence S. Kaplan, "Frederick Jackson Turner and Imperialism," *Social Science* 27, no. 1 (1952); William Appleman Williams, "The Frontier Thesis and American Foreign Policy," *Pacific Historical Review* 24, no. 4 (1955).

134. Lyons and Tengan, "Introduction: Pacific Currents," 545–6.

135. Lyons and Tengan, "Introduction: Pacific Currents," 567.

2. PLANTATION PEDAGOGY ON THE RESERVATION

1. For discussion of the lazy Indian stereotype in a variety of disciplines, see Robert J. Berkhofer Jr., *The White Man's Indian: Images of the American Indian from Columbus to Present* (New York: Vintage Books, 1979); Edward Burkley et al., "Structure and Content of Native American Stereotypic Subgroups: Not Just (ig)Noble," *Cultural Diversity and Ethnic Minority Psychology* 23, no. 2 (2017): 209; Robert A. Williams Jr., "Gendered Checks and Balances: Understanding the Legacy of White Patriarchy in an American Indian Cultural Context," *Georgia Law Review* 24 (1989): 1019; Robyn Taylor-Neu et al., "(De) Constructing The 'Lazy Indian': An Historical Analysis of Welfare Reform in Canada," *Aboriginal Policy Studies* 7, no. 2 (2019); K. Tsianina Lomawaima, "The Unnatural History of American Indian Education" in *Next Steps: Research and Practice To Advance Indian Education,* eds. Karen Gayton Swisher and John W. Tippeconnic III, 1–32, (Charleston, WV: Eric Clearinghouse on Rural Education and Small Schools, 1999).

2. "Why 'Pratt' Alone?" *The Red Man and Helper,* 19 no. 47, 48 (1904): 5.

3. Richard Henry Pratt, "The Indian No Problem," *Delaware County Institute of Science* 5, no. 1 (1909): 6.

4. Pratt, "The Indian No Problem," 10.

5. Katherine McKittrick, "Plantation Futures," *Small Axe: A Caribbean Journal of Criticism* 17, no. 3 (42) (2013).

6. At the same time that the reservation indexes the scope of Indigenous dispossession, it also has been repurposed as a space of sovereignty, resurgence, and survivance by Native peoples.

7. For a discussion of settler narratives, see Lorenzo Veracini, *Settler Colonialism: A Theoretical Outline* (Houndmills, UK: Palgrave Macmillan, 2010). For a discussion of settler colonialism and time, see Mark Rifkin, *Beyond Settler Time: Temporal Sovereignty and Indigenous Self-Determination* (Durham, NC: Duke University Press, 2017).

8. Houston A. Baker Jr., *Turning South Again: Re-thinking Modernism/Re-reading Booker T* (Durham, NC: Duke University Press, 2001); Katherine McKittrick, "On Plantations, Prisons, and a Black Sense of Place," *Social & Cultural*

Geography 12, no. 8 (2011); McKittrick, "Plantation Futures"; Sylvia Wynter, "Novel and History, Plot and Plantation," *Savacou* 5, no. 1 (1971).

9. I am, of course, focusing on Western concepts of education rather than Indigenous modes of learning, relationship, and resurgence. These alternate conceptions of education exist, thrive, resist, and contend with Western forms of education, but they are not the focus of this specific analysis.

10. David Wallace Adams, *Education for Extinction: American Indians and the Boarding School Experience, 1875–1928* (Lawrence: University Press of Kansas, 1995); Paul Francis Prucha, *Americanizing the American Indians: Writings by the "Friends of the Indian," 1880–1900* (Cambridge, MA.: Harvard University Press, 1973); K. Tsianina Lomawaima and Theresa L. McCarty, *To Remain an Indian: Lessons in Democracy from a Century of Native American Education* (New York: Columbia University Press, 2006).

11. Hollis Burke Frissell, "The Attitude of the Indian To White Civilization," n.d., Box 1, Hollis Burke Frissell Papers, Hampton University Archives, 5–6.

12. Frances Fisher Kane to Editor of the Washington Post, 22 August 1892, Box 1, Folder 37, Samuel Chapman Armstrong Papers, Williams College Archives, 3.

13. Frissell, "The Attitude of the Indian To White Civilization," 3.

14. Frissell, "The Attitude of the Indian To White Civilization," 14.

15. Frissell, "The Attitude of the Indian To White Civilization," 10.

16. Frissell, "The Attitude of the Indian To White Civilization," 3.

17. Maile Renee Arvin, *Possessing Polynesians: The Science of Settler Colonial Whiteness in Hawai'i and Oceania* (Durham, NC: Duke University Press, 2019), 4.; Phillip J. Deloria, *Playing Indian* (New Haven, CT: Yale University Press, 1998); Shari M. Huhndorf, *Going Native: Indians in the North American Cultural Imagination* (Ithaca, NY: Cornell University Press, 2015).

18. Arvin, *Possessing Polynesians,* 4.

19. Samuel Chapman Armstrong, *The Indian Question* (Hampton, VA: Normal School Steam Press, 1883), 4.

20. The term docility can also be related to the process of domestication, which I address with Juliet R. Kunkel in relation to genocide. Bayley J. Marquez and Juliet R. Kunkel, "The Domestication Genocide of Settler Colonial Language Ideologies," *American Quarterly Special Issue: The Politics of Language, Multilingualism, and Translation in American Studies,* 73 no. 3 (September 2021).

21. The Ghost Dance was a pan-Indian prophetic and ritualistic movement whose adherents believed, among many other things, that white colonization would be abolished. It contributed to Indigenous resistance to the settler colonial state's policies and frightened US government officials. BIA officials propagated the idea that Sitting Bull was the leader of the Ghost Dance movement, which led to the massacre at Wounded Knee. James Mooney, *The Ghost-Dance Religion and the Sioux Outbreak of 1890* (Lincoln: University of Nebraska Press, 1991).

22. Eric N. Olund, "From Savage Space to Governable Space: The Extension of United States Judicial Sovereignty over Indian Country in the Nineteenth Century," *Cultural Geographies* 9, no. 2 (2002).

23. Delos Sacket Otis, *The Dawes Act and the Allotment of Indian Lands* (Norman: University of Oklahoma Press, 2014); Leonard A. Carlson, "Federal Policy and Indian Land: Economic Interests and the Sale of Indian Allotments, 1900–1934," *Agricultural History* 57, no. 1 (1983); Emily Greenwald, *Reconfiguring the Reservation: The Nez Perces, Jicarilla Apaches, and the Dawes Act* (Santa Fe: University of New Mexico Press, 2002).

24. David A. Chang, *The Color of the Land: Race, Nation, and the Politics of Landownership in Oklahoma, 1832–1929* (Chapel Hill: University of North Carolina Press, 2010); Rose Stremlau, "'To Domesticate and Civilize Wild Indians': Allotment and the Campaign to Reform Indian Families, 1875–1887," *Journal of Family History* 30, no. 3 (2005); David J. Carlson and Charles Eastman, "'Indian for a While': Charles Eastman's 'Indian Boyhood' and the Discourse of Allotment," *American Indian Quarterly* 25, no. 4 (2001).

25. Chang, *The Color of Land*, 74–76.
26. Chang, *The Color of Land*, 75.
27. Chang, *The Color of Land*, 91.
28. Stremlau, "'To Domesticate and Civilize Wild Indians,'" 268.
29. Stremlau describes this consensus as a recognition that it was necessary to break up Indigenous kinship. However, she overemphasizes how this would impact Native families rather than the economic and material impacts of the policy. She notes that this cohesion may have been a result of the crisis of gender roles that was occurring in US society more generally during this time. Stremlau, "To Domesticate and Civilize Wild Indians."

30. Armstrong, *The Indian Question*, 46.

31. Samuel Chapman Armstrong, *Concerning Indians: Extracts from the Annual Report of the Principal of the Hampton Normal and Agricultural Institute, for the School Year Ending June 30th, 1883* (Hampton, VA: Normal School Steam Press, 1883), 20.

32. Wilbert H. Ahern, "The Returned Indians: Hampton Institute and Its Indian Alumni, 1879–1893," *The Journal of Ethnic Studies* 10, no. 4 (1983).

33. "Incidents in Indian Life at Hampton," *Southern Workman* 18, no. 2 (1889): 22, Hampton University Archives.

34. Leonard A. Carlson, "The Dawes Act and the Decline of Indian Farming," *Journal of Economic History* 38, no. 1 (1978); Leonard A. Carlson, *Learning to Farm: Indian Land Tenure and Farming Before the Dawes Act* (Lanham, MD: Rowman and Littlefield, 1992).

35. Frances Leon Quintana, *Ordeal of Change: The Southern Utes and Their Neighbors* (Walnut Creek, CA: AltaMira Press, 2004).

36. Frances Fisher Kane, letter to the editor, *Washington Post*, 4. In this quote, Fisher Kane frames Indigenous peoples who wander as "mad." In reading this quote I am inspired by La Marr Jurelle Bruce's understanding of Black radical creativity and madness, which connects madness to generation and creation. La Marr Jurelle Bruce, *How to Go Mad Without Losing Your Mind: Madness and Black Radical Creativity* (Durham, NC: Duke University Press, 2020).

37. Frances Fisher Kane, letter to the editor, *Washington Post*, 7–8
38. Frances Fisher Kane, letter to the editor, *Washington Post*, 7–8
39. Elaine Goodale, "The Attack Upon Indian Education in Congress," *Southern Workman* 15, no. 4 (1886): 45, Hampton University Archives.
40. Goodale, "The Attack Upon Indian Education in Congress," 45.
41. Elaine Goodale, "Hampton's Answer," *Southern Workman* 15, no. 4 (1886): 45, Hampton University Archives.
42. Goodale, "Hampton's Response," 46. The school described is one run by a former Native student who attended Hampton. Reports of this nature were common in Hampton's publications and the school tracked former students and their accomplishments in order to use them as examples of the transformative power of industrial education.
43. *The Indian Helper* 2, no. 39, May 6, 1887; "The Land in Severalty Bill Made Easy to Understand," *The Red Man* 14, no. 3, 1897; "'Dawes Bill Day,' February Eighth, Celebrated: The Dawes Act as Discussed by the Officials and Pupils of the Carlisle Indian School," *The Indian Helper* 4, no. 2, August 31, 1888; "Two Carlisle Boys at Pine Ridge Talk Over the Sioux Bill," *The Indian Helper* 4, no. 3 (1888): 1, 4.
44. *Annual Report of the Commissioner of Indian Affairs to the Secretary of the Interior for the Year 1884*, (Washington Government Printing Office, 1884), 187, Carlisle Indian School Digital Resource Center, http://carlisleindian.dickinson.edu/publications/excerpt-annual-report-commissioner-indian-affairs-1884.
45. *Annual Report of the Commissioner of Indian Affairs*, 187.
46. *Annual Report of the Commissioner of Indian Affairs*, 187.
47. William J. Bauer Jr., "Stories of American Indian Freedom: The Privatization of American Indian Resources from Allotment to Present," in *Allotment Stories: Indigenous Land Relations Under Settler Siege*, ed. Daniel Heath Justice and Jean M. O'Brien (Minneapolis: University of Minnesota Press, 2022), 202.
48. I am indebted to Rachel Williams's discussion of Deborah Thomas's palimpsest time in relation to her work on charter school reform in Memphis, TN. Rachel E. Williams, "The Political Economy of Subprime Education: Charter Schools and Black Communities," (paper presentation, University of Council for Educational Administration Convention, New Orleans, LA, November 2019); Deborah A. Thomas, *Exceptional Violence: Embodied Citizenship in Transnational Jamaica* (Duke University Press, 2011). Lomawaima and McCarty also point out this pendulum-like swing in their concept of safety zones which expand and contract as policy shifts, making the expression of Indianness less or more safe within schooling institutions. Lomawaima and McCarty, *To Remain and Indian*.
49. Richard Henry Pratt, *The Red Man and Helper* 19, no. 33 (1904): 2.
50. In this quote Pratt uses the phrasing "our own embryo society" to describe how educating Indigenous peoples in the East of the US is advantageous. This is an atemporal echo of the more famous usage of embryo and education found in John Dewey's 1907 text *The School and Society*, in which he asserts that the school must function as an "embryonic society." While this would seem to be the opposite idea

since Pratt argues that the school must be in the embryonic community of the Northeast and Dewey that the school community must echo society, they both connect the space of education to the achievement of a specific civil ideal. Scholars such as Elizabeth Carolyn Brown have argued that Dewey's progressive education was a continuance of the racial education coined at schools like Hampton, which I will address in chapter 7 and the conclusion. John Dewey, *The School and Society* (Chicago: University of Chicago Press, 1907); Elizabeth Carolyn Brown, "Pedagogies of U.S. Imperialism: Racial Education from Reconstruction to the Progressive Era," (PhD diss., English, University of Washington, 2016).

51. Francis E. Leupp, *Indian School Management: Reply to Attacks by Captain Pratt Upon the Introduction of Civil Service Reform Methods* (Philadelphia: Indian Rights Association, 1897); K. Tsianina Lomawaima and Jeffrey Ostler, "Reconsidering Richard Henry Pratt: Cultural Genocide and Native Liberation in an Era of Racial Oppression," *Journal of American Indian Education* 57, no. 1 (2018).

52. Richard Henry Pratt, "General Pratt's Own Statement," *The Red Man and Helper* 19, no. 47, 48 (1904): 1.

53. Pratt, "General Pratt's Own Statement," 1.

54. Pratt, "General Pratt's Own Statement," 1.

55. "Work," *The Indian Helper* 11, no. 32 (1896): 1, Carlisle Indian School Digital Resource Center. On Carlisle's use of didactic storytelling, see Elizabeth Carolyn Brown, "Pedagogies of U.S. Imperialism: Racial Education from Reconstruction to the Progressive Era" (PhD diss., English, University of Washington, 2016); Jessica Enoch, "Resisting the Script of Indian Education: Zitkala Ša and the Carlisle Indian School," *College English* 65, no. 2 (2002).

56. "Work," *The Indian Helper,* 1.

57. "Work," *The Indian Helper,* 1.

58. Brown, "Pedagogies of U.S. Imperialism"; Marianna Burgess, *Stiya: A Carlisle Indian Girl at Home* (Cambridge, MA: Riverside Press, 1891), Carlisle Indian School Digital Resource Center.

59. Lyman Abbott, "Our National Dealing with the Indians," *The Red Man,* 15 no. 4, (1899) 2, Carlisle Indian School Digital Resource Center.

60. Donald L. Fixico, *Termination and Relocation: Federal Indian Policy, 1945–1960* (Albuquerque: University of New Mexico Press, 1986).

61. Abbott, "Our National Dealing with the Indians," 2.

62. Abbott, "Our National Dealing with the Indians," 2.

63. William Link and Dictionary of Virginia Biography, "J. L. M. Curry (1825–1903)," Encyclopedia of Virginia, Virginia Humanities, last modified December 22, 2021, https://encyclopediavirginia.org/entries/curry-j-l-m-1825–1903/

64. Samuel Chapman Armstrong wrote a number of pieces in favor of the colonization movement; for example, see Samuel Chapman Armstrong, *Emigration to Liberia: An Address Delivered before the American Colonization Society, January 21, 1879* (Washington, DC: American Colonization Society, 1879).

65. J. L. M. Curry, "The Negro Problem," *The Red Man* 9, no. 4 (1889): 4, Carlisle Indian School Digital Resource Center.

66. Manu Karuka, *Empire's Tracks: Indigenous Nations, Chinese Workers, and the Transcontinental Railroad* (Berkeley: University of California Press, 2019), 19.

67. Bayley J. Marquez, "The Black Model Minority: Slavery, Settlement, and the Genealogy of the Model Minority," *Du Bois Review: Social Science Research on Race* 19, no. 1 (2022).

68. Robert Moton, "Indian Emancipation Day Address," Robert Moton Folder, Hampton University Archives.

69. W. N. Armstrong, "A Reoreant People," *Southern Workman* 7, no. 11 (1878): 82–83, Hampton University Archives.

70. D. A. Sanford, "A Missionary on the Indian Situations," *The Red Man and Helper* 18, no. 14 (1902): 1.

71. Richard Henry Pratt, "Colonel Pratt's Answer to Rev. Sanford's Letter," *The Red Man and Helper* 18, no. 14 (1902): 4.

72. Vine Deloria Jr., *We Talk, You Listen: New Tribes, New Turf* (Lincoln: University of Nebraska Press, 2007), 90. Yet school integration does not encompass all Black politics; for example, see Russell Rickford, *We Are an African People: Independent Education, Black Power, and the Radical Imagination* (Oxford: Oxford University Press, 2016).

73. Curry, "The Negro Problem," 4.

74. Pratt, "General Pratt's Own Statement," 1.

75. *The Red Man and Helper* 19, no. 20 (1903): 2.

76. Emma García, "Schools Are Still Segregated, and Black Children Are Paying a Price," *Economic Policy Institute* (2020); Tomas Monarrez, Brian Kisida, and Matthew M. Chingos, "The Effect of Charter Schools on School Segregation," *American Economic Journal: Economic Policy* 14, no. 1 (2022); Ann Owens, "Unequal Opportunity: School and Neighborhood Segregation in the USA," *Race and Social Problems* 12, no. 1 (2020).

77. William Edward Burghardt Du Bois, "Does the Negro Need Separate Schools?" *Journal of Negro Education* 4, no. 3 (1935); Vanessa Siddle Walker, "Valued Segregated Schools for African American Children in the South, 1935–1969: A Review of Common Themes and Characteristics," *Review of Educational Research* 70, no. 3 (September 2000); Vanessa Siddle Walker, *Their Highest Potential: An African American School Community in the Segregated South* (Chapel Hill: University of North Carolina Press, 1996).

78. Pratt, "General Pratt's Own Statement," 1.

79. Pratt, "General Pratt's Own Statement," 1.

80. Gillian Harkins and Erica R. Meiners, "Beyond Crisis: College in Prison through the Abolition Undercommons," *Lateral* 3 (2014); David A. Maldonado and Erica R. Meiners, "Due Time: Meditations on Abolition at the Site of the University," *Social Text* 39, no. 1 (146) (March 1, 2021).

81. This is also true of historical white abolitionist rhetoric prior to emancipation. I point out how Pratt disingenuously uses the language of abolition in relation to the reservation to demonstrate why Native peoples may react badly when abolition is used as an organizing construct for political action. This is not meant to

discount present-day prison and police abolitionist work, which I strenuously support. I also know that abolition is about imagining and moving towards a society that would not need police and prisons; it is not simply about abolishing police and prisons and then leaving society as it is. Thus, I know that Black calls for abolition prior to emancipation were radical in comparison to white calls for abolition of slavery. Yet, I also enter abolitionist spaces with one caution. When academics and activists imagine a world that would not need prisons or police, or slavery, for that matter, it is still possible for that world to exist on stolen Indigenous lands, and decolonization is not always an explicit part of these discussions (although sometimes it is, and I am grateful for these spaces). My desires for prison and police abolition necessitate that it occurs in relation to "land back." I believe my discussions of historical data in this section demonstrates that to not include decolonization in the conversations about abolition is a mistake.

82. "The Letter: Department of the Interior, Indian School Service," *The Carlisle Arrow* 4, no. 23 (1901), Carlisle Indian School Digital Resource Center.

83. W. M. Fishback, "The White Man's Side, and the Indian's," *The Red Man* 7, no. 5 (1895): 7.

84. Richard Henry Pratt, *The Red Man and Helper* 14, no. 33 (1904): 2.

85. Elaine Goodale, Amelia S. Quinton, and Herbert Welsh, "Indian Department," *Southern Workman* 15, no. 11 (1886): 115. Hampton University Archives.

86. "Setting the Negro Apart," *The Red Man* 12, no. 5 (1895): 5, Carlisle Indian School Digital Resource Center.

87. Tiffany Lethabo King, *The Black Shoals: Offshore Formations of Black and Native Studies* (Durham, NC: Duke University Press, 2019); Lorenzo Veracini, "Settler Collective, Founding Violence and Disavowal: The Settler Colonial Situation," *Journal of Intercultural Studies* 29, no. 4 (2008); Lisa Slater, *Anxieties of Belonging in Settler Colonialism: Australia, Race and Place* (New York: Routledge, 2019).

88. For example, see Joanne Barker, *Red Scare: The State's Indigenous Terrorist* (Berkeley: University of California Press, 2021); Ward Churchill and Jim Vander Wall, *Agents of Repression: The FBI's Secret Wars against the Black Panther Party and the American Indian Movement.* (Cambridge, MA: South End Press, 2002).

3. PACIFIC CURRENTS

1. A well-known example is Turner's frontier thesis: Frederick Jackson Turner, *The Frontier in American History* (New York: Henry Holt, 1921). For discussions of this discourse, see John Eperjesi, *The Imperialist Imaginary: Visions of Asia and the Pacific in American Culture* (Hanover, NH: Dartmouth College Press, 2004); Walter LaFeber, *The New Empire: An Interpretation of American Expansion, 1860–1898* (Ithaca, NY: Cornell University Press, 1998).

2. "Notes from Mrs. Cook's Journal," *The Red Man and Helper* 17, no. 5 (1901): 2, Carlisle Indian School Digital Resource Center.

3. N. DE G. Doubleday, "Aboriginal Industries," *Southern Workman* 30, no. 2 (1901): 81. I do not have space in this chapter to devote to the many geographic locations that US reformers sought to influence, and will focus specifically on Hawai'i and the Philippines rather than the Caribbean or China.

4. Nitasha Tamar Sharma, *Hawaii Is My Haven: Race and Indigeneity in the Black Pacific* (Durham, NC: Duke University Press, 2021), 15, 47.

5. For example, American-implemented education in the Philippines was often framed in relation to the education of Native peoples in the United States rather than the Black South. In Hawai'i, plantation histories often leave out a discussion of Hawai'i's Black population. Anne Paulet, "To Change the World: The Use of American Indian Education in the Philippines," *History of Education Quarterly* 47, no. 2 (2007); Elizabeth M. Eittreim, *Teaching Empire: Native Americans, Filipinos, and US Imperial Education, 1879–1918* (Lawrence: University Press of Kansas, 2019); Sharma, *Hawaii Is My Haven.*

6. J. Kēhaulani Kauanui, *Paradoxes of Hawaiian Sovereignty: Land, Sex, and the Colonial Politics of State Nationalism* (Durham, NC: Duke University Press, 2018); Dylan Rodriguez, *Suspended Apocalypse: White Supremacy, Genocide, and the Filipino Condition* (Minneapolis: University of Minnesota Press, 2010).

7. Robert Francis Engs, *Educating the Disfranchised and Disinherited: Samuel Chapman Armstrong and Hampton Institute, 1839–1893* (Knoxville: University of Tennessee Press, 1999); Carl Kalani Beyer, "The White Architects of Hawaiian Education," *American Educational History Journal* 44, no. 2 (2017).

8. Donal F. Lindsey, *Indians at Hampton Institute, 1877–1923* (Urbana: University of Illinois Press, 1994), 1.

9. Carl Kalani Beyer, "The Connection of Samuel Chapman Armstrong as Both Borrower and Architect of Education in Hawai'i," *History of Education Quarterly* 47, no. 1 (2007).

10. Katherine Margaret Cook, *Public Education in Hawaii* (Washington DC: United States Department of the Interior, Department of Education, 1935).

11. Cook, *Public Education in Hawaii.*

12. Sharma, citing Takara, identifies Black and formerly enslaved educator Betsy Stockton and her school for non-royal Hawaiian children on Maui as the model for the Hilo boarding school, which Armstrong cited as one of the key locations that inspired Hampton. Thus, Sharma attributes Hampton's inspiration in the Pacific to the educational connection between Native Hawaiians, white missionaries, and an enslaved Black women teacher, complicating the notion of a clear genealogy of Hampton's founding. Sharma, *Hawaii Is My Haven,* 45; Kathryn Takara, "The African Diaspora in Nineteenth Century Hawaii," in *They Followed the Trade Winds: African Americans in Hawaii,* ed. Miles Jackson (Honolulu: Hawaii University Press, 2014), 15.

13. Henry P. Judd, "The Practical Side of School Life," in *Building for the Future* (Hilo, HI: Hilo Boarding School Print, 1910), 6, Hawaiian Mission Children's Society Archive.

14. *Catalogue of the Hilo Boarding School for Boys, 1910–1911* (Hilo, HI: Hilo Boarding School Press 1910): 23, Hawaiian Mission Children's Society Archive.

15. Samuel Chapman Armstrong, "A Successful Work from 'Jubilee Notes, 1886'" in *Catalogue of the Hilo Boarding School for Boys 1907–1908* (Hilo, HI: Hilo Boarding School Press, 1907): 1, Hawaiian Mission Children's Society Archive.

16. Armstrong, "A Successful Work."

17. Margaret Kenwill, "Co-Education for the Hawaiians," *Hawaiian Gazette,* 11 August 1891, Box 1, Folder 10, Samuel Chapman Armstrong Papers, Williams College Archive.

18. *The Indian Helper* 15, no. 29 (1900): 2, Carlisle Indian School Digital Resource Center.

19. The Thomasites brought with them negative views of their students, referring to them as "barbarians" and "niggers." Fred W. Atkinson, "The Educational Problem in the Philippines," *The Atlantic,* March 1902, https://www.theatlantic.com/magazine/archive/1902/03/the-educational-problem-in-the-philippines/636646/.

20. Glenn A. May, "Social Engineering in the Philippines: The Aims and Execution of American Educational Policy, 1900–1913," *Philippine Studies* 24, no. 2 (1976); Atkinson, "The Educational Problem in the Philippines."

21. D. J. Fleming, "Some Aspects of the Philippine Educational System," *International Review of Mission* 10, no. 2 (1921); Shaunna Harrington, "The Philippine Normal School During US Colonial Rule, 1901–1916" (Arc of Teacher Education Conference, Bridgewater State University, March 26, 2015); J. J. Eaton, "The Manila Trade School," *The Annals of the American Academy of Political and Social Science* 33, no. 1 (1909). In addition to being the superintendent of education in the Philippines and later a university professor, David Barrows was also a promoter of eugenicist thought. Juliet R. Kunkel, "The Eugenic University," (PhD diss., University of California Berkeley, 2021).

22. May, "Social Engineering in the Philippines"; Paulet, "To Change the World."

23. Ingrid Dineen-Wimberly, "To Carry 'the Black Man's Burden': T. Thomas Fortune's Vision of African American Colonization of the Philippines in 1902 and 1903," *International Journal of Business and Social Science* 5, no. 10 (2014); Michele Mitchell, "'The Black Man's Burden': African Americans, Imperialism, and Notions of Racial Manhood 1890–1910," *International Review of Social History* 44, no. S7 (1999).

24. *The Indian Helper* 15, no. 29 (1900): 2.

25. Alyssa A. Hunziker, "Playing Indian, Playing Filipino: Native American and Filipino Interactions at the Carlisle Indian Industrial School," *American Quarterly* 72, no. 2 (2020): 423–448.

26. Pima student Daniel M. Thomas is discussed in the Carlisle publications as winning a speaking context in which the topic was independence in the Philippines. His argument states:

> We are not capable of governing the Filipinos on account of their distrust of us and the great difference in temperament of the Eastern and Western people, and also because the impulse for good government must come from within; We are robbing the Filipinos of their initiative and are dulling and weakening their powers, hopes,

and the very character of their race, and are taking from them the one condition necessary for economic advancement—freedom; The retention of the islands is advanced by large corporations of America to protect them in their selfish plans for gaining lands, mines, and wealth in various ways.

In this language you can see a critique of US imperialism couched in the discourse of freedom and individual struggle common to colonial narratives that sought to aggrandize colonizers and settlers. In "Pima Indian Argues for Philippine Independence," *The Carlisle Arrow* 10, no. 32 (1914): 4, Carlisle Indian School Digital Repository.

27. Lorenzo Alexander L. Puente, "Anti-US Imperialism as Assertion of Black Subjectivity at the Turn of the Last Century," *Kritika Kultura* 5 (2004).

28. William L. Brown, "The Mohonk Conference," *Southern Workman* 32, no 12 (1903): 585.

29. William L. Brown, "The Mohonk Conference," *Southern Workman* 33, no 11 (1904): 586.

30. William L. Brown, "The Mohonk Conference," *Southern Workman* 41, no. 12 (1912): 708–709.

31. Sharma, *Hawaii Is My Haven;* Sumner J. La Croix, "The Economic History of Hawaiʻi: A Short Introduction," (working paper, East West Center, University of Hawaii, 2002); Ralph S. Kuykendall, "Early Hawaiian Commercial Development," *Pacific Historical Review* 3, no. 4 (1934).

32. Noenoe K. Silva, *Aloha Betrayed: Native Hawaiian Resistance to American Colonialism* (Durham, NC: Duke University Press, 2004), 50.

33. Silva, *Aloha Betrayed,* 51.

34. Silva, *Aloha Betrayed,* 52.

35. Silva, *Aloha Betrayed,* 53.

36. Sharma, *Hawaii Is My Haven.*

37. Robert H. Stauffer, *Kahana: How the Land Was Lost* (Honolulu: University of Hawaii Press, 2003); Jocelyn Linnekin, "The Hui Lands of Keanae: Hawaiian Land Tenure and the Great Mahele," *The Journal of the Polynesian Society* 92, no. 2 (1983); Jocelyn Linnekin, "Statistical Analysis of the Great Māhele: Some Preliminary Findings," *The Journal of Pacific History* 22, no. 1 (1987).

38. Kate A. Berry, "Sovereign Sugar: Industry and Environment in Hawaiʻi," *Geographical Review* 108, no. 2 (2018).

39. Jennifer M. L. Chock, "One Hundred Years of Illegitimacy: International Legal Analysis of the Illegal Overthrow of the Hawaiian Monarchy, Hawaiʻi's Annexation, and Possible Reparations," *University Hawaii Law Review* 17 (1995); Sumner J. La Croix and Christopher Grandy, "The Political Instability of Reciprocal Trade and the Overthrow of the Hawaiian Kingdom," *The Journal of Economic History* 57, no. 1 (1997); William A. Russ, "The Role of Sugar in Hawaiian Annexation," *Pacific Historical Review* 12, no. 4 (1943); J. Kēhaulani Kauanui, "Colonialism in Equality: Hawaiian Sovereignty and the Question of US Civil Rights," *South Atlantic Quarterly* 107, no. 4 (2008); J. Kēhaulani Kauanui, "The Multiplicity of

Hawaiian Sovereignty Claims and the Struggle for Meaningful Autonomy," *Comparative American Studies: An International Journal* 3, no. 3 (2005).

40. "Hawaiian Problems," *Southern Workman* 31, no. 2 (1902): 58.

41. "Hawaiian Problems," 58.

42. "Hawaiian Problems," 61.

43. Samuel Chapman Armstrong, "Jubilee Address: To the Trustees, Faculty and Alumni of Oahu College and Former and Present Pupils at Punahou," *Hawaiian Gazette,* 30 June 1891, Box 1, Folder 10, Samuel Chapman Armstrong Papers, Williams College Archive.

44. Samuel Chapman Armstrong, "The Hawaiian Problem," *Hawaiian Gazette,* 30 August 1880, Box 1, Folder 10, Samuel Chapman Armstrong Papers, Williams College Archive.

45. Many of the youth sentenced to these industrial schools committed "crimes" such as being an orphan, vagrancy, or larceny. Girls were often sentenced to industrial schools not for actual crimes but in order to police their sexuality. "Industrial Schools, Administrative Files," Box 296, Folders 1–6, Hawaii State Archives.

46. Penal industrial schooling also had a connection to the Philippines. The Lake Mohonk conferences invited numerous speakers about the Philippines and the American educational programs there each year, one of whom was Mortimer L. Student, the director of the Bureau of Prisons in the Philippines, who spoke about the industrial programs at the Bilibid prison where "every prisoner is taught some trade of his own choosing and is so well taught that when he is dismissed and goes into town to get a job his certificate of discharge is considered so good a recommendation that he is usually given preference over other applicants." William L. Brown, "The Mohonk Conference," *Southern Workman* 41, no. 11 (1912): 708.

47. "Industrial Schools, Administrative Files," Box 296, Folders 1–6, Hawaii State Archives.

48. Correspondence from Wm. G. Irwin & Company (limited), Vice President W. M. Gifford to W. H. Babbit Superintendent of Public Instruction, 7 November 1906, Box 261, General Correspondence by Subject, Commissioner of Public Lands, Hawaii State Archives.

49. Correspondence from Wm. G. Irwin & Company (limited), Vice President W. M. Gifford to W. H. Babbit Superintendent of Public Instruction.

50. *Catalogue of the Hilo Boarding School for Boys 1907–1908* (Hilo HI: Hilo Boarding School Press, 1907): 18, Hawaiian Mission Children's Society Archive.

51. *Catalogue of the Hilo Boarding School for Boys,* 39.

52. *Catalogue of the Hilo Boarding School for Boys,* 39.

53. The Principals of the Manual and Preparatory, *Annual Report of the Kamehameha School for Boys for the Year 1894* (Honolulu, HI: Printed by Robert Grieve, Steam Book, and Job Printer 1895): 11, Hawaiian Mission Children's Society Archive.

54. *Annual Report of the Kamehameha School for Boys for the Year 1894,* 11.

55. *Annual Report of the Kamehameha School for Boys for the Year 1894,* 15.

56. *Annual Report of the Kamehameha School for Boys for the Year 1894*, 16.

57. Ch'eng-K'un Cheng, "Assimilation in Hawaii and the Bid for Statehood," *Social Forces* 30 (1951); Eric Tyrone Lowery Love, *Race Over Empire: Racism and US Imperialism, 1865–1900* (Chapel Hill: University of North Carolina Press, 2004); Arvin complicates this with her analysis of how Polynesians were situated vis-à-vis whiteness as well as the ways in which Hawai'i was positioned as a racial paradise as part of inclusion by possession. Maile Renee Arvin, *Possessing Polynesians: The Science of Settler Colonial Whiteness in Hawai'i and Oceania* (Durham, NC: Duke University Press, 2019).

58. This is inspired by Paul V. Kroskrity's discussion of ideologies of language that "index the political economic interests . . . and nation states." Paul V. Kroskrity, "Language Ideologies—Evolving Perspectives," *Society and Language Use* 7, no. 3 (2010): 192. Another close example of how written literacy in a language does not preclude settlement and dispossession is the creation and widespread use of the Cherokee Syllabary that preceded Cherokee removal. Jill Lepore, *A is for American: Letters and Other Characters in the Newly United States* (New York: Vintage, 2007); Theda Perdue and Michael D. Green, *The Cherokee Removal: A Brief History with Documents* (Boston, Bedford-St. Martin's, 1995).

59. Bayley J. Marquez and Juliet R. Kunkel, "The Domestication Genocide of Settler Colonial Language Ideologies," *American Quarterly Special Issue: The Politics of Language, Multilingualism, and Translation in American Studies*, 73 no. 3 (September 2021).

60. *The Polynesian*, June 15, 1861, Box 1, Folder 9, Samuel Chapman Armstrong Papers, Williams College Archives.

61. Samuel Chapman Armstrong, "The Hawaiian Problem," *Hawaiian Gazette*, 30 August 1880, Box 1, Folder 10, Samuel Chapman Armstrong Papers, Williams College Archive.

62. Additionally, "The development in both places of the classic pattern of very rich and very poor, millers and field hands, argues persuasively for the universal determinism of sugar in societal development." I would argue that this is a legacy of the plantation formation, which always has ties to slavery and settlement as sugar production inherently functions along the lines of antiblackness and colonialism once the plantation complex was formed. John A. Larkin, *Sugar and the Origins of the Modern Philippine Society* (Berkeley: University of California Press, 1993): 3, 6.

63. Larkin, *Sugar and the Origins of the Modern Philippine Society*, 51.

64. Larkin, *Sugar and the Origins of the Modern Philippine Society*, 54–60.

65. M. Friedman, "Teaching Farming in the Philippines," *Southern Workman* 34, no. 1. (1905): 22.

66. Friedman, "Teaching Farming in the Philippines."

67. An article in *Southern Workman* discussing Professor Kelly Miller's recent article in Arena of the same title. "The Anglo-Saxon and the African," *Southern Workman* 32, no. 1 (1903): 9.

68. "American Education in the Philippines," *Southern Workman* 34, no. 5 (1905): 261.

69. Calvin W. Woodward, "What Shall be Taught in an Indian School," *Southern Workman* 30, no. 8 (1901): 429.
70. Woodward, "What Shall be Taught in an Indian School," 431.
71. "Development or Repression," *Southern Workman* 34, no. 3 (1905): 131.
72. "American Education in the Philippines," *Southern Workman* 34, no. 5 (1905): 260.
73. "The Education of the Stranger," *Southern Workman* 33, no. 7 (1904): 371.
74. "The Education of the Stranger," 372.
75. This article published in *Southern Workman* states that it contains "extracts from a new book on the Philippines which will appear from the press of Ginn and Company in May 1905, by Dr. F. W. Atkinson, of the Brooklyn Polytechnic Institute and formerly General superintendent of Philippine Education." Fredrick W. Atkinson, "Education in the Philippine Islands," *Southern Workman* 34, no. 2 (1905): 74.
76. W. L. Brown, "The Mohonk Conference," *Southern Workman* 33, no. 11 (1904): 590.
77. Brown, "The Mohonk Conference," 589.
78. M. Friedman, "Industrial Education and the Development of the Filipinos," *Southern Workman* 33, no. 7 (1904): 381; Ranald P. Gleason, "Industrial Problems in the Philippines," *Southern Workman* 32, no. 11 (1903): 529.
79. Gleason, "Industrial Problems in the Philippines," 529.
80. Henry Flury, "Some Aspects of Philippine Education," *Southern Workman* 41, no. 3 (1912): 156–157.
81. Atkinson, "Education in the Philippine Islands," 78.
82. Friedman, "Industrial Education and the Development of the Filipinos," 382.
83. Washington and Du Bois, *The Negro in the South, His Economic Progress in Relation to His Moral and Religious Development*.
84. "Filipinos and American Methods of Education," *Southern Workman* 33, no. 2 (1904): 68.
85. Eaton, "The Manila Trade School."
86. Friedman, "Industrial Education and the Development of the Filipinos," 384.
87. Samuel Chapman Armstrong, "The Hawaiian Problem," *Hawaiian Gazette*, 30 August 1880, Box 1, Folder 10, Samuel Chapman Armstrong Papers, Williams College Archive.
88. Arvin, *Possessing Polynesians*.
89. W. N. Armstrong, "Current Comment," found as part of a family scrapbook in Box 2, Folder 14, Samuel Chapman Armstrong Papers, Williams College Archives.
90. *The Polynesian*, June 15, 1861, Box 1, Folder 9, Samuel Chapman Armstrong Papers, Williams College Archives.
91. Henry L. Flury, "Among the Igorots," *Southern Workman* 41, no. 11 (1912): 615. Igorot is a label given by colonizers for the people living in the mountains of northern Luzon. In the present day, Igorot people negotiate complex forms of identity in relation to the Philippine state that allow for them to maintain entitlements

to land and resources. Deirdre McKay, "Rethinking Indigenous Place: Igorot Identity and Locality in the Philippines," *The Australian Journal of Anthropology* 17, no. 3 (2006).

92. "Notes and Exchanges," *Southern Workman* 33, no. 11 (1904): 639.

93. William Allan Reed, "The Negritos of the Philippines," *Southern Workman* 33, no. 5 (1904): 273. Negrito was a term given to a large group of South Asian peoples by colonizers who classified them based on phenotype. The grouping included peoples living in the Andaman Islands and the Malay peninsula in Thailand. David R. Barrows, in a decidedly eugenic text, described them as a pagan people of the islands who had significantly intermixed with the Malay population. In reality, this population is comprised of a large number of groups with over thirty languages in the Philippines alone and of a variety of origins and cultures. David P. Barrows, "The Negrito and Allied Types in the Philippines," *American Anthropologist* 12, no. 3 (1910). Thomas N. Headland, "Thirty Endangered Languages in the Philippines," *Work Papers of the Summer Institute of Linguistics, University of North Dakota Session* 47, no. 1 (2003): 1.

4. ATLANTIC CURRENTS

1. Donald Spivey, *The Politics of Miseducation: The Booker Washington Institute of Liberia, 1929–1984* (Lexington: University Press of Kentucky, 1986), 19.

2. "Educational needs and opportunities in Liberia," International Education Board Records, Box 16, Folder 242, New York Colonization Society–Booker Washington Agricultural and Industrial Institute of Liberia, Rockefeller Archive Center.

3. Spivey, *The Politics of Miseducation*, 17.

4. Spivey, *The Politics of Miseducation*, 18.

5. Spivey, *The Politics of Miseducation*, 19, 31.

6. "Educational needs and opportunities in Liberia," 2.

7. Minutes of the Meeting of the Board of Trustees of the Booker Washington Agricultural and Industrial Institute of Liberia, September 7, 1938, International Education Board Records Box 16, Folder 241, New York Colonization Society–Booker Washington Agricultural and Industrial Institute of Liberia, Rockefeller Archive Center.

8. Some of the clearest examples of this occur in the work of Alexander Crummell. Anthony Appiah, "Alexander Crummell and the Invention of Africa," *The Massachusetts Review* 31, no. 3 (1990); Wilson Jeremiah Moses, *Alexander Crummell: A Study of Civilization and Discontent* (Oxford: Oxford University Press on Demand, 1989).

9. Andrew Zimmerman, *Alabama in Africa: Booker T. Washington, The German Empire, and the Colonization of the New South* (Princeton, NJ: Princeton University Press, 2010); Mahasan Offutt-Chaney, "'Black Crisis' and the 'Likely' Privatization of Public Education in New Orleans and Liberia," *Critical Studies in Education* (2019). Discussions of US education for Blacks applied to African contexts include Shoko Yamada, "Educational Borrowing as Negotiation: Re-Examining the

Influence of the American Black Industrial Education Model on British Colonial Education in Africa," *Comparative Education* 44, no. 1 (2008); Donald Spivey, "The African Crusade for Black Industrial Schooling," *The Journal of Negro History* 63, no. 1 (1978); Davis R. Hunt, "Charles T. Loram and an American Model for African Education in South Africa," *African Studies Review* 19, no. 2 (1976).

10. Lucy Jarosz, "Constructing the Dark Continent: Metaphor as Geographic Representation of Africa," *Geografiska Annaler: Series B, Human Geography* 74, no. 2 (1992); Patrick Brantlinger, "Victorians and Africans: The Genealogy of the Myth of the Dark Continent," *Critical Inquiry* 12, no. 1 (1985); Noah R. Bassil, "The Roots of Afropessimism: The British Invention of the 'Dark Continent,'" *Critical Arts* 25, no. 3 (2011).

11. Arit John, "Confusing a Country for a Continent: How We Talk About Africa," *The Atlantic,* August 29, 2013, https://www.theatlantic.com/international/archive/2013/08/confusing-country-continent-how-we-talk-about-africa/311621/

12. Robert J. Berkhofer Jr., *The White Man's Indian: Images of the American Indian from Columbus to Present* (New York: Vintage Books, 1979).

13. Thomas Jesse Jones, *Education in Africa: A Study of West, South, and Equatorial Africa by the African Education Commission, under the Auspices of the Phelps-Stokes Fund and Foreign Mission Societies of North America and Europe* (New York: Phelps-Stokes Fund, 1922).

14. Melinda Vaughn and Lori Verstegen Ryan, "Corporate Governance in South Africa: A Bellwether for the Continent?" *Corporate Governance: An International Review* 14, no. 5 (2006); Emmanuel Mogaji, "Africa Is Not a Country: Rebranding and Repositioning Africa as a Continent," in *Marketing Brands in Africa: Perspectives on the Evolution of Branding in an Emerging Market,* ed. Samuelson Appau (Cham, Switzerland: Palgrave Macmillan, 2021).

15. William H. Watkins, *The White Architects of Black Education: Ideology and Power in America, 1865–1954* (New York: Teachers College Press, 2001).

16. Jones, *Education in Africa.*

17. Thomas Jesse Jones, *Education in East Africa: A Study of East, Central, and South Africa by the Second African Education Commission, under the Auspices of the Phelps-Stokes Fund, in Cooperation with the International Education Board Phelps-Stokes Fund* (New York: Phelps-Stokes Fund, 1925).

18. For example, the British colonial office helped to fund the second trip of the Phelps-Stokes Africa commission, and the first commission report talked about securing cooperation with missionary societies and Great Britain as part of planning their trip. Jones, *Education in Africa;* Jones, *Education in East Africa.*

19. John Karefah Marah, "Educational Adaptation and Pan-Africanism: Developmental Trends in Africa," *Journal of Black Studies* 17, no. 4 (1987); Louis R. Harlan, "Booker T. Washington and the White Man's Burden," *The American Historical Review* 71, no. 2 (1966); David Sehat, "The Civilizing Mission of Booker T. Washington," *The Journal of Southern History* 73, no. 2 (2007); Andrew Barnes, *Global Christianity and the Black Atlantic: Tuskegee, Colonialism, and the Shaping of African Industrial Education* (Waco, TX: Baylor University Press, 2017).

20. Andrew Hayden Manson and Bernard Mbenga, "The African National Congress in the Western Transvaal/Northern Cape Platteland, c. 1910–1964: Patterns of Diffusion and Support for Congress in a Rural Setting," *South African Historical Journal* 64, no. 3 (2012); Thomas M. T. Dube, "Literature on African Resistance to Domination in South Africa: 1910–1966," *A Current Bibliography on African Affairs* 7, no. 2 (1974); Clarence G. Contee, "Du Bois, the NAACP, and the Pan-African Congress of 1919," *The Journal of Negro History* 57, no. 1 (1972).

21. Jarvis R. Givens, "A Grammar for Black Education Beyond Borders: Exploring Technologies of Schooling in the African Diaspora," *Race, Ethnicity and Education* 19, no. 6 (2015), 10–11.

22. Jackson Davis, "Confidential: Impressions of Liberia—March 31–April 12, 1935," International Education Board Records, Box 16, Folder 236, New York State Colonization Society–Booker Washington Institute of Liberia, Rockefeller Archive Center.

23. Davis, "Confidential: Impressions of Liberia."

24. E. D. Morel, "The Future of Tropical Africa," *Southern Workman* 41, no. 6 (1912): 355.

25. Robert E. Park, "Education by Cultural Groups," *Southern Workman* 41, no. 6 (1912): 370.

26. Charles Kirk Pilkington, "The Trials of Brotherhood: The Founding of the Commission on Interracial Cooperation," *The Georgia Historical Quarterly* 69, no. 1 (1985): 55–80.

27. Jones, *Education in Africa*, 12.

28. Jones, *Education in Africa*, 7.

29. Jones, *Education in Africa*, 7.

30. Jones, *Education in Africa*, 81.

31. Jones, *Education in Africa*, 13, quoting Robert Russa Moton.

32. Jones, *Education in Africa*, 95.

33. St. Clair Drake, "The Black Diaspora in Pan-African Perspective," *The Black Scholar* 7, no. 1 (1975); St. Clair Drake, *The Redemption of Africa and Black Religion*, (Chicago: Third World Press, 1970).

34. Charles Templeman Loram, *The Education of the South African Native* (New York: Negro Universities Press, 1917), 12.

35. Loram, *The Education of the South African Native*.

36. Maurice S. Evans, "Education among the Bantu of Southwest Africa," *Southern Workman* 41, no.6 (1912): 364.

37. Loram, *The Education of the South African Native*, 16, 19, 28.

38. Park cites a speech by Maurice Evans in which he describes these segregation debates in South Africa. Robert M. Park, "Notes and Reviews: Tuskegee International Conference on the Negro," *The Journal of Race Development* 3, no. 1 (1912): 119. James Emman Kwegyir Aggrey, an African intellectual who was compared to Booker T. Washington for his support of industrial education and conciliatory politics, was a member of the commission that authored the report on education in Africa with Thomas Jesse Jones. He gave a speech in South Africa telling Black

South Africans to deal with the segregation system as it was. This speech could be compared to Washington's Atlanta Exhibition speech, which called on Black Southerners to "cast down your buckets where you are at." Edward H. Berman, "American Influence on African Education: The Role of the Phelps-Stokes Fund's Education," *Comparative Education Review* 15, no. 2 (1971): 139.

39. Loram, *The Education of the South African Native*, 28, 29.
40. Loram, *The Education of the South African Native*, 28.
41. H. G. W. Wintersgill, "The Orchestras of Central Africa," *Southern Workman* 34, no. 12 (1905): 657.
42. Thomas Jesse Jones, "Excerpts from Principal Rupel's letter of August 2nd and comments," included in correspondence to Henry L. West from Thomas Jesse Jones, August 31, 1937, International Education Board Records, Box 16, Folder 239, New York State Colonization Society–Booker Washington Agricultural and Industrial Institute of Liberia, Rockefeller Archive Center.
43. R. L. Embree to Thomas Jesse Jones, "Extracts from Memoranda (of British Empire Advisory Committee on Education) on the Education of African Communities. (1935)," 18 September 1937, International Education Board Records, Box 16, Folder 240, New York Colonization Society–Booker T. Washington Agricultural and Industrial Institution of Liberia, Rockefeller Archive Center.
44. Thomas Jesse Jones, *Educational Adaptations: Report of Ten Years Work of the Phelps-Stokes Fund, 1910–1920* (New York: Phelps-Stokes Fund, 1920).
45. Jones, *Education in Africa*, 141–142.
46. Jones, *Education in Africa*, 1.
47. Jones, *Education in Africa*, 91.
48. Jones, *Education in Africa*, 1.
49. Robert E. Park, "Education by Cultural Groups," *Southern Workman* 41, no. 6 (1912): 371.
50. Park, "Education by Cultural Groups."
51. Park, "Education by Cultural Groups," 375.
52. Jones, *Education in Africa*, 26.
53. Saidiya Hartman, *Lose Your Mother: A Journey Along the Atlantic Slave Route* (New York: Farrar, Straus, and Giroux, 2008).
54. Loram, *The Education of the South African Native*, 38.
55. Booker T. Washington and William Edward Burghardt Du Bois, *The Negro in the South, his Economic Progress in Relation to his Moral and Religious Development*. The William Levi Bull Lectures for the Year 1907, (Philadelphia: GW Jacobs, 1907), 56.
56. Berkhofer, *The White Man's Indian;* Phillip J. Deloria, *Indians in Unexpected Places* (Lawrence: University Press of Kansas, 2004).
57. Loram, *The Education of the South African Native*, 35.
58. Loram, *The Education of the South African Native*, 149.
59. Loram, *The Education of the South African Native*, 150.
60. Loram, *The Education of the South African Native*, 16.
61. Jones, *Education in Africa*, 4.

62. Jones, *Education in Africa,* 2, 20.
63. Jones, *Education in Africa,* 20.
64. Jones, *Education in Africa,* 57.
65. For example, see Zimmerman, *Alabama in Africa;* Harlan, "Booker T. Washington and the White Man's Burden."
66. Josiah Tyler, "Among the Zulus," *Southern Workman* 23, no. 12 (1894): 213.
67. Report of R. R. Taylor upon the Booker T. Washington Agricultural and Industrial Institute at Kakata, Republic of Liberia, October 1929, International Education Board Records Box 16, Folder 235, New York Colonization Society–Booker Washington Agricultural and Industrial Institute of Liberia, Rockefeller Archive Center, 4.
68. Report of R. R. Taylor, 6, 8.
69. Report of R. R. Taylor, 13.
70. Report of R. R. Taylor, 17, 18.
71. Thomas Jesse Jones to Harvey S. Firestone Jr., 31 August 1937, International Education Board Records Box 16, Folder 239, New York Colonization Society–Booker Washington Agricultural and Industrial Institute of Liberia, Rockefeller Archive Center; L. A. Roy to Thomas Jesse Jones, Jackson Davis, Thomas S. Donahugh, and Henry L. West, 14 January 1939, International Education Board Records Box 17, Folder 243, New York Colonization Society–Booker Washington Agricultural and Industrial Institute of Liberia, Rockefeller Archive Center.
72. Copy of letter sent to Jackson Davis, W. T. Runals to Thomas Jesse Jones, 24 August 1937, International Education Board Records Box 16, Folder 239, New York Colonization Society–Booker Washington Agricultural and Industrial Institute of Liberia, Rockefeller Archive Center; Minutes of the Meeting of the Board of Trustees of the Booker Washington Agricultural and Industrial Institute of Liberia, 16 December 1937, International Education Board Records Box 16, Folder 240, New York Colonization Society–Booker Washington Agricultural and Industrial Institute of Liberia, Rockefeller Archive Center.
73. Simone Browne, *Dark Matters: On the Surveillance of Blackness* (Durham, NC: Duke University Press, 2015); Britt Rusert, "Plantation Ecologies: The Experimental Plantation in and against James Grainger's 'The Sugar-Cane,'" *Early American Studies,* 13, no. 2 (2015); Katherine McKittrick, "On Plantations, Prisons, and a Black Sense of Place," *Social & Cultural Geography* 12, no. 8 (2011).
74. Minutes of the Meeting of the Board of Trustees of the Booker Washington Agricultural and Industrial Institute of Liberia, 7 September 1938, International Education Board Records Box 16, Folder 241, New York Colonization Society–Booker Washington Agricultural and Industrial Institute of Liberia, Rockefeller Archive Center; Minutes of the Meeting of the Board of Trustees of the Booker Washington Agricultural and Industrial Institute of Liberia, 28 November 1939, International Education Board Records Box 17, Folder 243, New York Colonization Society–Booker Washington Agricultural and Industrial Institute of Liberia, Rockefeller Archive Center.

75. Christine Whyte, "Between Empire and Colony: American Imperialism and Pan-African Colonialism in Liberia, 1810–2003," *National Identities* 18, no. 1 (2016); Judson M. Lyon, "Informal Imperialism: The United States in Liberia, 1897–1912," *Diplomatic History* 5, no. 3 (1981); Cedric Robinson, "DuBois and Black Sovereignty: The Case of Liberia," *Race & Class* 32, no. 2 (1990).

76. Jessica M. Parr, "An African Republic: Black and White Virginians in the Making of Liberia," *Journal of the Early Republic* 29, no. 1 (2009); William Edward Burghardt Du Bois, "Liberia, the League and the United States," *Foreign Affairs* 11, no. 4 (1933).

77. Jones, *Education in Africa*, 10, 86.

78. Jones, *Education in Africa*, 86.

79. Jones, *Education in Africa*, 10, most likely referencing Lothrop Stoddard, *The Rising Tide of Color: The Threat Against White World-Supremacy* (New York: Charles Scribner's Sons, 1920) and Lothrop Stoddard, *The Revolt Against Civilization: The Menace of the Under Man* (New York: Charles Scribner's Sons, 1922). Stoddard was a white-supremacist eugenicist historian who believed in racial hierarchy.

80. Maurice S. Evans, "Education Among the Bantu of Southwest Africa," *Southern Workman* 41, no.6 (1912): 366, 368.

81. Hartman, *Lose Your Mother*.

82. Du Bois, "Liberia, the League and the United States."

83. Jackson Davis, "Confidential: Impressions of Liberia-March 31–April 12, 1935," International Education Board Records, Box 16, folder 236, New York State Colonization Society–Booker Washington Institute of Liberia, Rockefeller Archive Center, 2.

84. "Speech of the Hon. Chauncey M. Depew at Hampton Institute, Virginia," *Southern Workman* 21, no. 4 (1892): 63.

85. William I. Thomas, "Education and Racial Traits," *Southern Workman* 41, no. 6 (1912): 378, 386.

86. "Commencement Address Delivered by the Hon. Lester A. Walton, American Minister to Liberia to the Members of the Graduating Class of Liberia College, Monrovia, November 30, 1938," 4–5, International Education Board Records Box 17, Folder 243, New York Colonization Society–Booker Washington Agricultural and Industrial Institute of Liberia, Rockefeller Archive Center.

87. "An address by Dr. Thomas Jesse Jones, Educational Director of the Phelps-Stokes Fund ... Delivered at the League of Nations Association Convention, St. Louis, Missouri at 4 p.m., January 13, 1933. Liberia and the League of Nations," International Education Board Records Box 16, Folder 235, New York Colonization Society–Booker Washington Agricultural and Industrial Institute of Liberia, Rockefeller Archive Center.

88. "Address by Dr. Blyden, President of Liberia College, to the Students of Hampton," *Southern Workman* 12, no. 1 (1883): 9.

89. Annie E. Coombes, *Rethinking Settler Colonialism: History and Memory in Australia, Canada, New Zealand and South Africa* (Manchester, UK: Manchester

University Press, 2006); Thiven Reddy, *South Africa, Settler Colonialism and the Failures of Liberal Democracy* (London: Zed Books, 2015); Lorenzo Veracini, *Settler Colonialism: A Theoretical Outline* (Houndmills, UK: Palgrave Macmillan, 2010).

90. Loram, *The Education of the South African Native*, 2.
91. Loram, *The Education of the South African Native*, 3.
92. Loram, *The Education of the South African Native*, 6.
93. Loram, *The Education of the South African Native*, 7.
94. Loram, *The Education of the South African Native*, 8.
95. Loram, *The Education of the South African Native*, 9.
96. Loram, *The Education of the South African Native*, 235.
97. Loram, *The Education of the South African Native*, 236.
98. Maurice S. Evans, "Education Among the Bantu of Southwest Africa," *Southern Workman* 41, no.6 (1912): 364–365.
99. Jones, *Education in Africa*, 8.
100. Katherine McKittrick, "Plantation Futures," *Small Axe: A Caribbean Journal of Criticism* 17, no. 3 (42) (2013); Hartman, *Lose your Mother*.
101. Jackson Davis to Rebecca Davis, 2 March 1939, International Education Board Records Box 17, Folder 243, New York Colonization Society–Booker Washington Agricultural and Industrial Institute of Liberia, Rockefeller Archive Center.
102. Minutes of the Meeting of the Board of Trustees of the Booker Washington Agricultural and Industrial Institute of Liberia, September 9, 1936, International Education Board Records Box 16, Folder 238, New York Colonization Society–Booker Washington Agricultural and Industrial Institute of Liberia, Rockefeller Archive Center; Thomas Jesse Jones to Paul Rupel, 28 September 1937, International Education Board Records Box 16, Folder 240, New York Colonization Society–Booker Washington Agricultural and Industrial Institute of Liberia, Rockefeller Archive Center; Minutes of the Meeting of the Board of Trustees of the Booker Washington Agricultural and Industrial Institute of Liberia, April 8, 1938, International Education Board Records Box 16, Folder 241, New York Colonization Society–Booker Washington Agricultural and Industrial Institute of Liberia, Rockefeller Archive Center.
103. Jarvis R. Givens, *Fugitive Pedagogy: Carter G. Woodson and the Art of Black Teaching* (Cambridge, MA: Harvard University Press, 2021).
104. Thomas Jesse Jones, "Very Confidential Memorandum to Mr. Harvey S. Firestone, Jr., Dr. Anson Phelps Stokes, Mr. Henry L. West, Mr. Jackson Davis, Dr. Thomas S. Donohugh, and Mr. A. B. Parson," 20 January 1939, International Education Board Records Box 17, Folder 243, New York Colonization Society–Booker Washington Agricultural and Industrial Institute of Liberia, Rockefeller Archive Center.
105. Thomas Jesse Jones to F. D. Patterson, 21 February 1939, International Education Board Records Box 17, Folder 243, New York Colonization Society–Booker Washington Agricultural and Industrial Institute of Liberia, Rockefeller Archive Center.
106. Thomas Jesse Jones to H. L. West, Anson Phelps Stokes, Jackson Davis and Thomas S. Donohugh, 10 March 1939, International Education Board Records

Box 17, Folder 243, New York Colonization Society–Booker Washington Agricultural and Industrial Institute of Liberia, Rockefeller Archive Center.

107. Minutes of the Meeting of the Board of Trustees of the Booker Washington Agricultural and Industrial Institute of Liberia, November 28, 1939, International Education Board Records Box 17, Folder 243, New York Colonization Society–Booker Washington Agricultural and Industrial Institute of Liberia, Rockefeller Archive Center.

5. "OUT FROM CABIN AND TEPEE"

1. Hollis Burke Frissell, *Out from the Cabin and the Teepee,* (Hampton, VA: Hampton Institute Press, 1900), 13, https://catalog.hathitrust.org/Record/100787422.
2. Hollis Burke Frissell, "The Attitude of the Indian To White Civilization," n.d., Box 1, Hollis Burke Frissell Papers, Hampton University Archives, 10.
3. Samuel Chapman Armstrong, *Education for Life* (Hampton, VA: Press of the Hampton Normal and Agricultural Institute, 1913), 20.
4. I acknowledge that, in many ways, this comparison between Du Bois and Washington is a false one. For example, in *The Talented Tenth,* Du Bois famously writes, "I insist that the object of all true education is not to make men carpenters, it is to make carpenters men." This "making of men" echoes some of Armstrong's discussions of "making men and women," as discussed in chapter seven. Additionally, the debate between Du Bois and Washington does not often take into account Du Bois's change in political arguments during his later life. William Edward Burghardt Du Bois, *The Talented Tenth,* (New York: James Pott, 1903).
5. *Catalogue of the Hampton Normal and Agricultural Insitute for the Academic Year 1875–6,* Box 2, Folder 16, Samuel Chapman Armstrong Papers, Williams College Archives, 30–31.
6. James D. Anderson, *The Education of Blacks in the South, 1860–1935* (Chapel Hill: University of North Carolina Press, 1988); William H. Watkins, *The White Architects of Black Education: Ideology and Power in America, 1865–1954* (New York: Teachers College Press, 2001).
7. Edwin A. Start, "General Armstrong and the Hampton Institute," *The New England Magazine,* June 1892, Box 2, Folder 18, Samuel Chapman Armstrong Papers, Williams College Archives, 448.
8. Daiva Stasiulis and Nira Yuval-Davis, eds., *Unsettling Settler Societies: Articulations of Gender, Race, Ethnicity and Class* (London: Sage, 1995). A modern example of this is Canada's Indian Act and its 1951 amendments. An earlier example includes the arrival of European women creating new gender relations among white settlers and Indigenous peoples.
9. Rayna Green, "The Pocahontas Perplex: The Image of Indian Women in American Culture," *The Massachusetts Review* 16, no. 4 (1975).

10. Evelyn Nakano Glenn, "Settler Colonialism as Structure: A Framework for Comparative Studies of US Race and Gender Formation," *Sociology of Race and Ethnicity* 1, no. 1 (2015): 59, citing Rose Stremlau, "'To Domesticate and Civilize Wild Indians': Allotment and the Campaign to Reform Indian Families, 1875–1887," *Journal of Family History* 30, no. 3 (2005).

11. Other scholars who also make this argument include: Scott Lauria Morgensen, *Spaces between Us: Queer Settler Colonialism and Indigenous Decolonization* (Minneapolis: University of Minnesota Press, 2011); Mark Rifkin, *When Did Indians Become Straight?: Kinship, the History of Sexuality, and Native Sovereignty* (Oxford: Oxford University Press, 2010).

12. Maile Arvin, Eve Tuck, and Angie Morrill, "Decolonizing Feminism: Challenging Connections between Settler Colonialism and Heteropatriarchy," *Feminist Formations* 25, no. 1 (2013): 8.

13. Arvin, Tuck, and Morrill, "Decolonizing Feminism," 15.

14. Bayley J. Marquez, "'No Women Involved': Settler Colonial Racial Grammars in Black and Indigenous Education," *Feminist Formations* 33, no. 3 (2021).

15. Dorothy E. Roberts, *Killing the Black Body: Race, Reproduction, and the Meaning of Liberty* (New York: Vintage Books, 1999); Tiffany Lethabo King, "Black 'Feminisms' and Pessimism: Abolishing Moynihan's Negro Family," *Theory & Event* 21, no. 1 (2018); Roderick Ferguson, "The Nightmares of the Heteronormative," *Journal for Cultural Research* 4, no. 4 (2000).

16. Hortense J. Spillers, "Mama's Baby, Papa's Maybe: An American Grammar Book," *Diacritics* 17, no. 2 (1987).

17. Christina Sharpe, *In the Wake: On Blackness and Being* (Durham, NC: Duke University Press, 2016);

18. Margaret Kenwill, "Co-Education for the Hawaiians," *Hawaiian Gazette,* 11 August 1891, Box 1, Folder 10, Samuel Chapman Armstrong Papers, Williams College Archive.

19. Marquez, "No Women Involved"; Glenn, "Settler Colonialism as Structure."

20. Armstrong, *Education for Life,* 51.

21. Roberts, *Killing the Black Body.*

22. Start, "General Armstrong and the Hampton Institute," 453.

23. Amy Kaplan, "Manifest Domesticity," *American Literature* 70, no. 3 (1998); Beth H. Piatote, *Domestic Subjects: Gender, Citizenship, and Law in Native American Literature* (New Haven, CT: Yale University Press, 2013); Anne McClintock, *Imperial Leather: Race, Gender, and Sexuality in the Colonial Contest* (New York: Routledge, 1995).

24. Kaplan, "Manifest Domesticity," 582.

25. Ann Laura Stoler, *Carnal Knowledge and Imperial Power: Race and the Intimate in Colonial Rule* (Berkeley: University of California Press, 2010); Karen Sánchez-Eppler, "Raising Empires Like Children: Race, Nation, and Religious Education," *American Literary History* 8, no. 3 (1996): 399–425.

26. Kaplan, 584.

27. Piatote, *Domestic Subjects,* 4.

28. "Lexington Cottage," Indian Education Collection, Hampton University Archives.

29. Armstrong, *Education for Life,* 37–38.

30. Tuskegee utilized this same rhetoric of degradation of Black women. An article in *The Republic,* which reports on the Negro Yeomanry council at Tuskegee, notes that the goals of the council are "to elevate our women and broaden their field of labor. To practice more economy and sacrifice our useless expenditures, that we may get land and get out of debt. To urge it upon our ministers and teachers to give more attention to the home life." "Negro Yeomanry in Council: Conference at Tuskegee School," *The Republican* (n.d.), Box 2, Folder 19, Samuel Chapman Armstrong Papers, Williams College Archives.

31. Armstrong, *Indian Education in the East,* 114.

32. Edwin A. Start, "General Armstrong and the Hampton Institute," *The New England Magazine,* June, 1892, Box 2 Folder 18, Samuel Chapman Armstrong Papers, Williams College Archives, 453.

33. "Thirteenth Annual Report of the Principal, for the School and the Fiscal Year Ending July 1st, 1882," *Southern Workman* 11, no. 6 (1882), Hampton University Archives, 68.

34. "Thirteenth Annual Report of the Principal, for the School and the Fiscal Year Ending July 1st, 1882," 68.

35. Alexander Purves, "Capital and Labor in Co-operative Farming," in *Hampton Negro Conference* (Hampton, VA: Hampton Institute Press, 1999), 87.

36. Barbara Burlison Mooney, "The Comfortable Tasty Framed Cottage: An African American Architectural Iconography," *Journal of the Society of Architectural Historians* 61, no. 1 (2002).

37. William Edward Burghardt Du Bois, "The Home of the Slave (1901)," in *Cabin, Quarter, Plantation: Architecture and Landscapes of North American Slavery,* ed. Clifton Ellis and Rebecca Ginsburg (New Haven, CT: Yale University Press, 2010), 22, 24.

38. Du Bois, "The Home of the Slave," 24–35.

39. Clifton Ellis, "Building for 'Our Family, Black and White': The Changing Form of the Slave House in Antebellum Virginia," in *Cabin, Quarter, Plantation: Architecture and Landscapes of North American Slavery,* ed. Clifton Ellis and Rebecca Ginsburg (New Haven, CT: Yale University Press, 2010), 142, 146–47.

40. Valerie Sherer Mathes, "Nineteenth Century Women and Reform: The Women's National Indian Association," *American Indian Quarterly* 14, no. 1 (1990); Jane E. Simonsen, "'Object Lessons': Domesticity and Display in Native American Assimilation," *American Studies* 43, no. 1 (2002); Roger W. Buffalohead and Paulette Fairbanks Molin, "'A Nucleus of Civilization': American Indian Families at Hampton Institute in the Late Nineteenth Century," *Journal of American Indian Education* 35, no. 3 (1996).

41. Mathes, "Nineteenth Century Women and Reform," 76.

42. Mathes, "Nineteenth Century Women and Reform," 76.

43. Malea D. Powell, "Down by the River, or How Susan La Flesche Picotte Can Teach Us about Alliance as a Practice of Survivance," *College English* 67, no. 1 (2004); Dorothy Clarke Wilson, *Bright Eyes: The Story of Susette La Flesche, an Omaha Indian* (New York: McGraw Hill, 1974); Francis La Flesche, *The Middle Five: Indian Schoolboys of the Omaha Tribe* (Lincoln: University of Nebraska Press, 1978); Sherry L. Smith, "Francis La Flesche and the World of Letters," *American Indian Quarterly* 25, no. 4 (2001).

44. Buffalohead and Molin, "A Nucleus of Civilization."

45. Mathes, "Nineteenth Century Women and Reform," 76.

46. Mathes, "Nineteenth Century Women and Reform," 77.

47. Mathes, "Nineteenth Century Women and Reform," 77. The use of the term "erection" when referring to homes connects back to DeIsle and Diaz's "Itinerant Indigeneities" and their discussion of the "colonial erection." Christine Taitano DeLisle and Vicente M. Diaz, "Itinerant Indigeneities: Navigating Guahan's Treacherous Roads through CHamoru Feminist Pathways," in *Allotment Stories: Indigenous Land Relations Under Settler Siege*, ed. Daniel Heath Justice and Jean M. O'Brien (Minneapolis: University of Minnesota Press, 2022).

48. "Indian Families," Indian Education Collection, Hampton University Archives.

49. Buffalohead and Molin, "A Nucleus of Civilization."

50. "Indian Families," Hampton University Archives, 3.

51. Robert A. Trennert, "Educating Indian Girls at Nonreservation Boarding Schools, 1878–1920," *Western Historical Quarterly* 13, no. 3 (1982): 283.

52. "The Housekeeping Cottage," Indian Education Collection, Hampton University Archives, 1.

53. Watkins, *The White Architects of Black Education*.

54. Start, "General Armstrong and the Hampton Institute," 453.

55. "The Housekeeping Cottage," 1.

56. Cora Folsom, "Problem of the Indian Territory," *The Southern Workman* 13, no. 11 (1889), Hampton University Archives, 120.

57. Armstrong, *The Indian Question*, 17.

58. Maile Renee Arvin, *Possessing Polynesians: The Science of Settler Colonial Whiteness in Hawai'i and Oceania* (Durham, NC: Duke University Press, 2019).

59. Thomas Jesse Jones, *Education in Africa: A Study of West, South, and Equatorial Africa by the African Education Commission, under the Auspices of the Phelps-Stokes Fund and Foreign Mission Societies of North America and Europe* (New York: Phelps-Stokes Fund, 1922), 22.

60. Jones, *Education in Africa*, 23.

61. Jones, *Education in Africa*, 30.

62. Thomas Jesse Jones, "Excerpts from Principal Rupel's letter of August 2nd and comments," included in correspondence to Henry L. West from Thomas Jesse Jones, 31 August 1937, International Education Board Records, Box 16, Folder 239, New York State Colonization Society—Booker Washington Agricultural and Industrial Institute of Liberia, Rockefeller Archive Center.

63. Derek Taira, "Making 'Womenly Women' or 'Servants of Civilization': Ida May Pope, White Female Saviorhood, and Native Hawaiians at the Kamehameha School for Girls, 1894–1914," (presentation, History of Education Society Annual Meeting, Columbus, OH, 2019), 1.

64. Taira, "Making 'Womenly Women' or 'Servants of Civilization,'" 2, citing Ida May Pope, *Handicraft* 15, no. 8 (May 1910): 1.

65. Taira, "Making 'Womenly Women' or 'Servants of Civilization,'" 7, citing the Register of the Kamehameha Schools, 1913–1914, 44; Register 1921–1922, 32, KSA.

66. "Report of the Board of Industrial Schools of the Territory of Hawaii from the Period July 1, 1919 to December 31, 1920," *Honolulu Star Bulletin* (1921), 8, Folder on Hawaii (ter,) Industrial Schools, Board of Reports for 1882, 1920, Hawaiian Mission Children's Society Archive.

67. "Report of the Board of Industrial Schools," 24.

68. Barnes Riznik, "From Barracks to Family Homes: A Social History of Labor Housing Reform on Hawai'i Sugar Plantations," *The Hawaiian Journal of History* 33 (1999).

69. This is noted by both Fred W. Atkinson and David P. Barrows who were the first two heads of US-led education in the Philippines. Fred Washington Atkinson, *The Philippine Islands* (Washington, DC: United States Bureau of Education, 1902); Fred Washington Atkinson, *The Present Educational Movement in the Philippine Islands* (Washington, DC: United States Government Printing Office, 1902); David P. Barrows, "Education and Social Progress in the Philippines," *The Annals of the American Academy of Political and Social Science* 30, no. 1 (1907); David P. Barrows, "What May Be Expected from Philippine Education," *Journal of Race and Development* 1 (1910): 156; David P. Barrows, *A Decade of American Government in the Philippines, 1903–1913* (New York: World Book, 1914).

70. Funie Hsu, "Colonial Articulations: English Instruction and the 'Benevolence' of US Overseas Expansion in the Philippines, 1898–1916" (PhD diss., University of California, Berkeley, 2013), 69.

71. Anne Paulet, "To Change the World: The Use of American Indian Education in the Philippines," *History of Education Quarterly* 47, no. 2 (2007).

72. Emily Huntingdon, "Statement on Domestic Science Work and Expense," Box 2, Folder 16, Samuel Chapman Armstrong Papers, Williams College Archives, 2.

73. Memo, 26 September 1960. Hampton University Archives.

74. "Thirteenth Annual Report of the Principal, for the School and the Fiscal Year Ending July 1st, 1882," 68.

75. "Winona," *The Southern Workman* 11, no. 11 (1882), Hampton University Archives, 107.

76. "Fourteenth Annual Report of the Principal, for the School and Fiscal Year Ending July 1st, 1883," *The Southern Workman* 12, no. 6 (1883), Hampton University Archives, 69.

77. Cora Folsom, "Guiding the Indian," Cora Folsom Box, Hampton University Archives, 4. My emphasis.

78. Samuel Chapman Armstrong, *Concerning Indians: Extracts from the Annual Report of the Principal of the Hampton Normal and Agricultural Institute, for the School Year Ending June 30th, 1883* (Hampton, VA: Normal School Steam Press, 1883), 13–14.

79. David Wallace Adams, *Education for Extinction: American Indians and the Boarding School Experience, 1875–1928* (Lawrence: University Press of Kansas, 1995); Robert A. Trennert, "From Carlisle to Phoenix: The Rise and Fall of the Indian Outing System, 1878–1930," *Pacific Historical Review* 52, no. 3 (1983); Richard Henry Pratt, *Battlefield and Classroom: Four Decades with the American Indian, 1867–1904* (New Haven, CT: Yale University Press, 1964).

80. Eve Tuck, Allison Guess, and Hannah Sultan, "Not Nowhere: Collaborating on Selfsame Land," *Decolonization: Indigeneity, Education & Society* 26, (June 2014).

6. TEACHERS OF TEACHERS

1. G. S. Dickerman, "White Instructors and Negro Pupils," *Southern Workman* 32, no. 12 (1903): 615.

2. Dickerman, "White Instructors and Negro Pupils," 615. Nini Visaya and K. Wayne Yang argue that this extension of teacher education to Black communities was a form of "invasion by reform," which was a "version of colonial technologies that are almost always first experimented on raced people deemed deserving of colonization." These technologies "masquerade as innocent" while perpetuating systems of teaching that serve the ideologies of whiteness. Nini Visaya Hayes and K. Wayne Yang, "Decouple Your Train, or How Schools of Teacher Education May Yet Resist White Supremacy," in *Who Decides who Becomes a Teacher?: Schools of Education as Sites of Resistance*, ed. Julie Gorlewski and Eve Tuck (New York: Routledge, 2018): 145.

3. "Twenty-Fourth Annual Report of the Principal, for the School and Fiscal Year Ending in June 30th 1882," *The Southern Workman* 21, no. 6 (1882): 94, 102.

4. James D. Anderson, *The Education of Blacks in the South, 1860–1935* (Chapel Hill: University of North Carolina Press, 1988).

5. Julie Gorlewski and Eve Tuck, "Schools of Education as Sites of Resistance," in *Who Decides Who Becomes a Teacher?: Schools of Education as Sites of Resistance*, ed. Julie Gorlewski and Eve Tuck (New York: Routledge, 2018), 12.

6. Julie Gorlewski and Eve Tuck, "Who Decides Who Becomes a Teacher?" in *Who Decides Who Becomes a Teacher?: Schools of Education as Sites of Resistance*, ed. Julie Gorlewski and Eve Tuck (New York: Routledge, 2018), 94.

7. Anderson makes the argument that the establishment of Black normal schools in the South functioned to close off other educational and occupational possibilities for Black people. Thus, he frames normal schools as part of the many white led institutions that sought to maintain the power structures of the South in favor of white supremacy. I add to Anderson's poignant analysis that these institutions also sought to create Black teachers as individualized units of settlement and to create schools in

the shape of plantations. James D. Anderson, *The Education of Blacks in the South, 1860–1935* (Chapel Hill: University of North Carolina Press, 1988).

8. Jarvis R. Givens, *Fugitive Pedagogy: Carter G. Woodson and the Art of Black Teaching* (Cambridge, MA: Harvard University Press, 2021); K. Tsianina Lomawaima and Theresa L. McCarty, *To Remain an Indian: Lessons in Democracy from a Century of Native American Education* (New York: Columbia University Press, 2006); David Wallace Adams, *Education for Extinction: American Indians and the Boarding School Experience, 1875–1928* (Lawrence: University Press of Kansas, 1995).

9. David Labaree, "An Uneasy Relationship: The History of Teacher Education in the University," in *Who Decides Who Becomes a Teacher?: Schools of Education as Sites of Resistance,* ed. Julie Gorlewski and Eve Tuck, (New York: Routledge, 2018); Gorlewski and Tuck, "Who Decides Who Becomes a Teacher?"

10. Most histories of normal schools in general, outside of the work of scholars like Anderson who discuss Black normal schools, treat white-majority institutions as if they were representative of all teacher training. Nini Visaya Hayes and K. Wayne Yang call this out and argue that the history of normal schools is a history of the reproduction of settler whiteness. I add to their critique by showing that the production of Black teachers by places like Hampton was both a project of settlement and a part of slavery's reverberating afterlives. Anderson, *The Education of Blacks in the South.*

11. "The Questions They Ask," *Southern Workman* 21, no. 5 (1892): 70.

12. "The Questions They Ask," 70.

13. "Twenty-Fourth Anniversary of Hampton Institute," *Southern Workman* 21, no. 6 (1882): 80.

14. Silvia Schmid, "Pestalozzi's Spheres of Life," *Journal of the Midwest History Of Education Society* 24 (1997); J.A. Green, *The Educational Ideas of Pestalozzi* (Baltimore, MD: Warwick & York, 1914); Fredalene B. Bowers and Thom Gehring, "Johann Heinrich Pestalozzi: 18th century Swiss Educator and Correctional Reformer," *Journal of Correctional Education* 55, no. 4 (2004).

15. In this work, Beyer also states that industrial schooling models for Native peoples developed from missionary education programs and independently of Pestalozzi's influence. Carl Kalani Beyer, "Manual and Industrial Education for Hawaiians during the 19th Century," *The Hawaiian Journal of History* 38 (2004).

16. John P. Manning, "Rediscovering Froebel: A Call to Re-Examine His Life & Gifts," *Early Childhood Education Journal* 32, no. 6 (2005).

17. Eli Meyerhoff, *Beyond Education: Radical Studying for Another World* (Minneapolis: University of Minnesota Press, 2019), 15.

18. Meyerhoff, *Beyond Education,* 2.

19. Meyerhoff, *Beyond Education,* 58.

20. M. A. L., cartographer, *Map of Virginia and West Va., North & part of South Carolina, Maryland & Delaware, showing the situation in these states of schools taught by graduates of the Hampton Normal & Agricultural Institute from 1871 to 1876,* 1876, 48 × 74 cm (New York: Am. Photo-Lithographic, 1876), Library of Congress, Geography and Map Division, https://www.loc.gov/item/2003620479/.

21. *Southern Workman* 21, no. 1 (1882): 4.

22. *Southern Workman* 21, no. 2 (1882): 19.

23. "Speech of the Hon. Chauncey M. Depew at Hampton Institute, Virginia," *Southern Workman* 21, no. 4 (1892): 63.

24. B. C. Caldwell, "The Work of the Jeanes and Slater Funds," *The Annals of the American Academy of Political and Social Science* 49, no. 1 (1913).

25. Jackson Davis, "The Negro in Country Life," *Southern Workman* 40, no. 1 (1912): 24.

26. Jackson Davis, *The Jeanes Visiting Teachers: An Address Given at the Inter-Territorial Jeanes Conference Salisbury, Southern Rhodesia, May 27, 1935* (New York: Carnegie, 1926): 18–19.

27. Jackson Davis, "Rural Education and Social Efficiency," in *The Human Way: Addresses on Race Problems at the Southern Sociological Congress Atlanta, 1913*, ed. James E. McCulloch (Nashville, TN: Southern Sociological Conference, 1913), 80.

28. W. D. Weatherford, "Negro Training in the South," *Southern Workman* 41, no. 10 (1912): 522.

29. Davis, *The Jeanes Visiting Teachers*, 14.

30. Davis, *The Jeanes Visiting Teachers*, 14.

31. Davis, *The Jeanes Visiting Teachers*, 14.

32. Lance G. E. Jones, *The Jeanes Teacher in the United States, 1908–1933: An Account of Twenty-Five Years' Experience in the Supervision of Negro Rural Schools* (Chapel Hill: University of North Carolina Press, 2011): 61.

33. Jones, *The Jeanes Teacher in the United States*, 53.

34. Jones, *The Jeanes Teacher in the United States*, 54.

35. Jones, *The Jeanes Teacher in the United States*, 28.

36. Scholars have discussed how Gullah people have constructed themselves as Indigenous to the Americas. See, for example, Sharon Y. Fuller, *Gullah Geechee Indigenous Articulation in the Americas* (Berkeley: University of California, 2015).

37. Grace Biglow House, "The Need and Value of Industrial Education for Negroes," in *The Human Way: Addresses on Race Problems at the Southern Sociological Congress Atlanta, 1913*, ed. James E. McCulloch (Nashville, TN: Southern Sociological Conference, 1913), 94.

38. House, "The Need and Value of Industrial Education for Negroes."

39. Gorlewski and Tuck, "Schools of Education as Sites of Resistance."

40. Weatherford, "Negro Training in the South," 522.

41. Davis, *The Jeanes Visiting Teachers*, 13.

42. Davis, *The Jeanes Visiting Teachers*, 18–19.

43. Jones, *The Jeanes Teacher in the United States*, 49.

44. Caldwell, "The Work of the Jeanes and Slater Funds," 82.

45. Leo McGee and Dalton McAfee, "Role of the Traditionally Black Public Institution of Higher Learning in Extension Education," *The Journal of Negro Education* 46, no. 1 (1977); Felix James, "The Tuskegee Institute Movable School, 1906–1923," *Agricultural History* 45, no. 3 (1971).

46. Jackson Davis, "Rural Education and Social Efficiency," in *The Human Way: Addresses on Race Problems at the Southern Sociological Congress Atlanta, 1913*, ed. James E. McCulloch (Nashville, TN: Southern Sociological Conference, 1913), 82.

47. Caldwell, "The Work of the Jeanes and Slater Funds."

48. Gerda Lerner, "Early Community Work of Black Club Women," *The Journal of Negro History* 59, no. 2 (1974); Stephanie J. Shaw, *What a Woman Ought to Be and to Do: Black Professional Women Workers During the Jim Crow Era* (Chicago: University of Chicago Press, 1996).

49. la paperson, *A Third University Is Possible* (Minneapolis: University of Minnesota Press, 2017).

50. Caldwell, "The Work of the Jeanes and Slater Funds," 80.

51. House, "The Need and Value of Industrial Education for Negroes," 97.

52. Davis, "The Negro in Country Life," 25. This concept of "wealth of the state" is one that is neither specific nor complex. It merges a variety of possible institutions and processes into a single sign: "the state." I engage this phrasing here because it was the way it was termed by those describing this form of teaching and demonstrates an investment in the US state, and thus in the structures of settlement and slavery that uphold it.

53. Weatherford, "Negro Training in the South," 550–551.

54. House, "The Need and Value of Industrial Education for Negroes," 91.

55. House, "The Need and Value of Industrial Education for Negroes," 92.

56. Mahasan Offut-Chaney, "Discipline for the 'Educationally Deprived': ESEA and the Punitive Function of Federal Education Policy 1965–1998," (PhD diss., University of California Berkeley, 2020).

57. Davis, "Rural Education and Social Efficiency," 81.

58. Davis, *The Jeanes Visiting Teachers*, 17, 21; Caldwell, "The Work of the Jeanes and Slater Funds," 86; Weatherford, "Negro Training in the South," 550, 553, 534.

59. Robert E. Park, "Education by Cultural Groups," *Southern Workman* 41, no. 6 (1912): 375–377.

60. Thomas Jesse Jones, *Education in Africa: A Study of West, South, and Equatorial Africa by the African Education Commission, under the Auspices of the Phelps-Stokes Fund and Foreign Mission Societies of North America and Europe* (New York: Phelps-Stokes Fund, 1922).

61. Charles Templeman Loram, *The Education of the South African Native* (New York: Negro Universities Press, 1917).

62. Jones, *Education in Africa*, 30.

63. Jones, *Education in Africa*, 71.

64. Jones, *Education in Africa*, 72.

65. Helen Ludlow, "The Overtoun Institution: A Hampton in Africa," *Southern Workman* 33, no. 12 (1904): 669–676.

66. *The Indian Craftsman* 2, no. 4 (1909).

67. *The Indian Craftsman* 2, no. 4 (1909), 37.

68. Chris Kirk-Kuwaye, "Normal Schools and Haole Teachers," *Thinking Locally about Territorial Hawai'i* (blog), June 25, 2015. https://thinkinglocally.org/2015/06/25/normal-school-and-haole-teachers/

69. Correspondence with Normal Inspectors, Hawaii, 1905–1906, Folder 261, Hawaii State Archives.

70. Ma Teresa Pineda-Tinio, "Bearers of Benevolence: The Thomasites and Public Education in the Philippines," *Philippine Studies* 50, no. 4 (2002): 581–583; Peter James Tarr, *The Education of the Thomasites: American School Teachers in Philippine Colonial Society, 1901–1913* (Ithaca, NY: Cornell University, 2006); Dinah Roma-Sianturi, "'Pedagogic Invasion': The Thomasites in Occupied Philippines," *Kritika Kultura* 12 (2009): 100.

71. Fred Washington Atkinson, *Education in the Philippine Islands* (Washington, DC: United States Bureau of Education, 1902), 78.

72. David P. Barrows, "What May Be Expected from Philippine Education," *Journal of Race and Development* 1 (1910): 162.

73. M. Friedman, "Industrial Education and the Development of the Filipinos," *Southern Workman* 33, no. 7 (1904): 381.

74. Friedman, "Industrial Education and the Development of the Filipinos," 383.

75. Friedman, "Industrial Education and the Development of the Filipinos," 384.

76. Meyerhoff, *Beyond Education,* 59.

77. "Twenty-Fourth Anniversary of the Hampton Institute," *Southern Workman* 21, no. 6 (1892): 81.

78. "Twenty-Fourth Annual Report of the Principal, for the School and Fiscal Year Ending in June 30th 1982," *Southern Workman* 21, no. 6 (1882): 84.

79. "Twenty-Fourth Annual Report of the Principal," 94, 102.

80. James C. Albisetti, "The Feminization of Teaching in the Nineteenth Century: A Comparative Perspective," *History of Education* 22, no. 3 (1993); John G. Richardson and Brenda Wooden Hatcher, "The Feminization of Public School Teaching: 1870–1920," *Work and Occupations* 10, no. 1 (1983); Zeus Leonardo and Blanca Gamez-Djokic, "Sometimes Leaving Means Staying: Race and White Teachers' Emotional Investments," *Teachers College Record* 121, no. 13 (2019).

81. Labaree, "An Uneasy Relationship," 94.

82. Samuel Chapman Armstrong, *The Indian Question* (Hampton, VA: Normal School Steam Press, 1883), 17–18.

83. Hollis Burke Frissell, *Out from the Cabin and the Teepee,* (Hampton, VA: Hampton Institute Press, 1900), 13, https://catalog.hathitrust.org/Record/100787422.

84. Armstrong, *The Indian Question,* 17–18.

85. Black women teachers of Native women at Hampton felt like they were being placed into second class situations in which they were doing no real teaching, according to Paula Marie Seniors, *Beyond Lift Every Voice and Sing: The Culture of Uplift, Identity, and Politics in Black Musical Theater* (Columbus: The Ohio State University Press, 2009).

86. Armstrong, *The Indian Question,* 19.

87. Armstrong, *The Indian Question,* 17.

7. "BETTER LAND, BETTER STOCK, BETTER PEOPLE"

1. Robert F. Park, "International Conference on the Negro: An Account of the Conference Held at Tuskegee Institute April 17, 18, 19, 1912," *Southern Workman* 41, no. 6 (1912): 352.

2. Jackson Davis, "The Negro in Country Life," *Southern Workman* 41, no. 1 (1912): 15. The discussion in this article echoes the way Indigenous peoples of the Americas were described as not utilizing land appropriately, which becomes a justification for why they could be dispossessed of it. Schools like Hampton positioned themselves as the location where the "Negro Problem" and the "Indian Problem" could be solved. To do so they often relied on scientific language, likening their schooling model to an "experiment." This was often in direct contradiction to evidence that Indigenous peoples very much were using the land in ways that were not recognized by whites, whether purposefully or not—as were Black people.

3. Linda O. Hines, "George W. Carver and the Tuskegee Agricultural Experiment Station," *Agricultural History* 53, no. 1 (1979); Leo McGee, "Booker T. Washington and George Washington Carver: A Tandem of Adult Educators at Tuskegee," *Lifelong Learning* 8, no. 2 (1984): 16; Allen W. Jones, "The Role of Tuskegee Institute in the Education of Black Farmers," *The Journal of Negro History* 60, no. 2 (1975); Audra M. Akins, "An Introduction to Stem Courses and Careers through a Brief Historical Narrative of the Tuskegee Movable School," *Black History Bulletin* 76, no. 1 (2013); McGee and McAfee, "Role of the Traditionally Black Public Institution of Higher Learning in Extension Education"; Felix James, "The Tuskegee Institute Movable School, 1906–1923," *Agricultural History* 45, no. 3 (1971); B. D. Mayberry, "The Tuskegee Movable School: A Unique Contribution to National and International Agriculture and Rural Development," *Agricultural History* 65, no. 2 (1991).

4. There is evidence of non-cooperation with and resentment against Tuskegee demonstration agents. Karen J. Ferguson, "Caught in 'No Man's Land': The Negro Cooperative Demonstration Service and the Ideology of Booker T. Washington, 1900–1918," *Agricultural History* 72, no. 1 (1998).

5. Davis, "The Negro in Country Life."

6. "Light Ahead for the Southern Farmer," *Southern Workman* 35, no. 3 (1906): 131.

7. "Better Land, Better Stock, Better People," *Southern Workman* 35, no. 4 (1906): 199.

8. H. C. Knoblauch et al. *State Agricultural Experiment Stations: A History of Research Policy and Procedure* (Washington, DC: United States Department of Agriculture, 1962).

9. Bruno Latour and Steve Woolgar, *Laboratory Life: The Construction of Scientific Facts* (Princeton, NJ: Princeton University Press, 2013); Sandra Harding, *Whose Science? Whose Knowledge?: Thinking from Women's Lives* (Ithaca, NY: Cornell University Press, 1991); Mary Poovey, *A History of the Modern Fact: Problems of Knowledge in the Sciences of Wealth and Society* (Chicago: University of Chicago Press, 1998); Sylvia Wynter, "Unsettling the Coloniality of Being/Power/Truth

/Freedom: Towards the Human, After Man, its Overrepresentation—An Argument," *CR: The New Centennial Review* 3, no. 3 (2003).

10. Latour and Woolgar, *Laboratory Life*.

11. Latour and Woolgar, *Laboratory Life*.

12. Gabriella Gutiérrez y Muhs et al., *Presumed Incompetent: The Intersections of Race and Class for Women in Academia* (Logan: Utah State University Press, 2012); Bryan McKinley Jones Brayboy and Donna Deyhle, "Insider-Outsider: Researchers in American Indian Communities," *Theory into Practice* 39, no. 3 (2000); Robert Alexander Innes, "'Wait a Second. Who Are You Anyways?' The Insider/Outsider Debate and American Indian Studies," *American Indian Quarterly* 33, no. 4 (2009).

13. Denise Ferreira Da Silva, *Toward a Global Idea of Race* (Minneapolis: University of Minnesota Press, 2007); Britt Rusert, "'A Study in Nature': The Tuskegee Experiments and the New South Plantation," *Journal of Medical Humanities* 30 (2009): 155.

14. Wynter, "Unsettling the Coloniality of Being/Power/Truth/Freedom."

15. Despite Enlightenment thought being complicit in the separation between human and nature through defining science, it also conflates those defined as less than "man" with nature. In fact, Enlightenment thought breaks down when it rubs up against the being of Black and Indigenous bodies and the land that exceed its boundaries.

16. Daniel Merriman, "Armstrong the Christian Soldier," *Southern Workman* 35, no. 2 (1906): 167.

17. "Speech of the Hon. Chauncey M. Depew at Hampton Institute, Virginia," *The Southern Workman* 21, no. 4 (1892): 63.

18. Britt Rusert, "Plantation Ecologies: The Experimental Plantation in and against James Grainger's 'The Sugar-Cane,'" *Early American Studies,* 13, no. 2 (2015): 343–344.

19. Rusert, "Plantation Ecologies," 344.

20. Allen Kerr, *The Legacy: A Centennial History of the State Agricultural Experiment Stations, 1887–1987* (Columbia: Missouri Agricultural Experiment Station, University of Missouri-Columbia, 1987), 9.

21. Monica van Beusekom, "Colonial Agricultural Development Schemes," in *Oxford Research Encyclopedia of African History,* August 31, 2021, https://oxfordre.com/africanhistory/display/10.1093/acrefore/9780190277734.001.0001/acrefore-9780190277734-e-751?rskey=nSnSYc&result=1.

22. van Beusekom, "Colonial Agricultural Development Schemes."

23. Daniel R. Headrick, *The Tentacles of Progress: Technology Transfer in the Age of Imperialism, 1850–1940* (Oxford: Oxford University Press, 1988), 210.

24. Kerr, *The Legacy*.

25. Kerr, *The Legacy*, 5.

26. Kerr, *The Legacy*.

27. J. H. Blueford, "Negro Agricultural and Mechanical Colleges," *Southern Workman* 35, no. 1 (1906): 30.

28. Hines, "George W. Carver and the Tuskegee Agricultural Experiment Station"; Mark Hersey, "Hints and Suggestions to Farmers: George Washington Carver

and Rural Conservation in the South," *Environmental History* 11, no. 2 (2006); Stephen Gresham, "George Washington Carver and the Art of Technical Communication," *Journal of Technical Writing and Communication* 9, no. 3 (1979).

29. George Washington Carver, "How to Grow the Peanut: And 105 Ways of Preparing it for Human Consumption," *Bulletin,* no. 31 (Tuskegee, AL: Experiment Station, Tuskegee Normal and Industrial Institute, 1916), Tuskegee University Archives Repository, George Washington Carver Collection, http://archive.tuskegee.edu/repository/digital-collection/george-washington-carver/the-bulletins/gwc-bulletins-031/; Andrew F. Smith, *Peanuts: The Illustrious History of the Goober Pea* (Urbana: University of Illinois Press, 2002).

30. Smith, *Peanuts.*

31. George Washington Carver, "Fertilizer Experiments on Cotton," *Bulletin,* no. 3 (Tuskegee, AL: Experiment Station, Tuskegee Normal and Industrial Institute, 1899), Tuskegee University Archives Repository, George Washington Carver Collection, http://archive.tuskegee.edu/repository/digital-collection/george-washington-carver/the-bulletins/gwc-bulletins-003/; George Washington Carver, "Cow Peas," *Bulletin,* no. 5 (Tuskegee, AL: Experiment Station, Tuskegee Normal and Industrial Institute, 1903), Tuskegee University Archives Repository, George Washington Carver Collection, http://archive.tuskegee.edu/repository/digital-collection/george-washington-carver/the-bulletins/gwc-bulletins-005/; George Washington Carver, "How to Build up Worn Out Soils," *Bulletin,* no. 6 (Tuskegee, AL: Experiment Station, Tuskegee Normal and Industrial Institute, 1905), Tuskegee University Archives Repository, George Washington Carver Collection, http://archive.tuskegee.edu/repository/digital-collection/george-washington-carver/the-bulletins/gwc-bulletins-006/; George Washington Carver, "Cotton Growing on Sandy Upland Soils," *Bulletin,* no. 7 (Tuskegee, AL: Experiment Station, Tuskegee Normal and Industrial Institute, 1905), Tuskegee University Archives Repository, George Washington Carver Collection, http://archive.tuskegee.edu/repository/digital-collection/george-washington-carver/the-bulletins/gwc-bulletins-007/; George Washington Carver, "How to Make Cotton Growing Pay," *Bulletin,* no. 14 (Tuskegee, AL: Experiment Station, Tuskegee Normal and Industrial Institute, 1908), Tuskegee University Archives Repository, George Washington Carver Collection, http://archive.tuskegee.edu/repository/digital-collection/george-washington-carver/the-bulletins/gwc-bulletins-014/; George Washington Carver, "Study of the Soils in Macon County, Alabama, and Their Adaptability to Certain Crops," *Bulletin,* no. 25 (Tuskegee, AL: Experiment Station, Tuskegee Normal and Industrial Institute, 1913), Tuskegee University Archives Repository, George Washington Carver Collection, http://archive.tuskegee.edu/repository/digital-collection/george-washington-carver/the-bulletins/gwc-bulletins-025/; George Washington Carver, "How to Build up and Maintain the Virgin Fertility of Our Soils," *Bulletin,* no. 42 (Tuskegee, AL: Experiment Station, Tuskegee Normal and Industrial Institute, 1936), Tuskegee University Archives Repository, George Washington Carver Collection, http://archive.tuskegee.edu/repository/digital-collection/george-washington-carver/the-bulletins/gwc-bulletins-042/.

32. Carver, "Fertilizer Experiments on Cotton," 3.

33. Joanne Barker, "For Whom Sovereignty Matters," in *Sovereignty Matters: Locations of Contestation and Possibility in Indigenous Struggles for Self-Determination*, ed. Joanne Barker (Lincoln: University of Nebraska Press, 2005); Vine Deloria Jr., *Custer Died for Your Sins: An Indian Manifesto* (Norman: University of Oklahoma Press, 1969).

34. Carver, "Fertilizer Experiments on Cotton," 14.

35. Carver, "How to Build up Worn Out Soils," 4.

36. Carver, "How to Build up Worn Out Soils," 5.

37. Carver, "How to Build up Worn Out Soils," 5–6.

38. Carver, "How to Build up Worn Out Soils," 3.

39. Carver, "Cotton Growing on Sandy Upland Soils," 14, 25.

40. George Washington Carver, "Nature Study and Gardening for Rural Schools," *Bulletin*, no. 18 (Tuskegee, AL: Experiment Station, Tuskegee Normal and Industrial Institute, 1910), Tuskegee University Archives Repository, George Washington Carver Collection, http://archive.tuskegee.edu/repository/digital-collection/george-washington-carver/the-bulletins/gwc-bulletins-018/; George Washington Carver, "Cotton Growing for Rural Schools," *Bulletin*, no. 20 (Tuskegee, AL: Experiment Station, Tuskegee Normal and Industrial Institute, 1911), Tuskegee University Archives Repository, George Washington Carver Collection, http://archive.tuskegee.edu/repository/digital-collection/george-washington-carver/the-bulletins/gwc-bulletins-020/.

41. "History of the Hawai'i Agricultural Experiment Station" (website), University of Hawai'i, Manoa, College of Tropical Agriculture and Human Resources, accessed February 22, 2022, https://www.ctahr.hawaii.edu/site/HistoryRes.aspx.

42. *Catalogue of the Hilo Boarding School for Boys, 1910–1911* (Hilo, HI: Hilo Boarding School Press 1910), 44, Hawaiian Mission Children's Society Archive; "The Farm Department of the Hilo Boys Boarding School," Folder on Private Schools, Periodicals, Catalogs, Reports, etc., Hawaiian Mission Children's Society Archive.

43. Bureau of Agriculture, "Report of the Bureau of Agriculture for the Fiscal Year Ending June 30, 1907," *The Philippine Agricultural Review* 1, no. 1 (1908): 31, 39, 45.

44. William Coppinger, *The New Africa: Seventh Annual Paper* (Hampton, VA: Normal School Press, 1887): 17.

45. Thomas Jesse Jones, *Education in Africa: A Study of West, South, and Equatorial Africa by the African Education Commission, under the Auspices of the Phelps-Stokes Fund and Foreign Mission Societies of North America and Europe* (New York: Phelps-Stokes Fund, 1922), 131–133, 157, 188, 262; *Colonial Reports-Annual: Gold Coast, Report for 1916* (London: His Majesty's Stationary Office, 1918).

46. Minutes of the Meeting of the Board of Trustees of the Booker Washington Agricultural and Industrial Institute of Liberia, 22 January 1934, International Education Board Records, Box 16, Folder 235, New York Colonization Society-Booker Washington Agricultural and Industrial Institute of Liberia, Rockefeller

Archive Center; Mr. and Mrs. Paul Rupel to Thomas Jesse Jones, 6 November 1925, International Education Board Records, Appropriations, Box 16, Folder 237.

47. Jones, *Education in Africa*, 33.

48. Jones, *Education in Africa*, 91.

49. Jones, *Education in Africa*, 91.

50. Christophe Bonneuil, "Development as Experiment: Science and State Building in Late Colonial and Postcolonial Africa, 1930–1970," *Osiris* 15 (2000).

51. Thomas Jesse Jones, *The Navajo Indian Problem* (New York: The Phelps-Stokes Fund, 1939).

52. Jennifer Bess, "The New Egypt, Pima Cotton, and the Role of Native Wage Labor on the Cooperative Testing and Demonstration Farm, Sacaton, Arizona, 1907–1917," *Agricultural History* 88, no. 4 (2014).

53. Zhenmin Lu et al., "High Yields in Advanced Lines of Pima Cotton Are Associated with Higher Stomatal Conductance, Reduced Leaf Area and Lower Leaf Temperature," *Physiologia Plantarum* 92, no. 2 (1994); David M. Alberson and Victor Leo Stedronsky, *Roller Ginning American-Egyptian Cotton in the Southwest*, no. 257 (Agricultural Research Service, United States Department of Agriculture, 1964).

54. Alan L. Olmstead and Paul W. Rhode, "Cotton, Slavery, and the New History of Capitalism," *Explorations in Economic History* 67 (2018): 1–17; Sven Beckert, *Empire of Cotton: A Global History* (New York: Vintage, 2015).

55. Bess, "The New Egypt, Pima Cotton, and the Role of Native Wage Labor."

56. Bess, "The New Egypt, Pima Cotton, and the Role of Native Wage Labor," 501.

57. Khalil Anthony Johnson Jr., "Problem Solver or 'Evil Genius': Thomas Jesse Jones and the Problem of Indian Administration," *Native American and Indigenous Studies* 5, no. 2 (2018).

58. Daniel Perlstein, "Progressive Education for the Navajo: Re-Engineering a Subject Race" (paper presented at the History of Education Society Meeting, Albuquerque, NM, November 3, 2018).

59. Marsha Weisiger, *Dreaming of Sheep in Navajo Country* (Seattle: University of Washington Press, 2011).

60. The Navajo Life Way, "A Short History on Navajo-Churro Sheep," Diné Bé'Iiná, Inc, November 3, 2015, https://navajolifeway.org/a-short-history-on-navajo-churro-sheep/ (site discontinued); Susan Marie Strawn and Mary A. Littrell, "Returning Navajo-Churro Sheep for Navajo Weaving," *Textile* 5, no. 3 (2007); Susan Marie Strawn, *Restoring Navajo-Churro Sheep: Community-Based Influences on a Traditional Navajo Fiber Resource and Textile* (Iowa City: University Press of Iowa, 2004); David Elstein, "Making Sure Sacred Sheep Don't Become Extinct," *Agricultural Research* 53, no. 4 (2005); Weisiger, *Dreaming of Sheep in Navajo Country*.

61. Much like Lakota oral histories of horses, sheep are animals that preceded the Columbian exchange and European introduction according to Navajo epistemology.

62. Jones, *The Navajo Indian Problem*, 14, 16, 19–20.

63. Maile Renee Arvin, *Possessing Polynesians: The Science of Settler Colonial Whiteness in Hawai'i and Oceania* (Durham, NC: Duke University Press, 2019).

64. Rusert, "Plantation Ecologies."

65. Rusert, "A Study in Nature," 157.

66. Rusert, "A Study in Nature," 161.

67. Rusert, "A Study in Nature," 165.

68. Rusert, "A Study in Nature," 163.

69. Rusert, "A Study in Nature," 165.

70. For examples of Indigenous land-based pedagogy, see Wildcat et al., "Learning from the Land: Indigenous Land Based Pedagogy and Decolonization," *Decolonization: Indigeneity, Education & Society* 3, no. 3 (2014); Kate McCoy, Eve Tuck, and Marcia McKenzie, eds. *Land Education: Rethinking Pedagogies of Place from Indigenous, Postcolonial, and Decolonizing Perspectives* (New York: Routledge, 2017); Leanne Betasamosake Simpson, "Land as Pedagogy: Nishnaabeg Intelligence and Rebellious Transformation," *Decolonization: Indigeneity, Education & Society* 3, no. 3 (2014).

71. Bryan McKinley Jones Brayboy and Emma Maughan, "Indigenous Knowledges and the Story of the Bean," *Harvard Educational Review* 79, no. 1 (2009).

72. Thomas Jesse Jones, "Social Studies in the Hampton Curriculum: Civics and Social Welfare," *Southern Workman* 35, no. 1 (1906): 51.

73. Thomas Jesse Jones, "Social Studies in the Hampton Curriculum: III Economics and Material Welfare," *Southern Workman* 35, no. 2 (1905): 111.

74. Jones, "Social Studies in Hampton Curriculum: III Economics and Material Welfare," 15.

75. Jones, "Social studies in Hampton Curriculum: III Economics and Material Welfare," 16.

76. "Progress at St. Helena," *Southern Workman* 35, no. 4 (1906): 196.

77. John Dewey, *The School and Society and the Child and the Curriculum* (Chicago: University of Chicago Press, 1990).

78. Dewey, *The School and Society and the Child and the Curriculum.*

79. Paolo Freire, *Pedagogy of the Oppressed,* trans. Maya Bergman Ramos (New York: Continuum, 1996); Peter McLaren, "Critical Pedagogy and Class Struggle in the Age of Neoliberal Globalization: Notes from History's Underside," *Democracy & Nature* 9, no. 1 (2003).

80. Alyse Schneider, "Doing at the University of Chicago," (paper presented at the History of Education Society Meeting, Columbus, OH, November 8, 2020); Daniel Perlstein, "Community and Democracy in American Schools: Arthurdale and the Fate of Progressive Education," *Teachers College Record* 97, no. 4 (1996).

81. Brown makes the claim that Dewey drew directly from Washington's racialized education pedagogy. Elizabeth Carolyn Brown, "Pedagogies of U.S. Imperialism: Racial Education from Reconstruction to the Progressive Era" (PhD diss., English, University of Washington, 2016); Dewey, *The School and Society and the Child and the Curriculum;* Washington, *Up From Slavery.*

82. Dewey, *The School and Society and the Child and the Curriculum,* 8; Samuel Chapman Armstrong, *Education for Life* (Hampton, VA: Press of the Hampton Normal and Agricultural Institute, 1913).
83. Dewey, *The School and Society and the Child and the Curriculum,* 10–11.
84. Dewey, *The School and Society and the Child and the Curriculum,* 18.
85. Dewey, *The School and Society and the Child and the Curriculum,* 18.
86. Dewey, *The School and Society and the Child and the Curriculum,* 98.
87. Dewey, *The School and Society and the Child and the Curriculum,* 107.
88. Dewey, *The School and Society and the Child and the Curriculum.*
89. Jones, *The Navajo Indian Problem,* 24.

CONCLUSION: LEARNING BY (NOT) DOING?

1. Critical race theory famously posits that racism is endemic to the US. Bryan McKinley Jones Brayboy, "Toward a Tribal Critical Race Theory in Education," *The Urban Review* 37, no. 5 (2005); WTVM, "Update: Georgia State Board of Education Approves Resolution that Addresses how Race is Discussed in Public Schools," June 3, 2021, https://www.wtvm.com/2021/06/03/georgia-state-board-education-meeting-consider-resolution-that-addresses-how-race-is-discussed-public-schools/.
2. What seems to be missing in a discussion of "casting down one's bucket" is that the water that would be drawn up is salt water, which would only serve to poison the body with excess salt. This indicates the fundamental flaw in his reasoning. Whether Booker T. Washington meant for this flaw to be evident or not is unknown.
3. Recent examples of this debate include: Theodore Lewis, "Booker T. Washington's Audacious Vocationalist Philosophy," *Oxford Review of Education* 40, no. 2 (2014); Donald Generals, "Booker T. Washington and Progressive Education: An Experimentalist Approach to Curriculum Development and Reform," *Journal of Negro Education* 69, no. 3 (Summer 2000): 215–234; Ronald E. Chennault, "Pragmatism and Progressivism in the Educational Thought and Practices of Booker T. Washington," *Philosophical Studies in Education* 44 (2013); Blaine D. Pope et al., "Booker T. and the New Green Collar Workforce: An Earth-Based Reassessment of the Philosophy of Booker T. Washington," *Journal of Black Studies* 42, no. 4 (2011).
4. Booker T. Washington, *My Larger Education: Being Chapters From my Experience* (Garden City, NY: Doubleday, Page, 1911), 9–10.
5. Washington, *My Larger Education,* 7.
6. Washington, *My Larger Education,* 6.
7. Elizabeth Carolyn Brown, "Pedagogies of U.S. Imperialism: Racial Education from Reconstruction to the Progressive Era" (PhD diss., University of Washington, 2016).
8. Daniel Perlstein and Sam Stack, "Building a New Deal Community: Progressive Education at Arthurdale," in *"Schools of Tomorrow," Schools of Today: What Happened to Progressive Education,* eds. Susan F. Semel and Alan R. Sadovnik (New York: Peter Lang, 1999), 217.

9. Perlstein and Stack, "Building a New Deal Community," 224.
10. Perlstein and Stack, "Building a New Deal Community," 221.
11. Perlstein and Stack, "Building a New Deal Community," 232.
12. *Lexico*, s.v. "doing," accessed February 26, 2022. https://www.lexico.com/en/definition/doing.
13. *Lexico*, s.v. "doing;" *Lexico*, s.v. "do."
14. *Merriam Webster*, s.v. "do" accessed February 26, 2022. https://www.merriam-webster.com/dictionary/to%20do.
15. For example, see Diana B. Turk and Stacie Brensilver Berman, "Learning through Doing: A Project-Based Learning Approach to the American Civil Rights Movement," *Social Education* 82, no. 1 (2018); Jeff R. Crump, "Learning by Doing: Implementing Community Service-Based Learning," *Journal of Geography* 101, no. 4 (2002).
16. Samuel Bowles and Herbert Gintis, *Schooling in Capitalist America: Educational Reform and the Contradictions of Economic Life* (Chicago: Haymarket Books, 1976).
17. These structures can be discussed in relation to Foucault's formulations of disciplining the body. Michel Foucault, *Discipline and Punish* (New York: Vintage, 1977).
18. Jan O'Neill, "SMART Goals, SMART Schools," *Educational Leadership* 57, no. 5 (2000).
19. Theresa Burruel Stone, personal conversation, October 25, 2022.
20. Julius B. Fleming Jr., *Black Patience: Performance, Civil Rights, and the Unfinished Project of Emancipation* (New York: New York University Press, 2022).
21. Kevin Quashie, *The Sovereignty of Quiet: Beyond Resistance in Black Culture* (New Brunswick, NJ: Rutgers University Press, 2012), 334.
22. Quashie, *The Sovereignty of Quiet*.
23. Theresa Burruel Stone, personal conversation, October 25, 2022.
24. Henry Nash Smith, *Virgin Land: The American West as Symbol and Myth* (Cambridge, MA: Harvard University Press, 1970).
25. Daniel Perlstein, Funie Hsu, Judith Kafka, Jarvis R. Givens, Juliet R. Kunkel, personal conversation with authors, November 6, 2021; Funie Hsu, "What is the Sound of One Invisible Hand Clapping? Neoliberalism, the Invisibility of Asian and Asian American Buddhists, and Secular Mindfulness in Education," in *Handbook of Mindfulness: Culture, Context, and Social Engagement*, eds. Ronald E. Purser, David Forbes, and Adam Burke (New York: Springer, 2016).
26. Saidiya V. Hartman, *Lose Your Mother: A Journey Along the Atlantic Slave Route* (New York: Farrar, Straus, and Giroux, 2008).
27. In some ways, this work demonstrates one aspect of what can be meant by there being a social life within social death, as posited by Jared Sexton's work. Jared Sexton, "The Social Life of Social Death: on Afro-Pessimism and Black Optimism," *InTensions*, no. 5 (2011).
28. Once again, this isn't an answer. Don't take it as one. Watch some currents, try not doing, refuse things, learn at that limit, fuck some things up, sabotage them,

82. Dewey, *The School and Society and the Child and the Curriculum*, 8; Samuel Chapman Armstrong, *Education for Life* (Hampton, VA: Press of the Hampton Normal and Agricultural Institute, 1913).
83. Dewey, *The School and Society and the Child and the Curriculum*, 10–11.
84. Dewey, *The School and Society and the Child and the Curriculum*, 18.
85. Dewey, *The School and Society and the Child and the Curriculum*, 18.
86. Dewey, *The School and Society and the Child and the Curriculum*, 98.
87. Dewey, *The School and Society and the Child and the Curriculum*, 107.
88. Dewey, *The School and Society and the Child and the Curriculum*.
89. Jones, *The Navajo Indian Problem*, 24.

CONCLUSION: LEARNING BY (NOT) DOING?

1. Critical race theory famously posits that racism is endemic to the US. Bryan McKinley Jones Brayboy, "Toward a Tribal Critical Race Theory in Education," *The Urban Review* 37, no. 5 (2005); WTVM, "Update: Georgia State Board of Education Approves Resolution that Addresses how Race is Discussed in Public Schools," June 3, 2021, https://www.wtvm.com/2021/06/03/georgia-state-board-education-meeting-consider-resolution-that-addresses-how-race-is-discussed-public-schools/.
2. What seems to be missing in a discussion of "casting down one's bucket" is that the water that would be drawn up is salt water, which would only serve to poison the body with excess salt. This indicates the fundamental flaw in his reasoning. Whether Booker T. Washington meant for this flaw to be evident or not is unknown.
3. Recent examples of this debate include: Theodore Lewis, "Booker T. Washington's Audacious Vocationalist Philosophy," *Oxford Review of Education* 40, no. 2 (2014); Donald Generals, "Booker T. Washington and Progressive Education: An Experimentalist Approach to Curriculum Development and Reform," *Journal of Negro Education* 69, no. 3 (Summer 2000): 215–234; Ronald E. Chennault, "Pragmatism and Progressivism in the Educational Thought and Practices of Booker T. Washington," *Philosophical Studies in Education* 44 (2013); Blaine D. Pope et al., "Booker T. and the New Green Collar Workforce: An Earth-Based Reassessment of the Philosophy of Booker T. Washington," *Journal of Black Studies* 42, no. 4 (2011).
4. Booker T. Washington, *My Larger Education: Being Chapters From my Experience* (Garden City, NY: Doubleday, Page, 1911), 9–10.
5. Washington, *My Larger Education*, 7.
6. Washington, *My Larger Education*, 6.
7. Elizabeth Carolyn Brown, "Pedagogies of U.S. Imperialism: Racial Education from Reconstruction to the Progressive Era" (PhD diss., University of Washington, 2016).
8. Daniel Perlstein and Sam Stack, "Building a New Deal Community: Progressive Education at Arthurdale," in *"Schools of Tomorrow," Schools of Today: What Happened to Progressive Education*, eds. Susan F. Semel and Alan R. Sadovnik (New York: Peter Lang, 1999), 217.

9. Perlstein and Stack, "Building a New Deal Community," 224.

10. Perlstein and Stack, "Building a New Deal Community," 221.

11. Perlstein and Stack, "Building a New Deal Community," 232.

12. *Lexico*, s.v. "doing," accessed February 26, 2022. https://www.lexico.com/en/definition/doing.

13. *Lexico*, s.v. "doing;" *Lexico*, s.v. "do."

14. *Merriam Webster*, s.v. "do" accessed February 26, 2022. https://www.merriam-webster.com/dictionary/to%20do.

15. For example, see Diana B. Turk and Stacie Brensilver Berman, "Learning through Doing: A Project-Based Learning Approach to the American Civil Rights Movement," *Social Education* 82, no. 1 (2018); Jeff R. Crump, "Learning by Doing: Implementing Community Service-Based Learning," *Journal of Geography* 101, no. 4 (2002).

16. Samuel Bowles and Herbert Gintis, *Schooling in Capitalist America: Educational Reform and the Contradictions of Economic Life* (Chicago: Haymarket Books, 1976).

17. These structures can be discussed in relation to Foucault's formulations of disciplining the body. Michel Foucault, *Discipline and Punish* (New York: Vintage, 1977).

18. Jan O'Neill, "SMART Goals, SMART Schools," *Educational Leadership* 57, no. 5 (2000).

19. Theresa Burruel Stone, personal conversation, October 25, 2022.

20. Julius B. Fleming Jr., *Black Patience: Performance, Civil Rights, and the Unfinished Project of Emancipation* (New York: New York University Press, 2022).

21. Kevin Quashie, *The Sovereignty of Quiet: Beyond Resistance in Black Culture* (New Brunswick, NJ: Rutgers University Press, 2012), 334.

22. Quashie, *The Sovereignty of Quiet*.

23. Theresa Burruel Stone, personal conversation, October 25, 2022.

24. Henry Nash Smith, *Virgin Land: The American West as Symbol and Myth* (Cambridge, MA: Harvard University Press, 1970).

25. Daniel Perlstein, Funie Hsu, Judith Kafka, Jarvis R. Givens, Juliet R. Kunkel, personal conversation with authors, November 6, 2021; Funie Hsu, "What is the Sound of One Invisible Hand Clapping? Neoliberalism, the Invisibility of Asian and Asian American Buddhists, and Secular Mindfulness in Education," in *Handbook of Mindfulness: Culture, Context, and Social Engagement*, eds. Ronald E. Purser, David Forbes, and Adam Burke (New York: Springer, 2016).

26. Saidiya V. Hartman, *Lose Your Mother: A Journey Along the Atlantic Slave Route* (New York: Farrar, Straus, and Giroux, 2008).

27. In some ways, this work demonstrates one aspect of what can be meant by there being a social life within social death, as posited by Jared Sexton's work. Jared Sexton, "The Social Life of Social Death: on Afro-Pessimism and Black Optimism," *InTensions*, no. 5 (2011).

28. Once again, this isn't an answer. Don't take it as one. Watch some currents, try not doing, refuse things, learn at that limit, fuck some things up, sabotage them,

scavenge, lie about it, maybe don't write about it for academic journals. Have secret meetings, don't go to meetings, go and then refuse them. These aren't answers, just things I am willing to say here. Find me in a hallway at a conference, or in a coffee shop, or other venue so we can talk more. Or don't, depends on how much I trust you.

29. Vanessa Siddle Walker, *Their Highest Potential: An African American School Community in the Segregated South* (Chapel Hill: University of North Carolina Press, 1996); Vanessa Siddle Walker, "Organized Resistance and Black Educators' Quest for School Equality, 1878–1938," *Teachers College Record* 107, no. 3 (2005); Heather Andrea Williams, *Self-Taught: African American Education in Slavery and Freedom* (Chapel Hill: University of North Carolina Press, 2009); Brenda J. Child, *Boarding School Seasons: American Indian Families, 1900–1940* (Lincoln: University of Nebraska Press, 2000); K. Tsianina Lomawaima, *They Called it Prairie Light: The Story of the Chilocco Indian School* (Lincoln: University of Nebraska Press, 1994).

30. Katherine McKittrick, "Plantation Futures," *Small Axe: A Caribbean Journal of Criticism* 17, no. 3 (42) (2013).

31. Alyse Schneider, "Doing at the University of Chicago," (paper presented at the History of Education Society Meeting, Columbus, OH, November 8, 2020); Joanne Tien, "Teaching Identity vs. Positionality: Dilemmas in Social Justice Education," *Curriculum Inquiry* 49, no. 5 (2019).

32. Audra M. Akins, "An Introduction to Stem Courses and Careers Through a Brief Historical Narrative of the Tuskegee Movable School," *Black History Bulletin* 76, no. 1 (2013).

33. I take Nick Mitchell's critiques of Afropessimism seriously when I state this. Nick Mitchell, "The View from Nowhere: On Frank Wilderson's Afropessimism," *Specter* (Fall 2020).

34. Theresa Burruel Stone, personal conversation with author; Juliet R. Kunkel, "The Eugenic University," (PhD diss., University of California Berkeley, 2021).

35. Chad Infante et al., "Other Intimacies: Black Studies Notes on Native /Indigenous Studies," *Postmodern Culture* 31, no. 1 (2020), https://muse.jhu.edu/article/800013.

BIBLIOGRAPHY

PERIODICALS

Carlisle Indian School Periodicals
    The Carlisle Arrow
    The Indian Craftsman
    The Indian Helper
    The Red Man
    The Redman and Helper
Hampton Institute Periodicals
    Southern Workman
Negro History Bulletin
The Atlantic
Hawaiian Gazette
The Polynesian
The Republican

ARCHIVES AND COLLECTIONS

Carlisle Indian School Digital Resource Center
Hampton University Archives
Hawaii State Archives
    Records of the Department of Education
Hawaiian Mission Children Society Archive
The John Carter Brown Library Map Collection
Library of Congress
    Geography and Map Division
Newberry Digital Collections
Rockefeller Archive Center
    General Education Board Records
    International Education Board Records

Tuskegee University Archives
George Washington Carver Collection
Williams College Archives
Samuel Chapman Armstrong Papers

GOVERNMENT AND INTERNATIONAL REPORTS, PUBLICATIONS, AND RESOLUTIONS

Alberson, David M. and Victor Leo Stedronsky, *Roller Ginning American-Egyptian Cotton in the Southwest,* no. 257. Washington, DC: Agricultural Research Service, United States Department of Agriculture, 1964.

Annual Report of the Commissioner of Indian Affairs to the Secretary of the Interior for the Year 1884. Washington, DC: Government Printing Office, 1884.

Atkinson, Fred Washington. *Education in the Philippine Islands.* Washington, DC: United States Bureau of Education, 1902.

———. *The Present Educational Movement in the Philippine Islands.* Washington, DC: United States Government Printing Office, 1902.

Bureau of Agriculture. "Report of the Bureau of Agriculture for the Fiscal Year Ending June 30, 1907." *The Philippine Agricultural Review* 1, no. 1 (1908): 31, 39, 45.

Colonial Reports-Annual: Gold Coast, Report for 1916. London: His Majesty's Stationary Office, 1918.

Cook, Katherine Margaret. *Public Education in Hawaii.* Washington DC: United States Department of the Interior, Department of Education, 1935.

Knoblauch, H. C., E. M. Law, W. P. Meyer, B. F. Beacher, R. B. Nestler, and B. S. White Jr., *State Agricultural Experiment Stations: A History of Research Policy and Procedure.* Washington, DC: United States Department of Agriculture, 1962.

United Nations General Assembly, Resolution 61/295, United Nations Declaration on the Rights of Indigenous People A/61/L.67.1. September 13, 2007.

NON-PROFIT AND CORPORATE REPORTS AND PUBLICATIONS

Davis, Jackson. *The Jeanes Visiting Teachers: An Address Given at the Inter-Territorial Jeanes Conference Salisbury, Southern Rhodesia, May 27, 1935.* New York: Carnegie Corporation, 1926.

Jones, Thomas Jesse. *Educational Adaptations: Report of Ten Years Work of the Phelps-Stokes Fund, 1910–1920.* New York: Phelps-Stokes Fund, 1920.

———. *Education in Africa: A Study of West, South, and Equatorial Africa by the African Education Commission, under the Auspices of the Phelps-Stokes Fund and*

Foreign Mission Societies of North America and Europe. New York: Phelps-Stokes Fund, 1922.

———. *Education in East Africa: A Study of East, Central, and South Africa by the Second African Education Commission, under the Auspices of the Phelps-Stokes Fund, in Cooperation with the International Education Board Phelps-Stokes Fund.* New York: Phelps-Stokes Fund, 1925.

———. *The Navajo Indian Problem.* New York: Phelps-Stokes Fund, 1939.

Leupp, Francis E. *Indian School Management: Reply to Attacks by Captain Pratt Upon the Introduction of Civil Service Reform Methods.* Philadelphia: Indian Rights Association, 1897.

DISSERTATIONS

Brown, Elizabeth Carolyn. "Pedagogies of U.S. Imperialism: Racial Education from Reconstruction to the Progressive Era." PhD dissertation, English, University of Washington, 2016.

Chase, Sara. "Na: tinixwe Education as a Site for (Re)newed Words and Worlds." PhD dissertation, Education, University of California, Berkeley, 2020.

Dumas, Michael J. "Sitting Next to White Children. School Desegregation in the Black Educational Imagination." PhD dissertation, Urban Education, City University of New York, 2007.

Hsu, Funie. "Colonial Articulations: English Instruction and the 'Benevolence' of US Overseas Expansion in the Philippines, 1898–1916." PhD dissertation, Education, University of California, Berkeley, 2013.

King, Tiffany J. [Tiffany Lethabo King]. "In the Clearing: Black Female Bodies, Space, and Settler Colonial Landscapes." PhD dissertation, American Studies, University of Maryland, 2013.

Kunkel, Juliet B. "The Eugenic University." PhD dissertation, Education, University of California Berkeley, 2021.

Mason, Damien. "Command Presence: Video Observations of Police Civilian Encounters and the Practice of Coercive Force by Law Enforcement." PhD dissertation, Education, University of California, Berkeley, 2020.

Offut-Chaney, Mahasan. "Discipline for the 'Educationally Deprived': ESEA and the Punitive Function of Federal Education Policy 1965–1998." PhD dissertation, Education, University of California Berkeley, 2020.

WORKS CITED

Adams, David Wallace. *Education for Extinction: American Indians and the Boarding School Experience, 1875–1928.* Lawrence: University Press of Kansas, 1995.

Adas, Michael. "A Field Matures: Technology, Science, and Western Colonialism." *Technology and Culture* 38, no. 2 (1997): 478–487.
Ahern, Wilbert H. "The Returned Indians: Hampton Institute and Its Indian Alumni, 1879–1893." *The Journal of Ethnic Studies* 10, no. 4 (1983): 101–134.
Akins, Audra M. "An Introduction to Stem Courses and Careers through a Brief Historical Narrative of the Tuskegee Movable School." *Black History Bulletin* 76, no. 1 (2013): 20–25.
Albisetti, James C. "The Feminization of Teaching in the Nineteenth Century: A Comparative Perspective." *History of Education* 22, no. 3 (1993): 253–263.
Aldama, Arturo J., Elisa Facio, and Daryl Maeda, eds. *Enduring Legacies: Ethnic Histories and Cultures of Colorado.* Denver: University Press of Colorado, 2011.
Alexander, Michelle. *The New Jim Crow: Mass Incarceration in the Age of Colorblindness.* New York: The New York Press, 2010.
Anderson, James D. *The Education of Blacks in the South, 1860–1935.* Chapel Hill: University of North Carolina Press, 1988.
Anyon, Jean. *Ghetto Schooling: A Political Economy of Urban Educational Reform.* New York: Teachers College Press, 1997.
Appau, Samuelson, ed. *Marketing Brands in Africa: Perspectives on the Evolution of Branding in an Emerging Market.* Cham, Switzerland: Palgrave Macmillan, 2021.
Appiah, Anthony. "Alexander Crummell and the Invention of Africa." *The Massachusetts Review* 31, no. 3 (1990): 385–406.
Apple, Michael W. *Can Education Change Society?* New York: Routledge, 2012.
Armstrong, Samuel Chapman. *Emigration to Liberia: An Address Delivered before the American Colonization Society, January 21, 1879.* Washington, DC: American Colonization Society, 1879.
———. *Concerning Indians: Extracts from the Annual Report of the Principal of the Hampton Normal and Agricultural Institute, for the School Year Ending June 30th, 1883.* Hampton, VA: Normal School Steam Press, 1883.
———. *Education for Life.* Hampton, VA: Press of the Hampton Normal and Agricultural Institute, 1913.
———. *The Indian Question.* Hampton, VA: Normal School Steam Press, 1883.
Arvin, Maile. *Possessing Polynesians: The Science of Settler Colonial Whiteness in Hawai'i and Oceania.* Durham, NC: Duke University Press, 2019.
Arvin, Maile, Eve Tuck, and Angie Morrill. "Decolonizing Feminism: Challenging Connections between Settler Colonialism and Heteropatriarchy." *Feminist Formations* 25, no. 1 (2013): 8–34.
Barad, Karen. *Meeting the Universe Halfway: Quantum Physics and the Entanglement of Matter and Meaning.* Durham, NC: Duke University Press, 2007.
Baker Jr., Houston A. *Turning South Again: Re-thinking Modernism/Re-reading Booker T.* Durham, NC: Duke University Press, 2001.
Barker, Joanne, "Confluence: Water as an Analytic of Indigenous Feminisms." *American Indian Culture and Research Journal* 43, no. 3 (2019): 1–40.
———. *Red Scare: The State's Indigenous Terrorist.* Berkeley: University of California Press, 2021.

———, ed. *Sovereignty Matters: Locations of Contestation and Possibility in Indigenous Struggles for Self-Determination.* Lincoln: University of Nebraska Press, 2005.

Barnes, Andrew. *Global Christianity and the Black Atlantic: Tuskegee, Colonialism, and the Shaping of African Industrial Education.* Waco, TX: Baylor University Press, 2017.

Barrows, David P. *A Decade of American Government in the Philippines, 1903–1913.* New York: World Book, 1914.

———. "Education and Social Progress in the Philippines," *The Annals of the American Academy of Political and Social Science* 30, no. 1 (1907): 69–82.

———. "The Negrito and Allied Types in the Philippines." *American Anthropologist* 12, no. 3 (1910): 358–376.

———. "What May Be Expected from Philippine Education." *Journal of Race and Development* 1 (1910): 156–168.

Bassil, Noah R. "The Roots of Afropessimism: The British Invention of the 'Dark Continent.'" *Critical Arts* 25, no. 3 (2011): 377–396.

Bauer Jr., William J. *California Through Native Eyes: Reclaiming History.* Seattle: University of Washington Press, 2016.

Battiste, Marie. *Decolonizing Education: Nourishing the Learning Spirit.* Vancouver: University of British Columbia Press, 2017.

Beckert, Sven. *Empire of Cotton: A Global History.* New York: Vintage, 2015.

Berkhofer Jr., Robert J. *The White Man's Indian: Images of the American Indian from Columbus to Present.* New York: Vintage Books, 1979.

Berman, Edward H. "American Influence on African Education: The Role of the Phelps-Stokes Fund's Education." *Comparative Education Review* 15, no. 2 (1971): 132–145.

Berry, Kate A. "Sovereign Sugar: Industry and Environment in Hawai'i." *Geographical Review* 108, no. 2 (2018): 328–330.

Bess, Jennifer. "The New Egypt, Pima Cotton, and the Role of Native Wage Labor on the Cooperative Testing and Demonstration Farm, Sacaton, Arizona, 1907–1917." *Agricultural History* 88, no. 4 (2014): 491–516.

Beyer, Carl Kalani. "The Connection of Samuel Chapman Armstrong as Both Borrower and Architect of Education in Hawai'i." *History of Education Quarterly* 47, no. 1 (2007): 23–48.

———. "Manual and Industrial Education for Hawaiians during the 19th Century." *The Hawaiian Journal of History* 38 (2004): 1–34.

———. "The White Architects of Hawaiian Education." *American Educational History Journal* 44, no. 2 (2017): 1–18.

Bledsoe, Adam. "Marronage as a Past and Present Geography in the Americas." *Southeastern Geographer* 57, no. 1 (2017): 30–50.

Boggs, Abigail, Eli Meyerhoff, Nick Mitchell, and Zach Schwartz-Weinstein. "Abolitionist University Studies: An Invitation." *Abolition,* August, 28, 2019. https://abolitionjournal.org/abolitionist-university-studies-an-invitation/.

Bonekemper III, Edward H. "Negro Ownership of Real Property in Hampton and Elizabeth City County, Virginia, 1860–1870." *The Journal of Negro History* 55, no. 3 (1970): 165–181.

Bonneuil, Christophe. "Development as Experiment: Science and State Building in Late Colonial and Postcolonial Africa, 1930–1970." *Osiris* 15 (2000): 258–281.

Bosma, Ulbe, Juan Giusti-Cordero, and Roger Knight, eds. *Sugarlandia Revisited: Sugar and Colonialism in Asia and the Americas, 1800–1940*. New York: Berghahn Books, 2007.

Bourdieu, Pierre and Jean-Claude Passeron. *Reproduction in Education, Society and Culture*. Translated by Richard Nice. London: Sage, 1990.

Bowers, Fredalene B. and Thom Gehring. "Johann Heinrich Pestalozzi: 18th century Swiss Educator and Correctional Reformer." *Journal of Correctional Education* 55, no. 4 (2004): 306–319.

Bowles, Samuel and Herbert Gintis. *Schooling in Capitalist America: Educational Reform and the Contradictions of Economic Life*. Chicago: Haymarket Books, 1976.

Brantlinger, Patrick. "Victorians and Africans: The Genealogy of the Myth of the Dark Continent." *Critical Inquiry* 12, no. 1 (1985): 166–203.

Brayboy, Bryan McKinley Jones. "Toward a Tribal Critical Race Theory in Education." *The Urban Review* 37, no. 5 (2005): 425–446.

Brayboy, Bryan McKinley Jones and Donna Deyhle. "Insider-Outsider: Researchers in American Indian Communities." *Theory into Practice* 39, no. 3 (2000): 163–169.

Brayboy, Bryan McKinley Jones and Emma Maughan. "Indigenous Knowledges and the Story of the Bean." *Harvard Educational Review* 79, no. 1 (2009): 1–21.

Bristol, Laurette. "Practicing in Betwixt Oppression and Subversion: Plantation Pedagogy as a Legacy of Plantation Economy in Trinidad and Tobago." *Power and Education* 2, no. 2 (2010): 167–182.

Brophy, Alfred L. "Forum on Slavery and Universities: Introduction." *Slavery & Abolition* 39, no. 2 (2018): 229–235.

Brown, Nicole M., Ruby Mendenhall, Michael L. Black, Mark Van Moer, Assata Zerai, and Karen Flynn, "Mechanized Margin to Digitized Center: Black Feminism's Contributions to Combatting Erasure within the Digital Humanities." *International Journal of Humanities and Arts Computing* 10, no. 1 (2016): 110–125.

Browne, Simone. *Dark Matters: On the Surveillance of Blackness*. Durham, NC: Duke University Press, 2015.

Bruce, La Marr Jurelle. *How to Go Mad Without Losing Your Mind: Madness and Black Radical Creativity*. Durham, NC: Duke University Press, 2020.

Buffalohead, Roger W. and Paulette Fairbanks Molin. "'A Nucleus of Civilization': American Indian Families at Hampton Institute in the Late Nineteenth Century." *Journal of American Indian Education* 35, no. 3 (1996): 59–94.

Burgess, Marianna. *Stiya: A Carlisle Indian Girl at Home*. Cambridge, MA: Riverside Press, 1891. Carlisle Indian School Digital Resource Center.

Burkley, Edward, Federica Durante, Susan T. Fiske, Melissa Burkley, and Angela Andrade. "Structure and Content of Native American Stereotypic Subgroups: Not Just (ig)Noble." *Cultural Diversity and Ethnic Minority Psychology* 23, no. 2 (2017): 209–219.

Byrd, Jodi A. *The Transit of Empire: Indigenous Critiques of Colonialism.* Minneapolis: University of Minnesota Press, 2011.

Byrd, Jodi A., Alyosha Goldstein, Jodi Melamed, and Chandan Reddy. "Predatory Value: Economies of Dispossession and Disturbed Relationalities." *Social Text* 36, no. 2 (2018): 1–18.

Caldwell, B. C. "The Work of the Jeanes and Slater Funds." *The Annals of the American Academy of Political and Social Science* 49, no. 1 (1913): 173–176.

Carlson, David J. and Charles Eastman "'Indian for a While': Charles Eastman's 'Indian Boyhood' and the Discourse of Allotment." *American Indian Quarterly* 25, no. 4 (2001): 604–625.

Carlson, Leonard A. "The Dawes Act and the Decline of Indian Farming." *Journal of Economic History* 38, no. 1 (1978): 274–276.

———. "Federal Policy and Indian Land: Economic Interests and the Sale of Indian Allotments, 1900–1934." *Agricultural History* 57, no. 1 (1983): 33–45.

———. *Learning to Farm: Indian Land Tenure and Farming Before the Dawes Act.* Lanham, MD: Rowman and Littlefield, 1992.

Chang, David A. *The Color of the Land: Race, Nation, and the Politics of Landownership in Oklahoma, 1832–1929.* Chapel Hill: University of North Carolina Press, 2010.

Chen, Mel Y. *Animacies: Biopolitics, Racial Mattering, and Queer Affect.* Durham, NC: Duke University Press, 2012.

Chennault, Ronald E. "Pragmatism and Progressivism in the Educational Thought and Practices of Booker T. Washington." *Philosophical Studies in Education* 44 (2013): 121–131.

Cheng, Ch'eng-K'un. "Assimilation in Hawaii and the Bid for Statehood." *Social Forces* 30 (1951): 16–28.

Child, Brenda J. "The Boarding School as Metaphor." *Journal of American Indian Education* 57, no. 1 (2018): 37–57.

———. *Boarding School Seasons: American Indian Families, 1900–1940.* Lincoln: University of Nebraska Press, 2000.

Chock, Jennifer M. L. "One Hundred Years of Illegitimacy: International Legal Analysis of the Illegal Overthrow of the Hawaiian Monarchy, Hawai'i's Annexation, and Possible Reparations." *University Hawaii Law Review* 17 (1995): 463–512.

Churchill, Ward and Jim Vander Wall. *Agents of Repression: The FBI's Secret Wars against the Black Panther Party and the American Indian Movement.* Cambridge, MA: South End Press, 2002.

Clayton, Thomas. "Beyond Mystification: Reconnecting World-System Theory for Comparative Education." *Comparative Education Review* 42, no. 4 (1998): 479–496.

Clukey, Amy and Jeremy Wells. "Introduction: Plantation Modernity." *Global South* 10, no. 2 (2016): 1–10.

Clymer, Kenton J. "Humanitarian Imperialism: David Prescott Barrows and the White Man's Burden in the Philippines." *Pacific Historical Review* 45, no. 4 (1976): 495–517.

Contee, Clarence G. "Du Bois, the NAACP, and the Pan-African Congress of 1919." *The Journal of Negro History* 57, no. 1 (1972): 13–28.

Coombes, Annie E. *Rethinking Settler Colonialism: History and Memory in Australia, Canada, New Zealand and South Africa*. Manchester, UK: Manchester University Press, 2006.

Coppinger, William. *The New Africa: Seventh Annual Paper*. Hampton, VA: Normal School Press, 1887.

Corntassel, Jeff and Tiffanie Hardbarger. "Educate to Perpetuate: Land-Based Pedagogies and Community Resurgence." *International Review of Education* 65, no. 1 (2019): 87–116.

Crump, Jeff R. "Learning by Doing: Implementing Community Service-Based Learning." *Journal of Geography* 101, no. 4 (2002): 144–152.

Curtin, Philip D. *The Rise and Fall of the Plantation Complex: Essays in Atlantic History*. Cambridge: Cambridge University Press, 1998.

Dancy, T. Elon, Kirsten T. Edwards, and James Earl Davis. "Historically White Universities and Plantation Politics: Anti-Blackness and Higher Education in the Black Lives Matter Era." *Urban Education* 53, no. 2 (2018): 176–195.

Da Silva, Denise Ferreira. *Toward a Global Idea of Race*. Minneapolis: University of Minnesota Press, 2007.

David, Magdalene S. "The Love of Liberty Brought Us Here (an Analysis of the Development of the Settler State in 19th Century Liberia)." *Review of African Political Economy* 11, no. 31 (1984): 57–70.

Day, Iyko. "Being or Nothingness: Indigeneity, Antiblackness, and Settler Colonial Critique." *Critical Ethnic Studies* 1, no. 2 (2015): 102–121.

Dei, George Sefa. "Indigenous Anti-Colonial Knowledge as 'Heritage Knowledge' for Promoting Black/African Education in Diasporic Contexts." *Decolonization: Indigeneity, Education & Society* 1, no. 1 (2012): 102–119.

Deloria, Philip J. *Indians in Unexpected Places*. Lawrence, KS: University Press of Kansas, 2004.

———. *Playing Indian*. New Haven, CT: Yale University Press, 1998.

Deloria Jr., Vine. *Custer Died for Your Sins: An Indian Manifesto*. Norman: University of Oklahoma Press, 1969.

———. *We Talk, You Listen: New Tribes, New Turf*. Lincoln: University of Nebraska Press, 2007.

Dewey, John. *The School and Society: Being Three Lectures*. Chicago: University of Chicago Press, 1899.

Dineen-Wimberly, Ingrid. "To Carry 'the Black Man's Burden': T. Thomas Fortune's Vision of African American Colonization of the Philippines in 1902 and 1903." *International Journal of Business and Social Science* 5, no. 10 (2014): 69–74.

Drake, St. Clair. "The Black Diaspora in Pan-African Perspective." *The Black Scholar* 7, no. 1 (1975): 2–13.

———. *The Redemption of Africa and Black Religion*. Chicago: Third World Press, 1970.

Dube, Thomas M. T. "Literature on African Resistance to Domination in South Africa: 1910–1966." *A Current Bibliography on African Affairs* 7, no. 2 (1974): 156–168.

Du Bois, William Edward Burghardt. *Black Reconstruction: Toward a History of the Part Which Black Folk Played in the Attempt to Reconstruct Democracy in America, 1860–1880*. Philadelphia: A. Saifer, 1935.

———. "Does the Negro Need Separate Schools?" *Journal of Negro Education* 4, no. 3 (1935) 328–335.

———. "Liberia, the League and the United States." *Foreign Affairs* 11, no. 4 (1933): 682–695.

———. *The Talented Tenth*. New York: James Pott, 1903.

Dumas, Michael J. "Against the Dark: Antiblackness in Education Policy and Discourse." *Theory Into Practice* 55, no. 1 (2016): 11–19.

Dyson, Omari L. *The Black Panther Party and Transformative Pedagogy: Place-Based Education in Philadelphia*. Lanham, MD: Lexington Books, 2013.

Eagle Shield, Alayna, Django Paris, Rae Paris, Timothy San Pedro, eds. *Education in Movement Spaces: Standing Rock to the Chicago Freedom Square Movement*. New York: Routledge, 2020.

Eaton, J.J. "The Manila Trade School." *The Annals of the American Academy of Political and Social Science* 33, no. 1 (1909): 89–96.

Eittreim, Elizabeth M. *Teaching Empire: Native Americans, Filipinos, and US Imperial Education, 1879–1918*. Lawrence: University Press of Kansas, 2019.

Ellis, Clifton and Rebecca Ginsburg, eds. *Cabin, Quarter, Plantation: Architecture and Landscapes of North American Slavery*. New Haven, CT: Yale University Press, 2010.

Elstein, David. "Making Sure Sacred Sheep Don't Become Extinct." *Agricultural Research* 53, no. 4 (2005): 11.

Engs, Robert Francis. *Educating the Disfranchised and Disinherited: Samuel Chapman Armstrong and Hampton Institute, 1839–1893*. Knoxville: University of Tennessee Press, 1999.

Enoch, Jessica. "Resisting the Script of Indian Education: Zitkala Ša and the Carlisle Indian School." *College English* 65, no. 2 (2002): 117–141.

Eperjesi, John. *The Imperialist Imaginary: Visions of Asia and the Pacific in American Culture*. Hanover, NH: Dartmouth College Press, 2004.

Eshach, Haim. "Bridging In-School and Out-of-School Learning: Formal, Non-Formal, and Informal Education." *Journal of Science Education and Technology* 16, no. 2 (2007): 171–190.

Falzetti, Ashley Glassburn. "Archival Absence: The Burden of History," *Settler Colonial Studies* 5, no. 2 (2015): 128–144.

Ferguson, Karen J. "Caught in 'No Man's Land'": The Negro Cooperative Demonstration Service and the Ideology of Booker T. Washington, 1900–1918." *Agricultural History* 72, no. 1 (1998): 33–54.

Ferguson, Roderick. "The Nightmares of the Heteronormative." *Journal for Cultural Research* 4, no. 4 (2000): 419–444.

Fixico, Donald L. *Termination and Relocation: Federal Indian Policy, 1945–1960.* Albuquerque: University of New Mexico Press, 1986.

Fleming, D. J. "Some Aspects of the Philippine Educational System." *International Review of Mission* 10, no. 2 (1921): 249–259.

Fleming Jr., Julius B. *Black Patience: Performance, Civil Rights, and the Unfinished Project of Emancipation.* New York: New York University Press, 2022.

Foucault, Michel. *Discipline and Punish.* Translated by Alan Sheridan. New York: Vintage, 1977.

———. *Power/Knowledge: Selected Interviews and Other Writings, 1972–1977.* Edited by Colin Gordon. Translated by Colin Gordon, Leo Marshall, John Mepham, Kate Soper. New York: Pantheon Books, 1980.

Freire, Paolo. *Pedagogy of the Oppressed.* Translated by Maya Bergman Ramos. New York: Continuum, 1996.

Frissell, Hollis Burke. *Out from the Cabin and the Tepee.* Hampton, VA: Hampton Institute Press, 1900.

Fuller, Sharon Y. *Gullah Geechee Indigenous Articulation in the Americas.* Berkeley: University of California, 2015.

García, Emma. "Schools Are Still Segregated, and Black Children Are Paying a Price." *Economic Policy Institute* (2020): 1–5.

Gardner, Roberta Price, Sandra Lucia Osorio, Sara Carrillo, and Rachel Gilmore. "(Re) Membering in the Pedagogical Work of Black and Brown Teachers: Reclaiming Stories as Culturally Sustaining Practice." *Urban Education* 55, no. 6 (2020): 838–864.

Generals, Donald. "Booker T. Washington and Progressive Education: An Experimentalist Approach to Curriculum Development and Reform." *Journal of Negro Education* 69, no. 3 (Summer 2000): 215–234.

Ghaddar, Jamila J. "The Spectre in the Archive: Truth, Reconciliation, and Indigenous Archival Memory." *Archivaria* 82, no. 1 (2016): 3–26.

Ginsburg, Mark B., Susan Cooper, Rajeshwari Raghu, and Hugo Zegarra. "National and World-System Explanations of Educational Reform." *Comparative Education Review* 34, no. 4 (1990): 474–499.

Giroux, Henry A. *On Critical Pedagogy.* New York: Bloomsbury, 2011.

Givens, Jarvis R. *Fugitive Pedagogy: Carter G. Woodson and the Art of Black Teaching.* Cambridge, MA: Harvard University Press, 2021.

———. "A Grammar for Black Education Beyond Borders: Exploring Technologies of Schooling in the African Diaspora." *Race, Ethnicity and Education* 19, no. 6 (2015): 1288–1302.

Glancy, Diane and Rachel Gould. *Fort Marion Prisoners and the Trauma of Native Education.* Lincoln: University of Nebraska Press, 2014.

Glenn, Evelyn Nakano. "Settler Colonialism as Structure: A Framework for Comparative Studies of US Race and Gender Formation." *Sociology of Race and Ethnicity* 1, no. 1 (2015): 52–72.

Goeman, Mishuana. *Mark My Words: Native Women Mapping Our Nations*. Minneapolis: University of Minnesota Press, 2013.

Goodyear-Kaʻopua, Noelani. *The Seeds We Planted: Portraits of a Native Hawaiian Charter School*. Minneapolis: University of Minnesota Press, 2013.

Gorlewski, Julie and Eve Tuck, eds. *Who Decides Who Becomes a Teacher?: Schools of Education as Sites of Resistance*. New York: Routledge, 2018.

Gramsci, Antonio. *Prison Notebooks*. Edited and translated by Joseph A. Buttigieg. Vol. 2. New York: Columbia University Press, 2011.

Grande, Sandy. *Red Pedagogy: Native American Social and Political Thought*. Lanham, MD: Rowman and Littlefield, 2004.

Green, J. A. *The Educational Ideas of Pestalozzi*. Baltimore, MD: Warwick & York, 1914.

Green, Rayna. "The Pocahontas Perplex: The Image of Indian Women in American Culture." *The Massachusetts Review* 16, no. 4 (1975): 698–714.

Greenwald, Emily. *Reconfiguring the Reservation: The Nez Perces, Jicarilla Apaches, and the Dawes Act*. Santa Fe: University of New Mexico Press, 2002.

Gresham, Stephen. "George Washington Carver and the Art of Technical Communication." *Journal of Technical Writing and Communication* 9, no. 3 (1979): 217–225.

Gutiérrez y Muhs, Gabriella, Yolanda Flores Niemann, Carmen G. González, and Angela P. Harris, eds. *Presumed Incompetent: The Intersections of Race and Class for Women in Academia*. Logan: Utah University Press, 2012.

Hailu, Meseret and Amanda Tachine. "Black and Indigenous Theoretical Considerations for Higher Education Sustainability." *Journal of Comparative & International Higher Education* 13, (Summer 2021): 20–42.

Harkins, Gillian and Erica R. Meiners. "Beyond Crisis: College in Prison through the Abolition Undercommons." *Lateral* 3 (2014).

Harris, Leslie Maria, James T. Campbell, and Alfred L. Brophy, eds. *Slavery and the University: Histories and Legacies*. Athens: University of Georgia Press, 2019.

Hartman, Saidiya V. *Lose Your Mother: A Journey Along the Atlantic Slave Route*. New York: Farrar, Straus, and Giroux, 2008.

———. *Scenes of Subjection: Terror, Slavery, and Self-Making in Nineteenth-Century America*. Oxford: Oxford University Press, 1997.

———. *Wayward Lives, Beautiful Experiments: Intimate Histories of Riotous Black Girls, Troublesome Women, and Queer Radicals*. New York: W. W. Norton, 2019.

Hampton Institute and Richmond L. Miner. *Everyday Life at Hampton Institute*. Hampton, VA: Hampton Institute, 1907.

Harding, Sandra. *Whose Science? Whose Knowledge?: Thinking from Women's Lives*. Ithaca, NY: Cornell University Press, 1991.

Harlan, Louis R. "Booker T. Washington and the White Man's Burden." *The American Historical Review* 71, no. 2 (1966): 441–467.

Hawkins, Billy. *The New Plantation: Black Athletes, College Sports, and Predominantly White NCAA Institutions.* New York: Palgrave Macmillan, 2013.

Hayes, Sarah Kathryn Pitcher. "The Experiment at Fort Marion: Richard Henry Pratt's Recreation of Penitential Regimes at the Old Fort and Its Influence on American Indian Education." *Journal of Florida Studies* 1, no. 7 (2018): 1–22.

Headland, Thomas N. "Thirty Endangered Languages in the Philippines." *Work Papers of the Summer Institute of Linguistics, University of North Dakota Session* 47, no. 1 (2003): 1–12.

Headrick, Daniel R. *The Tentacles of Progress: Technology Transfer in the Age of Imperialism, 1850–1940.* Oxford: Oxford University Press, 1988.

Hersey, Mark. "Hints and Suggestions to Farmers: George Washington Carver and Rural Conservation in the South." *Environmental History* 11, no. 2 (2006): 239–268.

Hines, Linda O. "George W. Carver and the Tuskegee Agricultural Experiment Station." *Agricultural History* 53, no. 1 (1979): 71–83.

Hinrichsen, Lisa. "'A Curious Study': 'The Autobiography of an Ex-Coloured Man', Pedagogy, and the Post-Plantation Imagination." *African American Review* 48, no. 1/2 (2015): 175–189.

Hobbes, Thomas. *Leviathan: Or the Matter, Forme, and Power of a Commonwealth, Ecclesiastical and Civil.* Edited by A. R. Waller. Cambridge: University Press, 1904.

hooks, bell. *Belonging: A Culture of Place.* New York: Routledge, 2009.

Horne, Gerald. *The White Pacific: US Imperialism and Black Slavery in the South Seas After the Civil War.* Honolulu: University of Hawaii Press, 2007.

Hornsby Jr., Alton, ed. *A Companion to African American History.* Malden, MA: Blackwell, 2005.

Hugill, Peter J. "Communication and Empire," *The Geographical Review* 98, no. 3 (2008): 428–430.

Huhndorf, Shari M. *Going Native: Indians in the North American Cultural Imagination.* Ithaca, NY: Cornell University Press, 2015.

Hunt, Chester L. "Education and Economic Development in the Early American Period in the Philippines." *Philippine Studies* 36, no. 3 (1988): 352–364.

Hunt, Davis R. "Charles T. Loram and an American Model for African Education in South Africa." *African Studies Review* 19, no. 2 (1976): 87–100.

Hunziker, Alyssa A. "Playing Indian, Playing Filipino: Native American and Filipino Interactions at the Carlisle Indian Industrial School." *American Quarterly* 72, no. 2 (2020): 423–448.

Infante, Chad, Sandra Harvey, Kelly Limes Taylor, and Tiffany King. "Other Intimacies: Black Studies Notes on Native/Indigenous Studies." *Postmodern Culture* 31, no. 1 (2020). https://muse.jhu.edu/article/800013.

Innes, Robert Alexander. "'Wait a Second. Who Are You Anyways?' The Insider/Outsider Debate and American Indian Studies." *American Indian Quarterly* 33, no. 4 (2009): 440–461.

Issar, Siddhant. "Theorising 'Racial/Colonial Primitive Accumulation': Settler Colonialism, Slavery and Racial Capitalism." *Race & Class* 63, no. 1 (2021): 23–50.

Jackson, Miles, ed. *They Followed the Trade Winds: African Americans in Hawaii*. Honolulu: Hawaii University Press, 2014.

Jackson, Zakiyyah Iman. *Becoming Human: Matter and Meaning in an Antiblack World*. New York: New York University Press, 2020.

James, Felix. "The Tuskegee Institute Movable School, 1906–1923." *Agricultural History* 45, no. 3 (1971): 201–209.

Jarosz, Lucy. "Constructing the Dark Continent: Metaphor as Geographic Representation of Africa." *Geografiska Annaler: Series B, Human Geography* 74, no. 2 (1992): 105–115.

Johnson Jr., Khalil Anthony. "Problem Solver or 'Evil Genius': Thomas Jesse Jones and the Problem of Indian Administration." *Native American and Indigenous Studies* 5, no. 2 (2018): 37–69.

———. "'Recruited to Teach the Indians': An African American Genealogy of Navajo Nation Boarding Schools." *Journal of American Indian Education* 57, no. 1 (2018): 154–176.

Jones, Allen W. "The Role of Tuskegee Institute in the Education of Black Farmers." *The Journal of Negro History* 60, no. 2 (1975): 252–267.

Jones, Lance G. E. *The Jeanes Teacher in the United States, 1908–1933: An Account of Twenty-Five Years' Experience in the Supervision of Negro Rural Schools*. Chapel Hill: University of North Carolina Press, 2011.

Jung, Moon-Kie, and João H. Costa Vargas, eds. *Antiblackness*. Durham, NC: Duke University Press, 2021.

Justice, Daniel Heath and Jean M. O'Brien, eds. *Allotment Stories: Indigenous Land Relations Under Settler Siege*. Minneapolis: University of Minnesota Press, 2022.

Karuka, Manu. *Empire's Tracks: Indigenous Nations, Chinese Workers, and the Transcontinental Railroad*. Berkeley: University of California Press, 2019.

Kaplan, Amy. "Manifest Domesticity." *American Literature* 70, no. 3 (1998): 581–606.

Kaplan, Lawrence S. "Frederick Jackson Turner and Imperialism." *Social Science* 27, no. 1 (1952): 12–16.

Kauanui, J. Kēhaulani. "Colonialism in Equality: Hawaiian Sovereignty and the Question of US Civil Rights." *South Atlantic Quarterly* 107, no. 4 (2008): 635–650.

———. "Imperial Ocean: The Pacific as a Critical Site for American Studies." *American Quarterly* 67, no. 3 (2015): 625–636.

———. "The Multiplicity of Hawaiian Sovereignty Claims and the Struggle for Meaningful Autonomy." *Comparative American Studies: An International Journal* 3, no. 3 (2005): 283–299.

———. *Paradoxes of Hawaiian Sovereignty: Land, Sex, and the Colonial Politics of State Nationalism*. Durham, NC: Duke University Press, 2018.

Kempf, Arlo, ed. *Breaching the Colonial Contract: Anti-Colonialism in the US and Canada*. Dordrecht, NL: Springer, 2009.

Kerr, Allen. *The Legacy: A Centennial History of the State Agricultural Experiment Stations, 1887–1987*. Columbia: Missouri Agricultural Experiment Station, University of Missouri-Columbia, 1987.

King, Tiffany Lethabo. "Black 'Feminisms' and Pessimism: Abolishing Moynihan's Negro Family." *Theory & Event* 21, no. 1 (2018): 68–87.

———. *The Black Shoals: Offshore Formations of Black and Native Studies*. Durham, NC: Duke University Press, 2019.

———. "The Labor of (Re) Reading Plantation Landscapes Fungible(ly)." *Antipode* 48, no. 4 (2016): 1022–1039.

———. "Labor's Aphasia: Toward Antiblackness as Constitutive to Settler Colonialism." *Decolonization: Indigeneity, Education & Society*, 2014. https://decolonization.wordpress.com/2014/06/10/labors-aphasia-toward-antiblackness-as-constitutive-to-settler-colonialism/.

Kroskrity, Paul V. "Language Ideologies—Evolving Perspectives." *Society and Language Use* 7, no. 3 (2010): 192–205.

Kwet, Michael. "Digital Colonialism: US Empire and the New Imperialism in the Global South." *Race & Class* 60, no. 4 (2019): 3–26.

Kuykendall, Ralph S. "Early Hawaiian Commercial Development." *Pacific Historical Review* 3, no. 4 (1934): 365–385.

Labaree, David F. "The Winning Ways of a Losing Strategy: Educationalizing Social Problems in the United States." *Educational Theory* 58, no. 4 (2008): 447–460.

La Croix, Sumner J. and Christopher Grandy. "The Political Instability of Reciprocal Trade and the Overthrow of the Hawaiian Kingdom." *Journal of Economic History* 57, no. 1 (1997): 161–189.

LaFeber, Walter. *The New Empire: An Interpretation of American Expansion, 1860–1898*. Ithaca, NY: Cornell University Press, 1998.

La Flesche, Francis. *The Middle Five: Indian Schoolboys of the Omaha Tribe*. Lincoln: University of Nebraska Press, 1978.

la paperson. *A Third University Is Possible*. Minneapolis: University of Minnesota Press, 2017.

Larkin, John A. *Sugar and the Origins of the Modern Philippine Society*. Berkeley: University of California Press, 1993.

Latour, Bruno and Steve Woolgar. *Laboratory Life: The Construction of Scientific Facts*. Princeton, NJ: Princeton University Press, 2013.

Lefebvre, Henri. *The Production of Space*. Translated by Donald Nicholson Smith. Oxford: Blackwell, 1974.

Leonardo, Zeus and Logan Manning. "White Historical Activity Theory: Toward a Critical Understanding of White Zones of Proximal Development." *Race, Ethnicity and Education* 20, no. 1 (2017): 15–29.

Leonardo, Zeus and Blanca Gamez-Djokic. "Sometimes Leaving Means Staying: Race and White Teachers' Emotional Investments." *Teachers College Record* 121, no. 13 (2019): 1–22.

Lepore, Jill. *A is for American: Letters and Other Characters in the Newly United States*. New York: Vintage, 2007.

Lerner, Gerda. "Early Community Work of Black Club Women." *The Journal of Negro History* 59, no. 2 (1974): 158–167.

Lewis, Theodore. "Booker T. Washington's Audacious Vocationalist Philosophy." *Oxford Review of Education* 40, no. 2 (2014): 189–205.

Lindsey, Donal F. *Indians at Hampton Institute, 1877–1923.* Urbana: University of Illinois Press, 1994.

Linnekin, Jocelyn. "The Hui Lands of Keanae: Hawaiian Land Tenure and the Great Mahele." *The Journal of the Polynesian Society* 92, no. 2 (1983): 169–188.

———. "Statistical Analysis of the Great Māhele: Some Preliminary Findings." *The Journal of Pacific History* 22, no. 1 (1987): 15–33.

Logan, Frenise A. "The British East India Company and African Slavery in Benkulen, Sumatra, 1687–1792." *The Journal of Negro History* 41, no. 4 (1956): 339–348.

Lomawaima, K. Tsianina. *They Called It Prairie Light: The Story of the Chilocco Indian School.* Lincoln: University of Nebraska Press, 1994.

Lomawaima, K. Tsianina and Jeffrey Ostler. "Reconsidering Richard Henry Pratt: Cultural Genocide and Native Liberation in an Era of Racial Oppression." *Journal of American Indian Education* 57, no. 1 (2018): 79–100.

Lomawaima, K. Tsianina and Theresa L. McCarty. *To Remain an Indian: Lessons in Democracy from a Century of Native American Education.* New York: Columbia University Press, 2006.

Loram, Charles Templeman. *The Education of the South African Native.* New York: Negro Universities Press, 1917.

Love, Eric Tyrone Lowery. *Race Over Empire: Racism and US Imperialism, 1865–1900.* Chapel Hill: University of North Carolina Press, 2004.

Lowe, Lisa. *The Intimacies of Four Continents.* Durham, NC: Duke University Press, 2015.

Lu, Zhenmin, John W. Radin, Edgar L. Turcotte, Richard Percy, and Eduardo Zeiger. "High Yields in Advanced Lines of Pima Cotton Are Associated with Higher Stomatal Conductance, Reduced Leaf Area and Lower Leaf Temperature." *Physiologia Plantarum* 92, no. 2 (1994): 266–272.

Lüthi, Barbara, Francesca Falk, and Patricia Purtschert. "Colonialism without Colonies: Examining Blank Spaces in Colonial Studies." *National Identities* 18, no. 1 (2016): 1–9.

Lyon, Judson M. "Informal Imperialism: The United States in Liberia, 1897–1912." *Diplomatic History* 5, no. 3 (1981): 221–243.

Lyons, Paul and Ty P. Kāwika Tengan. "Introduction: Pacific Currents." *American Quarterly* 67, no. 3 (2015): 545–574.

Maldonado, David A. and Erica R. Meiners. "Due Time: Meditations on Abolition at the Site of the University." *Social Text* 39, no. 1 (146) (March 1, 2021): 69–92.

Manning, John P. "Rediscovering Froebel: A Call to Re-Examine His Life & Gifts." *Early Childhood Education Journal* 32, no. 6 (2005): 371–376.

Manson, Andrew Hayden and Bernard Mbenga. "The African National Congress in the Western Transvaal/Northern Cape Platteland, c. 1910–1964: Patterns of Diffusion and Support for Congress in a Rural Setting." *South African Historical Journal* 64, no. 3 (2012): 472–493.

Marah, John Karefah. "Educational Adaptation and Pan-Africanism: Developmental Trends in Africa." *Journal of Black Studies* 17, no. 4 (1987): 460–481.

Mathes, Valerie Sherer. "Nineteenth Century Women and Reform: The Women's National Indian Association." *American Indian Quarterly* 14, no. 1 (1990): 1–18.

Marquez, Bayley J. "'No Women Involved': Settler Colonial Racial Grammars in Black and Indigenous Education." *Feminist Formations* 33, no. 3 (2021): 116–139.

———. "The Black Model Minority: Slavery, Settlement, and the Genealogy of the Model Minority." *Du Bois Review: Social Science Research on Race* 19, no. 1 (2022): 129–145.

Marquez, Bayley J. and Juliet R. Kunkel, "The Domestication Genocide of Settler Colonial Language Ideologies." *American Quarterly Special Issue: The Politics of Language, Multilingualism, and Translation in American Studies* 73 no.3 (September 2021).

May, Glenn A. "Social Engineering in the Philippines: The Aims and Execution of American Educational Policy, 1900–1913." *Philippine Studies* 24, no. 2 (1976): 135–183.

Mayberry, B.D. "The Tuskegee Movable School: A Unique Contribution to National and International Agriculture and Rural Development." *Agricultural History* 65, no. 2 (1991): 85–104.

Mays, Kyle T. *An Afro-Indigenous History of the United States*. New York: Beacon Press, 2021.

McClintock, Anne. *Imperial Leather: Race, Gender, and Sexuality in the Colonial Contest*. New York: Routledge, 1995.

McCoy, Kate, Eve Tuck, and Marcia McKenzie, eds. *Land Education: Rethinking Pedagogies of Place from Indigenous, Postcolonial, and Decolonizing Perspectives*. New York: Routledge, 2017.

McCulloch, James E., ed. *The Human Way: Addresses on Race Problems at the Southern Sociological Congress Atlanta, 1913*. Nashville, TN: Southern Sociological Conference, 1913.

McGee, Leo. "Booker T. Washington and George Washington Carver: A Tandem of Adult Educators at Tuskegee." *Lifelong Learning* 8, no. 2 (1984): 16–18.

McGee, Leo and Dalton McAfee. "Role of the Traditionally Black Public Institution of Higher Learning in Extension Education." *The Journal of Negro Education* 46, no. 1 (1977): 46–52.

McGranahan, Carole. "Theorizing Refusal: An Introduction." *Cultural Anthropology* 31, no. 3 (2016): 319–325.

McKay, Deirdre. "Rethinking Indigenous Place: Igorot Identity and Locality in the Philippines." *The Australian Journal of Anthropology* 17, no. 3 (2006): 291–306.

McKittrick, Katherine. *Demonic Grounds: Black Women and the Cartographies of Struggle*. Minneapolis: University of Minnesota Press, 2006.

———. "Mathematics of Black Life." *The Black Scholar* 44, no. 2 (2014): 16–28.

———. "Plantation Futures." *Small Axe: A Caribbean Journal of Criticism* 17, no. 3 (42) (2013): 1–15.

———. "On Plantations, Prisons, and a Black Sense of Place." *Social & Cultural Geography* 12, no. 8 (2011): 947–963.
McLaren, Peter. "Critical Pedagogy and Class Struggle in the Age of Neoliberal Globalization: Notes from History's Underside." *Democracy & Nature* 9, no. 1 (2003): 65–90.
Meyer, John W., Francisco O. Ramirez, and Yasemin Nuhoḡlu Soysal. "World Expansion of Mass Education, 1870–1980." *Sociology of Education* 65, no. 2 (1992): 128–149.
Meyerhoff, Eli. *Beyond Education: Radical Studying for Another World*. Minneapolis: University of Minnesota Press, 2019.
Miles, Tiya and Sharon Patricia Holland, eds. *Crossing Waters, Crossing Worlds: The African Diaspora in Indian Country*. Durham, NC: Duke University Press, 2006.
Mitchell, Michele. "'The Black Man's Burden': African Americans, Imperialism, and Notions of Racial Manhood 1890–1910." *International Review of Social History* 44, no. S7 (1999): 77–99.
Mitchell, Nick. "The View from Nowhere: On Frank Wilderson's Afropessimism." *Specter* (Fall 2020): 110–122.
Moll, Luis. "Vygotsky's Zone of Proximal Development: Rethinking Its Instructional Implications." *Infancia y Aprendizaje* 13, no. 51–52 (1990): 157–168.
Monarrez, Tomas, Brian Kisida, and Matthew M. Chingos, "The Effect of Charter Schools on School Segregation." *American Economic Journal: Economic Policy* 14, no. 1 (2022): 301–340.
Mooney, Barbara Burlison. "The Comfortable Tasty Framed Cottage: An African American Architectural Iconography." *The Journal of the Society of Architectural Historians* 61, no. 1 (2002): 48–67.
Mooney, James. *The Ghost-Dance Religion and the Sioux Outbreak of 1890*. Lincoln: University of Nebraska Press, 1991.
Moreton-Robinson, Aileen. *The White Possessive: Property, Power, and Indigenous Sovereignty*. Minneapolis: University of Minnesota Press, 2015.
Morgensen, Scott Lauria. *Spaces between Us: Queer Settler Colonialism and Indigenous Decolonization*. Minneapolis: University of Minnesota Press, 2011.
Moses, Wilson Jeremiah. *Alexander Crummell: A Study of Civilization and Discontent*. Oxford: Oxford University Press on Demand, 1989.
Moten, Fred and Stefano Harney. "The University and the Undercommons: Seven Theses." *Social Text* 22, no. 2 (2004): 101–115.
Nee-Benham, Maenette Kapeʻahiokalani Padeken Ah and Ronald H. Heck. *Culture and Educational Policy in Hawaiʻi: The Silencing of Native Voices*. Mahwah, NJ: Lawrence Erlbaum, 1998.
Nelson, Cary and Lawrence Grossberg, eds. *Marxism and Interpretation of Culture*. Basingstoke, UK: Macmillan Education, 1988.
Nietzsche, Friedrich. *The Will to Power*. Edited by Walter Kaufmann. Translated by Walter Kaufmann and R. J. Hollingdale. New York: Vintage Books, 1967.
Nxumalo, Fikile. "Decolonial Water Pedagogies: Invitations to Black, Indigenous, and Black-Indigenous World-Making." *Occasional Paper Series*, no. 45 (2021).

Nxumalo, Fikile and Stacia Cedillo. "Decolonizing Place in Early Childhood Studies: Thinking with Indigenous Onto-Epistemologies and Black Feminist Geographies." *Global Studies of Childhood* 7, no. 2 (2017): 99–112.

Offutt-Chaney, Mahasan. "'Black Crisis' and the 'Likely' Privatization of Public Education in New Orleans and Liberia." *Critical Studies in Education* (2019): 1–16.

Olmstead, Alan L. and Paul W. Rhode. "Cotton, Slavery, and the New History of Capitalism." *Explorations in Economic History* 67 (2018): 1–17.

Olund, Eric N. "From Savage Space to Governable Space: The Extension of United States Judicial Sovereignty over Indian Country in the Nineteenth Century." *Cultural Geographies* 9, no. 2 (2002): 129–157.

O'Neill, Jan. "SMART Goals, SMART Schools." *Educational Leadership* 57, no. 5 (2000): 46–50.

Otis, Delos Sacket. *The Dawes Act and the Allotment of Indian Lands*. Norman: University of Oklahoma Press, 2014.

Owens, Ann. "Unequal Opportunity: School and Neighborhood Segregation in the USA." *Race and Social Problems* 12, no. 1 (2020): 29–41.

Paris, Django and Maisha T. Winn eds. *Humanizing Research: Decolonizing Qualitative Inquiry for Youth and Communities*. Thousand Oaks, CA: Sage, 2013.

Park, Robert M. "Notes and Reviews: Tuskegee International Conference on the Negro," *The Journal of Race Development* 3, no. 1 (1912): 119.

Parr, Jessica M. "An African Republic: Black and White Virginians in the Making of Liberia." *Journal of the Early Republic* 29, no. 1 (2009): 183–186.

Paulet, Anne. "To Change the World: The Use of American Indian Education in the Philippines." *History of Education Quarterly* 47, no. 2 (2007): 173–202.

Perdue, Theda and Michael D. Green, *The Cherokee Removal: A Brief History with Documents*. Boston, Bedford-St. Martin's, 1995.

Perlstein, Daniel. "Community and Democracy in American Schools: Arthurdale and the Fate of Progressive Education." *Teachers College Record* 97, no. 4 (1996): 625–650.

Phillips, Ulrich Bonnell. *Life and Labor in the Old South*. Columbia: University of South Carolina Press, 2007.

Piatote, Beth H. *Domestic Subjects: Gender, Citizenship, and Law in Native American Literature*. New Haven, CT: Yale University Press, 2013.

Pilkington, Charles Kirk. "The Trials of Brotherhood: The Founding of the Commission on Interracial Cooperation." *The Georgia Historical Quarterly* 69, no. 1 (1985): 55–80.

Pineda-Tinio, Ma Teresa. "Bearers of Benevolence: The Thomasites and Public Education in the Philippines." *Philippine Studies* 50, no. 4 (2002): 581–583.

Poovey, Mary. *A History of the Modern Fact: Problems of Knowledge in the Sciences of Wealth and Society*. Chicago: University of Chicago Press, 1998.

Pope, Blaine D., Ernie A. Smith, Samuel J. Shacks, and Joyce Keith Hargrove. "Booker T. and the New Green Collar Workforce: An Earth-Based Reassessment of the Philosophy of Booker T. Washington." *Journal of Black Studies* 42, no. 4 (2011): 507–529.

Posey, Josephine McCann. *Succeeding Against Great Odds: Alcorn State University in Its Second Century.* Jackson: University Press of Mississippi, 2017.
Powell, Malea D. "Down by the River, or How Susan La Flesche Picotte Can Teach Us about Alliance as a Practice of Survivance." *College English* 67, no. 1 (2004): 38–60.
Pratt, Richard Henry. *Battlefield and Classroom: Four Decades with the American Indian, 1867–1904.* New Haven, CT: Yale University Press, 1964.
Prucha, Francis Paul. *American Indian Policy in Crisis: Christian Reformers and the Indian, 1865–1900.* Norman: University of Oklahoma Press, 1976.
———. *Americanizing the American Indians: Writings by the "Friends of the Indian," 1880–1900.* Cambridge, MA: Harvard University Press, 1973.
Puente, Lorenzo Alexander L. "Anti-US Imperialism as Assertion of Black Subjectivity at the Turn of the Last Century." *Kritika Kultura* 5 (2004): 59–75.
Purser, Ronald E., David Forbes, and Adam Burke, eds. *Handbook of Mindfulness: Culture, Context, and Social Engagement.* New York: Springer, 2016.
Purves, Alexander. "Capital and Labor in Co-operative Farming." *Proceedings of the Hampton Negro Conference*, no. 3. Hampton, VA: Hampton Institute Press, 1899.
Quashie, Kevin. *The Sovereignty of Quiet: Beyond Resistance in Black Culture.* New Brunswick, NJ: Rutgers University Press, 2012.
Quintana, Frances Leon. *Ordeal of Change: The Southern Utes and Their Neighbors.* Walnut Creek, CA: AltaMira Press, 2004.
Raibmon, Paige. *Authentic Indians: Episodes of Encounter from the Late Nineteenth-Century Northwest Coast.* Durham, NC: Duke University Press, 2005.
Ramirez, Francisco O. "The World Society Perspective: Concepts, Assumptions, and Strategies." *Comparative Education* 48, no. 4 (2012): 423–439.
Ramirez, Francisco O. and John W. Meyer, "Comparative Education: The Social Construction of the Modern World System." *Annual Review of Sociology* 6, no. 1 (1980): 369–397.
Razack, Sherene, ed. *Race, Space, and the Law: Unmapping a White Settler Society.* Toronto: Between the Lines, 2002.
Reddy, Thiven. *South Africa, Settler Colonialism and the Failures of Liberal Democracy.* London: Zed Books, 2015.
Resendez, Andres. *The Other Slavery: The Uncovered Story of Indian Enslavement in America.* Boston: Houghton Mifflin Harcourt, 2016.
Richard, K. Keith. "Unwelcome Settlers: Black and Mulatto Oregon Pioneers." *Oregon Historical Quarterly* 84, no. 1 (1983): 29–55.
Richardson, John G. and Brenda Wooden Hatcher. "The Feminization of Public School Teaching: 1870–1920." *Work and Occupations* 10, no. 1 (1983): 81–99.
Rickford, Russell. *We Are an African People: Independent Education, Black Power, and the Radical Imagination.* Oxford: Oxford University Press, 2016.
Rifkin, Mark. *Beyond Settler Time: Temporal Sovereignty and Indigenous Self-Determination.* Durham, NC: Duke University Press, 2017.
———. *Fictions of Land and Flesh: Blackness, Indigeneity, Speculation.* Durham, NC: Duke University Press, 2019.

---. *When Did Indians Become Straight?: Kinship, the History of Sexuality, and Native Sovereignty.* Oxford: Oxford University Press, 2010.

Riznik, Barnes. "From Barracks to Family Homes: A Social History of Labor Housing Reform on Hawai'i Sugar Plantations." *The Hawaiian Journal of History* 33 (1999): 119–157.

Roberts, Dorothy E. *Killing the Black Body: Race, Reproduction, and the Meaning of Liberty.* New York: Vintage Books, 1999.

Roberts, Neil. *Freedom as Marronage.* Chicago: University of Chicago Press, 2015.

Robinson, Cedric. "DuBois and Black Sovereignty: The Case of Liberia." *Race & Class* 32, no. 2 (1990): 39–50.

Rodriguez, Dylan. *Suspended Apocalypse: White Supremacy, Genocide, and the Filipino Condition.* Minneapolis: University of Minnesota Press, 2010.

Roma-Sianturi, Dinah. "'Pedagogic Invasion': The Thomasites in Occupied Philippines." *Kritika Kultura* 12 (2009): 100–119.

Rudolph, Sophie. *Unsettling the Gap: Race, Politics and Indigenous Education.* New York: Peter Lang, 2019.

Rusert, Britt. "'A Study in Nature': The Tuskegee Experiments and the New South Plantation," *Journal of Medical Humanities* 30 (2009): 155–171.

---. "Plantation Ecologies: The Experimental Plantation in and against James Grainger's 'The Sugar-Cane.'" *Early American Studies* 13, no. 2 (2015): 341–373.

Russ, William A. "The Role of Sugar in Hawaiian Annexation." *Pacific Historical Review* 12, no. 4 (1943): 339–350.

Sánchez-Eppler, Karen. "Raising Empires Like Children: Race, Nation, and Religious Education." *American Literary History* 8, no. 3 (1996): 399–425.

Saunt, Claudio. *Black, White, and Indian: Race and the Unmaking of an American Family.* Oxford: Oxford University Press, 2005.

Schmid, Silvia. "Pestalozzi's Spheres of Life." *Journal of the Midwest History of Education Society* 24 (1997): 143–146.

Sehat, David. "The Civilizing Mission of Booker T. Washington." *The Journal of Southern History* 73, no. 2 (2007): 323–362.

Semel, Susan F. and Alan R. Sadovnik, eds. *"Schools of Tomorrow," Schools of Today: What Happened to Progressive Education.* New York: Peter Lang, 1999.

Seniors, Paula Marie. *Beyond Lift Every Voice and Sing: The Culture of Uplift, Identity, and Politics in Black Musical Theater.* Columbus: The Ohio State University Press, 2009.

Sexton, Jared. "The Vel of Slavery: Tracking the Figure of the Unsovereign." *Critical Sociology* 42, no. 4–5 (2016): 583–597.

---. "The Social Life of Social Death: on Afro-Pessimism and Black Optimism." *InTensions,* no. 5 (2011): 1–47.

Sharma, Nitasha Tamar. *Hawaii Is My Haven: Race and Indigeneity in the Black Pacific.* Durham, NC: Duke University Press, 2021.

Sharpe, Christina. *In the Wake: On Blackness and Being.* Durham, NC: Duke University Press, 2016.

Shaw, Stephanie J. *What a Woman Ought to Be and to Do: Black Professional Women Workers During the Jim Crow Era.* Chicago: University of Chicago Press, 1996.

Silva, Noenoe K. *Aloha Betrayed: Native Hawaiian Resistance to American Colonialism.* Durham, NC: Duke University Press, 2004.

Simonsen, Jane E. "'Object Lessons': Domesticity and Display in Native American Assimilation." *American Studies* 43, no. 1 (2002): 75–99.

Simpson, Audra. *Mohawk Interruptus: Political Life Across the Borders of Settler States.* Durham, NC: Duke University Press, 2014.

———. "On Ethnographic Refusal: Indigeneity, 'Voice' and Colonial Citizenship." *Junctures: The Journal for Thematic Dialogue* 9 (2007): 67–80.

Simpson, Leanne Betasamosake. "Land as Pedagogy: Nishnaabeg Intelligence and Rebellious Transformation." *Decolonization: Indigeneity, Education & Society* 3, no. 3 (2014): 1–25.

———. *As We Have Always Done: Indigenous Freedom Through Radical Resistance.* Minneapolis: University of Minnesota Press, 2017.

Slater, Lisa. *Anxieties of Belonging in Settler Colonialism: Australia, Race and Place.* New York: Routledge, 2019.

Smith, Andrew F. *Peanuts: The Illustrious History of the Goober Pea.* Urbana: University of Illinois Press, 2002.

Smith, Henry Nash. *Virgin Land: The American West as Symbol and Myth.* Cambridge, MA: Harvard University Press, 1970.

Smith, Linda Tuhiwai. *Decolonizing Methodologies: Research and Indigenous Peoples.* London: Zed Books, 1999.

Smith, Sherry L. "Francis La Flesche and the World of Letters." *American Indian Quarterly* 25, no. 4 (2001): 579–603.

Soja, Edward W. *Postmodern Geographies: The Reassertion of Space in Critical Social Theory.* London: Verso, 1989.

Spillers, Hortense J. "Mama's Baby, Papa's Maybe: An American Grammar Book." *Diacritics* 17, no. 2 (1987): 65–81.

Spivey, Donald. "The African Crusade for Black Industrial Schooling." *The Journal of Negro History* 63, no. 1 (1978): 1–17.

———. *The Politics of Miseducation: The Booker Washington Institute of Liberia, 1929–1984.* Lexington: University Press of Kentucky, 1986.

———. *Schooling for the New Slavery: Black Industrial Education, 1868–1915.* Westport, CT: Greenwood Press, 1978.

Stasiulis, Daiva and Nira Yuval-Davis, eds. *Unsettling Settler Societies: Articulations of Gender, Race, Ethnicity and Class.* London: Sage, 1995.

Stauffer, Robert H. *Kahana: How the Land Was Lost.* Honolulu: University of Hawaii Press, 2003.

Stein, Sharon. "Universities, Slavery, and the Unthought of Anti-Blackness." *Cultural Dynamics* 28, no. 2 (2016): 169–187.

Stoddard, Lothrop. *The Rising Tide of Color: The Threat Against White World-Supremacy.* New York: Charles Scribner's Sons, 1920.

———. *The Revolt Against Civilization: The Menace of the Under Man*. New York: Charles Scribner's Sons, 1922.

Stoler, Ann Laura. *Carnal Knowledge and Imperial Power: Race and the Intimate in Colonial Rule*. Berkeley: University of California Press, 2010.

Strawn, Susan Marie. *Restoring Navajo-Churro Sheep: Community-Based Influences on a Traditional Navajo Fiber Resource and Textile*. Iowa City: University Press of Iowa, 2004.

Strawn, Susan Marie and Mary A. Littrell. "Returning Navajo-Churro Sheep for Navajo Weaving." *Textile* 5, no. 3 (2007): 300–319.

Stremlau, Rose. "'To Domesticate and Civilize Wild Indians': Allotment and the Campaign to Reform Indian Families, 1875–1887." *Journal of Family History* 30, no. 3 (2005): 265–286.

Swisher, Karen Gayton, and John W. Tippeconnic III, eds. *Next Steps: Research and Practice to Advance Indian Education*. Charleston, WV: Eric Clearinghouse on Rural Education and Small Schools, 1999.

TallBear, Kim. "An Indigenous Reflection on Working Beyond the Human/Not Human." *GLQ: A Journal of Lesbian and Gay Studies* 21, no. 2–3 (2015): 230–235.

Tarr, Peter James. *The Education of the Thomasites: American School Teachers in Philippine Colonial Society, 1901–1913*. Ithaca, NY: Cornell University, 2006.

Taylor-Neu, Robyn, Tracy Friedel, Alison Taylor, and Tibetha Kemble, "(De) Constructing The 'Lazy Indian': An Historical Analysis of Welfare Reform in Canada." *Aboriginal Policy Studies* 7, no. 2 (2019): 65–87.

Thomas, Deborah A. *Exceptional Violence: Embodied Citizenship in Transnational Jamaica*. Durham, NC: Duke University Press, 2011.

Tien, Joanne. "Teaching Identity vs. Positionality: Dilemmas in Social Justice Education." *Curriculum Inquiry* 49, no. 5 (2019): 526–550.

Todd, Zoe. "Fish, Kin and Hope: Tending to Water Violations in Amiskwaciwâskahikan and Treaty Six Territory." *Afterall: A Journal of Art, Context and Enquiry* 43, no. 1 (2017): 102–107.

Trennert, Robert A. "Educating Indian Girls at Nonreservation Boarding Schools, 1878-1920." *Western Historical Quarterly* 13, no. 3 (1982): 271–290.

———. "From Carlisle to Phoenix: The Rise and Fall of the Indian Outing System, 1878-1930." *Pacific Historical Review* 52, no. 3 (1983): 267–291.

Trouillot, Michel-Rolph. *Silencing the Past: Power and the Production of History*. Boston: Beacon Press, 1995.

Tuck, Eve, Allison Guess, and Hannah Sultan, "Not Nowhere: Collaborating on Selfsame Land." *Decolonization: Indigeneity, Education & Society* 26, (June 2014): 1–11.

Tuck, Eve and Marcia McKenzie. *Place in Research: Theory, Methodology, and Methods*. New York: Routledge, 2015.

Tuck, Eve and K. Wayne Yang. "Decolonization Is Not a Metaphor." *Decolonization: Indigeneity, Education & Society* 1, no. 1 (2012): 1–40.

Turk, Diana B. and Stacie Brensilver Berman. "Learning through Doing: A Project-Based Learning Approach to the American Civil Rights Movement." *Social Education* 82, no. 1 (2018): 35–39.

Turner, Frederick Jackson. *The Frontier in American History.* New York: Henry Holt, 1921.

Tyler, Lyon G. *History of Hampton and Elizabeth City County, Virginia.* Hampton, VA: The Board of Supervisors of Elizabeth City County, 1922.

van Beusekom, Monica. "Colonial Agricultural Development Schemes." In *Oxford Research Encyclopedia of African History.* August 31, 2021, https://oxfordre.com/africanhistory/display/10.1093/acrefore/9780190277734.001.0001/acrefore-9780190277734-e-751?rskey=nSnSYc&result=12021.

Vaughn, Melinda and Lori Verstegen Ryan. "Corporate Governance in South Africa: A Bellwether for the Continent?" *Corporate Governance: An International Review* 14, no. 5 (2006): 504–512.

Veracini, Lorenzo. "Introducing: Settler Colonial Studies." *Settler Colonial Studies* 1, no. 1 (2011): 1–12.

———. "Settler Collective, Founding Violence and Disavowal: The Settler Colonial Situation." *Journal of Intercultural Studies* 29, no. 4 (2008): 363–379.

———. "'Settler Colonialism': Career of a Concept." *The Journal of Imperial and Commonwealth History* 41, no. 2 (2013): 313–333.

———. *Settler Colonialism: A Theoretical Outline.* Houndmills, UK: Palgrave Macmillan, 2010.

Walker Jr., Theodore. "The Black and the Red: Responding to Sioux and Other Native American Instructions on Red-Black Solidarity." *Journal of Religious Thought* 55, no. 2/1 (1999): 73–86.

Walker, Vanessa Siddle. *Their Highest Potential: An African American School Community in the Segregated South.* Chapel Hill: University of North Carolina Press, 1996.

———. "Valued Segregated Schools for African American Children in the South, 1935–1969: A Review of Common Themes and Characteristics." *Review of Educational Research* 70, no. 3 (September 2000): 253–285.

———. "Organized Resistance and Black Educators' Quest for School Equality, 1878–1938." *Teachers College Record* 107, no. 3 (2005): 355–388.

Warren, Calvin L. *Ontological Terror: Blackness, Nihilism, and Emancipation.* Durham, NC: Duke University Press, 2018.

Warren, Donald. "Slavery as an American Educational Institution: Historiographical Inquiries." *Journal of Thought* 40, no. 4 (2005): 41–54.

Warren, Joyce Pualani. "Reading Bodies, Writing Blackness: Anti-/Blackness and Nineteenth-Century Kanaka Maoli Literary Nationalism." *American Indian Culture and Research Journal* 43, no. 2 (2019): 49–72.

Warren, Joyce Pualani, Keith L. Camacho, Elizabeth Deloughrey, and Evyn Lê Espiritu Gandhi, "Genealogizing Pō: The Relational Possibilities of Blackness in the Pacific." *Ethnic Studies Review* 44, no. 3 (2021): 7–16.

Warren, Kim Cary. *The Quest for Citizenship: African American and Native American Education in Kansas, 1880–1935*. Chapel Hill: University of North Carolina Press, 2010.

Washburn, Kathleen. "New Indians and Indigenous Archives." *PMLA* 127, no. 2 (2012): 380–384.

Washburn, Wilcomb E. *The Assault on Indian Tribalism: The General Allotment Law (Dawes Act) of 1887*. Philadelphia: Lippincott, 1975.

Washington, Booker T. *My Larger Education: Being Chapters From my Experience*. Garden City, NY: Doubleday, Page, 1911.

———, ed. *The Negro Problem: A Series of Articles by Representative American Negroes of Today*. New York: James Pott, 1903.

———. "Relation of Industrial Education to National Progress." *The Annals of the American Academy of Political and Social Science* 33, no. 1 (1909): 1–12.

———. *Up From Slavery: An Autobiography*. New York: A. L. Burt, 1901.

Washington, Booker T. and William Edward Burghardt Du Bois, *The Negro in the South, his Economic Progress in Relation to his Moral and Religious Development*. The William Levi Bull Lectures for the Year 1907. Philadelphia: GW Jacobs, 1907.

Watkins, William H. *The White Architects of Black Education: Ideology and Power in America, 1865–1954*. New York: Teachers College Press, 2001.

Weisiger, Marsha. *Dreaming of Sheep in Navajo Country*. Seattle: University of Washington Press, 2011.

White, Derrick E. *Blood, Sweat, and Tears: Jake Gaither, Florida A&M, and the History of Black College Football*. Chapel Hill: University of North Carolina Press, 2019.

Whyte, Christine. "Between Empire and Colony: American Imperialism and Pan-African Colonialism in Liberia, 1810–2003." *National Identities* 18, no. 1 (2016): 71–88.

Wildcat, Matthew, Mandee McDonald, Stephanie Irlbacher-Fox, and Glen Coulthard. "Learning from the Land: Indigenous Land Based Pedagogy and Decolonization." *Decolonization: Indigeneity, Education & Society* 3, no. 3 (2014): i–xiv.

Wilder, Craig Steven. *Ebony and Ivy: Race, Slavery, and the Troubled History of America's Universities*. New York: Bloomsbury, 2014.

Wilderson, Frank B., III. *Red, White and Black: Cinema and the Structure of US Antagonisms*. Durham, NC: Duke University Press, 2010.

Williams, Bianca C., Dian D. Squire, and Frank A. Tuitt, eds. *Plantation Politics and Campus Rebellions: Power, Diversity, and the Emancipatory Struggle in Higher Education*. New York: SUNY Press, 2021.

Williams, Heather Andrea. *Self-Taught: African American Education in Slavery and Freedom*. Chapel Hill: University of North Carolina Press, 2009.

Williams, Joyce E. and Ron Ladd. "On the Relevance of Education for Black Liberation." *The Journal of Negro Education* 47, no. 3 (1978): 266–282.

Williams Jr., Robert A. *The American Indian in Western Legal Thought: The Discourses of Conquest*. Oxford: Oxford University Press, 1992.

———. "Gendered Checks and Balances: Understanding the Legacy of White Patriarchy in an American Indian Cultural Context." *Georgia Law Review* 24 (1989): 1019–1044.

Williams, William Appleman. "The Frontier Thesis and American Foreign Policy." *Pacific Historical Review* 24, no. 4 (1955): 379–395.

Willinsky, John. *Learning to Divide the World: Education at Empire's End.* Minneapolis: University of Minnesota Press, 1998.

Wilson, Dorothy Clarke. *Bright Eyes. The Story of Susette La Flesche, an Omaha Indian.* New York: McGraw Hill, 1974.

Wolfe, Patrick. "Settler Colonialism and the Elimination of the Native." *Journal of Genocide Research* 8, no. 4 (2006): 387–409.

———. "Land, Labor, and Difference: Elementary Structures of Race." *The American Historical Review* 106, no. 3 (2001): 866–905.

———. *Settler Colonialism and the Transformation of Anthropology: The Politics and Poetics of an Ethnographic Event.* London, New York: Cassell, 1999.

Wood, Anthony W. *Black Montana: Settler Colonialism and the Erosion of the Racial Frontier, 1877–1930.* Omaha: University of Nebraska Press, 2021.

Woodson, Carter G. *The Education of the Negro Prior to 1861: A History of the Education of the Colored People of the United States from the Beginning of Slavery to the Civil War.* Washington, DC: Association for the Study of Negro Life History, 1919.

———. *The Mis-education of the Negro.* Trenton, NJ: Africa World Press, 1933.

Wynter, Sylvia. "Novel and History, Plot and Plantation." *Savacou* 5, no. 1 (1971): 95–102.

———. "Unsettling the Coloniality of Being/Power/Truth/Freedom: Towards the Human, After Man, its Overrepresentation—An Argument." *CR: The New Centennial Review* 3, no. 3 (2003): 257–337.

Yamada, Shoko. "Educational Borrowing as Negotiation: Re-Examining the Influence of the American Black Industrial Education Model on British Colonial Education in Africa." *Comparative Education* 44, no. 1 (2008): 21–37.

Yokota, Kariann Akemi. "Transatlantic and Transpacific Connections in Early American History." *Pacific Historical Review* 83, no. 2 (2012): 204–219.

Zimmerman, Andrew. *Alabama in Africa: Booker T. Washington, The German Empire, and the Colonization of the New South.* Princeton, NJ: Princeton University Press, 2010.

INDEX

Abbott, Dr. Lyman, 71
Africa: and agricultural experimental stations, 181–82, 185–88; and Black settlement, 105–7; as "dark continent," 106, 108, 110; as "last frontier," 108; and resource extraction, 118–20; and settlement, 105–7, 121–26; and teacher training, 167–68; and US pro-colonial influences, 120–21; Western representations of, 105–9
Afropessimism, 13, 225n47
afterlife of slavery, 11, 117; in Africa, 122, 126–27; and the Pacific, 87; and proximity to whiteness, 35, 159; and survival, 163–64
agricultural experimental station. *See* experimental station
allotment: and agricultural experiment stations, 188–90; and Alice Fletcher, 6, 143; critiqued for failing to "civilize," 68–73; and domesticity, 133–34, 141–45; framed as freedom, 45, 68–71; as "herding," 61, 63, 66; as pedagogical, 39, 57, 61–66, 97–98; in the Philippines, 97–98; and private property relations, 77–79; and theorization of land and water, 15–17
American Colonization Society, 7
American Missionary Association, 6
anachronism. *See* time-space
animacy, 19
antiblackness: and Africa, 108–9, 113, 114; and the afterlife of slavery, 127; and

anti-Indigeneity, 12, 37–38, 56, 73; in archives, 21–24; as contextualizing complicity or coercing compliance, 12, 212n5; and currents of colonialism, 17; as distinct from colonialism or settler colonialism, 13, 31; and domesticity, 135; and European humanism, 156; and flesh, 134, 140, 226n66; and fungibility, 226n66; and "learning by doing," 203; in the Pacific, 81–82, 85; and pedagogy, 205; and the plantation, 30, 178, 242n62; and plantation pedagogy, 35, 48, 56, 73; spatial organization of, 31, 40, 78, 131; as upheld by education projects, 9, 37, 225n47
Armstrong, Richard, 4–5, 82–84, 87–88, 92, 169
Armstrong, Samuel Chapman: and Booker T. Washington, 103; and domesticity, 133, 144–45; founding of Hampton Institute, 5, 155; and Hawai'i, 4–5, 82, 89–90, 102; and slavery as educative, 34, 55; and teacher training, 173
Asian contract labor, 45–46, 88, 169
atemporality. *See* time-space
Atkinson, Frederick, 7, 85–86, 100, 169–70
Atlanta Compromise, 198

Barrows, David P., 7, 85–86, 170
Black Atlantic, 16
black-birding, 45
Black nationalism as alternate spatial vision, 77–79

297

Blackness: and comparison between US Black and African people, 105–9; as constitutive of Indigeneity, 14; contrasted with Indigeneity, 56; and Polynesian racialization, 14, 45–46, 82, 88–89, 95; and property, 38, 55; terminology, 211n1; and white anxieties, 165–66
Black Pacific, 80–81
Black Shoals, 16
Black Studies and Indigenous Studies, 12–20, 205–6
boarding schools: critiqued for lacking proximity to whiteness, 66–73; and domesticity, 141–45, 147; and outing programs, 150–51; as remedy for reservations, 58–59, 66; resistance in, 23; and teacher training, 168–69; as wasted resources, 66–68
Booker Washington Institute of Liberia. *See* Liberia, Booker Washington Institute of
Bureau of Indian Affairs (BIA): and allotment, 65, 188; critiques of, 68–71; and prisoners of war, 6; and proximity to whiteness, 56, 60

Calhoun School, 36
capitalist accumulation, 12, 38–39, 45, 56. *See also* allotment
carcerality: and criminality, 75–77, 90–91, 165–66; and labor as confinement or punishment, 33–34, 241n46; and prison and police abolition, 236n81; and reservations, 75–77; and surveillance through teacher programs, 165–66
Carlisle Indian School: and Alice Fletcher, 64; and failed "civilizing" efforts, 66–68; founding of, 5–6; and framings of slavery, 3–4, 68–71; outing program, 68, 113; and the Pacific, 7, 80, 85–86, 101, 171; and relationship to the Bureau of Indian Affairs, 67–70; and teacher training, 168–69
Carver, George Washington, 7, 176–77, 183–85
Christianity: and Black Ethiopianism, 112, 126; and domesticity, 145; in Hampton's industrial education, 32, 155; and Hawaiʻi, 5, 82–84; and slavery, 3, 37, 60; and teacher training, 172
cis-heteronormativity, 131–32; and Blackness, 134; as constructed through industrial education, 133–37
citizenship and enfranchisement: deferred promise of in the United States, 9, 33, 44; as differently conceived in Hawaiʻi, 82–83, 88–89
coeducation: at Hampton, 136–37; in Hawaiʻi, 134–35
colonialism as educative, 3–4
comparative racialization: and Africans as Black or Native, 106; and Blackness and Indigeneity, 14, 56; and Blackness and Polynesian racialization, 14, 45, 82, 88–89, 95
Councill, William Hooper, 3–4, 12
criminality: Black, 165–66; in Hawaiʻi, 90–91; on reservations, 75–77
Critical Race Theory, 197
crop rotation, 185
cultural difference, discourses of, 22–23
currents of colonialism: definition of, 17–18, 48–50; as organizational approach, 25–27, 51–52; in the Pacific, 80–82; and transit of plantation pedagogy, 46–50, 101; as methodology, 51–52
Curry, J. L. M., 71–72, 74

Davis, Jackson, 7; and the Firestone Rubber Company in Liberia, 110; and the "Negro problem," 176; and Southern educational structures, 164; and teachers, 158–160, 166
Dawes Severalty Act of 1887, 57, 62–64, 68, 141; and emancipation, 45; as pedagogical, 39; and the Philippines, 86
decolonizing education, 24
Depew, Chauncey M., 122, 157–58
Dewey, John, 193–95, 199, 203–4, 234n50
disappearance and death of the Native: and African life as doomed, 125; through gendered labor, 134; in Hawaiʻi, 101–3; as inevitable, 71; in the Philippines, 103–4; and possession by whiteness, 150–51

"doing," definition and refusal of, 200–202
domesticity: in Africa, 144–46; as civilizational, 137–39; and home expansion, 162–63; and homekeeping, 148–51; and homemaking, 141–47, 173–74; in the Pacific, 146–47; as spatial, 131–32; and targeting of non-human life, 189–90
Du Bois, W. E. B.: and Booker T. Washington, 35, 133, 251n4; on forced labor in Africa, 122; on integrated schools, 75; and Thomas Jesse Jones, 108

education: as creating Black and Native antagonisms, 18; theorization of, 8–10
Eliot, Dr. Samuel, 156–57
emancipatory education, 8
Embree, R. L., 114–15
English education: in Hawai'i, 83, 93–94, 102; and Native students, 154–55; in the Philippines, 7, 85; and race and nation, 93; as taught through slavery, 37, 60, 73
Enlightenment: ideologies of value, 164; philosophies of education, 155–56
experimental stations, 176–78; in Africa, 181–82, 186–188; in Indian Country, 188–90; in the Pacific, 185–86; as plantation laboratory, 190–95; roots in settlement and plantation slavery, 178–82; and scientific experimentation, 176–82; at Tuskegee, 182–85
experimentation: on Black bodies, 191–92; on land, 176–195

Firestone rubber plantation, 123; and "cooperation" with the Booker Washington Institute of Liberia, 110, 115, 146; and financial backing of Booker Washington Institute, 106, 119–120, 146
Fletcher, Alice, 6, 64, 141
Fort Marion, 6
Frissell, Hollis Burke, 7; and "cooperation," 111; and domestic education, 131, 150, 173; and proximity to whiteness, 59–61
Froebel, 155–56, 193
frontier: Africa as "last frontier," 108; as spatial formation in United States, 42, 50, 59–60
Frontier Thesis, 50

fugitivity: as assumed to be present, 22–23, 40; Black and Indigenous fugitivity, 43, 126, 153, 156, 225n53; and complicity, 198, 212n5; and Liberia, 123, 126; not found in the archive, 12
fungibility, 39, 43, 226n66
futurity: Indigeneity as outside colonial futures, 59; and Indigenous and Black conceptualizations of place, 40; reservations as plantation futures, 57–58; school integration discourse as plantation futures, 74–75; settlement and plantation futures, 44–46, 57–58, 204–205; prisons as plantation futures, 75–77; teacher training as expanding plantation futures, 153–54, 160

gender relations. *See* domesticity
General Allotment Act. *See* Dawes Severalty Act of 1887
Ghost Dance movement, 61–62
Goodale, Elaine, 66–67
Great Māhele, 88

Hampton Institute: coeducation, 133–37; domestic curriculum, 141–45; founding of, 4–6, 29–31; and Hawaiian schooling, 4–5, 82–87; as like a plantation, 29–34; as model for African schooling, 7–8, 105–7; as model for Filipino schooling, 7; model of industrial schooling, 29, 32–34; as model for Southern Black schooling, 6–7; relationship to Tuskegee, 6–7, 183; as a settlement, 29, 34; teacher training, 154–160, 171–174; as trafficking colonial technologies, 47–48
Hatch Act of 1887, 182
Hawai'i: coeducation in, 134–38; as comparison to US South, 89; English language education, 93–94; industrial schooling, 4–5, 82–87; missionary schooling, 4–5, 82–84; overthrow and annexation, 83, 88, 94; plantation economy, 45–46, 87–94; schools and plantations, 89–94
heteronormativity. *See* cis-heteronormativity
Hilo boarding school, 5, 83–84, 92, 186

imperialism, American as uniquely educational, 98–99. *See also* Manifest Destiny
incommensurability, 13–14
independence: deferred capacity for Filipino self-government, 86–87, 94–99; Liberian independence and influence of United States, 105–6, 120–21
"Indian problem": "Navajo problem" and livestock, 189–90; refusal to solve, 18–20, 22–24
Indian Rights Association, 59, 65–66
industrial education: in Africa, 108–9, 114–18; as allowing for openness to US markets, 99; as cultural uplift, 5; and gendered domesticity, 32–33, 133–45; in Hawai'i, 5, 89–94; in the Philippines, 7, 85–86, 99–101; as rooted in the Pacific, 82–87; for second-class citizenship status, 4, 33
Interracial Cooperation Commission (ICC), 111, 113

Jeanes Supervisory Teachers, 7, 131, 146, 154, 158–67
Jones, Thomas Jesse: and agricultural experimentation in Africa, 187; and classical education as slavery, 116; and the countrification of Africa, 108–9; and domestic education in Africa, 145–46; and educational "adaptation" in the US South, 115–18; on extraction of African resources as educational achievement, 118–19; and Indigenous industrial education, 192–194; and industrial education in Africa, 8, 26–27, 167–68, 193; justifying colonialism in Africa, 111–12, 120, 123; and the "Navajo Problem," 188–190; and teachers, 162, 171

Kamehameha school, 92–93, 146
Kane, Frances Fisher, 59, 65–66
Kenwill, Margaret, 84–85, 135
"kill the Indian to save the man," 3, 6
Knapp, Seaman, 177

labor: and "adaptation" in Africa, 114–18; contract labor in the Pacific, 45–46; in Hawai'i, 87–94; as necessary for off-reservation education, 66–73; as not valued by Filipinos, 99–101; as pedagogical, 55–57; in the Philippines, 95–96, 99–101; and proximity to whiteness, 36–39; on reservations, 62–66; for sake of itself, 33, 90, 194–195; and teacher training, 154–56; for white people, 28
Lake Mohonk conferences, 6, 71, 87, 99
land: and agricultural experimentation, 176–195; as connection between Black and Indigenous Studies, 15–18; as property, 38, 55; and school expansion, 160–62; transformed through domestic training, 141–45; transformed through pedagogy, 176–78; and water, 15–18, 50. *See also* allotment
land-grant college, 176–77, 182, 186; Black, 3, 7, 176; and land experimentation, 188
language education: English education, 7, 83–85, 93–94, 102, 154–55; English education and slavery, 37, 60, 73; Hawaiian language education, 83; and race and nation, 93
"learning by doing": in Liberia, 114–18; in progressive education, 193–95; refusal of, 197–206; and slavery, 197–200
Leupp, Francis E., 188–89
Liberia: and "cooperation" with Western business interests, 110; relationship to United States, 105–9; and self-determination, 120–21
Liberia, Booker Washington Institute of: and "adaptation" of labor as educative, 114–15, 119–20; and agricultural experimentation, 186–88; and "cooperation" as proximity to whiteness, 110, 159; and domestic education, 146; founding of, 7–8, 105–7, 126; and political conflict, 126–27
Loram, Charles T.: advocacy for industrial education, 117–118; and Black education as apolitical white "self-defense," 112–114; and justification of settlement, 124–125; as proponent of Jeanes teaching model, 167; and Thomas Jesse Jones, 8

marronage, 14, 43
Manifest Destiny, 50, 80, 106, 171
Manila Trade School, 7, 85–86, 101
Meriam Report, 189
missionary schools: in Africa, 119; in Hawai'i, 82–93; as precursor to plantation pedagogy, 10; and school segregation and integration discourse, 74
monocrop farming, 179
Morrill Acts, 176, 182
Moton, Robert, 7, 72, 111–12

Native American, terminology, 212n7
Navajo-Churro sheep genocide, 189–90
"Negro problem": as comparison to the Philippines, 86–87; as connected to land use, 176; as framed by white Southerners, 71–72; refusal to solve, 18–20, 22–24; as solved through didactic space, 132
New Deal education programs, 131, 199

outing programs, 148–151

pan-Africanism, 109
Park, Robert E., 110–11, 116, 166, 176
Peabody Fund, 6, 27, 71
peanut cultivation, 183–85
pedagogy: and allotment, 61–73; as liberatory, 19; and slavery, 10; theorization of, 10, 19
Penn School of St. Helena Island, 161–62, 193
Pestalozzi, 5, 84, 155, 181, 193
Phelps Stokes, Caroline, 148
Phelps Stokes, Olivia, 106, 148
Phelps-Stokes Fund: and African education, 108, 111–112, 119–120, 123, 146; and Black education in the South, 115, 146; and Booker Washington Institute of Liberia, 106, 119; and domestic education, 148; and teacher training, 158
Philippines: comparison to US South, 86–87; development of sugar plantations, 45–46, 95–96; establishment of industrial education, 85–87; independence and self-government, 86–87, 95–96, 186, 239n26; as liminal colonial possession, 94–96; racialization with respect to Black and Indigenous peoples, 95, 103–4
Pima cotton, 188–89
plantation: becoming school post-emancipation, 3; as colony or spatial iteration of settlement, 10, 34, 43–46; as contrasted with reservations, 55–61; definitions of, 43; and economic extraction in Africa, 118–20; economy in Hawai'i, 87–94; and the founding of Hampton, 29–32; and land transformation, 30–31; as school, 10, 34, 38–39; and scientific farming, 178–82; as site of Black immobilization, 33–34; spatiality and temporality, 42–46
plantation pedagogy, 12, 29, 35–38; and "adaptation" in Africa, 114–18; and allotment, 57, 62–73; and "cooperation" in Africa, 110–14; and currents of colonialism, 18, 80–82; and demonstration farming as targeting people, land, and non-human kin, 176–90; as extended through progressive education, 193–95; in Hawai'i, 89–96; and home as technology, 145–47, 162–63; and imagined relations of property, 38; and land as laboratory, 190–95; in the Philippines, 94–104; as rooted in the Pacific, 80–87; and school expansion, 160–62; and school integration or segregation, 74–75; as spatial formation, 40–42; and teacher training, 152–54; as technology of settlement, 46–48; transference to Africa, 105–9; transferred to reservations, 58–61
Polynesian racialization and Blackness, 14, 45–46, 82, 88–89, 95
Pratt, Richard Henry: and allotment, 68–69, 73–74, 77; and Carlisle Indian School, 6, 38, 68–69; and "contact" as violence, 3–4, 11; and criminality, 75–76; and proximity to whiteness, 73–77; and slavery as educative, 56–57, 69, 75, 198
primitive accumulation. See capitalist accumulation
prisons. See carcerality

progressive education, 41, 131, 193–95
proximity to whiteness: as civilizing, 11; and "cooperation" in Africa, 110–14, 126–27; as degraded through Blackness, 112–13; and density, 56–57, 61–66, 78; as educational by definition, 34–37; and English language education in Hawaiʻi, 93–94; as leading to death, 101–4, 150–51; as necessary in the training of teachers, 152–54, 158–60; in the Philippines, 94–99; and possession by whiteness, 144–45, 150–51; and the reservation, 55–73; and school integration or segregation, 36–37, 74–75; and slavery, 34–39; as transferring a proximity to Blackness, 61; and zones of proximal development, 224n45

Reel, Estelle, 6
refusal: of "doing," 201–2; ethnographic refusal as methodology, 21–24, 51–52; of framing schooling as possible of abolition/decolonization, 205–206; as politic, 23–25, 204–6, 268n28; to solve Black and Indigenous peoples as educational problems, 20–25, 51–52, 202, 205
reservations: and allotment, 61–66; and boarding schools, 66–73; as carceral space, 75–77; and connection to colonial schooling in the Philippines, 85–87; and connection to land policies in the Philippines, 97–98; as containment, 58; and contradictory framings of educational value, 55–61; as contrasted with plantations, 55–61; as disappearing, 58–61; as idleness and debauchery, 70; as space of criminality, 75–77
Rockefeller Foundation, 6–7, 27, 112, 146; Rockefeller General Education Board, 106, 110, 158, 161; Rockefeller International Education Board, 8, 119–22
Rosenwald schools, 6–7, 146
Rudolph, Virginia, 158, 160, 162
Rupel, Paul, 114, 146

settlement: in Africa, 121–26; definition of, 11, 107; as educational, 8–10

sexuality, 17, 132–138, 180, 200, 241n45. See also cis-heteronormativity
settler colonialism, 11. See also settlement
school integration, 36–37, 74–75
school segregation, 8, 58, 74–75, 113, 154
scientific farming techniques, 33; roots in settlement and plantation slavery, 178–82; as teaching land, 176–78
scientific method, critique of, 179–80
Shellbanks farm and plantation, 33
Slater fund, 6, 27, 71, 158
slave cabin: as didactic space, 131–32, 199–200; framed as space of Black degradation, 131–32, 139–40
slavery: and carcerality, 75–77; classical education as, 116–17; compared to Filipinos needing to work, 99–101; and conscripted labor in Liberia, 122–23; contrasted framings in Africa and the US South, 116–17; as educative, 8, 34, 37–39; as educative post-emancipation, 20; as engendering moral debt to whites, 72; as "learning by doing," 197–200; as more educational than the reservation, 55–61; as transformation of land, 42–46, 55–56
Smith-Lever Act of 1914, 177, 182
South Africa: implementing industrial schooling, 8, 117; as related to slavery and settlement, 124–25; segregation and "cooperation," 112–14; and US support for apartheid, 121
space, theorization of, 40–42

teacher training: in Africa, 167–68, 171; as capitalist/colonial worldmaking, 154–56; in Hawaiʻi, 168–71; in Indian Country, 168–69; in the Philippines, 99, 169–71; as scaling whiteness as ideology, 152–54, 156–60; as suppression of Black rebellion, 165–66
teaching: as feminized, 171–73; land, 176–78; theorization of, 9–10
terra nullius, 44
Thomasites, 169
time-space: and atemporality of slavery, 126; "au," 51–52; of Black labor, 123, 167; in book organization, 25–27; and currents, 48–50; and flight across time, 14;

in Hawai'i, 81, 85; and "learning by doing," 200–201; and methodology, 25; in the Philippines, 94–95; of plantations, 42–46, 56–59, 74–75, 178; and plantation pedagogy, 38, 195, 200; and proximity to whiteness, 102, 224n45; refusing notions of progress, 25; of reservations, 58–61, 74

Turner's Thesis, 50

Tuskegee Institute: Agricultural Experiment Station, 163, 176–78, 183–86; and Black criminality, 165–66; and Booker Washington Institute of Liberia, 26, 105–6; as example of Black school under white influence, 36; and experimentation, 180; and experimentation on Black bodies, 191–92; founding of, 3, 183; as inspired by Hampton, 6–7, 183; and "learning by doing," 204; relationship to Africa, 109, 116, 127; teacher training, 158, 161, 166

Up From Slavery, 28

US Department of Agriculture, 177, 179, 182, 186, 188

Washington, Booker T.: Atlanta Compromise, 197–98, 267n2; on Black criminality, 165; and laboring for white people, 28, 38–39, 199; and "learning by doing," 197–99, 204; and racial uplift through property ownership, 44–45; relationship to Samuel Armstrong, 183, 194; and teaching "wants," 100, 117, 164; and W. E. B. Du Bois, 133, 251n4; work with Indigenous students, 34–35, 39

Whipple farm, 33

white people, useless. *See* Armstrong, Samuel Chapman; Jones, Thomas Jesse; Pratt, Richard Henry

Woodson, Carter G., 29–30, 109, 169

Women's National Indian Association, 6, 131–32, 141–42

AMERICAN CROSSROADS

Edited by Earl Lewis, George Lipsitz, George Sánchez, Dana Takagi, Laura Briggs, and Nikhil Pal Singh

1. *Border Matters: Remapping American Cultural Studies,* by José David Saldívar
2. *The White Scourge: Mexicans, Blacks, and Poor Whites in Texas Cotton Culture,* by Neil Foley
3. *Indians in the Making: Ethnic Relations and Indian Identities around Puget Sound,* by Alexandra Harmon
4. *Aztlán and Viet Nam: Chicano and Chicana Experiences of the War,* edited by George Mariscal
5. *Immigration and the Political Economy of Home: West Indian Brooklyn and American Indian Minneapolis, 1945–1992,* by Rachel Buff
6. *Epic Encounters: Culture, Media, and U.S. Interests in the Middle East since 1945,* by Melani McAlister
7. *Contagious Divides: Epidemics and Race in San Francisco's Chinatown,* by Nayan Shah
8. *Japanese American Celebration and Conflict: A History of Ethnic Identity and Festival, 1934–1990,* by Lon Kurashige
9. *American Sensations: Class, Empire, and the Production of Popular Culture,* by Shelley Streeby
10. *Colored White: Transcending the Racial Past,* by David R. Roediger
11. *Reproducing Empire: Race, Sex, Science, and U.S. Imperialism in Puerto Rico,* by Laura Briggs
12. *meXicana Encounters: The Making of Social Identities on the Borderlands,* by Rosa Linda Fregoso
13. *Popular Culture in the Age of White Flight: Fear and Fantasy in Suburban Los Angeles,* by Eric Avila
14. *Ties That Bind: The Story of an Afro-Cherokee Family in Slavery and Freedom,* by Tiya Miles
15. *Cultural Moves: African Americans and the Politics of Representation,* by Herman S. Gray
16. *Emancipation Betrayed: The Hidden History of Black Organizing and White Violence in Florida from Reconstruction to the Bloody Election of 1920,* by Paul Ortiz

17. *Eugenic Nation: Faults and Frontiers of Better Breeding in Modern America,* by Alexandra Stern
18. *Audiotopia: Music, Race, and America,* by Josh Kun
19. *Black, Brown, Yellow, and Left: Radical Activism in Los Angeles,* by Laura Pulido
20. *Fit to Be Citizens? Public Health and Race in Los Angeles, 1879–1939,* by Natalia Molina
21. *Golden Gulag: Prisons, Surplus, Crisis, and Opposition in Globalizing California,* by Ruth Wilson Gilmore
22. *Proud to Be an Okie: Cultural Politics, Country Music, and Migration to Southern California,* by Peter La Chapelle
23. *Playing America's Game: Baseball, Latinos, and the Color Line,* by Adrian Burgos, Jr.
24. *The Power of the Zoot: Youth Culture and Resistance during World War II,* by Luis Alvarez
25. *Guantánamo: A Working-Class History between Empire and Revolution,* by Jana K. Lipman
26. *Between Arab and White: Race and Ethnicity in the Early Syrian-American Diaspora,* by Sarah M. A. Gualtieri
27. *Mean Streets: Chicago Youths and the Everyday Struggle for Empowerment in the Multiracial City, 1908–1969,* by Andrew J. Diamond
28. *In Sight of America: Photography and the Development of U.S. Immigration Policy,* by Anna Pegler-Gordon
29. *Migra! A History of the U.S. Border Patrol,* by Kelly Lytle Hernández
30. *Racial Propositions: Ballot Initiatives and the Making of Postwar California,* by Daniel Martinez HoSang
31. *Stranger Intimacy: Contesting Race, Sexuality, and the Law in the North American West,* by Nayan Shah
32. *The Nicest Kids in Town:* American Bandstand, *Rock 'n' Roll, and the Struggle for Civil Rights in 1950s Philadelphia,* by Matthew F. Delmont
33. *Jack Johnson, Rebel Sojourner: Boxing in the Shadow of the Global Color Line,* by Theresa Rundstedler
34. *Pacific Connections: The Making of the US-Canadian Borderlands,* by Kornel Chang

35. *States of Delinquency: Race and Science in the Making of California's Juvenile Justice System,* by Miroslava Chávez-García

36. *Spaces of Conflict, Sounds of Solidarity: Music, Race, and Spatial Entitlement in Los Angeles,* by Gaye Theresa Johnson

37. *Covert Capital: Landscapes of Denial and the Making of U.S. Empire in the Suburbs of Northern Virginia,* by Andrew Friedman

38. *How Race Is Made in America: Immigration, Citizenship, and the Historical Power of Racial Scripts,* by Natalia Molina

39. *We Sell Drugs: The Alchemy of US Empire,* by Suzanna Reiss

40. *Abrazando el Espíritu: Bracero Families Confront the US-Mexico Border,* by Ana Elizabeth Rosas

41. *Houston Bound: Culture and Color in a Jim Crow City,* by Tyina L. Steptoe

42. *Why Busing Failed: Race, Media, and the National Resistance to School Desegregation,* by Matthew F. Delmont

43. *Incarcerating the Crisis: Freedom Struggles and the Rise of the Neoliberal State,* by Jordan T. Camp

44. *Lavender and Red: Liberation and Solidarity in the Gay and Lesbian Left,* by Emily K. Hobson

45. *Flavors of Empire: Food and the Making of Thai America,* by Mark Padoongpatt

46. *The Life of Paper: Letters and a Poetics of Living Beyond Captivity,* by Sharon Luk

47. *Strategies of Segregation: Race, Residence, and the Struggle for Educational Equality,* by David G. García

48. *Soldiering through Empire: Race and the Making of the Decolonizing Pacific,* by Simeon Man

49. *An American Language: The History of Spanish in the United States,* by Rosina Lozano

50. *The Color Line and the Assembly Line: Managing Race in the Ford Empire,* by Elizabeth D. Esch

51. *Confessions of a Radical Chicano Doo-Wop Singer,* by Rubén Funkahuatl Guevara

52. *Empire's Tracks: Indigenous Peoples, Racial Aliens, and the Transcontinental Railroad,* by Manu Karuka
53. *Collisions at the Crossroads: How Place and Mobility Make Race,* by Genevieve Carpio
54. *Charros: How Mexican Cowboys are Remapping Race and American Identity,* by Laura R. Barraclough
55. *Louder and Faster: Pain, Joy, and the Body Politic in Asian American Taiko,* by Deborah Wong
56. *Badges without Borders: How Global Counterinsurgency Transformed American Policing,* by Stuart Schrader
57. *Colonial Migrants at the Heart of Empire: Puerto Rican Workers on U.S. Farms,* by Ismael García Colón
58. *Assimilation: An Alternative History,* by Catherine S. Ramírez
59. *Boyle Heights: How a Los Angeles Neighborhood Became the Future of American Democracy,* by George J. Sánchez
60. *Not Yo' Butterfly: My Long Song of Relocation, Race, Love, and Revolution,* by Nobuko Miyamoto
61. *The Deportation Express: A History of America through Mass Removal,* by Ethan Blue
62. *An Archive of Skin, An Archive of Kin: Disability and Life-Making during Medical Incarceration,* by Adria L. Imada
63. *Menace to Empire: Anticolonial Solidarities and the Transpacific Origins of the US Security State,* by Moon-Ho Jung
64. *Suburban Empire: Cold War Militarization in the US Pacific,* by Lauren Hirshberg
65. *Archipelago of Resettlement: Vietnamese Refugee Settlers across Guam and Israel-Palestine,* by Evyn Lê Espiritu Gandhi
66. *Arise! Global Radicalism in the Era of the Mexican Revolution,* by Christina Heatherton
67. *Resisting Change in Suburbia: Asian Immigrants and Frontier Nostalgia in L.A.,* by James Zarsadiaz
68. *Racial Uncertainties: Mexican Americans, School Desegregation, and the Making of Race in Post–Civil Rights America,* by Danielle R. Olden

69. *Pacific Confluence: Fighting over the Nation in Nineteenth-Century Hawaiʻi,* by Christen T. Sasaki
70. *Possible Histories: Arab Americans and the Queer Ecology of Peddling,* by Charlotte Karem Albrecht
71. *Indian Wars Everywhere: Colonial Violence and the Shadow Doctrines of Empire,* by Stefan Aune
72. *Plantation Pedagogy: The Violence of Schooling across Black and Indigenous Space,* by Bayley J. Marquez

Founded in 1893,
UNIVERSITY OF CALIFORNIA PRESS
publishes bold, progressive books and journals
on topics in the arts, humanities, social sciences,
and natural sciences—with a focus on social
justice issues—that inspire thought and action
among readers worldwide.

The UC PRESS FOUNDATION
raises funds to uphold the press's vital role
as an independent, nonprofit publisher, and
receives philanthropic support from a wide
range of individuals and institutions—and from
committed readers like you. To learn more, visit
ucpress.edu/supportus.